The Coalitions against Napoleon

The Coalitions against Napoleon

How British Money, Manufacturing and Military Power Forged the Alliances that Achieved Victory

William R. Nester

AN IMPRINT OF PEN & SWORD BOOKS LTD
YORKSHIRE – PHILADELPHIA

First published in Great Britain in 2023 by
FRONTLINE BOOKS
an imprint of Pen & Sword Books Ltd
Yorkshire – Philadelphia

Copyright © William R. Nester, 2023

ISBN 978-1-39904-302-1

The right of William R. Nester to be identified as the author of this work has been asserted by him in accordance with the Copyright, Designs and Patents Act 1988.

A CIP catalogue record for this book is available from the British Library.

All rights reserved. No part of this book may be reproduced or transmitted in any form or by any means, electronic or mechanical including photocopying, recording or by any information storage and retrieval system, without permission from the Publisher in writing.

Typeset by Concept, Huddersfield, West Yorkshire, HD4 5JL.
Printed and bound in England by CPI Group (UK) Ltd, Croydon CR0 4YY.

Pen & Sword Books Ltd incorporates the Imprints of Aviation, Atlas, Family History, Fiction, Maritime, Military, Discovery, Politics, History, Archaeology, Select, Wharncliffe Local History, Wharncliffe True Crime, Military Classics, Wharncliffe Transport, Leo Cooper, The Praetorian Press, Remember When, White Owl, Seaforth Publishing and Frontline Books.

For a complete list of Pen & Sword titles please contact
PEN & SWORD BOOKS LTD
47 Church Street, Barnsley, South Yorkshire, S70 2AS, England
E-mail: enquiries@pen-and-sword.co.uk
Website: www.pen-and-sword.co.uk
or
PEN & SWORD BOOKS
1950 Lawrence Rd, Havertown, PA 19083, USA
E-mail: uspen-and-sword@casematepublishers.com
Website: www.penandswordbooks.com

Contents

List of Plates vii
List of Tables ix
Acknowledgements xi
Introduction 1

Part I: Developments

1. Political 11
2. Economic 21
3. Imperial 31

Part II: Coalitions

4. First, 1793–97 49
5. Second, 1798–1802 87
6. Third, 1803–05 109
7. Fourth, 1806–07 119
8. Fifth, 1808–11 129
9. Sixth, 1812–14 149
10. Seventh, 1815 175
11. Legacies 189

Notes 195
Bibliography 227
Index 245

List of Plates

Bank of England, from *Microcosm of London*, c.1808.

The 'Old Lady of Threadneedle Street', the Bank of England today.

Bust of Nathan Rothschild.

Recruiting for the British Army, by Thomas Rowlandson.

Bond of the Russian Government, issued 1 March 1822, signed by Nathan Mayer Rothschild.

Pitt the Younger in 1804, by John Hoppner.

Shot stacked up outside the Royal Laboratory gates and rows of guns arrayed in the background, Royal Arsenal.

East India Company soldiers at the Battle of Seringapatam, by Alexander Allan.

HMS *Shannon* leading the captured American frigate *Chesapeake* into Halifax, Nova Scotia, in June 1813, by John Christian Schetky.

Old Mill, built as a steam-powered mill in Ancoats in 1798, is the oldest-surviving cotton mill in Manchester.

The Thirteen Factories, the area of Guangzhou to which China's Western trade was restricted in 1757–1842.

An old carronade, part of a now neglected display in the archway of the old clocktower of the Carron Works.

Prussia's Friedrich Wilhelm II, painting by Anton Graff.

William Wyndham Grenville, 1st Baron Grenville, succeeded his cousin William Pitt as Prime Minister in 1806.

Portrait of Friedrich Wilhelm II of Prussia, by Anton Graf.

The signed Treaty of Amiens.

List of Tables

2.1. Comparisons of Yearly Average Growth in Different Sectors ... 22
2.2. Comparisons of Real Average Yearly Growth Per Person 22
2.3. Adult Literacy, 1500 and 1800 24
2.4. Country Population Shares by Location, 1500 and 1800 25
2.5. British Inanimate Energy Power Sources, 1760 and 1800 28
2.6. Distribution of Professions by Families and Incomes in England and Wales, 1801–03 29
3.1. Exports and Re-exports from Britain to its Empire and World in Pounds Sterling 37
3.2. The Logistics of War: Men 41
3.3. The Logistics of War: Money 41
3.4. Military Spending as a Share of Government Spending 42
4.1. British Government Spending and Private Investment, 1790–1813 56
4.2. Estimated National Income, Total Revenue, and Indirect Taxes . 56
4.3. Military Spending Select Years in Pound Sterling 57
4.4. British Army Numbers Select Years 59
4.5. Growth of British Seapower, 1792–1802 63
4.6. Bank of England Specie Reserves, First Coalition 66
9.1. Portuguese Recipients of Subsidies and Supplies 158
11.1. Comparison of Naval Power by Tonnage of Ships over 550 Tons 191
11.2. Population of Britain's West Indian Colonies, 1815 192
11.3. The Expansion of the East India Company's Army, 1793–1815 . 192

Acknowledgements

I want to acknowledge my deep gratitude and pleasure at having had this latest opportunity to work with the outstanding Frontline editorial team including Lisa Hooson, John Grehan, Martin Mace and Paul Middleton. I am especially grateful to John and Martin for finding the illustrations.

Introduction

While our countrymen retain their love of their country, and by industry and commerce administer to our naval superiority, we have little to dread from the military enterprise of any continental power. [*Henry Dundas*]

[I]t is our business ... to teach the world ... whenever ... the true balance of the world comes to be adjusted, we are the natural mediators for them all, and it is only through us alone that they can look for secure and effectual tranquillity. [*George Canning*]

All wars are a contention of purse. [*Henry Dundas*]

Power is the ability to get what one wants. In conflicts among nations that involves the assertion of both 'hard' physical power like personnel, production, organisations, and allies; and 'soft' psychological power like morale, unity, ideas, plans, and leadership, to name a few of each. Ideally, among power's many ends is more power to get more of the same or other desired goals.[1]

Money is hard power's literal and figurative bottom line, especially for wars. No one expressed that better than British Secretary at War Henry Dundas: 'all wars are a contention of purse.'[2] William Wickham, a British spymaster, succinctly captured the dilemma and essence of wealth and power behind a coalition: 'In a word, money you must give them; for without money, they cannot possibly go on, and without them we can do nothing.'[3]

Faced with a rising foreign power and thus potential threat, a nation state can either 'bandwagon' with it or 'balance' against it by forging an alliance to deter or, if need be, defeat it. For centuries, Britain's leaders balanced rather than bandwagoned against a series of threats that arose on the continent.[4] Foreign Secretary George Canning explained that core British national interest and strategy in 1807: [I]t is our business ... to teach the world ... that ... whenever ... the true balance of the world comes to be adjusted, we are the natural mediators for them all, and it is only through us alone that they can look for secure and effectual tranquillity.'[5]

Britain never performed that balancing act more intensively and eventually decisively than from 1793 to 1815. During those years, Whitehall, the seat of government, underwrote seven coalitions in wars against first revolutionary then Napoleonic France that cost Britain £1,657,854,518 as the national debt tripled from £290,000,000 to £860,000,00.[6] Of that, British subsidies to around thirty allies were £65,830,228, along with staggering amounts of war supplies mass produced by British factories and shipped to them. For instance, in 1813 alone, Whitehall dispersed £2,000,000 worth of war supplies including 1,000,000 muskets and £11,100,000 of subsidies, including £2,000,000 to Portugal, £1,333,333 to Russia, £1,200,000 to Sweden, £1,000,000 to Spain, £1,000,000 to Austria, £666,666 to Prussia, £400,000 to Sicily, and the rest to an array of smaller states and groups.[7] Ambassadors to recipient countries combined the traditional duties of diplomat and spy with those of paymaster, accountant, and spending watchdog.

Britain's allies had mixed feelings about all that aid. They at once eagerly took and detested it, then demanded more. They hated being so dependent and often projected their self-loathing on their supplier. Naturally, Britons bristled at their allies' ingratitude and hypocrisy, but kept distributing money, arms, uniforms, and other supplies vital to enticing allies to war or keeping them in the fight against the French empire. Foreign Secretary Richard Wellesley called for those frustrated by Spain's especially egregious behaviour to think instead of what was at stake: 'However the conduct of the Spanish Government may increase the difficulties of co-operation, alienate the spirit of the English from their cause, and even apparently justify a total separation of the interest of the two nations, yet it must never be forgotten that in fighting the cause of Spain, we are struggling for the last hope of continental Europe.'[8]

Britain's leading role in Europe did not end with Waterloo. Immediately following the Sixth Coalition and amidst the Seventh Coalition, Britain constructed with the other great powers a security system of co-operation and consultation called the concert of Europe that prevented a serious war among them for two generations and a war that engulfed most of the continent for nearly a century.

Britain's power to underwrite those coalitions came from a related series of revolutions – agrarian, mercantile, financial, technological, manufacturing, cultural, and political – that developed over the proceeding century.[9] That happened in Britain and not elsewhere for many reasons.[10] Of them, cultural values may be most crucial. Constraints were fewer and incentives greater for enterprising Britons to invest, invent, buy, and sell in ways that enriched themselves and their nation more than in any other state except the Netherlands for a while. Indeed, Dutch and British merchants competed to capture markets and colonies around the world during the seventeenth century and that culminated in three naval wars between them. Britain emerged victorious from those wars, having broken the back of Dutch naval and thus mercantile power.

Britain's industrial revolution did not take off for another century. When it did, unrivalled mercantile and naval power let traders reap profits from sales of mass-produced goods in markets to the ends of the earth. The government skimmed a portion of that profit as revenues with which to expand the navy that protected British merchants and decimated rivals. Few men during this era better understood the dynamic among financial, mercantile, manufacturing, diplomatic, and military power than Dundas, who proudly asserted: 'While our countrymen retain their love of their country, and by industry and commerce administer to our naval superiority, we have little to dread from the military enterprise of any continental power.'[11]

During the eighteenth century, Britain's leaders mastered a virtuous power cycle of victorious wars, expanding production, captured territories and markets, and more revenue. Trade soared with exports increasing 560 per cent, re-exports 900 per cent, and imports 500 per cent.[12] Thus did Britain achieve the mercantilist goal of perennial trade surpluses that enriched the nation by reaping sales from foreign rivals in an expanding array of products, most importantly, manufactures. Businessmen reinvested most of their revenues in ways that further swelled productivity, comparative advantages, and profits. Whitehall invested much of its tariff revenues in the navy that protected the nation's merchant ships. William Mildmay explained that dynamic in his 1765 book *Laws and Policy of England Relating to Trade*: 'A nation cannot be safe without Power; Power cannot be obtained without Riches; nor Riches without Trade ... And increase in National Wealth may be procured by enforcing such laws as are most agreeable to the Maxims and Principles ... with regard to the exigences of our own government; the state of foreign affairs, and the different interests of each independent kingdom.'

Thomas Mortimer, another eighteenth century thinker, also elaborated that wealth and power dynamic: 'The great increase and extent of the commercial connections of Great Britain, arising from the augmentation of her maritime power from new territorial acquisitions, and from the flourishing state of her colonies having ... given to the monied interest, great weight and influence in the state ... the public revenues, and ... public funds.'[13]

The British empire was a vital means and end of power.[14] Like virtually all empires, Britain's developed sporadically and opportunistically over centuries. Whitehall mostly franchised the process to private companies with royal charters that authorised them to colonise specific regions, monopolise specific products, and protect that with military force. Usually only when a company went bankrupt did Whitehall name its possessions crown colonies and directly oversee them by appointing their governors. Most colonies eventually proved to be well worth all the investments of money and men to conquer, exploit, and defend them. The empire produced a diversified array of goods and markets. Britain did not depend on any one colony for any one product, but the navigation laws ensured that colonists had to buy a lengthening list of British manufactured goods conveyed in British vessels. Britain suffered a terrible economic and strategic blow when thirteen American colonies revolted and won independence to become the United States between 1775 and 1783. Yet, within a decade, Britain's economy had recovered to the point where it could finance the first of seven coalitions against revolutionary and later Napoleonic France. Britain's empire greatly expanded during its wars between 1793 and 1815, a gain at the expense of enemies and allies alike including Spain, France, the Netherlands, Portugal, Denmark, and Sweden.

An 1800 intelligence report from Malta revealed how Britain assessed, created, and exploited wealth from conquered foreign peoples, and thus the foundation for asserting power. First, the writer analysed the strengths and weaknesses of Malta's political and economic system. He disparaged the former rulers, the Knights of St John, as 'perfect Sybarites; they had lost the spirit of their predecessors, they lived luxuriously on the revenues they derived from the possessions of their Order in other countries and paid no attention to the cultivation and commerce of Malta'. The result was wasted potential wealth that Britain could develop – 'all these branches of revenue may be improved to an amount much more considerable, and this island by proper management would in a few years produce a surplus of revenue to any power who can protect its commerce and encourage its cultivation'. He cited cotton, pepper, sugar, indigo, wine, and salt as key exports to generate business wealth and government revenues. Finally, he lauded the Maltese as 'good seamen' who 'in time of war would furnish excellent sailors for our fleet'.[15]

As an island nation, Britain enjoyed an enormous economic, military, and political advantage over continental enemies. The first line of defence was the 'wooden wall' of warships in the English Channel.[16] British defence policy was to maintain a fleet as large as the combined fleets of the continent's two largest naval powers – usually Spain and France. As long as the navy deterred or defeated any would-be invaders, Whitehall could avoid the financial cost and potential political peril of maintaining a large standing army. During wars, the relatively small army was fleshed out with native recruits and hired foreign regiments. The government also saved enormous sums by relying on a naval militia or privateers. Before the eighteenth century, most of the Royal Navy's fleet were armed merchant ships licensed for privateering duty and potential profit. For instance, the English fleet that staved off the 1588 Spanish Armada numbered thirty-four crown and 163 private warships.[17] The Navigation Acts starting in 1651 strengthened the merchant fleet by requiring all trade between England and its colonies for a lengthening list of products to be carried in the nation's vessels.

London was Britain's greatest port with a vast complex of wharfs, warehouses, coffee houses, pubs, residences, and brothels on both sides of the Thames River below the Tower of London. In 1792, 13,033 vessels entered and 13,891 vessels departed British ports, with most to or from London. The 16,079 registered vessels included 12,776 with owners in Britain, 1,558 in Ireland, the Channel Islands, and the Isle of Man, and 1,745 in the colonies. Most were small vessels for intercostal trade or fishing. The largest were thousand-ton East Indies behemoths.[18] After going to war in 1793, Whitehall mobilised its resources steadily and vastly to expand its merchant and naval power.

Of course, hard economic and military power is not enough to win a war. Leadership – good, bad, mediocre – then as always was crucial in determining what did or did not happen. Napoleon Bonaparte's military genius crushed the first five coalitions.[19] The sixth coalition briefly and the seventh coalition definitively defeated Napoleon for many reasons, of which the sheer weight of overwhelming numbers of coalition troops was perhaps most vital. Yet, without British finance and factories along with the brilliance of Admiral Horatio Nelson at sea and General Arthur Wellesley, Duke of Wellington, on land, the allies could never have mustered, armed, equipped, and fed enough men eventually to overwhelm Napoleon. Nearly as vital was William Pitt, Prime Minister from 1783 to 1801 and 1804 to 1806. During his first decade in office, Pitt pushed through reforms that boosted the economy and government revenues while slashing corruption and inefficiency. Financially, Britain was in excellent shape when it went to war in 1793. Pitt then worked with talented ministers and diplomats to forge coalitions that warred against France. Thus, Pitt was critical for the ultimate victory, although he did not live to see it.

When it came to power, no Briton during the Age of Revolution and Napoleon had a more sophisticated understanding than Secretary at War Henry Dundas. For Dundas, British power was ultimately grounded in commerce. The nation's power swelled with the spread of British-manufactured goods in ever more markets around the world. Markets were worth fighting for, and the more lucrative the market, the more worthy the fight. He explained: 'The prosperity of this country knows no bounds, unless ... its industry and commercial enterprise shall outrun the extension of its foreign markets.'[20] He could have been describing British policy after acquiring any colony when he mulled taking Portugal's Goa: 'If ... the country comes totally into our hands, and we apply the same salutary principles of administration and government which we practice with regard to our own Indian territories, we may fairly hope that, ere long, the people will be rendered happy and prosperous, and the country produce at least adequate to its own defence.'[21] The winning strategy was clear: 'Great Britain can at no time propose to maintain an extensive and complicated war but by destroying the colonial resources of our enemies and adding proportionately to our own commercial resources which are and must ever be the sole basis of our maritime strength. By our commerce and our fleet, we have been enabled to perform those prodigies of exertion which have placed up in the proud state of preeminence we now hold.'[22]

As for France's revolutionary ideology, Dundas did 'not feel the same alarm of danger to this country from the situation of France that I once did; nor do I think the contagion of its example, in any material degree, longer dangerous to us. When the delusive and intoxicating system of liberty and equality and the natural rights of man were in full fashion, and uncontrolled by external power or their own consequent misfortunes, the neighbourhood of France to this country was seriously dangerous and justly alarming; but I am not afraid of men in this country being captivated by a military despotism, or wishing to exchange the mild and happy government of this country for the cruel, unprincipled, and ignominious slavery and oppression which reigns in France. Every nation on the continent of Europe have just cause to dread a great concentrated military power existing among them, and threatening devastation and military ... but ... Britain is the last that has reason to tremble.'[23]

After Britain declared war against France, the key question was what strategy would best win that war. Given Dundas's views of power and national interests, he naturally sought a victory that enriched Britain economically and imperially at France's expense. To that end, he advocated a 'maritime strategy' of blockading French ports, capturing French colonies, and sweeping the seas of French war and merchant vessels while underwriting allied armies that fought France on the continent. In contrast, Secretary of State William Grenville sought a victory that restored France's monarchy. To that end, he insisted on a 'continental strategy' of massing a British army with European allies that invaded France as counter-revolutionary forces rebelled to destroy and replace the regime. The policy result for the next two decades was a hybrid of the maritime and continental strategies. The emphasis varied with the shifting threats, opportunities, and what worked or failed.

The most controversial strategy was in the West Indies.[24] Here Dundas's view prevailed of conquering as many French colonies as possible to weaken France and aggrandise Britain and its empire. Expeditions took and held most of the colonies whose sugar, tobacco, coffee, cocoa, and ginger production enriched Britain but at a vast cost in lives – mostly disease killed 45,250 of 88,969 British soldiers and sailors who served in the West Indies from 1792 to 1801. The fighting devastated the West Indian economies, which took years and sometimes decades to be profitable again.[25]

Espionage and nationalism were two other key sources of British soft power. The Foreign, War, and Home ministries collaborated to spy, catch spies, and conduct covert operations to influence politics in foreign lands. Each had its own bureau devoted to those ends that ultimately involved manipulating individual and collective hearts and minds. Of those, the Foreign Secretary's Alien Office launched the most widespread and daring operations. Whitehall ensured that its covert operations were well funded even if the results rarely matched the hopes that inspired them. Nationalism was another crucial British advantage. Although class, ethnic, religious, and regional conflicts beset Britain, they were less severe than in most other realms. Perhaps only the Dutch and the Americans held similar unified visions of themselves as nations. Relatively high literacy rates and plenty of newspapers to satisfy cravings to learn helped inform and unite Britons as they did Dutch and Americans.

Of course, the quirks of human nature and unique individuals distorted the views and acts of that era's British statesmen as thoroughly as anyone else at any time. Ideally, careful calculations by governments of their relative interests and power in relation to other states determines their respective foreign policies. Practically, other forces often divert or impede that rational process. Harold Nicolson, a British diplomat at the 1919 Versailles conference and author of a book on the Congress of Vienna, gave an insider's view: 'Nobody who has not actually watched statesmen dealing with each other can have any real idea of the immense part played in human affairs by such unavowable and often unrecognisable causes as lassitude, affability, personal affection or dislike, misunderstanding, deafness or incomplete command of a foreign language, vanity, social engagements, interruptions, and momentary health. Nobody who has not watched "policy" expressing itself in day-to-day action can realise how seldom is the course of events determined by deliberately planned purpose or how often what in retrospect appears to have been a fully conscious intention was at the time governed and directed by that most potent of all factors – "the chain of circumstances". Few indeed are the occasions on which any statesmen sees his objective clearly before him and marches toward it with undeviating stride.'[26] That certainly characterised British diplomacy during the revolutionary and Napoleonic era.

* * *

During a speech before Congress in December 1940, President Franklin Roosevelt called on Americans to be an 'arsenal of democracy' for Britain and other countries imperiled by the 'Axis alliance' of Japan, Germany, and Italy. He argued that American national interests demanded arming and funding resistance against those 'Axis' powers even if the United States was then neutral. Within a year, America joined that world war and through its vast manufacturing, financial, and population powers was able to forge and lead an alliance to victory. Although that alliance included dictatorships as well as democracies, the key point was that America served as its arsenal.

Britain played exactly the same role during the Napoleonic era with allies that either were constitutional or absolute monarchies. *The Coalitions against Napoleon* explores how Britain developed and asserted the financial, manufacturing, and military power to do so.[27]

PART I
DEVELOPMENTS

Chapter 1

Political

> I glory in the name of Britain; and the peculiar happiness of my life will ever consist in promoting the welfare of a people whose loyalty a warm affection to me I consider as the greatest and most permanent security of my throne. [*George III*]

> [T]he essence of a free state is to manage the party warfare as to reconcile it with the safety of the sovereign ... to do this, the king must give contending parties facilities against each other, and not embark himself too deeply with any. [*Robert Stewart, Viscount Castlereagh*]

State building and nation building are related but distinct. State building involves developing institutions and laws to govern people within a territory and protect them from foreign and domestic enemies.[1] Nation building involves developing a common identity for those people to better govern them.[2] Obviously, institutions – governmental, political, economic, social, and religious – are less challenging to develop than identities. One's identity is a unique mix of genes and relations with others starting with one's family. In preliterate peasant societies one's clan and village vitally shaped personal identity. Nationalism, or an emotional attachment to one's nation or people sharing a language, culture, history, and institutions, is mostly a modern identity forged by mass armies, media, and education. Political unity against foreign enemies often precedes and develops nationalism. Foreign conquest can certainly provoke nationalism for the conquerors and conquered alike.

Among Britain's array of key powers during the revolutionary and Napoleonic era was being a state and nation relatively more unified than most other European nation states. Yet Britain's existence let alone its power was not preordained. Looking back through a country's time, perhaps no event or result was inevitable other than death. Existential threats can arise, overwhelm, and transform a country's leaders and people.

The development of an English state and nation that became Britain developed slowly, sporadically over a millennium, during which at times it faced possible extinction. That began with the Germanic tribes of Angles,

Saxons, and Jutes that invaded the island in the fifth and sixth centuries. Eventually those tribes conquered and assimilated themselves and the existing Gallo-Roman peoples in what today is most of England. The word English came from the Angles and the English language developed from the mingling of the tongues of the invaders with that of the peoples they absorbed.

Beginning in the late ninth century, the English faced a series of invasions by Vikings that persisted for four hundred or so years that threatened their existence. England's first great king, Alfred, led the resistance from 871 to his death in 899. He and his successors managed to defeat or co-opt most invaders. That ended in 1066 when William, the Duke of Normandy, invaded and conquered England. He and his men were descendants of Vikings that the kingdom of France had subdued by giving them title to Normandy. William had a tenuous familial claim to the English throne that was the excuse for his invasion. For a century or so, the royal family spoke French while most of their subjects retained their English language and identity; the English language was enriched by countless French words. Gradually the monarchy became Anglicised.

A turning point in England's history came with the 1215 Magna Carta or Great Charter. A group of barons revolted against King John's tyrannical and inept rule, and forced him to sign a contract that guaranteed their rights of speech, assembly, property, and freedom from arbitrary arrest. The Magna Carta became Parliament's foundation that gradually expanded those considered eligible to vote for or be members. Eventually Parliament split between a House of Lords and a House of Commons. Parliament's powers also slowly expanded, with its greatest approving the king's requests for money and determining how most of it was spent.

The English eventually dominated the Gaelic-speaking Welsh and Scots living in the western and northern regions of their island and the Irish on their neighbouring island by sheer weight of population, victory in wars, and marriages between powerful families. Gradually English replaced Welsh, Scot, and Irish as the first or sole language. By the eighteenth century, nearly everyone in the British Isles spoke English and most as their first language. That represented more than a millennium of conquests and mingling of peoples.

As England united linguistically, it split religiously. Henry VIII ruled England from 1509 to 1547. When he took the throne, Christianity was split between the Catholic and Orthodox versions in western and eastern Europe with their respective capitals at Rome and Constantinople and leaders the pope and patriarch. In 1534, Henry denounced the papacy and declared himself the head of a Church of England after the pope refused to recognise his divorce from his first wife. Although Parliament recognised Henry's claim with its Act of Supremacy, religious conflicts and at times wars plagued England, Scotland, and Ireland for another century and a half. Most English people accepted the liturgy and authority of the Church of England and became known as Anglicans. A growing minority became known as Puritans for their belief that each congregation's members should govern and interpret the Bible for themselves. Most Scots embraced a version articulated by John Knox called Presbyterianism that involved pre-destination. Most Irish remained Catholic. The Protestant Anglican, Puritan, and Presbyterian sects promoted literacy because of their belief that faith must be grounded on the ability to read and interpret the Bible.

The realm's ruling family dynasty changed from Tudor to Stuart in 1603 when Elizabeth I died childless. The claimant with the closest lineage was Scottish King James VI, who was crowned James I, thus uniting the English and Scottish thrones. He achieved renown for two decisions. He ended a war with Spain that had lasted for decades. He authorised a translation of the Bible from its original Hebrew Old and Greek New Testaments; the subsequent 'King James Bible' provided an eloquent source of linguistic unity even if the sects interpreted it differently.

His son Charles I, who became king in 1625, sought to be an absolute monarch that treated Parliament as a rubberstamp to approve tax increases to pay for his lavish court and wars against France. Charles also tried to suppress the Puritans that dominated Parliament and threatened the Church of England's supremacy. The result was a civil war between royalists and parliamentarians from 1642 to 1649. The parliamentarians won, executed the king, and formed a republic they called the Commonwealth headed by Lord Protector Oliver Cromwell, their most brilliant general. Cromwell and his coterie purged any opponents from Parliament, transforming a nascent republic into a dictatorship. They also suppressed not just Anglicans but Scottish Presbyterians and Irish Catholics.

England's Civil War overlapped with the Thirty Years' War on the continent that largely pitted Protestant and Catholic countries against each other. The fighting was most severe and prolonged in central Europe, where perhaps one of three people perished from battle, disease, or starvation. In the 1648 Peace of Westphalia, the belligerents agreed to transfer sovereignty, or ultimate political authority, from the Roman papacy to each realm's ruler. That began the modern system of nation states.

After Cromwell died in September 1658, Parliament accepted his son Richard as Lord Protector. Unfortunately, Richard Cromwell proved to be a weak, inept, and divisive leader. General George Monck and a coterie deposed him in May 1659 then, in May 1660, convinced Parliament to invite the former king's son to take the throne as Charles II after he promised to respect Parliament's rights and powers.

Parliament passed a series of laws approved by Charles II that essentially made Britain a theological dictatorship. The 1661 Corporation Act required all public officials to take the Anglican sacraments. The 1662 Uniformity Act forbade worship outside the Anglican Church and required everyone to use the Book of Common Prayer for liturgy. The Test Acts of 1673 and 1678 required all public officials to repudiate the Catholic belief in transubstantiation. Officially, Catholics could not serve in the armed forces, although countless did.

The accession of James II to the throne in 1685 after his older brother died appeared to threaten the Anglican Church's domination. James was a Catholic who sought to overturn those restrictions on his faith. His oldest daughter Mary, an Anglican, had wed William, the Dutch stadtholder or ruler. In June 1688, a cabal in Parliament invited William to lead an army to England and depose James, after which William and Mary would be crowned the rightful monarchs. A civil war ensued. The decisive battle was at the Boyne in Ireland on 1 July 1690, when William's Protestant army defeated James's Catholic army, later called Jacobites. James fled to France. William's army completed its conquest of Ireland with the battle of Aughrim in 1691.

Meanwhile, William and Mary agreed to a series of parliamentary laws that curtailed their power. The 1689 Bill of Rights allowed a small standing army subject to annual parliamentary reauthorisation and oversight. The 1689 Toleration Act let members of any Protestant sect freely worship as long as they believed in the Holy Trinity, accepted the Anglican Church's Thirty-Nine Articles, and established religious schools for their children, and they could vote and run for public office if they met the property standards for either; Catholics were denied those rights until 1829.[3] The 1694 Triennial Act required parliamentary elections within three years from previous ones; the 1716 Septennial Act expanded the time between elections to seven years. Regardless, Parliament annually met for several months rather than its previous sporadic usually short sessions when summoned by the monarch.

England became Great Britain with the 1707 Act of Union that merged Scotland's parliament with England's.[4] The document legally required that the peoples be 'united into one kingdom by the name of Great Britain' with one sovereign, Parliament, legal system, and market. The inhabitants would be known as 'Britons'. The founders acquired that identity from the Romans, who had named the island Britannica and the peoples Britons. Ever since Britons have debated just what their identity means and how it complements or conflicts with their other ethnic identities of being English, Welsh, Scot, or Irish. Nonetheless, despite the deep cleavages among them, British nationalism steadily expanded during the eighteenth century.[5] Of course, frequent wars boosted British identity against their enemies, mostly France.[6]

Britain's sovereignty, however, lay in the monarchy, not the people, who were the monarch's subjects not citizens. Nonetheless, Britons insisted that they had inherent rights like a trial by a jury of one's peers, equal protection before the law, the legal sanctity of one's home and other property, and freedom of speech, press, and petition, in contrast to most foreigners who were repressed and exploited by despotic regimes. They attributed their greater national and personal wealth to their greater liberties and rights.[7]

A dynamic flourished among steadily rising rates of literacy, literature, prosperity, liberalism, and nationalism.[8] Eighteenth-century Britons enjoyed relative freedom of the press.[9] Censorship ended in 1695. Publications were subject to libel laws but very few cases went to court. Thereafter the number of newspapers and journals rose steadily. By 1790, London had fourteen dailies, seven tri-weeklies, and two bi-weeklies. The most influential publications were journals with articles on politics, art, literature, history, and practical advice. The first was *The Spectator*, founded by Joseph Addison and Richard Steele in 1711. Others included *Gentlemen's Magazine*, *London Magazine*, and *Scots Magazine*.

Some writers and painters explicitly promoted nationalism. Novels that did so by contrasting virtuous, naive young Britons abroad with often intriguing foreigners included Henry Fielding's *Joseph Andrews* (1742) and Thomas Smollett's *Roderick Random* (1748) and *The Expedition of Humphrey Clinker* (1751), while plays included Samuel Foote's 'The Englishman in Paris' (1753) and 'The Englishman Returned from Paris' (1756), and Arthur Murphy's 'The Pouter'. Some among those who took the Grand Tour returned to publish accounts that lambasted foreigners, especially the French, as with Smollett's *Travels through France and Italy* (1766). Historians espousing nationalism included John Brown with his *Estimate of the Manners and Principles of the Times* (1758) written amidst the Seven Years' War and John Andrew's *Comparative View of the French and English Nations* (1785). Samuel Johnson promoted national pride through his *Dictionary* (1755), *Encyclopedia Britannica* (1768–71), and *Lives of the Poets* (1779–81). Artists and patrons founded a series of institutions to promote British creativity including the Saint Martin's Lane Academy (1735), the Society for the Encouragement of the Arts, Manufacturing, and Commerce (1755), the Society of Artists of Great Britain (1761), and, most importantly, the Royal Academy of Arts (1768), chartered by George III. Some painters explicitly promoted national sentiments. William Hogarth did so by mocking those Britons who aped foreign styles as in his 'Masquerades and Operas' (1724) and 'Marriage at la Mode' (1743), and mocking foreigners who publicly disdained and secretly admired Britain, as in 'The Gate of Calais, O the Roast Beef of Old England' (1749). Two American-born painters produced two of that century's most patriotic works of art, Benjamin West with his 'Death of Wolfe' (1770) and John Copley with his 'Death of Major Pierson' (1781). A generation later, Arthur Devis painted a dramatic 'Death of Nelson' (1806).

* * *

By 1789, Britain's political system had three power centres – Whitehall, Westminster, and Buckingham – for, respectively, the administration, Parliament, and king.

The king headed both Britain and the Church of England. He picked a Privy Council to advise him and a cabinet headed by a chief minister, usually the First Lord of the Treasury, to govern on his behalf. Politics often forced him to tap men whose personalities, behaviours, or views he found odious. And that was critical to making the king a constitutional rather than absolute monarch. Foreign Secretary Robert Stewart, Viscount Castlereagh, explained that element of Britain's political system: 'Tyrants may poison or murder an obnoxious character, but the surest and only means a constitutional sovereign has to restrain such a character is to employ him ... the essence of a free state is to manage the party warfare as to reconcile it with the safety of the sovereign ... to do this, the king must give contending parties facilities against each other, and not embark himself too deeply with any.'[10]

The king still retained the power to declare war, negotiate peace, and call or dismiss Parliament. He enjoyed a Civil List or annual allowance that reached £900,000 in the late eighteenth century; he could spend it any way he liked without parliamentary oversight. Kings wielded some of that largess for bribing politicians and officials to do their bidding. For instance, the 1809 Civil List of £906,911 included £365,000 for the royal family itself and for the king to distribute such vague unsupervised categories as £93,990 for compensation or services, £63,000 for England and Wales, £35,588 for Scotland, £92,049 for Ireland, £32,000 for former ministers, £28,248 for 4½ per cent duties, £97,271 as pensions for superannuation, and £101,265 as pensions for compensation.[11]

After inheriting the crown at age twenty-two in 1760, George III exclaimed before Parliament that: 'I glory in the name of Britain; and the peculiar happiness of my life will ever consist in promoting the welfare of a people whose loyalty a warm affection to me I consider as the greatest and most permanent security of my throne.'[12] For patriotic Britons that was a welcome contrast with his father and grandfather, whose identities were much more German than British. He was Britain's king from 1760 to 1820, although he did not reign that entire time. Tragically, he suffered from porphyria in which the body masses rather than flushes chemical toxins that attack the nervous system. Porphyria rendered him insane for bouts in 1765, 1788, 1795, 1801, and 1804, and permanently from 1810 to his death in 1820.[13] During those periods the crown prince, George, the Duke of Wales, served as regent and eventually replaced him as king. Americans view George III as a stubborn, intolerant, uncompromising tyrant who provoked their war for independence.[14] Britons tend to sympathise with George III for his sufferings while condemning his son's regency and reign for his decadence and gambling debts.

Lucid, George III asserted his monarchial powers. He moved the royal residence from St James's Palace to Buckingham Palace shortly after he took the throne. He closely followed the issues and policies, and vented his views with his ministers. He was a stickler for etiquette at court and church. Astronomy, mechanics, clocks, and botany fascinated him, and for leisure with Queen Charlotte, he enjoyed music, theatre, paintings, and literature. He was shy, pious, moderate in eating and drinking, and, unlike virtually all monarchs, faithful to his wife, with whom he sired fifteen children: nine boys and six girls. He and his first-born son George, the Prince of Wales, came to detest each other, with the former a moralist and the latter a libertine, spendthrift, gambling addict, and drunkard. He favoured his compliant second son, Frederick, the Duke of York, who he made the army's commander and wished could have followed him on the throne.

The king's ministers rather than the king actually governed Britain and its empire. The formal office of Prime Minister did not then exist. Instead, the First Lord of the Treasury, who usually was also Chancellor of the Exchequer, served as Chief or Prime Minister. The cabinet included him and the other key ministers. The cabinet met infrequently to debate policy. Usually, the Prime Minister discussed what to do with one or more ministers with duties for that issue as an inner cabinet.

Most ministers headed a bureaucracy whose ranks expanded during the eighteenth and early nineteenth centuries. For instance, from 1708 to 1783, officials in customs rose from 1,830 to 2,205, excise from 2,247 to 4,908, and treasury and exchequer from 124 to 200.[15] The number of government employees remained stable from 1783 to 1793, then quadrupled over the twenty-two years to 1815 as Britain forged seven coalitions against France. Given the politics that determined so many promotions and posts, a dilemma often haunted policymakers. The need for more officials was undercut by their varied competence. Foreign Secretary William Grenville captured this dilemma in a letter to ambassador Gilbert Minto in Vienna: 'I have been on the point of sending you one or more military assistants, but I have hesitated from the fear of burthening you with inefficient and sometimes troublesome instruments.'[16]

The king selected his Prime Minister and others from the leaders of the party that appeared to dominate Parliament. Exact counts of party members were nearly impossible because the Whigs and Tories were not formal institutions, but instead were loose coalitions of factions headed by rich, charismatic leaders.[17] Generally, Whigs favoured greater parliamentary power with the king a figurehead, while Tories wanted a power balance between the king and Parliament. Tories tended to represent landed aristocratic and Anglican Church interests while Whigs represented mercantile, urban, and dissident Protestant interests. As such the Whigs and Tories respectively leaned liberal and conservative in the eighteenth-century sense of those terms. Clubs like White's, Goosetree's, and Brooks's overlapped with parties as political associations.[18] Goosetree's and White's leaned Tory, while Brooks was a Whig bastion. White's was especially notorious for its gambling and dissipation.

Of Parliament's two houses, the Commons had greater power because it determined spending and revenues.[19] All money bills originated and had to be approved by the Commons. There were 513 seats before the 1707 Union when forty-five Scottish seats joined, making 558 seats, then the 1801 Union when 100 Irish seats joined for 658 altogether. From 1780 to 1801, the House of Commons had 558 seats from 314 constituencies. England enjoyed the lion's share with 489 members from 245 constituencies, including 203 boroughs, forty counties with two members each, and two universities, followed by forty-five Scottish and twenty-three Welsh constituencies each with one member. The boroughs varied from the smallest, Sarum, with seven electors to several hundred. Those who aspired to vote or hold a public-appointed or -elected office had to be Anglican Church members who owned at least £100 of assessable property. They also had to be rich because parliamentarians received no salary. In 1801, Britain's electorate numbered only about 250,000, or 7 per cent of adult males. Elections were notoriously corrupt.[20] The smaller a constituency's voting population, the more susceptible it was to bribes from candidates. Politically, aristocratic families dominated the Commons as their sons or other picked candidates enjoyed enormous advantages in winning local seats, often with rigged elections that cost from £3,000 to £4,000 to win. For instance, in 1807, 234 members of the Commons, or about one of three, had that backing.[21]

Military officers comprised the largest profession represented in the House of Commons, with lawyers the second largest, and equal to merchants, bankers, and manufacturers. The military share gradually rose during the eighteenth century from fifty-eight army and eleven navy officers or 9.3 per cent among 739 members from 1715 to 1722 to 208 army and seventy-nine navy officers or 14.7 per cent among 1,964 members from 1754 to 1790. From 1714 to 1763, 152 of 374 regimental colonels held seats. That rise reflected Britain's expanding empire and victorious wars. However, those officers were not organised in a party, faction, or club nor did any among them became noted parliamentary leaders.[22]

The House of Lords mostly had the power to delay measures initiated by the House of Commons.[23] Usually only a fraction of those entitled to sit in the Lords actually attended. In 1800, the official ranks included 267 English and Welsh nobles, sixteen Scottish nobles, and twenty-six Anglican bishops. By one count those men represented 0.0000857 per cent of Britain's population.[24] They differed in rank and wealth. Their titles included in ascending order barons, viscounts, marquesses, earls, and dukes. When the 12,000 to 13,000 extended families of those peers are added they still numbered less than one per cent of the population but owned half of all land.[25]

Aristocrats retained their wealth and power by marrying among themselves.[26] Another way was the primogeniture inheritance system whereby the eldest son took title to the land and any younger siblings had to find other sources of wealth. Daughters sought the wealthiest available husbands. The other sons had to rely on their wits to survive and ideally thrive. Usually, all the sons attended elite lower or 'public schools' like Harrow, Winchester, Westminster, and Eton. A relatively precocious or privileged few went on for university studies at Oxford and Cambridge. Young aristocratic men finished up their education with the Grand Tour of months and sometimes years travelling around Europe, especially places like Paris, Venice, Florence, Rome, and Naples.

A few thousand Britons enjoyed enormous wealth without titles, mostly successful merchants and financiers. A steadily expanding minority of Britons were middle-class shopkeepers, landowners, doctors, and lawyers. Most people were relatively poor rural peasants or urban labourers. Many of Britain's leading entrepreneurs were banned from polite society and corrupt politics. Members of nonconformist sects like Quakers could not attend universities, vote, run for office, or receive royal charters for business companies. They valued hard work, honesty, saving for the future, and educating their children. They established their own schools that emphasised the practical application of knowledge. A few sought to promote civil rights for themselves and others who were excluded by forming organisations like the Society of the Supporters of the Bill of Rights (1769), the Constitutional Society (1771), and the Society for Constitutional Information (1780).[27]

Corruption is the illegal or unethical use of public resources for private gain. Corruption permeated British politics at all levels.[28] That might include those holding public offices selling licences, information, property, posts, access, or other favours to outsiders. That pay for play system saps a nation's power by promoting selfish over national interests and venality over competence and efficiency. In Britain, no one corrupted politics more than the king. The monarch could raise money by creating and selling offices. Recipients reaped varying revenues, fees, and bribes from their posts. For instance, 242 sinecures cost £297,095 in 1810.[29] The king further corrupted politics by wielding much of his Civil List or expense account to buy the votes of parliamentarians. During this era, some in power tried to reduce corruption. Prime Minister William Pitt cut the number of sinecures. Prime Minister Spencer Perceval pushed through an 1809 law that forbade buying, soliciting, and selling public offices.

As for local government, the king appointed the mayors of most cities and a Lord Lieutenant to head each of the forty English counties. Mayors appointed boards of aldermen and Lord Lieutenants appointed justices of the peace, sheriffs, and lieutenants from the rich local elite who served without pay aside from a share of fees imposed for court decisions and business licences. The justice of the peace decided misdemeanours in Petty Sessions and annually convened four Quarter Sessions or Assizes with juries to try serious criminal cases.

Britain's criminal justice system then had over 200 death penalty offences. In practice, relatively few people were executed each year. The reason was a lack not of criminals but police to capture them and prisons to keep them. Gradually cities established constabularies with salaried officers. Usually, it was up to victims to somehow apprehend criminals and bring them before a Justice of the Peace. Sentences for those found guilty was usually transportation rather than execution. Crime rose during the revolutionary and Napoleonic wars with worsening inflation, poverty, homelessness, depletion of strong local men who might deter crime, and increased numbers of widows with children.

The deficiencies of Britain's government and population were at once blatant yet relatively less severe than those of most other nation states. Indeed, the relative efficiency of Britain's political system and the unity of its people were among an array of reasons why Britain was able to fight nearly non-stop and forge seven coalitions against France from 1793 to 1815.

Chapter 2

Economic

Nothing has wrought an alteration in this order of people as the introduction of trade. This hath ... almost totally changed the manners, customs, and habits of the people, especially of the lower sort. The narrowness of their future is changed into wealth, their frugality into luxury, their humility into pride, and their subjection into equality.

[*Henry Fielding*]

If a revolution involves rapid, systematic change, then Britain's industrial version was not that but evolutionary.[1] Nonetheless, in the late-eighteenth century, British entrepreneurs and innovators pioneered the transformation of manufacturing from small-scale, slow-paced 'cottage' production to large-scale, fast-paced 'factory' production. That change unfolded steadily over the next half century until mass manufacturing skyrocketed in an array of products, most notably textiles. The industrial revolution depended on related preceding cultural, agrarian, financial, mercantile, transportation, energy, and machinery developments that together can be called an industrious revolution.[2]

The Renaissance, with its core value of humanism, seeded that dynamic three centuries earlier. Humanism is the belief that every individual is a unique mix of potentialities, mostly for good. Our moral imperative is to nurture the best in each other within a community. One achieves meaning by fulfilling one's potential. That outlook diametrically opposed the Medieval Christian view that devotion to God might bring salvation after one's death. Humanism was a renaissance or rebirth of the outlook propounded by most ancient Greek and Roman thinkers. Of course, the ability to achieve that ideal was confined to those wealthy enough to afford it, a minority in the ancient and early modern worlds. A Renaissance man or woman was witty in several languages, dabbled in painting, composed sonnets, played a musical instrument, and read enlightening and often provocative works of literature.

The Renaissance symbolically began around 1450 when Johannes Guttenberg used movable type to mass produce books and pamphlets. As production rose, prices fell, giving more people an incentive to learn to read if they could

2.1. Comparisons of Yearly Average Growth in Different Sectors[3]

	Industry	Commerce	Government Defence	Rent Services	Agriculture
1700–60	0.71%	0.69%	1.91%	0.38%	0.60%
1760–80	1.51%	0.70%	1.29%	0.69%	0.13%
1780–1801	2.11%	1.32%	2.11%	0.97%	0.75%
1801–31	3.00%	2.13%	n.a.	n.a.	1.18%

2.2. Comparisons of Real Average Yearly Growth Per Person[4]

	Wages	Productivity	Consumption
1780–1821	0.71%	0.42%	0.47%
1821–51	0.94%	1.19%	1.24%
1780–1851	0.80%	0.75%	0.80%

afford a tutor. The circulation of knowledge spurred an ongoing expansion of trade and a middle class of shopkeepers, artisans, money-changers, lawyers, and doctors. Universities founded as theology schools in the Middle Ages expanded their curriculums to include law and natural sciences. Visually, the humanist ideal was best realised in painting and sculpture that depicted individual characters realistically, a revolutionary artistic change from the stylised depictions of types of people by Medieval artists. On the continent, scientists like Nicolas Copernicus and Galileo Galilei discovered through telescopes that the earth circled the sun, debunking the Catholic Church's insistence that the earth was at the centre of the universe. Researchers became 'scientific' with controlled experiments, careful measurements, extensive reports, and repeated results before drawing conclusions, then sharing them through publications and conferences.

If the Renaissance promoted an individual's freedom to express himself creatively, the Reformation asserted one's right freely to interpret the Bible and express one's religious beliefs. Martin Luther, a priest, sparked that revolution in 1517 when he nailed his Ninety-Five Thesis or criticisms of the Catholic Church to the front door of his church in Wittenberg in central Germany. The pope soon excommunicated him and anyone else who dared challenge Rome's theological and political domination of western Christendom. Ever more monarchs, including English King Henry VIII, either cynically or faithfully embraced Protestantism to free themselves from Rome's authority. That led to a series of worsening religious wars between Catholics and Protestants that culminated with the Thirty Years' War from 1618 to 1648. In the Peace of Westphalia, the belligerents agreed to disagree; thereafter each head of state could determine his own realm's version of Christianity. That transfer of sovereignty or ultimate authority from the pope to the princes inaugurated the modern nation state system.

The Enlightenment was the third revolution in thought and behaviour that developed the modern world. From 1648 to 1789, or symbolically from the Peace of Westphalia to the Parisian mob's storming of the Bastille, humanists emphasised individual economic and political freedom. Symbolically, the Enlightenment peaked in 1776. In Philadelphia, American patriots issued a Declaration of Independence from Britain justified by an eloquent and succinct expression of natural laws and rights of life, liberty, the pursuit of happiness, and government grounded on democratic principles. In London, Adam Smith's nearly thousand-page tome, *An Inquiry into the Wealth of Nations*, argued that each person's freedom to produce and consume best promoted the wealth of each and thus all people.

In Britain, Smith was only the latest thinker who expressed Enlightenment ideals. Scientists like Francis Bacon, Thomas Harriot, Robert Boyle, Isaac Newton, and Joseph Priestly through experiments discovered and explained many principles that governed the natural world. Through philosophy and literature, thinkers like John Locke, Jonathan Swift, Daniel Defoe, and David Hume explored notions of individual political liberty and representative government. A series of organisations arose that promoted discovery and knowledge, including the Royal Society in 1660, the Chelsea Physic Garden in 1673, the Society for the Encouragement of the Arts, Manufacturers, and Commerce in 1754, the Birmingham Lunar Society in 1765, the Manchester Committee for the Protection and Encouragement of Trade in 1774, the Manchester Literary and Philosophical Society in 1781, the Derby Philosophical Society in 1784, the Linnean Society in 1788, and the Society for Philosophical Experiments and Conversations in 1794. Each had its share of brilliant members that shared information, ideas, projects, and inspiration with each other. For instance, among the Lunar Society's most esteemed members were Josiah Wedgewood, James Watt, Joseph Priestly, and Erasmus Darwin. Secret Masonic lodges promoted free thinking among members for the good of society. Whitehall advanced knowledge by launching naval expeditions to map the world, most vitally those of Captain George Anson's three-year and nine-month circumnavigation of the earth from 1740 to 1743 and Captain James Cook's three voyages to the Pacific Ocean from 1768 to 1771, 1772 to 1775, and 1776 to 1780. In 1714, Parliament offered a reward for anyone who could invent a device that measured longitude; John

Harrison won that prize with the chronometer he invented in 1730 and thereafter improved.[3]

Britain's cultural freedom for precocious individuals to tinker with ideas and devices was a critical reason why the industrial revolution began there and not elsewhere.[4] Britons were far more interested than their French counterparts in experimenting and finding practical and profitable applications for scientific concepts. Another key element was that ever more Britons could read, write, and calculate. Productivity and literacy tend to rise together. Although there was no public education system, parish churches often provided basic schooling for boys and girls, while wealthier families hired tutors. As for higher education, Oxford and Cambridge were renowned more for being finishing schools for the elite while Scotland's universities at Edinburgh and Aberdeen provided students with ample opportunities to learn an array of subjects and, more importantly, learn better how to learn.

An agrarian revolution that produced more crops and livestock with fewer workers preceded and helped make possible the industrial revolution.[5] Redundant farm workers found non-farm work in the countryside or migrated to cities for diverse jobs. Most people enjoyed more nutritious diets that boosted their productivity, creativity, and longevity. That had positive military as well as economic and cultural effects. Late eighteenth-century British army recruits averaged 172cm, compared with 162cm for French recruits.[7]

A series of innovations boosted productivity. Grain harvests got easier with the switch from sickles to scythes. Jethro Tull devised new farming techniques like soil aeration, crop hybrids, fruit grafts, seed drills, and light plows that expanded production; he shared his discoveries in his 1733 book *Horse-Hoeing Husbandry*. Robert Bakewell's selective sheep-breeding produced more wool and mutton. Viscount Charles 'Turnip' Townshend got his nickname by popularising that crop as cheap fodder for people and livestock. New crops like clover, sainfoin, turnips, and lucerne restored minerals to depleted soils. Crop rotations replenished soils, with the most productive being the four-year Norfolk system of wheat, turnips or potatoes, barley, and clover.

2.3. Adult Literacy, 1500 and 1800[5]

	1500	1800		1500	1800
England	6%	53%	Austria/Hungary	6%	21%
Netherlands	10%	68%	Poland	6%	21%
Belgium	10%	49%	Italy	9%	22%
Germany	6%	35%	Spain	9%	20%
France	7%	37%			

The demand for food from swelling numbers of urban dwellers and factory workers encouraged aristocrats to 'enclose' more of their land and entrepreneurs to buy and drain marshlands for crops and livestock. To do so required a parliamentary act. The first came in 1604 and the number steadily increased to peak at 3,828 enclosures for more than 7 million acres from 1750 to 1819. Simply pulling stones from the earth and fitting them into walls around a pasture enriched soil as grass replaced rock and when plowed for crops the soil stayed rather than washed away. Enclosed fields were 30 to 40 per cent more productive than open fields. The new crops flourished on marginal lands to feed people and livestock. Agrarian lands increased from 59 to 91 per cent, productivity per acre from 15 to 38 per cent, and labour productivity from 41 to 70 per cent. That caused the share of agrarian workers – landowners, farmers, and labourers –in the economy to fall from 45 per cent or 2.25 million of 5 million people in 1700 to 36 per cent or 3 million of 8.5 million in 1800.[8]

Not everyone benefited from these changes. Tenant land rents rose 80 per cent from 1790 to 1813.[10] Enclosures forced tens of thousands of tenants from their plots to even worse poverty in city slums. Nature was as fickle as ever. During the Napoleonic era, poor harvests caused food shortages and high prices in 1792–93, 1794–95, 1799–1801, 1812–13, and 1815–16. However, the worst fears were not realised. In 1798, Thomas Malthus predicted in his 'Essay on Population' that the population would grow faster than the food supply, leading eventually to chronic mass starvation and violence for the scraps. In the early nineteenth century that appeared to be happening in Britain. Whitehall eventually alleviated worsening shortages in

2.4. Country Population Shares by Location, 1500 and 1800[9]

	1500			1800		
	Urban	Rural Non-Farm	Farm	Urban	Rural Non-Farm	Farm
England	7%	18%	74%	29%	36%	35%
Netherlands	30%	14%	56%	34%	25%	41%
Belgium	28%	14%	58%	22%	29%	49%
Germany	8%	18%	73%	9%	29%	62%
France	9%	18%	73%	13%	28%	59%
Austria/Hungary	5%	19%	76%	8%	35%	57%
Poland	6%	19%	75%	5%	39%	56%
Italy	22%	16%	62%	22%	20%	58%
Spain	19%	16%	65%	20%	16%	64%

1846 by abolishing the Corn Laws that protected Britain's farmers from imported food. That combined with the latest generation of agriculture technological innovations, brought the food supply back in sync with rising demand.

Investments were critical to the industrial revolution. Those depended on a stable expanding financial system.[11] In 1694, William III took a decisive step toward that when he chartered the Bank of England as a corporation to be the government's chief lender at interest rates never to exceed 5 per cent.[12] The Bank of England enjoyed a monopoly on joint stock banking. In England, no other bank could have more than six partners or be incorporated, which meant they were personally liable for any bad loans or bankruptcies. The Crown did charter the Bank of Scotland in 1695 and the Royal Bank of Scotland in 1727 with no limits to partners but the same restrictions as other banks. The Bank of England held most of the nation's gold reserves, which made its banknotes good as gold, thus served as a stable paper currency. That monopoly lasted until 1826.

Despite the restrictions on private banking, the number of banks steadily grew from around a dozen in 1750 to as many as 780 across the country in 1810. Bankers devised more sophisticated means like letters of credit and bills of exchange to transfer and invest money deposited by businesses and households in their vaults. Capital formation soared from £83,000 in 1760 to £776,000 in 1810.[13]

Marine insurance provided a rising share of British finance. Leading firms formed the Society of Underwriters in 1760 to organise and publish an annual Register of Shipping. By 1793, the industry was centred at London's Royal Exchange with offices for Lloyd's Coffee House, the Subscribers' Room, the Captains' Room, the Jerusalem, the Jamaica, the Virginia and Maryland, and Sam's. Of them, Lloyd's, founded in 1774, was the most powerful. Other ports like Liverpool, Bristol, Glasgow, Newcastle, and Hull had their own marine insurance underwriting companies. Many firms had offices overseas in Amsterdam, Hamburg, Copenhagen, New York, and Philadelphia.

In the substratum of regions across the British Isles lay ample veins of minerals. Two critical problems with mining were aquifer water filling the hole, and diminishing air for miners to breathe. The development of steam-powered pumps resolved that problem by extracting water and circulating air. Miners now could dig deeper and extract more coal, iron ore, tin, lead, and copper. For instance, from 1780 to 1806, iron production skyrocketed from 67,000 tons to 265,000 tons. Mineral prices dropped as more was extracted, refined, and transported to factories.[14] Most industrialisation occurred in cities like Leeds, Manchester, Birmingham, and Sheffield near mining districts.

A transportation revolution literally carried the industrial revolution.[15] Parliament led that by licensing turnpike and canal companies. When completed, the turnpikes usually halved travel times for wagons and carriages. For instance, a mail coach clattering the 114 miles from London to Bristol took forty hours in 1750 and eleven hours and forty-five minutes in 1811. That increased business profits and government revenues. Yearly postal revenues soared from £196,000 in 1784 to £391,000 in 1793 to £1,000,000 by 1800. Profits rose for completed canals as barges held far more than horse-drawn wagons. A barge guided by two men could carry 24 tons of iron that otherwise would need twelve wagons drawn by forty-eight horses and guided by twenty-four men. Rivers like the Trent, Severn, and Mersey drained from mining country. Canals extended navigation deep into the interior, where boats were loaded with ore that was brought downstream to refineries. From 1760 to 1800 alone, Parliament passed 165 canal acts with £113 million worth of construction costs, which stimulated the overlapping local, regional, and national economies. The most important canals linked the Mersey with the Trent in 1772 and the Severn in 1777. A canal linked the Thames and Severn in 1789 and them with the Mersey in 1790. By 1815, Britain had 2,000 navigable river miles and 2,200 canal miles. That internal web of canals was especially appreciated from 1793 to 1815 when French privateers prowled Britain's inter-coastal trade routes.[16]

A series of inventions and innovations expanded mass production in ever more products.[17] For textile production, John Kay invented the flying shuttle in 1733, James Hargreaves the spinning jenny in 1766, Richard Arkwright the water frame in 1769, Samuel Crompton the mule spinner in 1778, Edmund Cartwright the power loom in 1788, and William Marshall worsted spinning in 1790. In metallurgy, John Wood invented the potting process for producing pig iron in 1761, John Wilkinson a cannon barrel boring device with unprecedented precision that was eventually applied to steam engine cylinders in 1774, and Henry Cort the puddling furnace and rolling mill for refining pig iron in 1784. For steam power, Thomas Newcomen invented an engine to drain mines in 1712, and James Watt a rotary engine many times more efficient than previous ones in 1781. As engineers improved steam engines, they burned less coal, which raised profits. By 1800, over 2,500 steam engines pumped mines and ran machines across the nation. Nonetheless, falling rather than steamed water still produced more inanimate energy.

Improvements in measuring time helped propel industrialisation. 'Clockwork' for workers to begin and end their workdays at precise times and

2.5. British Inanimate Energy Power Sources, 1760 and 1800[18]

	1760	1800
Steam	5,000	35,000
Water	70,000	120,000
Wind	10,000	15,000
Total	85,000	170,000

produce a quota in between came to personify the industrial revolution. Dutchman Christian Huygens's 1656 invention of the pendulum for tall clocks cut their average daily inaccuracy from fifteen minutes to fifteen seconds, and improvements further shaved those seconds. Watchmaking involves cutting and assembling precise, tiny, delicate brass wheels, springs, gears, screws, and hands that made them work; watchmakers transferred their precision skills to cutting industrial-strength brass and iron gears that replaced straps for turning machines.

Factory production destroyed cottage production. Workers running machines that rapidly churned out parts for a final product assembled by others replaced craftsmen who carefully, lovingly created or refined all the parts that they joined into the finished product. The number of jobs soared far beyond those they displaced, but drudgery, danger, and alienation dominated the workplace. Factory owners treated workers as interchangeable and ultimately discardable as the parts they endlessly produced twelve hours a day, six days a week. They preferred more docile women and children as labourers even if they lacked the physical strength of men.

Britain's population expanded from around 5.5 million in 1688 to 9.9 million in England and Wales and 1.5 million in Scotland in 1801, the first official census. Greater prosperity lowered the average age of marriage and raised the portion of people who married that led to more children. First marriages for women fell from 26.5 to 23.5 and the mean age for giving birth from 33 to 31 years.[19] Annual food production usually exceeded population increases. Better nutrition reduced miscarriages and let more children survive. Edward Jenner's mastery of smallpox inoculation in 1796 would eventually further swell the population as more people received vaccinations.

Cities bloated with people.[21] Urbanisation both spurred and was spurred by industrialisation. London's population rose from 200,000 in 1600 to 630,000 in 1715, then to a precise census count of 1,096,789 in 1801, and to 1,400,000 in 1815. About one of ten Britons lived in London. By 1801, fourteen other cities held more than 20,000 people, and thirty-three cities had

2.6. Distribution of Professions by Families and Incomes in England and Wales, 1801–03[20]

	Family Numbers	Share of Total	Income	Share of Total
High Titles/Gentlemen	27,203	1.2%	£27,540,000	13.9%
Professions	74,840	3.4%	£17,310,000	8.7%
Military/Maritime	244,348	11.1%	£10,380,000	5.2%
Commerce	205,800	9.4%	£39,210,000	19.7%
Industry Construction	541,026	24.7%	£51,070,000	25.7%
Agriculture	320,000	14.6%	£38,000,000	19.1%
Labourers	340,000	15.5%	£10,500,000	5.4%
Cottagers/Paupers	260,179	11.9%	£2,600,000	1.3%
Vagrants	179,718	8.2%	£1,920,000	1.0%
Total	2,193,114		£198,580,000	

from 10,000 to 20,000 people. Over the preceding century the share of people living in cities with 10,000 or more people rose from 13.4 per cent to 24.0 per cent.[22] Those rising populations worsened already dismal problems of pollution, poverty, homelessness, crime, prostitution, and disease.

Yet in cities, towns, and villages alike, a middle class of shopkeepers, traders, artisans, farmers, innkeepers, lawyers, and doctors steadily expanded and their demand for goods and services at once fuelled national economic development and enriched themselves. They owned houses that they filled with Chippendale furniture, Wedgewood porcelain, and Bateman silverware, to name the most esteemed of numerous producers. They wore the latest fashions in silk, cotton, and wool. They subscribed to the leading journals of high culture like *The Gentleman's Magazine* (1731) and *The Lady's Magazine* (1770). Jane Austen beautifully described that world in her novels *Sense and Sensibility* (1811), *Pride and Prejudice* (1813), *Mansfield Park* (1814), *Emma* (1815), *Northanger Abbey* (1818), and *Persuasion* (1818). Henry Fielding observed that phenomena seven decades earlier: 'Nothing has wrought an alteration in this order of people as the introduction of trade. This hath ... almost totally changed the manners, customs, and habits of the people, especially of the lower sort. The narrowness of their future is changed into wealth, their frugality into luxury, their humility into pride, and their subjection into equality.'[23]

The industriousness of Britons empowered them to wage a global war and forge seven coalitions from 1793 to 1815.

Chapter 3

Imperial

As the alliances entered into by the late king, my father, with foreign powers, have contributed to restoring the tranquillity, and preserving the balance of Europe, I shall endeavour to cultivate those alliances, and to improve and perfect this great work, for the honour, interest, and security of my people. [*George II*]

How shall we be able to render these Colonies more subservient to this Island, and more obedient to the Laws and Government of the Mother Country, than they voluntarily choose to be. [*Josiah Tucker*]

This vast empire on which the sun never sets and whose bounds nature has not yet ascertained. [*George Macartney*]

Imperialism is the conquest and colonisation of one people by another. Most empires evolve haphazardly over time as fear and greed motivates a state's leaders to war to successfully vanquish foreign threats and seize foreign opportunities. Ideally colonies provide consumers, producers, and fighters that enrich the conqueror beyond the costs of governing, policing, and protecting the conquest. Imperialism tends to beget imperialism as leaders perceive their new conquests vulnerable to neighbouring powers who must be subdued.

England's overseas empire began with Ireland. England's Norman rulers invaded Ireland in 1169 and established a Lordship over it in 1171. In 1541, Henry VIII designated Ireland a kingdom with himself and his successors its rightful monarchs. That began the notorious apartheid system based on religion with Anglicans dominating political, economic, social, and religious power, followed by Presbyterian Scot immigrants, and Irish Catholics at the bottom with no rights, only duties.

Beyond Ireland, England's empire followed the wakes of other Europeans.[1] In the mid-fifteenth century, the Portuguese launched a series of expeditions down Africa's west coast that traded with various states and tribes along the way in the hope of eventually rounding the continent's southern end then crossing the Indian Ocean to pack their vessels with spices and other exotic goods from Southeast Asia. Vasco da Gama succeeded in 1498, leading the way for steady Spanish trade with Asia. Then, in 1492, Christopher Columbus sailed west to discover an unknown hemisphere.

During the sixteenth century, the Catholic Habsburg Empire threatened England. That empire reached its height with Emperor Charles V, who reigned over Austria, Spain, the Netherlands, and an array of smaller realms. Of them, Spain was the most powerful. It had a vast expanding empire in the western hemisphere and in 1580 absorbed Portugal. In 1568, the Dutch began a rebellion against Habsburg rule that took eighty years before they finally achieved independence.

English Queen Elizabeth I, who ruled from 1558 to 1603, counterbalanced the Habsburg threat by first secretly and then in 1585 openly aiding the Dutch revolt. She authorised John Hawkins, Francis Drake, and other sea captains to attack Spanish merchant and war vessels wherever they could be found, including the New World. Hawkins and Drake brought back scores of captured vessels packed with gold, silver, and other riches that enriched England's wealth and power. From 1577 to 1580, Drake sailed around the world, capturing Spanish vessels and mapping the way. 1588, Spanish King Philip II launched an armada of 130 warships packed with 7,000 troops to invade England. The English and Dutch fleets defeated the armada and a series of storms destroyed most of the rest of it before its remnants returned to Spain.

From the late sixteenth century through the early eighteenth, the English crown issued royal charters to companies to explore, trade, settle, and even war in designated foreign lands. Most consequential were those for the Virginia Company, Massachusetts Company, West India Company, East India Company, Hudson's Bay Company, and Royal Africa Company.

The first successful settlement was Jamestown, Virginia, founded in 1607. Gradually, English companies established or conquered other colonies along North America's east coast, including Plymouth in 1620, Massachusetts in 1628, Maryland in 1634, Connecticut and New Hampshire in 1635, Rhode Island in 1636, North Carolina in 1663, New York, East Jersey, and West Jersey in 1664, South Carolina in 1670, Pennsylvania in 1681, Nova Scotia in 1710, and Georgia in 1732. Those became England's most economically diverse and prosperous colonies in which most people were the middling sort who enjoyed property and income. Although slaves existed in each colony, the share of the population and thus economic importance varied from around 2 per cent in the New England colonies and Nova Scotia, 15 per cent in the mid-Atlantic colonies, and 40 per cent in the southern colonies.

Britain's West Indian and Atlantic colonies were settled or taken, starting with Bermuda in 1607 then St Christopher's/St Kitts in 1624, Barbados in 1627, Nevis in 1628, Antigua in 1632, Montserrat in 1632, and the Bahamas in 1648, while an expedition captured Jamaica in 1655.[2] Those colonies' planters and shippers produced about 10 per cent of the British Empire's economy and so reaped vast wealth and thus power. Cash crops included sugar, coffee, cotton, cocoa, indigo, ginger, and tobacco. Sugar, dubbed 'white gold', was the most lucrative crop. Europeans imported 90 per cent of their sugar from the West Indies in the 1780s, with 43.3 per cent coming from French colonies and 36.7 per cent from British ones.[3] Crops grew year-round, yielding two and sometimes three harvests. Soil was rich and deep. Slaves were expensive to buy but cheap to maintain; masters squeezed every penny of profit from them. Refining, storing, and shipping crops was relatively easy. Profits were enormous from sales in Europe and other markets. The West Indies were important markets as well for some products as the planter elite demanded the latest luxury goods, wines, and fashions. There was huge demand for cheap clothing for slaves.

Spanning the Atlantic basin was a triangular trade of British manufactured goods, African slaves, and West Indian crops. There was also trade between the American and West Indian colonies whereby the former exchanged salt beef, rice, flour, dried fish, and lumber for the latter's rum, molasses, and sugar whose respective values were £848,934 and £762,053 in 1770. In 1787, Britain's West India trade involved 13,976 sailors manning 689 vessels totaling 148,176 tons of about 1 million total tons of shipping. British sugar imports rose from 8,176 tons in 1663 to 97,000 tons in 1775. Britain consumed portions of each crop and re-exported the rest. For instance, around 70 per cent of sugar was re-exported. By 1789, the West Indies trade provided 23.9 per cent of Britain's imports, 9.6 per cent of its exports and re-exports, and 15.5 per cent of its total trade. Two forces potentially threatened this prosperous commerce – war and slave revolts, with the former far more common than the latter.[4]

Spain initiated the triangular Atlantic trade of exchanging European manufactured goods for West African slaves, slaves for West Indian plantation crops, and those crops for more manufactured goods. By the eighteenth century, Britain's triangular trade surpassed that of not just Spain but also Portugal, France, and the Netherlands. Liverpool's merchants amassed the most wealth from the slave trade, followed by those of London then Bristol. From 1662 to 1807, British merchants purchased 3,415,500 slaves from African owners and conveyed them in 131,200 vessels across the Atlantic; 450,700 of the slaves or about 13.2 per cent died on the voyage, leaving

2,964,800 to be sold. That was about half the total transatlantic trade during that time. Around 1790, the slave trade represented about £1.5 million in investments and profits of about £150,000 or 10 per cent. Although the trade was lucrative, it was less than 1 per cent of Britain's economy and thus negligible in financing the industrial revolution.[5]

For both financial and humanitarian reasons, slave ship captains followed procedures to minimise deaths during the voyage. Slaves received three meals a day, including a dram of brandy for breakfast, and every day they had to bathe and exercise, including dance. A 1789 act required a surgeon on each slave vessel. Nonetheless, deaths from disease and suicide remained high. However, more crew may have died than slaves. From September 1784 to January 1790, 350 slave trade vessels from Bristol and Liverpool lost 2,283 of 12,263 crew members or 21.5 per cent.[6]

The power pyramid of the West Indian colonies was necessarily rigid and steep, with perhaps 50,000 whites exploiting 10,500 free mulattos and 465,000 slaves in the 1780s.[7] Slave revolts were rare but naturally feared by the tiny ruling white elite.[8] Maroons were communities of escaped slaves living in the Jamaican mountains. From 1700 to 1729, the Maroons raided the settlements to rob, murder, and rape whites, and free slaves. The British fought back with a series of campaigns from 1729 to 1739 known as the Maroon War. In 1739, a treaty between British officials and Maroon leader Captain Cudjoe acknowledged Maroon autonomy in return for an end to Maroon raids and the return of any escaped slaves for rewards.

* * *

As in the western hemisphere, the British did not begin to trade in the Indian and Pacific basins until nearly a century after Portugal and Spain led the way.[9] In 1600, Elizabeth I granted the East India Company a charter with a monopoly on all trade east of Africa's Cape of Good Hope. To develop that trade, the charter authorised the East India Company to wield diplomatic and military power.[10] The Company led the way to Britain's eventual conquest of South Asia during the nineteenth century. That was never the intention. As in other regions, empire in India developed haphazardly over centuries as the English defeated threats and seized opportunities from European rivals and native states.

India was never unified before the British empire. It was a geographic term for a subcontinent with a feudalistic hodge-podge of different states, languages, religions, and loyalties. During the seventeenth and eighteenth centuries, the stagnant Mogul empire with its capital at Delhi was the largest realm but faced an array of restive suzerain and outright enemy states.

Initially, like the Portuguese, Dutch, and French, the English cut deals with the Moguls or other rulers to lease land for trading posts, which gradually expanded in population and fortification. The most important acquisitions were Madras in 1639, Bombay in 1662, and Calcutta in 1686, called presidencies. From those city-states, the Company's trade expanded across the local region and overseas to ports around the Indian Ocean basin, Southeast Asia, and China. Each was governed by a president with an advisory council and defended by a small army and navy. Gradually those enclaves acquired more adjacent and then distant territories and thus transformed from weak city-states into increasingly powerful states.

Inevitably, the English and other European traders got caught up in local rivalries and wars.[11] They won most of those conflicts with their early modern advantages in organisation, firepower, and leadership over the feudal Indian levies. For instance, the rate of fire of a European cannon crew was ten times that of Indian gunners. Europeans fought with flintlock muskets with attachable bayonets, while Indians mostly used antiquated matchlocks and wheellocks. European officers drilled their troops in precise, swift manoeuvres, rapid, accurate fire, and fierce, cohesive charges that devastated Indian armies. To augment their ranks, Europeans trained and armed native or sepoy troops. With time, Indian leaders hired Europeans to instil European training and arms in their troops. Victories usually reaped reparations, trade, taxes, and territory from the defeated.

The most important products were Indian saltpeter, silk, cotton, calicos, indigo, and rice; East Indies spices; and Chinese tea, porcelain, and silk. India's most important product was saltpeter, an ingredient for gunpowder. The East India Company was required annually to send 2,000–3,000 tons at a fixed price to London. The most valuable product was Chinese tea, whose importation soared from £8,000 in 1699–1700 to £848,000 in 1772–74.[12]

The British suffered chronic trade deficits with China. British consumers highly desired Chinese tea, silk, lacquerware, and porcelain but the Chinese disdained any British products. As a result, British merchants had to pay coin for Chinese goods. Compounding that was the law that forced foreigners to trade only at Canton (Quandong) with a syndicate of Chinese merchants called the Co-Hong that kept prices high.

Whitehall dispatched two missions to China with four key goals; to exchange embassies in each other's capitals, end the Co-Hong system, open new ports, and purchase a small coastal island. Colonel Charles Cathcart died en route to China in 1787. Former Madras Governor George Macartney reached Beijing and met the emperor in August 1792, but the Chinese rejected all his requests. Eventually, the British merchants resolved the trade deficit with Indian opium, in violation of Chinese law. That began with the opium trade's authorisation with the 1813 Charter Act, led to the Opium War from 1839 to 1842, and culminated with the 1842 Treaty of Nanjing that forced China to open five ports, exchange embassies, and cede Hong Kong island to Britain.

About a hundred vessels plied the East Indies trade annually. The largest vessels sailed the furthest, the 1,200-ton ships bound to and from Canton, China. Smaller 800-ton and 500-ton vessels served the Indian trade. Construction costs for the 1,200-ton, 800-ton, and 500-ton vessels were around £70,000, £50,000, and £30,000, respectively. Ships usually lasted for six round trip voyages before rot rendered them fit only for scrap. Ships carried cannon and small arms as well as cargo. Crews were trained to man the cannon, fire muskets and pistols, and slash with cutlasses. The 1,200-ton, 800-ton, and 500-ton vessels mounted up to thirty-eight, thirty-two, and twenty cannon, respectively. Captains got rich with allocations of cargo space for their own goods. For instance, of an 800-ton vessel, a captain enjoyed 56 tons for himself.[13]

* * *

Trade rose steadily between Britain and its expanding empire. From 1686 to 1815, the tonnage of British merchant ships rose from 340,000 to 2,477,000, while the tonnage of those that sailed for America, the Caribbean, or Asia rose from 82,000 to 467,000.[14] Key imports from the empire were tropical commodities like tobacco, sugar, tea, coffee, cocoa, rice, and spices; textiles like cotton, silk, linen, nanqueen, and calico; raw materials for shipbuilding like hemp, flax, tar, pitch, turpentine, masts, bowsprits, and spars; and Indian saltpeter. In return, Britain exported a broadening array of manufactured goods, with textiles the most valuable.

Whitehall increasingly regulated trade to protect and promote it and British manufacturing.[15] The Navigation Acts of 1651, 1660, 1661, 1663, 1673, 1696, 1733, 1763, 1765, 1767, 1770, 1774, and 1786 either prevented foreigners from shipping and selling products in Britain and its colonies or prevented colonists from making a longer list of finished products and forced them to sell only to Britain. Thus, did the Navigation Acts benefit British merchants and manufacturers at the expense of colonials and foreigners in a vast captive market. For instance, it was mostly London merchants that reaped fortunes by selling American rice, tobacco, lumber, rum, salt beef, salt pork, and cotton to other European countries. The increasingly onerous trade and production restrictions were among the reasons why the Americans eventually rebelled against Britain.

3.1. Exports and Re-exports from Britain to Its Empire and World in pounds sterling[16]

	Exports		Re-exports	
	1700–01	1789–90	1700–01	1789–90
North America	256,000	3,295,000	106,000	468,000
West Indies	205,000	1,690,000	131,000	202,000
East Indies	114,000	2,096,000	11,000	77,000
Africa	81,000	517,000	64,000	282,000
Imperial Total	656,000	7,598,000	312,000	1,029,000
World	4,461,000	14,350,000	2,126,000	5,380,000

Many entrepreneurs formed groups to lobby Whitehall, Parliament, and influential politicians either to win support for them or end favours for others. William Shipley, a London artist, gathered sixteen like-minded associates to found the Society for the Encouragement of Arts, Commerce, and Manufacturers in 1754; within a decade, it boasted 2,100 members including members of the political elite.[17] Jonas Hanway formed with twenty-two other merchants the Marine Society to promote foreign trade and Royal Navy enlistments in 1756. By 1793, Whitehall had revoked the monopolies of most companies that had originally received them like the Royal Africa, Hudson's Bay, and Levant firms. Companies competed for business in most regions and colonies around the globe. That did not stop rivals from co-operating to pressure Whitehall to support their common interests. The Committee of West Indian Merchants was an especially powerful lobby group that shaped British policy toward the Caribbean. As the name implied, the General Shipowners Society lobbied for industry-wide interests like protecting sources of building supplies and trade routes.

Britain's growing empire was a refuge for Britons who sought economic or religious freedom, and a dumping ground for convicts. Nearly a million Britons emigrated to the colonies from 1689 to 1815. Under the Transportation Act, authorities exiled 49,000 male and female felons to the American colonies from 1718 to 1775 and 29,400 to Botany Bay, Australia, from 1787 to 1820.[18]

Whitehall did not run its empire, it supervised it. No one bureaucracy was in charge, but several had overlapping imperial duties. The Privy Council handled colonial affairs through its Lords of the Committee of Trade and Plantations known as the Board of Trade, established in 1696; its twenty appointed members issued commissions and instructions to and corresponded with colonial governors, gathered information on colonial affairs, and accepted colonial assembly petitions. The Treasury Department collected trade duties, excise taxes, postal revenues, and other official fees. The Admiralty defended the sea lanes, operated courts for maritime cases like smuggling, issued letters of marque to privateers, and oversaw colonial production of naval stores like masts, spars, pitch, hemp, and tar. In 1660, Charles II established two offices each headed by a Secretary of State. The Southern Department oversaw southern England, Wales, the American colonies, and relations with Catholic sovereigns. The Northern Department oversaw northern England, Scotland, Ireland, and relations with Protestant countries.

In 1782, George III rationalised the confusing system. He abolished the Southern and Northern Departments and replaced them with the Home Department for the United Kingdom and the Foreign Affairs Department. In 1784, he established the Privy Council for Trade and Plantations to supplement the Board of Trade.

In the western hemisphere, each colony had a governor with the king appointing all except those of Connecticut and Rhode Island, whose assemblies elected them and their councils. Royal governors selected a council of half a dozen of the colony's most powerful leaders. Each American colony and the West Indian colonies of Jamaica and Barbados had assemblies elected by men with property valued above a certain varying level. Victory in the Seven Years' War reaped new colonies through the 1763 Treaty of Paris. George III authorised governors, councils, and assemblies for Canada, East Florida, West Florida, and the Windward Islands of Saint Vincent, Tobago, Grenada, and Dominica. In 1791, the crown split Canada between Lower or mostly French-speaking Canada in the Saint Lawrence valley and Upper or mostly English-speaking Canada north of the Great Lakes.

Over time, the East India Company became a state within a state as its power expanded with its wealth. At the London headquarters, two institutions governed the company: the executive Court of Committees with its governor, deputy governor, and twenty-four directors, and the legislative General Court (later the Court of Proprietors) of shareholders, initially with at least £200 and later with £500 worth of stock. Officials returned from India very rich. The record for such so-called 'nabobs' was the £72,000 that Warren Hastings brought home in 1785; a parliamentary impeachment trial of Hastings for corruption acquitted him, although it lasted nearly a decade and the legal fees bankrupted him. Not only did the Company have the deepest of pockets with which to buy parliamentarian votes but from sixty to a hundred members of Parliament were stockholders.

Fearing that power, Whitehall tried to curb it with a series of laws. The 1773 Regulating Act transformed the presidents appointed by the Company Court into governors-general appointed by the king. The 1784 India Act established a crown-appointed seven-man Board of Commissioners, known as the Board of Control, mostly cabinet ministers to oversee the East India Company's operations and a governor-general over all British possessions there.

Whitehall had a relatively simple set of foreign policy ends and means. The goal was to expand overseas markets and colonies for British goods while preventing any one European realm or alliance from dominating the continent. To those ends, British policymakers tried to maintain a navy with twice as many warships as the combined fleets of the two next largest naval powers and forged coalitions against the dominant European state or alliance. The worst threat shifted from the Spaniards from the mid-sixteenth century to the early seventeenth century, the Dutch in the mid-seventeenth century, and the French from the late seventeenth century until 1815. Britain decisively defeated each of those threats.

Wars were frequent and could be ruinous. Those that began in Europe inevitably spread to the colonies, while some erupted between England and other rivals overseas then engulfed Europe. Regardless, England's colonies were lightly defended and relatively easy prey to the side that first mounted a major expedition. For instance, the French captured seven of Britain's ten West Indian colonies when it fought with the Americans during their war for independence. To defend its colonies, the British deployed two squadrons in the West Indies at Port Royal, Jamaica and English Harbour, Antigua. To the victor went the spoils. Conquerors emptied treasure chests and warehouses, then often heavily taxed merchants and planters. Privateering was another way to reap vast wealth at the enemy's expense. Ships sailed with the winds and currents. With intelligence of the routes and schedules, privateers often waited for the prey to sail past. To thwart that, each belligerent organised its merchant ships into convoys protected by warships. Time was money even then and plenty was lost during the weeks or months it took to collect a convoy and then sail across the ocean as fast as the slowest vessel.

The 1714 accession of Elector George of Hanover to become King George I complicated British foreign policy. His son, George II, who succeeded him, and, much less enthusiastically, his grandson who would be George III sought to protect their ancestral realm of Hanover in northern Germany from aggressive neighbours. Several wars led to commitments of British armies to Germany that most foreign policymakers would have preferred deploying elsewhere. Nonetheless, the three Georges understood and backed the core aims of British foreign policy. In his 1729 inaugural address to the Privy

Council, George II offered these reassuring words: 'As the alliances entered into by the late king, my father, with foreign powers, have contributed to restoring the tranquillity, and preserving the balance of Europe, I shall endeavour to cultivate those alliances, and to improve and perfect this great work, for the honour, interest, and security of my people.'[19]

* * *

Britain warred for seventy-three of 126 years from 1689 to 1815 and won all but one of those wars.[20] The enemy was nearly always France and its allies: King William's War or War of the Augsburg League (1689–97), Queen Anne's War or War of Spanish Succession (1702–13), King George's War or War of the Austrian Succession (1744–48), French and Indian War or Seven Years' War (1754–63), War of American Independence (1775–83), and Wars of the French Revolution and Napoleon (1793–1801, 1803–14, 1815). Spain was Britain's second most persistent enemy as they fought from 1702 to 1713, 1739 to 1748, 1762 to 1763, 1780 to 1783, 1796 to 1802, and 1803 to 1808. The Seven Years' and French revolutionary and Napoleonic wars were global struggles with fighting across Europe, North America, Latin America, the West Indies, the East Indies, West Africa, and seas linking those far-flung lands. In every war but one, against America, British naval and mercantile power was decisive for the result. To varying degrees, Britain organised and financially underwrote an alliance in each war. The most vital wars before 1793 were the Spanish Succession, Seven Years', and American Independence.

England allied with the Netherlands and Austria against France during the war to determine whether a French Bourbon or Austrian Habsburg took the Spanish throne. England won that war because John Churchill, who Queen Anne named the Duke of Marlborough for his victories, commanded the army on the continent. He inflicted decisive defeats on the French at Blenheim in 1704, Ramillies in 1706, Oudenarde in 1708, and Malplaquet in 1709. Under the 1713 Treaty of Utrecht, Britain won from France Newfoundland, Hudson Bay, and Acadia, today's Nova Scotia, and eastern New Brunswick, and from Spain Gibraltar, Minorca, and the Asiento or right to sell slaves in Spain's empire.

Before 1815, Britain's most decisive victory was in 1763. The Seven Years' War began in the upper Ohio River valley in spring 1754 when rival French and Virginian forces fought for supremacy. Then Lieutenant Colonel George Washington actually instigated that war when he ordered his Virginian troops to fire at a encamped French patrol. Learning of the fighting, Whitehall and Versailles sent ever more troops to North America and their warships against each other at sea. That war overlapped with one that erupted between

3.2. The Logistics of War: Men[21]

War	Navy	Army	Total
Nine Years' War, 1689–97	40,262	76,404	116,666
War of the Spanish Succession, 1702–13	42,938	92,708	135,646
War of the Austrian Succession, 1739–48	50,313	62,373	112,686
Seven Years' War, 1756–63	74,800	92,676	167,476
American War, 1775–83	82,022	108,484	167,476

Prussia and Austria over Silesia in 1756. Eventually Britain allied with Prussia, the Netherlands, and Portugal against France, Bavaria, Austria, Russia, and Spain. British forces not only conquered Canada by 1760 but captured most of France's West Indian, Indian, and African colonies, as well as Spain's Havana and Manila by 1762. Under the Treaty of Paris, Britain took Canada, Louisiana east of the Mississippi River, Goree, Senegal, and the West Indian colonies of Grenada, St Vincent, Dominica, and Tobago from France, and East and West Florida from Spain. The most lucrative gains were in India, where British forces defeated the French and asserted control over Bengal and the Carnatic south-east coast.

Britain's trade and tariff revenues soared during the Seven Years' War, letting Whitehall supply war goods and money to its allies. From 1756 to 1763, exports rose 33 per cent from £11.6 million to £14.7 million, imports 39 per cent from £8 million to £11.1 million, and tariff receipts 31 per cent from £3.6 million to £4.8 million. Although the national debt nearly doubled from £73.6 million to £132.6 million, Whitehall was able to service it at reasonable levels of taxes, tariffs, and interest rates that did not overburden the economy. The demand for war goods stimulated the economy without causing crippling inflation.[23]

3.3. The Logistics of War: Money[22]

War	Average Yearly Expenditure	Average Year Tax Revenue	Beginning National Debt	Ending National Debt
Nine Years' War, 1689–97	£5,456,555	£3,640,000	n.a.	£16,700,000
War of the Spanish Succession, 1702–13	£7,063,923	£5,355,583	£14,100,000	£36,200,000
War of the Austrian Succession, 1739–48	£8,778,900	£6,422,800	£46,900,000	£76,100,000
Seven Years' War, 1756–63	£18,036,000	£8,641,125	£74,600,000	£132,600,000
American War, 1775–83	£20,272,799	£12,154,700	£127,300,000	£242,900,000

3.4. Military Spending as a Share of Government Spending[24]

War	Total Spending	Military Spending	Military Share
Nine Years' War, 1689–97	£49,109,000	£36,270,000	74%
War of the Spanish Succession, 1702–13	£98,207,000	£64,718,000	66%
War of the Austrian Succession, 1739–48	£87,789,000	£55,814,000	64%
Seven Years' War, 1756–63	£116,664,000	£82,727,000	71%
American War, 1775–83	£178,482,000	£109,368,000	61%

Britain's unrivalled global power inspired Sir George Macartney to boast about 'this vast empire on which the sun never sets and whose bounds nature has not yet ascertained'.[25] Secretary of State Henry Conway of the Northern Department feared that paradoxically British power might backfire against the nation: 'The unparalleled successes of the last war ... have set England in so high a point of light, that the envy of our neighbours is more to be dreaded than a contrary sentiment; and the great object of our ministers is rather to abate the jealousy of the European powers, than to increase their reverence toward us.'[26]

Ironically, a core value of English identity contributed to America's war for independence. From the first settlement at Jamestown in 1607, the colonists asserted their rights as English subjects including life, liberty, and property, due legal process including jury trials and habeas corpus, the sanctity of one's home and business from arbitrary search and seizure, and for propertied men to vote and run for a seat in a representative assembly or serve in a civil post. Politically, before 1763, they expressed these rights peacefully through their colonial assemblies and lobbyists like Benjamin Franklin in London. And neither the king nor Parliament challenged those rights.

That changed following the 1763 Treaty of Paris. Britain's imperial gains came at a vast financial cost as the national debt doubled from £74.6 million in 1754 to £132.6 million in 1763. How to pay interest on that debt was a key post-war challenge for British policymakers. Another worry was that the colonial Americans were acquiring ever more wealth, population, and identity to the point where they might one day seek independence. Josiah Tucker expressed that dilemma in his 1763 book *The True Interest of Great Britain Set Forth in Regard to the Colonies*: 'How shall we be able to render these Colonies more subservient to this Island, and more obedient to the Laws and Government of the Mother Country, than they voluntarily choose to be.'[27] Whitehall conceived a plan that ideally would both alleviate the debt and suppress American autonomy by imposing taxes, barriers to westward expansion, and troops on the colonies. That policy actually accelerated rather than deterred American independence. Americans reacted to the taxes in three ways: loyalists accepted them, moderate patriots protested against them; and radical patriots like the Sons of Liberty committed violence that included tar and feathering tax officials, smashing the windows of governors' mansions, and brawling with redcoats in the streets.

Two policies tried to geographically contain the colonies. The 1763 Proclamation forbade Americans from settling west of the Appalachian Mountains and the 1774 Quebec Act extended that colony's frontier to the Ohio River, thus eliminating the claims of American colonies to that vast territory, and the liberty of hunters, trappers, merchants, land speculators, and settlers to exploit it. Taxes included the 1765 Stamp Act, 1767 Townshend Act, and 1773 Tea Act and East India Company Regulating Act. The 1766 Declaratory Act asserted Parliament's power over the colonies including the imposition of taxes. All that infuriated ever more Americans.

Moderate and radical patriots succeeded in pressuring Parliament to rescind the Stamp and Townshend Acts. Boycotts against British goods and terrorism against British officials were effective strategies of American moderates and radicals, respectively. From 1768 to 1769, Britain's exports to the thirteen colonies plummeted 38 per cent from £2.1 million to £1.3 million.[28] Parliament yielded to demands by British exporters to lift all the taxes except that on tea as a principled assertion of its right and power to do so. The Tea Act and East India Company Regulating Act saved that company from bankruptcy by giving it a monopoly directly to sell tea in the colonies. American radicals committed their most destructive act on 16 December 1773, when they swarmed aboard three merchant ships packed with crates of tea in Boston harbour and dumped £10,000 worth of tea in the water. Whitehall responded by suspending Massachusetts's charter and assembly, imposing martial law with General Thomas Gage as governor, severing any trade with Boston except food and firewood, and doubling the number of troops to 7,000 in Boston. Those measures would remain until Massachusetts repaid the full value of the destroyed tea. By harshly penalising Massachusetts, Whitehall hoped to cow the other colonies. Instead, those 'intolerable acts', as critics dubbed them, enflamed American nationalism, resistance, and organisation. The First Continental Congress with delegations from twelve colonies met at Philadelphia in September and October 1774. The delegates agreed to set up committees of correspondence to co-ordinate policy among themselves, enforce the boycott of British goods, and prepare their militias for possible fighting.

War erupted on 19 April 1775, when British troops marching to capture military supplies at Concord 20 miles west of Boston, fired on and routed American militia at Lexington. Although the redcoats did reach Concord and burn supplies, militia companies converged to battle the British there and all the way back to Boston. Militia from across New England and eventually most other colonies massed around Boston to besiege the British army. Congress appointed George Washington that American army's commander. Congress sent an 'olive branch petition' to George III, asking him to guarantee American rights and withdraw British troops. The king ignored the petition, declared the Americans rebels, and mobilised a vast army and navy to crush that rebellion.

The war lasted eight years. The Americans declared independence on 4 July 1776. They captured a British army of 6,000 troops led by General John Burgoyne at Saratoga, New York, on 17 October 1777. That enabled Benjamin Franklin in Paris to negotiate treaties of alliance and trade between the United States and France. Massive French money, supplies, troops, and warships enabled the Americans to win independence when and how they did. King Louis XVI enticed Spanish King Charles III to join the alliance against Britain. Washington commanded the American–French army that forced General George Cornwallis to surrender his 7,500 troops at Yorktown on 19 October 1781. That surrender was inevitable after Admiral Francois de Grasse's fleet defeated Admiral Thomas Grave's fleet that was attempting to rescue Cornwallis on 5 September.

Elsewhere, the French captured the British colonies of Dominica in 1778, Saint Vincent and Grenada in 1779, and Tobago in 1781. In a series of campaigns, the Spanish captured West Florida from 1779 to 1781. The British won only two decisive victories, both at sea. The Royal Navy deterred an invasion by a joint French–Spanish armada in 1779, and Admiral George Rodney devastated Admiral de Grasse's fleet at the Battle of the Saintes from 9 to 12 April 1782.

The war cost Britain its most economically developed colonies. Under the Treaty of Paris signed on 3 September 1783, Britain recognised American independence for a country that stretched west to the Mississippi River, south to the 31st parallel, and north to mid-channel through the Great Lakes of Superior, Huron, Erie, and Ontario, then east to the Atlantic Ocean. Spain retained East and West Florida. Britain had suffered a devastating financial, strategic, and emotional defeat. One member of Parliament presciently feared that America would surpass Britain in commercial power: 'American independence must tend to great convulsions in our commerce, the emigration of manufacturers, the loss of seamen, and all the evils of a declining country,' including 'the carrying trade'.[29] Much of that would indeed come to pass, but not for a century. Meanwhile, within a decade, far-sighted decisive leadership rebuilt Britain's financial, mercantile, and naval power to the point where it could forge, finance, and lead seven coalitions against first revolutionary then Napoleonic France.

* * *

George III asked William Pitt to form a government on 19 December 1783. Then just twenty-three years old, Pitt would become Britain's longest-serving and arguably greatest Prime Minister.[30] His father and namesake was William Pitt, Lord Chatham, Prime Minister from 1756 to 1761 and 1766 to 1768. That was a tough act to follow but the son's intellect and character rivalled that of his father, although his aloof and introverted personality could not have differed more. He entered Cambridge University's Pembroke College aged thirteen, studied law at Lincoln's Inn, and was elected to Parliament in January 1781 at twenty-one. He was a brilliant orator and networker. He was also a workaholic and alcoholic; he drowned his chronic tensions, especially during the war years, in wine-soaked banquets with close friends at Goostree's Club. William Petty, Earl Shelburne, welcomed Pitt to his faction. After Shelburne became First Lord of the Treasury and thus Prime Minister in 1783, he convinced the king to name Pitt Chancellor of the Exchequer. Pitt resigned with Shelburne in March 1783 but nine months later the king recalled him to the Exchequer and made him First Lord of the Treasury, thus figuratively handing him the keys to 10 Downing Street.

Prime Minister Pitt's priority was raising revenues and cutting spending to pay down Britain's national debt, which nearly doubled during the American War from £131 million in 1775 to £245 million in 1783. In 1786, he did so with higher taxes and tariffs that went to a Sinking Fund that paid the interest and part of the principle. In 1787, he established a Consolidated Fund run by a Board of Commissioners for Reducing the National Debt that regulated the array of government budgets. He tried to ensure that only competent, honest men served in the 600 or so customs and excise bureau positions. He purged other bureaucracies in Britain and India of many corrupt and inept officials and sinecure positions. Those reforms reaped the most spectacular gains in India, which enriched the government's coffers by £500,000 in 1793 alone. He expanded exports with a series of trade treaties with European countries, most vitally with France that cut its tariffs to 10–15 per cent for British goods in September 1786.[31] From 1783 to 1792, British exports doubled in value to Europe and a £2.5 million trade deficit became a £2 million surplus as revenues rose 56 per cent. The Bank of England's bullion balance rose from

£590,000 in August 1783 to £8,056,000 in August 1791. Meanwhile, Pitt restricted the government's annual budget to around £5,500,000 from 1784 to 1792; of that, military and non-military spending was around £4,000,000 and £1,500,000, respectively. The result was a dynamic, virtuous economic cycle of expanding production, exports, incomes, government revenues, and middle class, and diminishing unemployment, poverty, and government debt.[32]

Without Pitt's financial reforms, Britain could not have distributed a fraction of the subsidies and supplies it did to each of the seven coalitions it forged from 1793 to 1815. Without those massive infusions of coin and arms, the continental powers most likely would have accepted rather than fought Napoleon's expanding hegemony. And that would have decisively altered the history of Britain, Europe, and the world beyond.

PART II
COALITIONS

Chapter 4

First, 1793–97

We shall lose some money for having believed in the good faith and probity of the Austrian government. The Court of Vienna will forever lose its credit, its honour, and the chance of finding here any financial aid which it might require in the future. All things considered I really believe that if we are the dupes, it is the duper whose will be the loser.
[*William Grenville*]

It now remains to be seen whether ... the efforts of a free, brave, loyal people, aided by their allies, will not be successful in checking the progress of a system, the principles of which, if not opposed, threaten the most fatal consequences to the tranquillity of this country, the security of its allies, the good order of every European government and the happiness of the whole human race. [*William Pitt*]

'England will never consent that France shall arrogate the power of annulling at her pleasure, and under the pretence of a pretended natural right, of which she makes herself the only judge, the political system of Europe.' [*William Grenville*]

Whitehall, Parliament, and the informed public marvelled at the revolutionary series of events that engulfed France from May 1789.[1] Like that of Britain, France's national debt skyrocketed during the eighteenth century from a succession of expensive wars. Unlike Britain, France did not have someone like William Pitt with the will, skill, and power to enact reforms that reduced the debt and expanded the economy. French Finance Minister Jacques Necker had the will and skill but lacked the power, so France faced bankruptcy. In May 1789, to approve Necker's proposed reforms, King Louis XVI convened at Versailles Palace 12 miles west of Paris the Estates General, an assembly with three classes or estates with roughly equal numbers of nobles, clergy, and commoners that had last gathered in 1614. The third estate of commoners – mostly lawyers and merchants – had no intention of rubberstamping the king's taxation decrees. Instead, they sought to transform France from an absolute into a constitutional monarchy like Britain. On

17 June, they declared themselves the National Assembly. The king ordered the National Assembly to disperse. The assemblymen stood firm. Eventually, Louis reluctantly yielded and had the clergy and nobles join the National Assembly on 27 June.

Violence erupted on 14 July when a mob in Paris first seized weapons at Les Invalides, a veteran's hospital, then captured Bastille castle, an arms depot and symbol of royal despotism, and massacred most of the garrison. From then, the revolution was an increasingly violent tug of war between reformers and radicals. The National Assembly announced the abolition of feudalism and noble privileges on 4 August; issued the Declaration of the Rights of Man and the Citizen, inspired by America's Declaration of Independence, on 16 August; and nationalised the Catholic Church's property on 2 November. Meanwhile, on 5 October a Parisian mob marched on Versailles and forced the royal family to move to Tuileries Palace in the centre of Paris the following day. Reforms continued throughout 1790, including the National Assembly's 22 May declaration that: 'The French nation renounces the undertaking of any war with a view to making conquests and [declares that] it will never use its force against the liberty of any other people.'[2]

Although France's revolution eventually posed ominous related ideological and military challenges to Britain, understandably, most Britons initially reacted with elation.[3] The French Revolution appeared to emulate Britain's a century earlier by transforming an absolute monarchy into a constitutional one with most power held by a parliament. The pledge of France's leading revolutionaries to international peace and brotherhood was reassuring, even inspiring. Whig leader Charles James Fox joyfully celebrated the French Revolution: 'How much the greatest event it is that ever happened in the history of the world! & how much the best!'[4]

One prominent Casandra stood out. Edmund Burke lambasted the events in France in his *Reflections on the Revolution* that appeared in November 1790.[5] He pointed out that the French Revolution was devouring itself and warned Britons to avoid doing the same: 'The French had shown themselves the ablest architects of ruin that had hitherto existed in the world. In that very short space of time, they had completely pulled down to the ground their church, their nobility, their law, their revenue, their army, their navy, their commerce, their arts, and their manufactures. They had done their business for us as rivals in a way which twenty Ramillies or Bleinheims could never have done.'[6] What Burke did not foresee was the more powerful government, military, and nation that the revolutionaries planted, nurtured, and controlled in those ruins. Thomas Paine, who had rhetorically aided America's Revolution, rebuked Burke and extolled the unfolding revolution with its 'liberty, equality, and fraternity' ideals in his *Rights of Man*, with parts one and two published respectively in March 1791 and February 1792. He then journeyed to Paris to join the revolution.[7]

Whether they were enthusiasts or sceptics, all British observers agreed that France's potential foreign aggression diminished as political turmoil and divisions engulfed its government and regions. Prime Minister Pitt issued a neutrality proclamation toward France and its unfolding revolution in July 1789. Over the next two years, he and his ministers worried most about possible wars first with Spain over its seizure of British merchants at Nootka Sound on Vancouver Island in 1790 and then with Russia over its retention of the strategic fortress of Ochakov on the Black Sea in 1791 after a victorious war with the Ottoman Empire. Each time, Whitehall announced the Royal Navy's war preparations while sending diplomats to find a face-saving solution. That muscular diplomacy resolved both crises.

Radicals increasingly seized the upper hand in France's unfolding revolution. To the rage of the king and other devout Catholics, the National Assembly, now named the Legislative Assembly, passed laws that nationalised the Church's property and forced priests to swear allegiance to the government. The government's refusal to let Louis and his family attend mass at Saint Cloud Palace convinced him that they must flee France.

Two coaches clattered from Tuileries Palace on the night of 20 June 1791. One contained Louis XVI and his family, the other his brother Louis, comte Provence, his wife, and several attendants. Beyond the city's wall, they separated on different routes to the Austrian Netherlands. Provence's coach made it. Alert National Guards stopped the king's coach at Varennes just miles from the frontier on 21 June. The National Guard brought the royal family back to Tuileries Palace, where they were guarded constantly.

That aborted flight tipped the balance from moderates to radicals among the revolutionaries. Virtually no one believed the lie promoted by the Legislative Assembly's moderate majority that counter-revolutionaries had kidnapped the royal family and they were happy to be back. The moderates wanted a constitutional monarchy, while the radicals sought a republic.

Queen Marie Antoinette secretly sent letters to her brother Emperor Leopold II beseeching him to form an allied army to rescue them and restore their rule. On 6 July, Leopold II issued the Padua Circular that urged all monarchs 'to vindicate the liberty and honour of the Most Christian King and his family, and to limit the dangerous extremes of the French revolution'.[8] On 27 August, Prussian King Frederick William II joined Leopold to issue the Declaration of Pillnitz that echoed the Padua Circular. To that, Whitehall announced that King George III 'has determined not to take any part in supporting or opposing' operations on behalf of Louis XVI.[9]

French royalist exiles were an increasingly numerous and noisy group that pressured Europe's governments to oppose the revolutionary regime, ideally by uniting and warring against it. The most important concentration of émigrés was at Coblenz, where the Moselle River joins the Rhine. There Louis Joseph, prince de Conde, struggled to form a brigade of counter-revolutionary French troops amidst squabbling political factions and infiltration by revolutionary agents. The two most prominent exiles were the king's brothers. The youngest brother, Charles, Comte d'Artois, fled with his family in late July 1789 after the Bastille fell. Louis, Comte de Provence, escaped Paris with the king that same night of June 1791, but reached Brussels safely. Like most refugees, Charles and Louis led peripatetic lives over the next two decades, although they spent little time together. Louis became the heir apparent when Louis XVII, then seven years old, died in prison on 10 June 1795. The exiled brothers could not have differed more. Louis was obese, passive, and homosexual. Charles was a handsome, lean womaniser, and a lobbyist for the French royalist cause in Europe's capitals. He sought money, arms, and recognition of his brother as Louis XVIII.

France's Legislative Assembly threatened to send an army to destroy the émigré army at Coblenz. Austrian Foreign Minister Wenzel Anton von Kaunitz informed the French ambassador in Vienna that war would result if the French attacked. The Legislative Assembly forced Louis XVI to approve an attack. Vienna sent a blunt warning to Paris to stand down on 17 February 1792.

Amidst this worsening crisis, Prime Minister Pitt reassured Parliament and the nation on the same day that 'there never was a time in the history of this country when from the situation of Europe, we might more reasonably expect fifteen years of peace than we may at the present moment'.[10] He soon rued those heady words.

With Louis XVI forced to approve, the Legislative Assembly declared war against Austria and Prussia on 20 April 1792. Over the next several months, the belligerents mobilised their troops and propaganda for war. The allied plan was for an army of Prussian, Austrian, Imperial, and royalist troops commanded by Wilhelm, Duke of Brunswick, to mass at Coblenz, then march up the Moselle River valley against France. On 25 July, the duke issued what was called the Brunswick Manifesto, warning that if the revolutionaries harmed the royal family, the allies would destroy Paris. That enraged rather than intimidated most revolutionaries. On 10 August, a radical mob attacked

Tuileries Palace, slaughtered the Swiss Guards, and incarcerated the royal family.

Brunswick's army marched into France on 19 August and captured the fortress city of Verdun on 1 September. Two French armies commanded by Generals Charles Dumouriez and Francois Kellerman converged to block the allied advance at Valmy. The opposing armies were matched in numbers with about 35,000 troops each, but diseases and food shortages weakened the allies. On 20 September, after an exchange of artillery fire and several hundred casualties on each side, Brunswick ordered his army to retreat. Although the battle of Valmy was little more than a skirmish, it had crucial results. Johann Wolfgang von Goethe witnessed the battle and understood its significance: 'From here and today there begins a new epoch in the history of the world.'[11]

French armies followed up that victory by advancing to the Rhine, and into the Austrian Netherlands and the Piedmont-Sardinian Kingdom's province of Savoy. Meanwhile, on 21 September, the Legislative Assembly, now called the Convention, declared France a republic. On 10 October, Dumouriez declared before the Convention that: 'Liberty is triumphant everywhere; led by philosophy, it will sweep the universe; it will establish itself on every throne once it has crushed despotism and enlightened the people ... This present war will be the last, and all tyrants and privileged, their criminal plots exposed, will be the only victims of this struggle between arbitrary power and reason.'[12] The Convention issued four proclamations that threatened British national security interests: free navigation on the Scheldt River forbidden by the 1648 Treaty of Westphalia on 16 November; aid for any people rebelling against monarchial oppression on 19 November; the intended overthrow of all monarchies and establishment of republics on the ruins on 15 December; and the exploitation for war of any countries that French armies conquered on 16 December.

Pitt and his key ministers decided on 13 November that Britain would war against France if it invaded the Netherlands. Foreign Secretary William Grenville issued French ambassador Bernard-Francois, marquis de Chauvelin, a powerful letter on 31 December 1792, that was one step short of an ultimatum. First, he stated that Chauvelin was an accredited ambassador of Louis XVI, and thus lost that status when the French government deposed the king on 10 August 1792. He then condemned France's revolution without frontiers policy that targeted every monarchy for destruction and replacement with a republic. He blasted France's opening of the Scheldt River to trade and threats against the Netherlands. In sum: 'England will never consent that France shall arrogate the power of annulling at her pleasure, and under the pretence of a pretended natural right, of which she makes herself the only judge, the political system of Europe, established by solemn treaties, and guaranteed by the consent of all the powers. This Government, adhering to the maxims which it has followed for more than a century, will also never see with indifference that France shall make herself, either directly or indirectly, sovereign of the Low Countries, or general arbitress of the rights and liberties of Europe.'[13]

The Convention charged Louis XVI with thirty-three counts of treason on 3 December, unanimously found him guilty on 15 January, voted 361 to 355 for his unconditional execution on 17 January, and had him guillotined on 21 January. Word of the king's execution reached London on 23 January. Pitt had Grenville summon Chauvelin and declare him persona non grata and diplomatic relations with France ended. He then publicly called on France's government to withdraw to its 1789 borders and repudiate its revolution without frontiers and opening of the Scheldt River assertions, with two months to comply. On 24 January, Whitehall agreed to help the Dutch hire 13,000 Hanoverian troops to bolster their defence.

Paris declared war against Britain and the Netherlands on 1 February. The same day Pitt revealed the nature of the French threat in a speech before the House of Commons: 'They mean to carry their principles into every nation, without exception subvert and destroy every government, and to plant on their ruins their sacred tree of liberty ... England will never consent that France shall arrogate the power of annulling at her pleasure and under the pretence of a natural right of which she makes herself the only judge, the political system of Europe, established by solemn treaties, and guaranteed by the consent of all the powers.'[14] The day after George III declared war on 11 February, Pitt elaborated that threat's nature: 'It now remains to be seen whether ... the efforts of a free, brave, loyal, and happy people, aided by their allies, will not be successful in checking the progress of a system, the principles of which, if not opposed, threaten the most fatal consequences to the tranquillity of this country, the security of its allies, the good order of every European government and the happiness of the whole human race.'[15]

Three men initially spearheaded Britain's war effort as an inner cabinet: Prime Minister William Pitt, Home Secretary Henry Dundas, and Foreign Secretary William Grenville, with important inputs by Ordnance Master Charles Lennox, Duke Richmond and Secretary at War William Windham, both in secondary posts. In July 1794, Pitt established the cabinet-level post Secretary for War and gave it to Dundas. William Cavendish-Benedict, Duke of Portland, became Home Secretary.

William Grenville was an Eton, Oxford, and Lincoln Inn law graduate.[16] He was Pitt's cousin, friend, and fellow Goosetree's Club member. Much like Pitt, Grenville was highly intelligent, well-read, articulate, and reserved. He won his first parliamentary seat in 1782 as the American War was winding down with Britain's loss of those thirteen colonies. Pitt dispatched Grenville on troubleshooting diplomatic missions, starting with the Hague and Paris in 1787 when he helped resolve a military crisis among the Netherlands, Prussia, France, and Britain over disputed Dutch territory and political succession. In 1788, Britain signed with Prussia and Austria a treaty to guarantee the Netherlands' independence. Grenville was the House of Commons' Speaker from 1 January 1789 to 5 June 1789. Pitt appointed Grenville Paymaster of the Forces from 1784 to 5 June 1789, then Home Secretary until 6 June 1791, and finally Foreign Secretary until 20 February 1801.

Unlike most parliamentarians, Henry Dundas had a brilliant legal and academic career before he entered politics.[17] He was born in Edinburgh and studied law at Edinburgh University. He became Scotland's Solicitor General in 1766 and its Lord Advocate in 1775, Glasgow University's Lord Rector in 1781, Edinburgh University's dean of the Faculty of Advocates in 1784, Aberdeen University's chancellor in 1788, and received his doctorate from Edinburgh University in 1789. He first won a parliamentary seat in 1779. Pitt named Dundas Treasurer of the Navy in 1784, Home Secretary in 1791, and Secretary for War in 1794. Dundas was renowned for his backroom dealmaking.

For the next two decades, Britain's strategy was an amalgam that shifted between two alternatives depending on circumstances. Grenville advocated a 'continental' strategy whereby Britain massed an army with its allies that invaded France, crushed the rebellion, and reimposed the Bourbons. Dundas advocated a 'maritime' strategy whereby British armadas systematically captured one French colony after another to expand British and diminish French power.

To fight that war, Britain had enormous advantages. Most importantly, Britain was an island nation with a navy twice as powerful as France's. Economically, Britain far surpassed France by most measures of productivity, income, and, most critically, finance. Paris had no equivalent of London's financial district known as the City that included the Bank of England, Royal Exchange, Stock Exchange, and dozens of banks and insurance companies. In 1788, the average Briton was around 30 per cent wealthier than the average Frenchman. However, Britain's national debt was three times greater per person and the tax burden was double at 12.4 per cent of the economy compared with France's 6.8 per cent, and that greatly worsened over the next quarter century.[18] Britain's leadership of seven coalitions against first revolutionary then Napoleonic France from 1793 to 1815 officially cost £1,657,854,518 and caused the national debt to triple from £290,000,000 to £860,000,000.[19]

Whitehall financed those soaring expenditures with a mix of loans, taxes, excises, tariffs, fines, and confiscations. Excise taxes came from an expanding list that eventually included salt, soap, candles, beer, malt, hops, leather, hats, silk gloves, carriages, horses, servants, newspapers, wills, probates, licences, and windows. In 1799, Whitehall imposed a graduated income tax that began at £60. The most vital overall source was the Bank of England that lent money to the government at low interest rates. The sinking fund that annually paid not just the national debt's interest but some of the principal gave lenders the confidence to keep lending. From 1793 to 1815, the sinking fund took £81,000,000 of £578,000,000 in new debt.[20]

Nonetheless, Whitehall would need time to build up its army and navy for war. Fortunately, Pitt had not neglected the military over the decade from the American war's end and French war's beginning. Military spending was around £4,00,000 of the government's annual £5,500,000 budget from 1784

4.1. British Government Spending and Private Investment, 1790–1813[21]

Average	Military Spending Millions	Civilian Spending Millions	Total Spending Millions	Private Investment Millions	Private Spending Share of Economy	Military Spending Share of Economy
1790–95	£5.27	£3.12	£8.39	£12.90	8.8%	3.6%
1796–99	£28.22	£3.56	£31.78	n.a.	n.a.	n.a.
1800–04	£30.56	£5.30	£35.89	£17.04	6.9%	10.4%
1805–09	£35.96	£6.43	£42.39	n.a.	n.a.	n.a.
1810–12	£50.89	£7.29	£58.18	£28.50	7.9%	14.1%
1813	£64.36	£8.07	£72.42	n.a.	n.a.	n.a.

4.2. Estimated National Income, Total Revenue, and Indirect Taxes[22]

Year	National Income	Total Revenue	Total Revenue as Share of National Income	Indirect Taxes as Share of Total Taxes
1791	£153,920,000	£17,890,000	11.62%	67.3%
1799	£232,480,000	£32,470,000	13.96%	59.5%
1806	£271,410,000	£51,770,000	19.07%	60.5%
1810	£358,980,000	£63,490,000	17.68%	56.9%

4.3. Military Spending Select Years in Pound Sterling[23]

Years	Total	Army	Navy	Militia	Ordnance	Subsidies
1803	38,956,917	8,935,753	10,211,378	2,889,976	1,128,914	n.a.
1808	48,319,807	19,428,189	17,496,047	n.a.	4,534,571	1,100,000
1812	97,521,371	24,987,362	20,500,339	n.a.	4,252,409	8,204,028
1813	117,587,979	33,795,556,	21,961,566	138,494	4,480,729	10,024,618

to 1793. The shipbuilding budget was £2,400,000, the navy launched thirty-three ships of the line, and the number of sailors rose from 15,000 to 18,000 from 1784 to 1790.[24]

The Ordnance Board procured artillery and munitions for the army and navy. It was headquartered in the Tower of London and had a cannon foundry at Woolwich and gunpowder mills and cannon foundries at Waltham Abbey and Faversham. Although the state factories satisfied peacetime demand for ordnance, during wars the Ordnance Board contracted orders from private producers. The most important cannon producers during this era were the East India Company, Walker and Company of Rotherham, and Carron and Company of Falkirk, Scotland. From 1779, the Carron Company produced a new type of cannon called the carronade with a short barrel whose weight was around one third that of regular cannon. The carronade was nicknamed the 'smasher' for the short-range and slow-velocity but powerful impact of its balls against a ship's hull. Most muskets came from a half dozen or so factories in Birmingham, with the East India Company's .75 calibre India Pattern musket – affectionately called the 'Brown Bess', by soldiers – the prototype.

The industrial revolution led to better and more quickly made and less-expensive firearms. Mass-produced interchangeable parts for a musket's lock, stock, and barrel were swiftly assembled into finished firearms. The recent invention of the horizontal boring machine rendered British cannon superior in accuracy and range in each class because of the tighter windage or fit of balls in bores. British gunpowder was the world's finest because Bengal's conquest secured the richest saltpeter reserves.

* * *

Although the king officially headed the army, actually, he rarely had more to do with troops than attend parades in London, appoint generals, and issue commissions.[25] The last time a king accompanied an army on campaign was George II, who witnessed the battle of Dettingen in 1743. Nonetheless,

George III was interested in military affairs and often asked his ministers to explain issues and policies made in his name. During the Napoleonic era, three men served as commanders-in-chief: Jeffrey Amherst from January 1793 to February 1795; the king's second son, Frederick Augustus, Duke of York, from April 1795 to March 1809; David Dundas from March 1809 to May 1811; and York again from May 1811 to January 1828.[26] Unfortunately, none was acclaimed for his leadership while York bungled his field campaigns and resigned in 1809 after an embarrassing sex and corruption scandal. Yet if York failed as a field commander, he excelled as an army reformer by improving rations and housing for soldiers, reducing punishments, standardising drill, promoting light infantry tactics, instituting in 1801 the Royal Military College at Sandhurst to professionalise the officers' corps, and in 1809 requiring minimal years of experience before promotions to higher ranks for officers.

The commander's key subordinates included his Military Secretary, Adjutant General, Quartermaster General, Master General of Ordnance, Paymaster General, Barrack Master General, and Storekeeper General. For amphibious operations he had to work with the Admiralty's Transport Board. For cannon he competed with the navy for orders from the Ordnance Board. The Secretary at War was a minor non-cabinet post that did not administer the army but instead was a liaison with Parliament who helped promote and craft army bills. In 1794, William Pitt established the Secretary for War to provide civilian oversight and direction of the military although the commander remained autonomous.

That era's only enduring army organisation was the regiment – brigades, divisions, corps, and armies were established and dissolved as needed. A colonel headed each regiment as a mostly ceremonial post, with his most important duty supplying the men's uniforms. The lieutenant colonel actually commanded the regiment at home and abroad. Most regiments had two battalions each with ten hundred-man companies including eight 'centre' and two 'flank' companies, one 'light' of the swiftest and best shots for skirmishing, and the other 'grenadier' of the largest, strongest as shock troops; one battalion usually served on campaign, while the other was stationed at home to defend and recruit.

The king often established new regiments during wartime and abolished regiments with officers on half-pay during peacetime. In 1793, when Britain went to war, the existing regiments numbered up to seventy-seven. Over the next twenty-two years, the king commissioned the 78th through 133rd regiments. Of the army's regiments, twelve were Scottish and the troops of one, the 95th, wore green rather than red coats, fired a Baker rifle rather than

4.4. British Army Numbers Select Years[27]

Year	Cavalry	Infantry	Total
1793	4,681	34,262	38,945
1794	14,527	70,570	85,097
1795	28,810	100,452	129,262
1804	16,729	119,751	136,480
1806	23,396	142,177	165,573
1809	27,391	183,223	210,614
1813	28,983	201,528	239,469

'Brown Bess' musket, and trained to be light infantry skirmishers. Establishing a new regiment took a lot of money and time. It was easier and cheaper to hire foreign regiments for a war's duration, then send them home. An important innovation in 1793 was establishing the Royal Waggoners with soldiers to replace the previous hiring of civilian teamsters and wagons.

Army officers bought and sold commissions from lieutenant to lieutenant colonel, with supply and demand determining the price. Nearly all were nobles. Lords often bought a commission for a second son at a young age. In 1809, York required commissioned officers to be at least sixteen years old who had to start at the bottom and buy their way up after serving three years for captain, seven for major, and nine for lieutenant colonel. He also opened purchases to anyone recommended by a higher officer from major on up. An officer could receive a higher rank by recruiting enough men for that command. Lieutenant colonels could recommend heroic non-commissioned officers for a king's commission, although such cases were rare.

Officers received pay for their rank but the amount was so measly they needed alternative incomes. Officers did lead from the front and suffered casualty rates around 20 per cent higher than the enlisted men. Training was mostly on the job as new officers observed and emulated veterans. A few attended the engineer and artillery school at Woolrich, founded in 1714, or the Royal Military Academy, founded in 1741 and transformed into the Royal Military College at Sandhurst in 1801.

Most members of Whitehall, Parliament, and the public had mixed feelings about the army. The tradition was 'no standing army' both to save costs and avoid potential coups, and a limited militia to avoid populist insurrections. The unprecedented threat posed by Napoleon forced government leaders to reconsider that policy. Prime Minister Pitt explained in 1803 that: 'There was a time ... when it would have been dangerous to entrust arms with a great portion of the people of the country ... but that time is now past.'[28]

The crown requested rather than demanded service; there was no draft for the regular army. Desertion, disease, and combat depleted regiments, with most less than half their official 1,000-man contingents. Each regiment was responsible for filling its own ranks. Recruiting parties consisted of a captain, sergeant, several privates, and a drummer boy who journeyed from town to town usually during the winter months. In the town square, the boy's whirling hands drummed up a crowd. The captain made a stirring speech. The sergeant invited those interested to a pub for informal pitches by him and the privates over a pint or two. Recruits had to be able-bodied and at least 5ft 4in for line regiments and 5ft 7in for Royal Guard or cavalry regiments. A recruit palmed the 'the king's shilling' and had twenty-four hours to reconsider and repay, otherwise he was brought before a magistrate to swear an oath to serve his king and country. Before 1806, he enlisted for life, although he could be discharged if he became crippled or his regiment was decommissioned. From 1806, to receive a pension, an infantrymen had to serve three seven-year stints; a cavalrymen a ten-year then two seven-year stints; and an artillerymen a twelve-year then two five-year stints.

Why would anyone enlist? The army provided minimal food, board, and shelter; companionship; a sense of identity and purpose; and, for some, a refuge from the law. Soldiers received a new coat, waistcoat, trousers, two pairs of socks, and two pairs of shoes annually, and a shako every two years, but their pay was deducted for that clothing. The regiment did furnish a musket, cartridge box, bayonet, haversack, blanket, and great coat. Discipline was harsh with dozens, scores, and even hundreds of whippings against one's naked back depending on the offence; those who deserted, struck an officer, or mutinied could be executed.

The army's 'wastage' or replacement rate was stunning – 225,000 men, including 188,000 British, from 1803 to 1814 alone.[29] What happened to all those men? Although combat was relatively rare even in wartime, tens of thousands were killed or maimed. Far more men died from disease than battle, especially those posted in the tropics. Others were discharged, crippled from battle or sickness. Every year thousands of men got away with deserting.

Militia supplemented home defence and freed most regiments for foreign service. Able-bodied men from age eighteen to forty-five years old in England and Wales were required to register with their local militia company. In 1757 amidst the Seven Years' War, a law required the names of each county's militiamen to be placed in a hopper and a quota selected for a year of training and service in Britain. The initial national number was 30,000. The 1796 Supplementary Militia Act authorised the recruitment of 60,000 militiamen from England and 4,400 from Wales, and in 1797 6,000 from Scotland. The

1798 Defence of the Realm Act required each county to compile lists of all inhabitants and for militiamen their physical fitness, weapons, and equipment. Fencible regiments were a halfway house between regulars and militia; their soldiers were organised, trained, and served as long as regulars but, with a few exceptions, never had to leave Britain. Many Fencible companies were deployed to guard prisoner-of-war camps.

The year 1811 was typical for that era's deployments of redcoat and mercenary troops. There were 12,050 cavalry, 1,568 foreign cavalry, 3,748 Foot Guards, 45,501 infantry, 2,746 foreign infantry, and 77,159 militia at home and 11,719 cavalry, 2,135 foreign cavalry, 3,130 Foot Guards, 99,735 infantry, and 36,320 foreign infantry abroad. Combat and disease killed 19,019 British and 3,441 foreign troops.[30]

As for combat, the British army had some handicaps to overcome over the next two decades. One was conflicting schools of tactics among officers based on whether they had mostly served in the Old or New World. The 'Prussian School' emphasised continental style parade-ground slow-moving, mass-firing three-man-deep formations. The 'American School' emphasised no more than two-man-deep, quick-moving formations covered by light infantry. Eventually the American School prevailed but only after a steep, blood-soaked learning curve. Light infantry tactics were critical to finding and fighting enemy troops and guerrillas in the jungles and mountains of West Indian islands. Arthur Wellesley, Duke of Wellington, largely followed the American School first during half a dozen years in India, then perfected those tactics during half a dozen years in the Peninsula. He established a light infantry brigade; wielded the expanding battalions of the 95th Rifle Regiment to pick off the enemy; and carefully deployed his troops to take best advantage of terrain to kill and avoid being killed.

* * *

The Admiralty planned and implemented naval strategy usually in collaboration with the Secretary for War since many operations involved transporting, protecting, and supplying troops in foreign lands.[31] A First Lord headed and an Admiralty Board of half dozen officers oversaw the Admiralty. The bureaucracy consisted of usually seven-man committees including the Navy Board that oversaw the dockyards, ships, and recruiting, the Ordnance Board, the Victualling Board, the Transport Board that supplied ships for army expeditions, the Sick and Hurt Board, the Longitude Board that supplied and upgraded sea charts with the latest information, and the Royal Navy Academy at Plymouth founded in 1733. The Treasurer of the Navy had an impressive title but no real duties and was subordinate to the Navy Board.

The personnel of the respective administrations expanded steadily throughout the era.

In a rather blatant case of nepotism, the Prime Minister's older brother, John Pitt, Earl Chatham, was the First Lord when the war began. Unfortunately, he was inept and corrupt, so Pitt replaced him with George, Earl Spencer in December 1794. Spencer served ably in that stressful post until 1801. Thereafter there was a rapid turnover for the First Lord with John Jervis, Earl Saint Vincent, serving from 1801 to 1804; Henry Dundas, Viscount Melville, from 1804 to 1805; Charles Middletown, Baron Barham, from 1805 to 1806; Charles Grey, Viscount Howick, in 1806; Thomas Grenville from 1806 to 1807; Henry Phipps, Baron Mulgrave, from 1807 to 1810; Charles Yorke from 1810 to 1812; then Robert Dundas, Viscount Melville, with the longest tenure from 1812 to 1827.

The Royal Navy began the war with only twenty-six ships of the line, thirty-two frigates, and thirty-four sloops on duty. Warships that needed officers, sailors, and supplies included eighty-seven ships of the line and twenty-nine frigates.[32] Most ships of the line had two decks packed with seventy-four or sixty-four cannon, but a few were three-deck behemoths with a hundred or more cannon. Ideally each ship sailed from port with its hull packed with five months of provisions, including barrels of salt beef, dried biscuits, lemon juice, rum, and wine. Barrels of gunpowder and cannon cartridges were stored below the waterline. With a steady wind at its stern, most vessels plowed the waves at a leisurely 5 mph, or 120 daily miles.

The number of sailors rose from 16,000 in 1789 to 140,000 in 1812. Many, perhaps most, served against their will. Given a choice, virtually any sailor would prefer serving on a merchant ship rather than a warship because the pay, conditions, and chances of survival were much better. The Royal Navy filled empty hammocks by impressing or essentially kidnapping able-bodied men in ports. Sometimes magistrates helped by sentencing miscreants to the navy. Prize money was a powerful incentive for enlisting in the navy during wartime. Of course, that depended on whether one's warship captured any enemy vessels. Merchants ships naturally yielded the most money when they and their cargo were auctioned. The prize was split eight ways, with two eighths to the captain, four eighths among junior officers, and two eights among the crew.

Recent Admiralty reforms greatly enhanced British naval power. From 1778 hulls were copper-sheathed to prevent sea worms from boring into them, thus prolonging the lives and speeds of British warships beyond those of foreign warships. Another was ensuring that each sailor had a daily ration of lime or lemon juice that prevented scurvy on long voyages. That rendered

4.5. Growth of British Seapower, 1792–1802[33]

Year	Merchant Shipping			Royal Navy		
	Ships	Tons	Men	Ships	Tons	Men
1792	14,334	1,437,000	118,286	304	299,409	16,613
1802	16,552	1,797,000	138,721	505	416,566	129,340

British crews far healthier than foreign crews, and thus more numerous and capable for sailing and fighting. The British developed a flag signalling system that let fleet commanders issue tactical instructions to captains during battles. British gunners received far more training and practice than those of any other navy, giving them a rate of fire two to four times faster.

Britain's accelerating industrial revolution enabled the Admiralty to finance, build, arm, supply, and repair its vessels quicker than its rivals. The Royal Dockyards at Portsmouth, Plymouth, Deptford, Chatham, and Woolwich were immense complexes of warehouses, dry docks, workshops, offices, and residences with 3,000 shipwrights and 8,000 labourers. During this era, the British constructed warships at a cost 25 per cent less than French shipbuilders.[34]

'Break the line' tactics were another British advantage. For centuries, the tactic had been for opposing fleets to sail in long single-ship lines either in the same or opposite directions and broadside each other with all facing cannon. Indeed, the Admiralty's 1653 'Fighting Instructions' to captains made that mandatory. Admiral George Rodney was the first to violate that orthodoxy and get celebrated rather than court martialled. Before his fleet battled a French fleet commanded by Admiral de Luc-Urbain de Guichen near Dominica on 17 April 1780, he ordered all captains to break off the line and square off with an individual ship, thus shattering the enemy line. That tactic made the most of superior British seamanship, gunnery, and carronade 'smashers'. Unfortunately, his order confused rather than inspired his captains and the French evaded serious damage. It took a while to master that tactic. Two years later, on 12 April 1782, Rodney's thirty-six warships devastated Admiral de Grasse's thirty-four warships near the Saintes Islands, capturing four ships of the line, destroying one, battering the others, inflicting 3,000 dead and wounded, and capturing 5,000 while suffering 1,000 casualties and no ship losses; de Grasse was among the captives. The success emboldened other fleet commanders to emulate it and the Admiralty to render the Fighting Instructions a dead letter.

No one wielded that new tactic more brilliantly than Horatio Nelson, Britain's greatest naval commander.[35] Not just the tactics but the tactical goal had changed from merely battering to destroying the enemy. Nelson explained that it was 'annihilation that the country wants, and not merely a splendid victory ... Numbers alone can annihilate'. And he pursued that goal ruthlessly, most spectacularly at the Nile in 1798, Copenhagen in 1801, and Trafalgar in 1805. Atop all that, Nelson understood that military and diplomatic power were inseparable and mutually reinforcing: 'A fleet of British ship of war are the best negotiators in Europe; they always speak to be understood, and generally gain the point.'[36]

The Royal Navy had a potential Achilles heel. Domestic production of a widening array of raw materials and food increasingly fell short of demand. Over the centuries, the demand for wood products had deforested much of the British Isles.[37] That worsening shortage most severely affected shipbuilding. Just one 74-gun ship of the line demanded 3,000 loads of timber from 57 forest acres, with a load of 50 cubic feet. Naval and merchant ship construction annually consumed around 60,000 and 72,500 respective loads.[38] Britain increasingly depended on foreign sources of oak for planks, tall pines for masts and spars, and scrub pines for turpentine. Nearly all oak now came from the old-growth forests of Scandinavia, Russia, and Canada. Two products – flax for sailcloth and wool for uniforms – were especially important for the military, and supplies of those were often tight. Whitehall could only fill that gap with imports. The Royal Navy could protect most of those shipments unless Britain was warring against a nation that was the source.

The most important fleet was the Western Squadron that variously anchored at Torbay, Plymouth, and Spithead or Saint Helens near Portsmouth. The Western Squadron's mission was to guard the English Channel's broad west entrance and threaten France's Atlantic coast naval bases of Brest and Rochefort. The Royal Navy's key overseas bases for operations in its surrounding region included Gibraltar for the Mediterranean, Antigua and Port Royal, Jamaica for the Caribbean, Halifax, Nova Scotia for the north Atlantic Ocean, and Madras and Bombay for the Indian Ocean.

Blockading squadrons had two strategies. A close blockade was just beyond cannon shot of the enemy port to intercept any vessels sailing to or from that port. A far blockade had most warships lurking beyond the horizon with a few small vessels acting as sentinels within view of the enemy port. Ideally that strategy enticed enemy war or merchant ships to venture to sea where they could be pursued and taken.

Merchant ships were as vital to Britain's naval power as warships. Merchant ships enriched the nation with trade and during wars transported troops and supplies to overseas fronts. Britain's merchant fleet expanded steadily from 14,500 registered vessels with 114,000,000 total tons in 1793 to 22,000 and 2,500,000 in 1815. It was actually cheaper to transport soldiers and supplies by merchant than navy vessels, for instance, respectively £24 versus £55 per man and £12 versus £27 per ton from London to Alexandria. The number of vessels swelled partly from shipbuilding and the rest from Britain's warships and privateers capturing more foreign merchant ships than the enemy captured the nation's ships.[39]

It was as vital to protect one's own merchant vessels as to scour the enemy's from the seas.[40] For that, the Admiralty re-established the convoy system that it had deployed in previous wars. The Admiralty worked with leading shipowners in the Committee of Shippers to arrange sailing times, rendezvous sites, and signal codes for Britain, the West Indies, and the East Indies. Mostly brigs and sloops guarded convoys since privateers with similarly sized vessels posed the worst threat. The Admiralty only assigned frigates and ships of the line to guard convoys with exceptionally valuable cargos like gold and silver. Joining a convoy was voluntary until 1798 when the Compulsory Convoy Act made it mandatory unless a shipowner received a license from the Admiralty. For West Indies bound convoys, vessels sailing from London or ports in east England and Scotland, or south England gathered at Spithead while those from west England and Scotland and Ireland gathered at Cork. Convoys sailing from the West Indies gathered at Port Royal, Jamaica or Barbados.

* * *

Espionage or secretly gathering, analysing, and using information about one's friends, rivals, and enemies is critical to security for individuals, groups, organisations, and nation states alike. Britain's government did not have a unified intelligence system but instead had parallel intelligence organisations that mostly competed and at times co-operated with each other. The Home, Foreign, and, from 1794, War Ministries each had intelligence bureaux. Secretaries took secrecy oaths when they assumed those offices and overseeing intelligence was among their many duties. Key bureaux before 1792 included the Private Office, also called the Foreign Letter Office, and the Secret Deciphering Office that worked together to intercept, decode, and release correspondence. In 1793, the Home Ministry established the Alien Office first to conduct counterespionage at home and soon espionage abroad. The Treasury financed some of these operations, while much money came from the king's Civil List whose spending was free of parliamentary oversight. Money for foreign operations was often transferred through intermediaries like Boyd, Benfield, and Company or Herries, Farquahar and Company.

From 1793 to 1815, Whitehall's intelligence services steadily grew more sophisticated and successful at espionage, counter-espionage, and an array of covert actions designed to change the policies and power of other countries in Britain's favour.[41] Yet that development could never overcome the core dilemma of intelligence: the information one most wants is either unobtainable or unreliable. First Lord of the Admiralty George, Earl Spencer explained that dilemma in a 1798 report: 'All the intelligence received from time to time has constantly been circulated for the information of the Cabinet.' The perennial intelligence trouble was that it 'cannot always be known what degree of reliance should be placed upon any particular piece of information, and it is only from a general view and comparison of the whole that anything like a tolerable judgement of it can be formed.'[42]

* * *

Foreign Secretary Grenville swiftly constructed a coalition. British envoys signed alliance treaties with Sardinia-Piedmont on 25 April, Spain on 25 May, Naples on 12 July, Prussia on 14 July, and Austria on 30 August. Whitehall underwrote 50,000 Piedmontese troops for £200,000 in 1793 and 1794. The British got 6,000 Neapolitan troops in exchange for shipping them to the nearest front, which in the autumn of 1793 was Toulon. Initially, the British refused to subsidise the Prussian, Spanish, and Austrian troops, arguing that those great powers were fully capable of paying for their own wars.

Ambassador Charles Whitworth failed to cut a deal with Tsarina Catherine for 12,000 Russian troops. She demanded £600,000 for 10,000 troops. In London, Ambassador Alexander Vorontzoff slashed that demand in half, but Grenville for now declined it. Catherine could not spare more as she, Prussian King Frederick William, and Austrian Archduke Francis I each took territory from Poland in 1793 and would completely partition Poland's remnants in 1795.

4.6. Bank of England Specie Reserves, First Coalition[43]

1793	February	£4,011,000	1796	February	£2,540,000
	August	£5,322,000		August	£2,123,000
1794	February	£6,987,000	1797	February	£1,086,000
	August	£6,770,000		August	£4,090,000
1795	February	£6,128,000			
	August	£5,136,000			

The immediate strategic priority was defending the Netherlands. Having overrun most of the Austrian Netherlands, French armies invaded the Dutch republic on 16 February 1793, and within weeks advanced deep into the country. Whitehall dispatched 2,500 Royal Guardsmen to the Netherlands on 25 February, and eventually eight other British regiments joined them. That army's numbers doubled with German regiments. Envoys negotiated deals whereby Hanover, Hesse-Cassel, and Hesse-Darmstadt furnished 10,000, 12,000, and 3,000 troops, respectively. The Hanoverians annually cost £455,851 and the Hessians £7 4s for infantrymen and £19 5s for cavalrymen. The British also hired 754 troops from Baden for an annual payment of £5,013. The total cost for all foreign troops was £1,169,000 in 1794. Foreign contingents composed one quarter of Britain's army by 1795.[44]

Frederick Augustus, Duke of York and the king's second son, received command of the 35,000-man army in Flanders. The allies launched an offensive in mid-July. York supported an Austrian–Dutch army that recaptured the fortress city of Valenciennes on 28 July. Days earlier on 23 July, a Prussian army retook Mainz. Those successes prompted Whitehall to order York to take Dunkirk to serve as a depot for both his army and the navy. York's army invested Dunkirk on 24 August but lacked heavy cannon to breach the walls. French General Jean Houchard advanced and routed York's covering force at Hondschoote on 6 September, forcing York to hastily break off the siege and withdraw. Dunkirk was the furthest York advanced in the Low Countries. Strategically, for the next year and a half he and his diminishing army would take two steps backward for every step forward along with the other allied armies until the French revolutionary armies overran both the Austrian and Dutch Netherlands. Deeply frustrated, York turned over his army's command to General William Harcourt on 2 December 1794. Harcourt eventually withdrew to Bremen, where the navy evacuated the army's remnants in April 1795.[45]

* * *

France's revolutionary regime faced growing opposition in regions across the country. Some were federalists who favoured a republic with limited powers and regional autonomy. Others were royalists who wanted the Bourbons returned to the throne, although they bickered over whether the king's powers should be absolute or constitutional. Devout Catholics hated the revolutionaries for desecrating their churches and purging their priests. North-west rebel groups included the Chouans in Normandy and Brittany, and the Vendeans in the lower Loire River valley. In the lower Rhône valley, royalists and federalists formed an uneasy alliance as they took power in Lyon, Marseille, and Toulon.

London and Madrid agreed in March 1793 to jointly blockade Toulon, France's main Mediterranean naval base.[46] On 16 July, Admiral Samuel Hood's fleet that eventually peaked with 21 ships of the line and 19 frigates and brigs appeared off Toulon. Soon joining Hood was a Spanish fleet of eighteen ships of the line first commanded by Admiral Juan de Langara, then by Admiral Frederico Gravina. On 23 August, Hood received a rebel delegation from Toulon that requested its aid against the revolutionary regime and offered to surrender the port. Hood readily agreed. The Toulon fleet, including thirty-one ships of the line and twenty-seven smaller warships, was now in allied hands. Eventually, the allies deployed more than 17,000 troops in a dozen forts on the hills surrounding Toulon, including 2,114 British, 6,846 Spanish, 4,832 Neapolitans, 1,584 Piedmont Sardinians, and 1,542 royalists.[47]

Paris mobilised an army to crush the southern revolt. The French revolutionary army recaptured Avignon on 24 July, Marseilles on 25 August, and opened a siege of Toulon on 30 August. Eventually, 40,000 French troops ringed Toulon. Captain Napoleon Bonaparte received command of the siege army's artillery when his predecessor was wounded, and was eventually promoted to brigadier general. Bonaparte devised a plan that captured a series of key positions, culminating on 16 December with Fort l'Eguillette that overlooked the bay packed with allied warships. That forced Hood to hastily evacuate Toulon and sail on 18 December. Of course, no one then, including Bonaparte, could imagine that he would become the nemesis for Britain and all other states that opposed his ambitions. Nonetheless, the allies inflicted a devastating blow to the Toulon fleet as they withdrew. The British took three French ships of the line, three frigates, and seven smaller warships with them while setting fires to the rest of the French fleet. The French rushed in and managed to extinguish the fires with minor damage to eighteen ships of the line, while nine were destroyed.

* * *

Amidst the coalition and royalist offensives in 1793, the Convention issued a decree on 23 August that revolutionised warfare, the *levee en masse* or mobilisation of nearly all able-bodied citizens: 'From now on, until the complete repulsion of all our enemies from the territory of the Republic of France, all French people are subject to military service. The young men will march to the battlefield; the married men will forge the arms and transport supplies; the women will produce tents and clothes and serve in the hospitals; the children will make dressing material from old linen; the old men will be carried to public places to encourage the warriors and to preach hatred of kings and the unity of the Republic.'[48]

The Convention's governing Committee of Public Safety officially launched 'the terror' to destroy all domestic enemies on 5 September. Revolutionaries executed captured rebels, slaughtered men, women, and children of rebellious towns, then destroyed the buildings, and eventually guillotined thousands of real and imagined subversives in Paris and other city squares.

Reports of those atrocities horrified Britain's leaders and public. When war erupted in February, Pitt explained that Britain fought not to destroy the revolutionary regime or return the Bourbons to power, but to restore peace to Europe and France to its pre-war boundaries. He and the other ministers feared that publicly calling for the French republic's destruction would only stiffen the revolutionaries' will to fight to the last cartridge. Peace would be grounded on returning France territorially before April 1792, not ideologically before September 1789. Now France's total war strategy atop its commitment to destroy all monarchies and replace them with republics provoked a policy debate over ends and means. Pitt and the other ministers changed Britain's war goal from tolerating to overthrowing the revolutionary regime. On 29 October 1793, King George III issued a proclamation whereby he 'invites the Co-operation of the People of France ... to join the Standard of a hereditary Monarchy ... in this Moment of Disorder, Calamity, and public Danger ... to unite themselves once more under the Empire of Law, of Morality, and of Religion.'[49] In other words, Britain would ally with France's royalists against its republicans and re-establish a constitutional monarchy in France.

France's total war strategy posed a dilemma for Britain and other monarchies. If they tried to conjure mass nationalism could they control it or would it rise against and overthrow them? Poet Samuel Coleridge explained how total war at once inspired patriotism, social levelling and extremism in Britain: 'Is the nation in danger? Every man is called into play; every man feels his interest as a citizen predominating over his individual interests; the high, and the low, and the middle classes all alike politicians; the majority carry the day; and Jacobinism is the natural consequence. Every state in which all the inhabitants without distinction of property are roused to the exertions of a public spirit is, for the time, a Jacobin state.'[50]

* * *

Foreign Secretary Grenville forged a coalition in 1793, but it was ineffectual. Throughout 1794, he struggled to get the allies to commit specific numbers of troops to specific co-ordinated offensives. Most negotiations took place at the Hague, but Grenville also had to co-ordinate diplomacy with ambassadors James Harris, Earl Malmesbury, in Berlin and Morton Eden, Baron Henley, in Vienna.

The Prussians demanded the most. Initially, the British, Dutch, and Austrians agreed to provide 'bread and forage' for 52,000 Prussian troops in the Low Countries, an annual £1,000,000 cost that they split equally. In November 1793, Frederick William II demanded from Britain £3,500,000 for 100,000 troops. Grenville countered by offering £800,000 if the Prussians deposited £400,000 with the allies as a sign of good faith and security against any depredations committed by Prussian soldiers. He also asked the Dutch and Austrian governments to each pledge £400,000 to Berlin. The Dutch and Austrians rejected his request, pleading a lack of money. The haggling persisted. On 19 April, British and Prussian envoys signed at the Hague a treaty whereby King Frederick William II promised 62,400 troops in return for £400,000 in preparation costs and annually £1,350,000. That same day the British and Dutch signed a treaty whereby the Hague would pay £100,000 of the preparation money and £400,000 of the annual subsidy.[51]

Grenville had Malmesbury, General Charles Cornwallis, and Commissary General Brook Watson journey to Prussian General Otto von Mollendorf's headquarters at Mainz to co-ordinate operations. On their way, Prussian ambassador Christian von Haugwitz met them at Maastricht, where he rejected Watson's offer for sixty days of rations, instead insisting on the money promised by the treaty. Watson explained that he had no money to give, only credit to supply provisions. The British envoys continued to Mainz, where they found only 40,000 Prussian troops. The Prussians matched their failure to provide all the troops they promised with refusing to march against the French for most of the summer.

Meanwhile, the Austrians also sought British money. Ambassador Georg Adam Starhemberg tried to raise a £3,000,000 loan in London's financial markets but got only a fraction of what was wanted. He asked Pitt for his government to guarantee the loan. Pitt agreed if Vienna fielded 160,000 Austrian and Imperial troops in the Low Countries. Chancellor Johann Amadeus von Thugut countered by demanding £6,000,000 for 100,000 troops. After consulting Grenville, Pitt offered to guarantee £4,000,000 for 160,000 troops. On 4 May 1795, diplomats signed a treaty whereby Britain underwrote a £4,600,000 loan at 6 per cent interest if Vienna fielded 170,000 in the Low Countries and Rhine valley. This was the first of numerous loans by British financiers to foreign powers that Whitehall guaranteed.

William Wickham was then Britain's liaison with the Austrian army in the Low Countries. Grenville issued him this instruction: 'We can appropriate a million to procure reinforcements for the Austrian army. You are on the spot, and best understand how to apply this in the most beneficial manner; to make the money go as far, and to derive as much benefit from it as possible. Do so according to the best of your judgment and be persuaded that ... will be approved and adopted here.'[52] Wickham replied with pointed advice on how to play the allies: 'Consider them only as instruments employed to fight the French (though in their own way), and do not either cross them at headquarters, blame their operations, or submit plans to their consideration.'[53]

Of course, having enough money to pay for a campaign does not guarantee its success. French armies drove back the allies across the Low Countries and Rhine Valley in 1794, inflicting devastating defeats at Tourcoing on 18 May and Fleurus on 26 June, capturing Brussels on 10 July, and retaking nearly all of the Austrian Netherlands by 18 September. York retreated his small, battered army into the Netherlands along with other allied forces. In July Vienna asked London to provide £3 million for another 60,000 Austrian reinforcements that year and 160,000 in 1795. Pitt countered with £200,000 to finance those immediate reinforcements. Negotiations stalled.

The only potentially positive development in 1794 was the coup from 27 to 28 July that overthrew and executed Maximilien Robespierre and his henchmen that had inflicted the terror against their real and imagined domestic enemies. Moderates controlled the new government, which would be called the Directory. The hope in Whitehall and other capitals warring against France was that the Directors would be amenable to a peace without retaining France's conquests. That hope would prove futile.

* * *

Word that Toulon had fallen prompted a Whitehall debate over whether to capture another mid-Mediterranean naval base from France. The decision was to seize Corsica in alliance with rebels led by Pasquale Paoli. Admiral Samuel Hood had wintered his fleet near the Hyères Islands just beyond Toulon's south-eastern horizon. The Admiralty ordered him to take Bastia, Corsica's largest port, as the first step in the island's conquest. Hood put Captain Horatio Nelson in command of the 1,500 marines and sailors mobilised to besiege Bastia. The French surrendered the port on 22 May. On 22 June, Paoli announced the shift of Corsica's allegiance from France to Britain. After several weeks of siege, the expedition captured the port of Calvi on 10 August. The British now effectively controlled Corsica.

The Admiralty replaced Hood with Admiral William Hotham, a cautious commander. Over the following months, the Toulon squadron sailed toward Corsica twice, ideally to drive away the British fleet and retake the island. Each time Nelson spearheaded attacks that captured French warships but Hotham restrained him from pursuing the French for more captures. In November Admiral Hyde Parker replaced Hotham but was just as timid. To Nelson's disgust, Parker recalled him from battles and pursuits that could have resulted in more prizes.

During May, several French and British fleets and convoys converged several hundred miles west of Brittany. The convoys included a French one sailing from the West Indies via Norfolk, Virginia to France; a British one from Britain that would split into three smaller convoys with different destinations; another British one from Newfoundland back to Britain; and a Dutch one from the West Indies back to the Netherlands. Two French squadrons, one led by Admiral Joseph Nielly from Rochefort and the other by Admiral Louis Villaret-Joyeuse from Brest, sailed to intercept the French convoy and escort it home but had orders to capture any British convoys they encountered. Admiral Richard Howe's squadron was to escort the British convoy until its split, then find and capture the French convoy that spies had sent word was approaching. Both French admirals spotted British convoys, pursued, and captured dozens of vessels.

Howe's fleet of twenty-six ships of the line and seven frigates encountered and chased Villaret-Joyeuse's twenty-five ships of the line, six frigates, and prizes on 28 May. During the pursuit and battles over several days that were called the Glorious First of June, the British captured six ships of the line with 3,000 sailors and sank one, inflicting 4,000 dead and wounded while suffering 1,200 casualties and eleven severely battered warships.

* * *

All along, War Secretary Dundas advocated systematically conquering France's colonies to impoverish France and enrich Britain.[54] France's West Indian colonies produced enormous wealth, especially Saint-Domingue with its huge sugar cane plantations. In 1790, colonial revenues accounted for 65 million livres of the French government's 450 million livre budget, contributed 37 per cent of the nation's imports and consumed 22 per cent of its exports.[55] Dundas sought to transfer all that wealth to Britain.

France's revolution inadvertently weakened its grip over its West Indian colonies. The colonists demanded equality and sent delegations to the National Assembly. In 1790, slaves revolted in Saint-Dominque and Martinique. It took 6,000 troops nearly a year to crush those revolts, during which around 2,000 whites and 10,000 blacks died, and hundreds of plantations, warehouses, and homes were looted and burned. Although the Convention declared equality for free mulattos and blacks in 1792 and abolished slavery on 4 February 1794, the chaos and violence persisted. Most planters were royalists who opposed the republic, equality for free blacks, and abolition for slaves. In 1793, the colonists on Saint-Domingue, Martinique, Guadeloupe, and Tobago denounced the revolution and asked for British aid.

The first British offensive in the West Indies was designed to secure those islands. Dundas assigned that mission to General Cornelius Cuyler and Admiral Alan Gardner who, at Barbados, commanded British army and naval forces in the West Indies. Although French General Donatien de Rochambeau was able to crush the colonial revolt and repel the British attack on Martinique, the British expedition did extract around 6,000 refugees. For Saint-Domingue, a smaller expedition led by General Adam Williamson, Jamaica's governor, and the flotilla by Commodore John Ford took Jeremie and Mole Saint Nicolas but failed to capture Tiburon in late 1793. That began a campaign to control Saint-Domingue that the British eventually abandoned in 1798 after squandering vast amounts of treasure and lives.[56]

Dundas organised a larger expedition that sailed from Portsmouth in November 1793, with Admiral John Jervis commanding the fleet and General Charles Grey the 16,000 troops. They captured Martinique on 25 March, Saint Lucia on 4 April, and Guadeloupe on 22 May 1794. Meanwhile, Williamson captured several Saint-Domingue ports, then asked Grey for reinforcements. Grey sent General John Whyte to join Williamson and they took Port-au-Prince on 4 June. The spoils of those captures were vast, with £65,000 of ordinance and £25,000 of engineer supplies alone and eventually £289,000 in prize money distributed. However, the human price mounted steadily from the first landfall as malaria, dysentery, typhoid, and other deadly tropical disease killed or debilitated thousands of men.[57]

The French launched a counter-attack. The first came in February 1794 when the Convention abolished slavery in France's colonies and sent agents to British colonies to provoke slave revolts in Grenada, Saint Vincent, and Jamaica. Now British colonists suffered the same death and destruction as their French counterparts. The devastation for Grenada alone was £2,500,000, with exports to Britain plummeting from an average £460,000 from 1792 to 1794 to £91,000 from 1795 to 1797.[58] Atop those losses an expedition led by General Victor Hugues recaptured Guadeloupe on 10 December 1794, and Saint Lucia on 19 June 1795.

* * *

As France's revolution radicalised, British dissidents asserted some of Edmund Burke's worst fears.[59] They demanded similar rights for themselves that all Frenchmen now enjoyed. On 14 July 1790, the Bastille's anniversary, they held celebratory dinners in London and other major cities. They signed petitions for the abolition of the Test and Corporation Acts that barred Protestant nonconformists from holding office. In 1791, they sought to unify themselves by refounding the then moribund Society for Constitutional Information. In April 1792, after France's war declarations, they formed the Society of Friends of the People that lauded France's revolution and called for civil rights including universal manhood suffrage, secret ballots, constituencies with equal populations, abolition of property qualifications to vote and hold office, and salaries for members of Parliament. Radical newspapers emerged like the *Edinburgh Gazette*, *Manchester Herald*, and *Sheffield Register* to criticise the government and espouse radical reforms. Mary Wollstonecraft insisted on equal rights for all with her *Vindication of the Rights of Women* that appeared in 1792. John Tooke, Thomas Hardy, William Godwin, and Major John Cartwright were the most prominent dissident leaders during these decades.

Conservatives formed clubs like the Church and King Club, the Association for the Protection of Liberty and Property against Levelers and Republicans, and the Loyal Association to counter the Friends of the People clubs.[60] Riots erupted between conservatives and radicals. A conservative mob burned dissident Joseph Priestley's Birmingham home in July 1791.

George III issued a proclamation that outlawed seditious writings and speeches in May 1792. The king and Parliament passed a series of laws to crush dissent and aid to France, including the 1792 Libel Act, the 1793 Traitorous Correspondence Act, the 1795 Two Acts against Treasonable and Seditious Practices and Seditious Meetings, the 1797 Act Condemning Seduction from Duty, the 1797 Act against Administering Unlawful Oaths, the 1798 and 1799 Newspaper Act, the 1799 Act for more Effective Suppression of Societies Established for Seditious and Treasonous Purposes, and the 1799 and 1800 Combination Acts that forbade labour unions. Whitehall steadily tightened controls over the press. Threat of prosecution forced the editorial boards of initially radical newspapers like the *Newcastle Chronicle*, *Morning Post*, *Sheffield Iris*, and *Chester Chronicle* to wave the Union Jack. Meanwhile, from 1792, the government secretly spent around £5,000 annually on subsidising pro-government newspapers, especially *The Sun* and *True Briton*.[61]

Whitehall worried about links between French revolutionary agents and British dissidents. They feared that agent provocateurs lurked among the thousands of French refugees fleeing the revolution. The Police Bill of June 1792 empowered the government to spy on dissident groups. The Alien Act of January 1793 required all foreigners to apply for residency with the customs house, surrender any weapons, and then await a decision from either the Home Office or local magistrate over whether a visa would be issued. Foreigners who arrived after 1 January 1792, but before 10 January 1793, had to apply for Home Office approval if they wanted to change their residence. The Home Office could deport any undesirable aliens. Officers had police powers but wore no uniforms and often worked undercover.

Grenville had agents infiltrate the London Corresponding Society and Society for Providing Constitutional Information to search for ties with French revolutionaries. On 12 May 1794, he had the papers of those two organisations seized. Although those papers did not reveal any direct link with French revolutionary agents, Pitt called for the suspension of habeas corpus on 1 May. The House of Commons and House of Lords each formed a Secret Committee to investigate British radicals and subversion.

Pitt named William Wickham the Alien Office's Superintendent of Aliens in 1794. Wickham was an excellent choice. He was educated at Harrow, Oxford University, and Geneva University, where he received a law degree. He was naturally gifted at assessing and nurturing potential sources of critical information or connections. In 1794 he was among those that Grenville had infiltrate the London Corresponding Society. That autumn, Grenville dispatched Wickham to Bern to determine whether secret peace overtures from Paris were legitimate and to assess the counter-revolutionary forces. Wickham reported the overtures as unofficial, and the counter-revolutionaries as divided. He advised ignoring the overtures and uniting the opposition.

Back in London, Wickham developed the Alien Office into a national intelligence agency. He sought agents who were discreet, intelligent, courageous, creative, and perceptive. Although the acronym MICE was not yet coined, he taught his men to understand what motivated a potential recruit – money, ideology, compromise, and/or ego – and then subtly provide him or her that in return for critical information and actions. Within Britain, he developed a network of agents who infiltrated dissident groups and sometimes provoked them into protests that led to arrests and interrogations. He dispatched agents to key foreign cities, where they recruited agents, stole secrets, and sent back reports using the classic array of techniques like ciphers, secret ink, dead drops, honey traps, and the 'three Bs' – burglary, blackmail, and bribery. He planned an array of covert foreign operations to shift the policies and power of foreign countries in Britain's favour by spreading propaganda, bribing officials, and, at times, fomenting revolts and even assassinations, including targeting Napoleon Bonaparte. He often joined his agents on the continent, especially in Switzerland and Bavaria.

All Along, Wickham faced the same dilemmas as anyone else involved in espionage. The most vital information was the most elusive, obscured by lies, exaggerations, and misplaced hopes and fears, especially of double agents. Indeed, lurking within the Alien Office was a mole, Le Clerc de Noisy, who thwarted some plots by passing word of them back to Paris. Wickham knew of his existence but not his identity. He urged a subordinate: 'You must find the spy in our midst, the man who is said to be a spy of the Directory, for there is no spy as good as a double spy.'[62]

Money was one vital resource that Wickham and other intelligence officers worried little about. Peacetime funding for the spy bureaux was £48,600 from 1784 to 1789, rose to £76,750 from 1790 to 1794, then skyrocketed to £665,222 from 1795 to 1799. Of that, Wickham and his agents expended £302,994.[63] That much money at once inspired creative ideas about how to spend it and a lot of wasted efforts. Most funding came from the king's Civil List or the Consolidated Fund, and any questions over spending came from the king and his ministers rather than Parliament.

On the continent Francis Drake was Britain's spymaster. He usually had diplomatic cover. When the war opened, he was Britain's minister at Genoa. There he nurtured ties with Louis de Launay, Comte d'Antraigues, an exile leader dedicated to organising resistance in France. Antraigues was a constitutional monarchist critical of absolutists and republicans alike.

Among the Alien Office's most enduring coups were helping establish two royalist front organisations in Paris, the Philanthropic Institute (*Institut Philanthropic*) and Paris Agency (*Amis de Paris*). Although each survived, they faced continual threats of being penetrated by police agents or blown by their own rogue agents. For instance, Paris Agency Pierre Jacques Lemaitre was a flamboyant journalist who alarmed his more discreet colleagues with what they considered his hair-brained revolt schemes. Police caught, tried, and executed Lemaitre in 1795. Nonetheless, the Paris Agency eventually expanded beyond the capital to eight regions with headquarters in Rouen, Senlis, Beauvais, Orleans, Melun, Le Mans, Evreux, and Tours, each led by a president. Ideally, each president received £10,000 annually to fund operations including printing propaganda, buying arms, paying agents, and bribing officers, bureaucrats, politicians, police, and voters. Meanwhile, Whitehall subsidised the Philanthropic Institute with £20,000 annually.[64]

Although Pitt initially denied backing the Bourbon claim to the French throne, British agents worked with émigrés to build a secret royalist army. Francis Rawdon-Hastings, Marquess of Moira, received command of that army on 12 October 1793. Moira proved a capable general during the American War but failed in his mission to capture Saint Malo or Noirmoutiers.

Pitt got around to asking Parliament's permission to do what he had already been doing on 7 April 1794. He called for establishing an émigré army to depose the revolutionary regime in Paris. That proved a daunting challenge over the next two decades as British officers and agents contended with competing exile factions who demanded huge sums to fund ambitious promised operations that usually came to naught.

Louis XVII died in prison on 8 June 1795. The succession passed to his uncle, Louis, Count of Provence, who would become Louis XVIII. At the time, Louis was in exile in Verona in the Venetian republic. Grenville sent venerable diplomat Lord George Macartney there to talk him out of declaring himself the heir and authorisation to buy the cash-strapped claimant's silence for up to £10,000. By the time he got there, Louis had issued the Verona Declaration that asserted his title to France's throne, condemned the republicans, and promised that he would overthrow them and become the rightful monarch.

In mid-summer 1795, Grenville had Ambassador Morton Eden in Vienna underwrite an invasion of France's Franc-Comte region by an exile army led by Louis Joseph, Prince de Conde. Eventually, Whitehall appropriated the extraordinary sum of £140,000 to fund it. He instructed Wickham to organise revolts in conjunction with that invasion. Wickham conceived a plan for revolt in Lyon and other towns across the region. He was confident that enough Lyonnais were ready to rebel despite rather than because the government had crushed insurrections there and elsewhere in the Rhône valley in 1793, 1794, and as recently as February 1795. In Lyon, he had a network of agents led by Louis Francois Perrin, Comte de Précy, and dispatched the exiled leader Louis Gabriel, chevalier d'Artez, from Turin to mobilise them. He had the rebels try to bribe General Charles Serizat, Lyon's National Guard commander, to join them. Meanwhile, he dispatched an agent to organise smaller revolts in Besançon, Mâcon, Montbrison, and Bourg-en-Bresse. He got Sardinia-Piedmont King Victor Amadeus III to launch an invasion by General Joseph Nikolaus Freiherr de Vins to invade Savoy to distract French forces across south-eastern France. He dispatched Louis Augusta Victor de Ghaisne, marquis de Bourmont, to stir the latest revolt in the Vendée. Whitehall underwrote Wickham's operations with £50,000.[65]

Planning such a series of invasions and revolts was challenging enough; implementing them was beyond the plotters' powers. Austrian General Dagobert Sigmund von Wurmser refused to assist Conde, while General de Vins's invasion stalled. Wickham pushed back the insurrection's timing to early autumn. French intelligence uncovered and arrested one set of plotters after another. By the year's end, Whitehall's investment of men and money was an abject failure.

The worst debacle came at Quiberon Bay on Brittany's south coast. Admiral Alexander Hood, Lord Bridport, led an armada of nine warships and sixty transports packed with 5,437 émigré royalist troops whose command Generals Joseph, Comte de Puisaye, and Louis Charles d'Hervilly squabbled over. That émigré army landed at Carnac on 27 June 1795. The plan was to link with around 15,000 Chouans and overrun Brittany. Upon hearing of the landing, Republican General Lazare Hoche quick-marched 13,000 troops to the region, routing several Chouan forces en route. The decisive battle came on 21 July with Hoche's attack on the émigré and Chouan army. The republicans slaughtered around 5,000 royalists and captured 6,332; Hood managed to evacuate around 2,500 to the transports while other survivors fled into the countryside. The Republicans executed 751 prisoners. In Parliament, Pitt defended the operation by lamely arguing that 'no English blood had been shed'. To that, member Richard Sheridan replied: 'That is true, but English honour has been shed from every pore.'[66]

The only clear success that Whitehall's covert operations may have assisted was France's 1795 elections. Among the delegates who won seats in both houses were eighty-eight absolute and seventy-three constitutional monarchists. Bizarrely, the royalists aligned with the radical Jacobins rather than moderate republicans who dominated the assemblies and Directory. Thus did the expediency of that classic political maxim 'the enemy of my enemy is my friend' trump the ideologies that committed each to the other's destruction. Wickham marvelled that 'the Royalists ... are far more disposed to compromise with the Jacobins than with any other party. All views of humanity, policy, justice, and interest are nothing when opposed to the desire of humbling and of publishing the first authors of the revolution.'[67]

* * *

To stay in the war for 1795, Vienna demanded a £4 million loan to field 120,000 troops on the Rhine and 40,000 troops on the northern Italian front. Pitt countered by offering £4.5 million with a 7.5 per cent interest rate to underwrite 200,000 Austrian troops split between those fronts. The Austrians asked for a much lower interest rate. Pitt agreed to 6 per cent. The final deal was signed on 4 May 1795.

Grenville had Ambassador Charles Whitworth offer Catherine £500,000 for 55,000 troops to join the Austrians on the Rhine. Catherine was willing to provide those troops for £1,000,000. He tried to soften the tsarina by having

George III send her a 10ft telescope and selection of exotic plants from Kew Garden. Catherine rejoiced at those gifts and did enter an alliance in 1795, but with Austria against the Ottoman Empire in a treaty signed on 3 January. With Russian troops about to march into what was left of Poland and against the Turks, Catherine could spare none to Britain at any price. However, on 18 February, she did accept a treaty that established a defensive alliance between St Petersburg and London whereby she would send 12,000 troops to join the British, while twelve Royal Navy ships of the line would sail to the Baltic if either were attacked by a third country. For now, Catherine agreed to dispatch a fleet of twelve ships of the line and six frigates to join Admiral Adam Duncan's fleet in the North Sea. Her intention for the fleet was not to fight but learn better seamanship by sailing with the Royal Navy.

By early 1795, the French overran most of the Netherlands and the Rhine's west bank. Under the Treaty of the Hague, signed on 16 May, the Dutch had to pay France 100,000,000 guilders; cede Maastricht, Venlo, and Dutch Flanders; and underwrite a French occupation army of 25,000 troops until all belligerents made peace with Paris. The remnants of Britain's army sailed home from Bremen in April. The Prussians and Spaniards respectively signed peace treaties with France on 5 April and 22 July at Basel. Hesse-Cassel withdrew its troops from British service. Although the Austrians held out, the French had conquered their Netherlands territory. Amidst those coalition debacles, the Russians, Prussians, and Austrians completed their partition of Poland in 1795, with each having previously taken large swaths in 1774 and 1793.

Ambassador Whitworth was able to convince Catherine and her ministers to commit 60,000 troops to bolster Austria's armies against France in return for a £300,000 preparation payment and thereafter £100,000 monthly subsidies. But before those terms were written in a formal treaty, Catherine died on 17 November. Her son Paul took the throne and scuttled the deal. That prompted Pitt to quip that: 'It is difficult to say whether one ought to regret that she had not died sooner or lived longer.'[68]

Grenville tried to entice Prussia back into the war with this argument to Ambassador Haugwitz: 'Europe can be saved only by a reunion of the Great Powers, which would have for its purpose the re-establishment of the general peace and thereupon the maintenance of the common tranquillity, and the guarantee of possessions by the respective governments. As long as war exists in part, the interest will be divided; as long as a general concert does not exist for the maintenance of peace, nothing can halt the designs of a government which dominates by disunion.'[69]

Word that Spain had signed an alliance with France on 18 August 1796, forced Whitehall to revise its strategy. A combined Franco–Spanish fleet outgunned Britain's Mediterranean fleet commanded by Admiral John Jervis. Reluctantly, the Admiralty ordered Jervis to abandon Corsica, concentrate the fleet at Gibraltar, and send a squadron to blockade Cadiz. Spies revealed a plan by the French and Spanish to conquer and split Portugal between them. Lisbon asked London for a fleet and enough arms to equip a 16,000-man corps. Whitehall had Jervis sail with most of the fleet to Lisbon. From 1796 to 1801, the British sent 31,000 muskets, 11,300 carbines, 3,300 pistols, 14,300 swords, 900,000 pounds of gunpowder, and twenty cannon worth £210,688 to Portugal.[70] General Charles Stuart arrived with 3,000 redcoats in February 1797 to furnish and train the Portuguese army.

* * *

The West Indies continued to be the graveyard for the reputations of most commanders and the lives of their sailors and soldiers. A storm devastated the expedition of Admiral Hugh Christian and General Ralph Abercromby after it departed Gosport, England, in November 1795, with one ship sunk and thirty of 110 returning to port for repairs. In December, the expedition sailed again, this time with 218 war and transport vessels and again storms battered it. By late January 1796 only forty-nine vessels accompanied Christian, so he turned back to Portsmouth to regroup. In March, he made his third attempt, this time with six warships and forty-one transports. They reached Barbados in early April, then Abercromby captured Dutch Demerara on 23 April and French Saint Lucia on 25 May 1796. The cost in lives, most killed by disease, was high – 6,484 from March to December 1796.[71] Abercromby resumed his campaign in 1797, captured Spanish Trinidad on 21 February but was repulsed at San Juan, Puerto Rico, on 1 May. Meanwhile, British attempts to conquer Saint-Dominigue were thwarted by black resistance leaders Francois Dominique Toussaint Louverture and Andre Rigaud, compounded by devastating diseases. After withdrawing the last redcoats in 1798, General Maitland summed up the self-defeating campaign to seize what was once the world's richest source of 'white gold' or sugar but now with its plantations destroyed and the overseers and merchants murdered or exiled: 'Thank God I have at last got Great Britain rid of the whole of the incumbrance of this island.'[72]

The British found a way to fill some of their empty ranks. A consensus built in Whitehall that regiments of black troops were the best means of fighting in the Caribbean.[73] First, most blacks were more inured to the tropical diseases that devastated regiments sent from Britain, with death rates one quarter to one half. Second, co-opting blacks with pay, dignity, and discipline in regular regiments was better than trying to intimidate them into continued suppression. Third, they better endured the sweltering heat and picked their way through jungle and mountains easier than white troops. Eventually, the British raised twelve black Caribbean regiments with only centre companies. Recruitment was slow so from 1795 to 1808, Whitehall paid around £1 million for 13,000 slaves from West Indian owners for those regiments; those men would be freed after they served their time.[74]

British expeditions in the Indian Ocean basin nearly all succeeded. Upon learning of the war, British forces in India swiftly captured France's vulnerable entrepôts of Pondicherry, Chandernagore, and Mahé, and their trading posts at Calicut, Surat, and Masulipatam. Dutch colonies became fair game after French revolutionary armies conquered the Netherlands and transformed it into the Batavian Republic in 1795. British expeditions captured the Dutch fortresses at Trincomalee, Ceylon and Malacca, on the Penang Peninsula in August 1795, and Columbo, Ceylon, Amboina, and Banda in February and March 1796. British squadrons blockaded the islands of French Mauritius and Dutch Java. The cost in lives in the East Indies was a fraction of that in the West Indies because the diseases were not as virulent.

A British expedition led by Admiral George Elphinstone and General James Craig appeared off Cape Town on 10 June 1795, and sent a demand for the governor to yield. After being refused, Craig landed his troops on 15 July and began a siege that ended with Cape Town's surrender on 15 September. Britain now strategically straddled the sea lanes between the Atlantic and Indian Oceans.

* * *

Napoleon Bonaparte was arguably Britain's most formidable enemy across its history.[75] He first made himself known to Whitehall by devising and asserting the plan that drove an allied armada from Toulon in December 1793. After that, he secured the Directory's backing, especially that of Director Paul Barras, by crushing a Parisian rebellion on 5 October 1795. The Directors rewarded Bonaparte by giving him command of the Army of Italy with its headquarters at Nice. His mission was to defeat the allied Piedmont-Sardinian and Austrian armies in north-western Italy. Starting in mid-April 1796, Bonaparte did so in a brilliant series of campaigns that first split the allied armies and decisively defeated each. In a peace treaty, Piedmont-Sardinia yielded treasure, territory, fortresses, and right of military passage to France. Bonaparte chased the Austrians eastward and overran all of Lombardy except for the fortress city of Mantua. He defeated Neapolitan,

Papal, and Venetian armies sent against him, forcing those countries to sign treaties that yielded treasure, territory, and art. From July 1796 to February 1797, he repelled four invasions by Austrian armies and eventually captured Mantua. He then marched north-east toward Vienna, repeatedly trouncing the Austrian army before finally, just 75 miles from the capital, the Austrians accepted an armistice for peace negotiations. In between campaigns he reorganised Lombardy, first into the Cisalpine and Cispadane republics, then joined them into the Italian republic with its army subordinate to France, and he transformed the Genoan Republic into the Ligurian Republic allied with France.

Bonaparte's extraordinary military, diplomatic, and political feats contrasted with the lacklustre campaigns of generals commanding much larger and better-equipped French armies against Austrian armies along the Rhine valley. The Treaty of Leoben, signed on 18 April 1797, ended Britain's first coalition. Austria ceded its Netherlands (Belgium) and Lombard regions in return for Mantua and most of Venetia, leaving Venice little more than a city-state. The Directory rejected Bonaparte's treaty as too lenient. He then returned to the diplomatic table. Under the Treaty of Campo Formio, signed on 17 October 1797, in addition to the previous deal, Austria got all of mainland Venetia while France took its four Ionian Islands and Albania; Austria ceded Mantua to the Italian republic. A congress at Rastatt, Baden, in December among France, Austria, and the Holy Roman Empire would convene to settle other territorial issues in Germany, Switzerland, and the Low Countries.

* * *

Meanwhile, the British hoped to undo Bonaparte's conquests by overthrowing the Directory. Wickham convinced Whitehall that enticing Jean Charles Pichegru, the revolution's most successful general before Bonaparte, to defect would be a great coup. Through intermediaries, he asked what might tempt Pichegru to turn coat. The stunning reply was 500,000 gold louis. Wickham dutifully sent the request to Grenville, who reluctantly approved. Wickham never made the pay-off. Rumours of Pichegru's treason provoked the Directory to pressure him into resigning on 19 March 1796. Wickham saw that not as a setback but as an opportunity to gain Pichegru's allegiance at a lower cost. Pichegru did provide intelligence to agents dispatched by Wickham but still hesitated to defect. Wickham's agents also established a link with General Jean Moreau, who replaced Pichegru.[76]

Secret British subsidies affected France's 1797 election as they had the previous 1795 election. The number of constitutional or absolute monarchists in both houses soared to 269. Among those who won a seat was Pichegru, who was elected president of the Council of Five Hundred on 1 June, although he was voted out of that post the following month. Those stunning results were partly obtained by bribes to newspaper publishers and groups. Wickham's funds helped establish the royalist newspapers *Journal General de France*, *Orateur Constitutionel*, *Ami de l'Ordre et du Repos Public*, *Quotidienne*, *Gazette Francaise*, *Nouvelles Politiques*, *Censeur des Journaux*, and *Tribune Politique*. Most money was funnelled through the Philanthropic Institute and the Paris Agency.[77]

That electoral success encouraged Louis XVIII and his ministers to replace the Paris Agency with a seven-man Council with a president who would secretly communicate with the king, Charles Comte d'Artois, and Conde. The Council would act like a royalist shadow government prepared to take power should the republic collapse from invasion and/or revolt. The Council wanted British money without oversight let alone direction. Whitehall refused and thereafter mostly worked through the Philanthropic Institute. With British money the Institute expanded its branches to fifty-eight departments by late 1797.[78]

Britain's covert war suffered a blow when French troops captured royalist leader Louis Alexandre de Launay, Comte d'Antraigues, in Trieste on 21 May 1797. Bonaparte had him brought to his headquarters at Milan and on 11 June interrogated him, making threats and promises. D'Antraigues told Bonaparte about a pending royalist coup in Paris in return for being allowed to escape. Bonaparte sent General Pierre Augereau to Paris to warn the Directory. The Directory declared martial law, had the police arrest around seventy suspects, forced 140 National Assembly deputies to resign their seats, annulled elections in forty-nine departments, and closed forty-two newspapers.[79] That decimated the Alien Office's spy network. Pichegru was among the few able to escape. D'Antraigues also 'escaped' from his Milan prison but thereafter the British, royalists, and other foreign powers shunned him.

* * *

The Royal Navy scored a stunning victory in 1797. Admiral Don Josef de Cordova commanded the Cadiz fleet of twenty-seven ships of the line. After learning that Cordova was preparing to sortie, Admiral John Jervis sailed with his fleet from Lisbon. The fleets sighted each other off Cape Saint Vincent on 14 February 1797. Although Jervis had only fifteen ships of the line, Horatio Nelson commanded one of them. When told how much the Spanish fleet outgunned his own, Jervis replied: 'The die is cast and if there are fifty I will go through them. England badly needs a victory at present.'[80] And he did just that. The British fleet captured four ships of the line and pummelled most of the rest as they fled to Cadiz, inflicting 800 casualties and capturing 3,000 sailors while suffering 300 dead and wounded. For his victory, George III knighted Jervis the Earl of Saint Vincent.

A crisis muted celebration of that victory. One by one, strikes engulfed Britain's home-based fleets, those at Portsmouth and Spithead on 13 April, Plymouth on 26 April, Nore on 7 May, and Sheerness and Woolwich on 28 May. In each fleet, the sailors elected two delegates from each warship to collectively demand better pay, food, health care, shore leave, and prize money. They promised to return to duty if the French fleet sailed but otherwise the strike would persist until the Admiralty approved their demands. First Lord of the Admiralty Earl George Spencer sent Admiral Richard Howe to negotiate with the mutineers. Howe conveyed their demands to Whitehall. Pitt and the inner cabinet approved most of them. On 9 May, Pitt asked Parliament for a supplementary budget to fund pay raises for sailors. Upon learning of that request, the sailors began to resume their duties. The mutinies at Spithead and Nore lasted from 15 April to 17 May and 12 May to 12 June, respectively. Court martials tried 412 mutineers, imprisoned twenty-nine, flogged nine, condemned fifty-nine to death, and hanged twenty-nine from their warships' yardarms, while acquitting the rest.[81]

The sailors proved their skill and loyalty later that year when Dutch Admiral Jan de Winter sailed with fifteen ships of the line and six frigates into the North Sea. The Admiralty ordered Admiral Adam Duncan with sixteen ships of the line and two frigates to intercept him. The fleets fought off the Dutch coast near Camperdown on 11 October. It was another lopsided devastating victory as the British captured nine ships of the line and two frigates, inflicted 1,100 casualties, and captured several thousand sailors while suffering 825 casualties.

* * *

Britain suffered a potential financial crisis in 1797. From 1793 to 1797, Whitehall had dispersed £13,000,000 in bills or specie among various foreign governments and groups, of which Vienna pocketed £10,000,000. Whitehall also spent £4,000,000 purchasing foreign grain to supply the army and fleet. Fortunately, annual government revenues rose from £23,000,000 to £35,000,000 during those four years.[82] The trouble was that expenses soared far beyond revenues. Grenville cautioned his colleagues that 'our financial resources [are] not ... unlimited or inexhaustible as at first sight would appear to be'.[83] With most of that spending covered by borrowed money, the national debt rose £116,300,000 from £242,900,000 in 1792 to £359,200,000 in 1797.[84] Over the next two years, Pitt alleviated the worsening debt with the Triple Assessment of taxes that varied on annual incomes from £60 to £200.

Atop that, the Austrians repudiated their loan guaranteed by Britain, thus forcing Whitehall to pay for it. That naturally enraged the British. Grenville observed that: 'We shall lose some money for having believed in the good faith and probity of the Austrian government. The Court of Vienna will forever lose its credit, its honour, and the chance of finding here any financial aid which it might require in the future. All things considered, I really believe that if we are the dupes, it is the duper who will be the loser.'[85] British national interests soon mooted that otherwise reasonable assessment. Whitehall would have to forgive Austrian perfidy to underwrite its next round of campaigns against France.

The key reason why the Bank of England haemorrhaged so much specie was the long-standing rule that it had to redeem its notes in hard cash. That forced the directors to curtail issues and thus the amount of money circulating. The 1797 Restriction Act ended that gold standard rule. Thereafter the Bank of England freely issued notes to finance expenditures and lowered the minimal issue from £5 to £1. The Royal Mint began stamping copper coins. The downside was soaring prices with the paper money unbacked gold or silver coins.

Despite this array of financial troubles, Whitehall would muster enough funds to underwrite the next coalition.

Chapter 5

Second, 1798–1802

[T]he appearance of a British squadron in the Mediterranean is a condition on which the fate of Europe may ... depend ... [W]e are disposed to ... run some risk ... to bring about a new system of affairs in Europe, which shall save us all from being overrun by the exorbitant power of France ... [I]f by our appearance in the Mediterranean, we can encourage Austria to come forward again, it is ... probable that the other powers will seize the opportunity of acting at the same time.

[John Jervis, Earl Saint Vincent]

The man who defeated the coalition that cost Britain so much treasure and blood to form returned to Paris triumphant and exhausted in December 1797. Parisians celebrated Napoleon Bonaparte as a hero and the French Institute made him a member. The Directory assigned him the mission of determining whether Britain could be invaded. He spent several weeks along the English Channel inspecting forces and mulling intelligence reports. He informed the Directory that for the foreseeable future France's navy would not be powerful enough to control the English Channel long enough for an army to sail across and invade Britain. He then pitched an alternative. The Directory agreed to his plan to conquer Egypt, an Ottoman Empire province, for its riches and as a stepping stone to invade British India.

At Toulon and several minor ports, Bonaparte assembled an armada packed with 38,000 troops, 1,200 horses, and supplies among 280 transports escorted by thirteen ships of the line and two score smaller warships commanded by Admiral Francois Brueys. The armada departed on 21 May 1798. The first objective was Malta, strategically sited between Sicily and Tunisia and ruled by the Knights Hospitallers. The armada dropped anchor before the bay leading to Valletta, Malta's capital, on 9 June. After a short siege, Malta surrendered on 19 June. After garrisoning Malta, the armada sailed to Egypt, arriving off Alexandria on 28 June. Bonaparte landed his army and captured Alexandria on 2 July. It took a week to disembark all the men and supplies. Before heading toward Cairo, Bonaparte told Brueys either to crowd his fleet in Alexandria's small harbour or sail to French-held Corfu. Brueys did neither. Bonaparte marched his army up the Nile River valley and routed the Egyptian army led by the ruling caste called Mamelukes. He triumphantly led his army into Cairo on 24 July. He soon received catastrophic news.

Spy reports of the armada massing at Toulon reached Whitehall. First Admiral Spencer directed John Jervis, Earl of Saint Vincent, who commanded the fleet at Lisbon, to assign Horatio Nelson, then commanding the squadron blockading Cadiz, to find and destroy it. He explained that mission's geopolitical importance: '[T]he appearance of a British squadron in the Mediterranean is a condition on which the fate of Europe may ... depend ... [W]e are disposed to ... run some risk ... to bring about a new system of affairs in Europe, which shall save us all from being overrun by the exorbitant power of France ... [I]f by our appearance in the Mediterranean, we can encourage Austria to come forward again, it is ... probable that the other powers will seize the opportunity of acting at the same time.'[1] And that was indeed what happened.

Nelson eventually gathered fourteen ships of the line as he sailed first to Gibraltar and then eastward. He guessed that Bonaparte had targeted Egypt but actually reached Alexandria before the slow-moving armada. He then sailed toward Constantinople, imagining that Bonaparte sought its conquest. Learning that Bonaparte had indeed invaded Egypt, he returned to Alexandria on 1 August to find Brueys's fleet anchored in a long row in Aboukir Bay a dozen miles east of the city. He caught Brueys by surprise as, inexplicably, the French admiral had failed to post frigates as pickets on the horizon to warn of an approaching enemy. Nelson split his fleet in two to sail along each side of the French warships and broadside them. The British destroyed two ships of the line, including Brueys's 120-gun flagship, which exploded, and battered nine more into surrender. Only two ships of the line escaped. The British inflicted around 2,000 casualties and captured several thousand sailors while suffering 218 dead and 678 wounded but losing no ships.

The Battle of the Nile as it was called decisively shifted the Mediterranean's naval balance to favour Britain. The British steadily expanded that advantage. Bonaparte was now marooned in Egypt. The Ottoman Empire joined what became the Second Coalition because the French had conquered their province of Egypt. The Austrians and Russians signed an alliance treaty against France in July 1798. Whitehall steadily developed the second coalition with diplomacy, money, and supplies. Foreign Secretary William Grenville was confident that militarily an alliance of Britain, Austria, Russia, German states, and royalists was powerful enough to prevail if each fulfilled his duty. And therein lay the rub.

Although Prime Minister William Pitt had originally wanted to limit all subsidies to £2,000,000, he eventually had to raise that to £3,500,000 to accommodate the demands and mostly genuine needs of the allies. And once again, Pitt and most other ministers considered Austria the key ally. Only Secretary for War Henry Dundas objected: 'We have nothing to gain and much to lose by entwining ourselves round the desperate fortunes of Austria.'[2] Dundas proved to be prescient.

Vienna was eager to play Britain's leading land warfare role. The Austrians had no sooner ratified their peace treaty with France than they prepared to break it and demand that Whitehall underwrite their latest war. On 1 April 1798, Ambassador George Adam, Prince Starhemberg, asked Foreign Secretary Grenville to underwrite another huge loan for Austria to fight France. Pitt and his cabinet had already decided to do exactly that. The question was how much at what interest rate.

With Austria, a perfect storm of deviousness and incompetence fouled its relations with Britain. Alien Office chief Wickham warned Whitehall that with Johann von Thugut as chancellor, 'we shall be tricked and teased and tormented ... as long as that man shall remain in place. But there is no one to succeed him.'[3] He explained that: 'Thugut's ill-humour arises principally from bills coming in upon him faster than he can pay them; and indeed, when I witness the enormous expenses incurred for the support of the army here, it is a matter of astonishment to me how they can possibly go on as they do with their finances in so very disordered a state.'[4] Grenville reckoned that Vienna's assertion of its full military power 'depends on the windings of a policy so perverse and crooked that my mind is utterly unable to follow them'.[5]

In St Petersburg, British Ambassador Charles Whitworth negotiated subsidy treaties with Austria and Russia. On 13 December 1798, he and Austrian Ambassador Louis Cobenzl signed a treaty whereby Whitehall underwrote a £3,600,000 loan to Austria. In doing so, he defied Grenville's instructions. He did so because Tsar Paul promised to reward him with a treaty whereby Russia supplied 45,000 troops in return for a preparation payment of £225,000 and monthly subsidies of £75,000. There was a catch. Russia would only join the coalition if Prussia also did so. After signing that treaty on 29 December, Whitworth sent both to London. Pitt accepted the Russian treaty and rejected the Austrian treaty.

Grenville dispatched his brother Thomas Grenville to Berlin to pressure Prussian King Frederick William III to join the coalition. Frederick William was willing to commit 60,000 troops for £200,000 in preparation money and £1,000,000 for a six-month campaign. That was too much for Whitehall, but the king refused any lesser amount. Although Frederick William remained neutral, Paul joined the coalition.

* * *

Just as the British tried to foment insurrections in France, the French sought to inflict the same on the British Isles. No part of Britain was more susceptible to subversion and revolt than Ireland. England's Norman rulers invaded Ireland in 1169 and from 1171 ruled Ireland as a Lordship.[6] In 1542, Henry VIII transformed that into the kingdom of Ireland whereby England's king was also Ireland's king, but of the Anglican rather than Catholic version of Christianity and represented in Dublin, the capital, by a viceroy. What followed was a three-tiered apartheid system based on religion with Anglican landlords and merchants about 10 per cent of the population, Presbyterian Scots who migrated mostly to northern Ireland about 10 per cent, and indigenous Irish Catholics 80 per cent. An Irish parliament evolved that by 1800 had 300 members, although only wealthy Anglicans and some Presbyterian landowners could vote or run for a seat. Catholics could not vote or hold public office, possess weapons, practise law, teach, or acquire land from Protestants; Catholic land had to be equally split among sons when the father died. Only one priest was allowed in each parish.

Dissident Presbyterians, Catholics, and free thinkers established the Society of United Irishmen to voice support for the French Revolution and advocate civil rights in 1791.[7] Worried about the worsening threat of revolt, Ireland's parliament passed the Insurrection Act that empowered the government to impose curfews, search homes, and arrest and charge dissidents as traitors in 1796.

Wolf Tone was a United Irishmen leader who fled to exile in Paris in February 1796. Tone talked the Directory into mustering an armada to invade Ireland as the Irish rebelled against the British.[8] On 11 December 1796, Admiral Justin Morard de Galles's fleet of seventeen ships of the line, thirteen frigates, and seven transports packed with 15,000 troops led by General Lazare Hoche sailed from Brest. They ran a gauntlet of prowling British squadrons including frigates off Brest, ships of the line off Ushant, and the Channel fleet led by Admiral Alexander Hood, Lord Bridport, sailing from Spithead. Storms scattered the armada and only eight ships including Tone's reached the invasion point of Bantry Bay on 22 December. With Hoche among the missing warships and transports, Tone and the captains agreed to call off the invasion and sail back to France.

Word of the near invasion alarmed the Irish government and inspired the underground United Irishmen. Tone and the Directory planned an even larger invasion to join an Irish revolt in 1798. In April, the rebellion erupted in County Leinster and soon spread across the island. British regulars and militia routed rebel armies at Tara on 26 May, Curragh on 29 May, New Ross on 5 June, Ballynahinch on 13 June, and, most decisively, Vinegar Hill on 21 June. Thousands of Irish were killed during combat or executed after surrendering. The French invasion armada belatedly dropped anchor at Kilcumin in County Mayo on 22 August. General Jean Humbert marched inland with 2,000 French troops in search of rebel armies that no longer existed. General Gerald Lake intercepted and forced Humbert to surrender at Ballinamuck on 8 September. Theobald Wolf Tone was part of a ten-ship armada led by Admiral Jean Bompart that a British fleet cornered near Lough Swilly on 22 October. He was on one of the seven captured ships. Condemned to death for treason, he cheated the hangman by slitting his own throat on 7 December.

British troops and militia may have slaughtered as many as 30,000 Irish to crush that rebellion and hopefully deter future ones. General Lake ordered his officers and men to carry out 'summary' executions of any armed rebels and their supporters. General Edward Cornwallis tried to restrain atrocities by his 'troops who delight in murder' and so 'powerfully counteract all plans of conciliation'. Their looting and burning also devastated the economy. Eventually survivors petitioned the British government for £1,023,337 in claims, a fraction of the total destruction. The war grossly worsened Ireland's pervasive poverty and stagnation. Ireland may have been a strategic asset but was an enormous drain of treasure and troops for Whitehall to suppress and defend.[9]

* * *

In the Mediterranean, the next British victory came on Spain's island province of Minorca. A British armada led by Admiral John Duckworth and General Charles Stuart dropped anchor there on 7 November 1798. Stuart led the troops ashore to invest the major port, Ciutadella. On 16 November, General Juan de Quesada surrendered his 4,000 troops, four frigates, and the island.

Meanwhile, British diplomats and admirals tried to reverse a recent French conquest in Italy but ended up provoking another. The Papal States had joined its small army to the first coalition. Bonaparte's troops routed it and under the Treaty of Tolentino, signed on 19 February 1797, the papacy ceded to Paris reparations, paintings, and a protectorate. A Roman uprising that killed General Mathurin Duphot on 28 December 1797 became the excuse for invasion. General Louis-Alexandre Berthier marched unopposed into Rome on 10 February 1798, declared the Republic of Rome on

18 February, and captured and carried Pope Pius VI away on 20 February, eventually keeping him under guard in a small palace at Valence, France.

Ferdinand IV and Maria Carolina ruled the Kingdom of Naples, which included southern Italy and Sicily. The queen figuratively wore the pants in that royal couple as she adeptly manipulated her husband's flimsy mind and will to her own purposes. She was the daughter of Austrian Empress Maria Theresa and older sister of French Queen Marie Antoinette, guillotined by France's revolutionaries. Hatred for the French Revolution primarily shaped her foreign policy. The royal couple's prime minister was John Acton, an expatriate Englishman who did whatever he could to advance both Neapolitan and British interests. Britain was officially represented by its ambassador, Sir William Hamilton, then sixty-eight, and unofficially by his vivacious, pretty, coquettish wife, Emma, then thirty-three.

Horatio Nelson and Emma had flirted during his previous fleeting visits to Naples. They consummated their desires shortly after his triumphant return to Naples from the Battle of the Nile. Amidst a global war, what ensued was among history's most famous adulterous affairs. And their torrid romance mattered because at times it distorted the love-sick captain's decisions. Nelson was just as deeply immersed in political affairs. The kingdom's incompetence, sloth, and corruption appalled him. He explained to Jervis that: 'This country by its system of procrastination will ruin itself; the Queen sees it and thinks as we do ... War at this moment alone can save these kingdoms ... I have scolded; anger is necessary.'[10]

Nelson spearheaded the British and Austrian diplomatic effort to convince the royal couple to join the coalition against France. Ferdinand agreed to have Austrian General Karl Mack command the Neapolitan army. On 22 November 1798, the king issued France an ultimatum to withdraw from the Papal States and Malta. He did not await an answer but instead authorised Mack to invade the Roman Republic on 23 November. Outnumbered, French General Jean-Etienne Championnet withdrew north into Tuscany. The Neapolitan army marched into Rome on 29 November. After receiving reinforcements, Championnet marched on Rome. The Neapolitan army abandoned Rome on 12 December and hurried back to Naples. Championnet pursued relentlessly. The royal family, court, and diplomatic community packed into Nelson's flotilla and sailed to Palermo. Championnet received Naples' surrender on 12 January and helped liberal Neapolitans establish the Parthenopean Republic on 21 January. He then garrisoned two forts and withdrew to Rome.

At Palermo, Ferdinand committed his one successful act of war. He had Cardinal Fabrizio di Ruffo di Baranello and eight aides transported across the

Messina Straits to a beach near Reggio di Calabria on the night of 7 February 1799. Ruffo was a charismatic, fearless leader who inspired and led a rebellion against the French. By May, rebel groups had captured much of Italy south of Naples, including Calabria, Basilicata, and Puglia. On 13 June, Ruffo's army stormed into Naples and routed the republican defenders. The French commander and Neapolitan republicans signed a convention with Ruffo and British and Russian envoys that allowed them to be repatriated to France.

Nelson's squadron dropped anchor off Naples on 24 June. Determined to deter future republican revolts, he repudiated the convention and had the rebel leaders tried for treason. Trials eventually resulted in the execution of ninety-nine rebels, 222 given life imprisonment, 300 lesser prison terms, and 288 deported. Ferdinand rewarded Nelson by naming him the Duke of Bronte with a £3,000 annual stipend. The East India Company was even more generous; in gratitude for destroying whatever threat Bonaparte's conquest of Egypt posed to India, it granted the captain £10,000. Nelson returned to Britain, where he was feted and acclaimed by a grateful Parliament and public.[11]

* * *

The Low Countries were as much the graveyard of generals' reputations if not as voracious of soldiers' lives as the West Indies. Pitt and Grenville devised a plan to restore exiled Stadtholder William V to the Netherlands, renamed the Batavian Republic under French domination. They dismissed Dundas's warning that the expedition had little chance of succeeding but later likely rued their decision. Britain's second coalition effort there was as ignominious as that of the first coalition's effort with the Dutch, Austrians, Prussians, and various German states. This time, the British had only one partner. Foreign Minister Grenville instructed Ambassador Whitworth to hire a Russian army. On 22 June 1799, Whitworth got Paul to pledge 17,583 troops for a £88,000 preparation subsidy and thereafter monthly payments of £44,000 along with a monthly £19,642 for Russia's transport fleet. In all, Britain paid Russia £1,934,459 from June 1799 to June 1800. Paul eagerly took the money but shortchanged Whitehall on the soldiers he promised.

Once again Commander-in-Chief William, Duke of York, led the expedition, with General Ralph Abercromby heading the British contingent. The flotilla of 150 or so ships packed with 15,000 troops sailed from Margate on 13 August. Contrary winds prevented the troops from disembarking at the tiny Dutch port of Callantsoog before 27 August. They routed a Dutch force and invested the port of Helder. The Dutch naval commander capitulated the port and his fleet of sixteen ships of the line and five frigates on

30 August. That same day, the first Russian contingent of 17,500 troops led by General Ivan Hermann began landing. General Guillaume Brune commanded the 16,000 army of French and Dutch troops scattered across the Batavian Republic that he tried to concentrate against the invaders. In a seesaw campaign, the Anglo–Russian army defeated the Franco–Dutch army at Krabbendam on 10 September and Alkmaar on 2 October, but suffered defeats at Bergin on 19 September and Castricum on 6 October. Strategically the Franco–Dutch army hemmed in the Anglo–Russian army. York agreed to cut his losses and withdraw. Under the Convention of Alkmaar, signed on 19 October, the coalition troops had to embark before 1 December, while each side had to release its prisoners. Overall, the campaign was a British victory since they kept the Dutch fleet they captured and incorporated it into the Royal Navy.

Initially on other European fronts, the coalition scored stunning victories in 1799. They repelled spring offensives by Generals Andre Masséna in Switzerland, Barthelemy Scherer in northern Italy, and Jean-Baptiste Jourdan in the Rhine valley. British-subsidised Russian armies led by Generals Alexander Suvorov and Alexander Korsakov were critical to the coalition success in northern Italy and Switzerland, respectively. The French Republic rushed reinforcements and supplies to the endangered fronts. The campaign's turning point came when Masséna routed Korsakov's army at Zurich on 25 September. Suvorov withdrew eastward. The French recaptured most of their lost conquests.

Pitt and his ministers debated whether to subsidise Russian armies for campaigns in 1800. Grenville saw Russia's role as crucial to the war's outcome: 'Without a Russian army we shall make no solid impression on the French, and without these arrangements the most numerous Russian army will, I fear, rather be productive of triumph to our enemies than of advantage to ourselves.'[12] Paradoxically, Russia was powerful partly because of its weaknesses. Grenville recognised that and saw no end of diplomatic and operational challenges in dealing with the Russians, 'the most shabby set of people in Europe. It will require no small degree of firmness ... to convince them that we are not at their mercy, which we really are in this respect, though we must not let them think so.'[13]

Dundas was typically sceptical about any major commitments to offensives in Europe and readily agreed that Russia was the coalition's weakest link. He acknowledged that their troops 'are brave men, and are, I suppose as good materials as can be for the formation of a powerful army,' unfortunately 'it is in vain to look for any effectual aid from the armies of Russia in the ... next campaign ... If they are to act either in Italy or Switzerland, they must be totally new modelled and every principle in their formation ... must be altered and new arranged.' The trouble was that doing so would take time, money, and, above all, St Petersburg's full commitment. Until then, the Russians were perhaps best deployed to garrison fortresses and depots in the rear of the Austrian armies, thus freeing up more of the latter's troops to fight at the front. The first step was to ensure that the Russians were 'regularly fed and deprived of the means of plundering'.[14]

Spymaster William Wickham had observed Suvorov's operations and sent Whitehall a caveat. He saw the Russian army as a potential asset, but only if it was essentially run by British and Austrian officers, and adequately paid and provisioned. Otherwise, the Russian troops would harm rather than enhance the coalition. He condemned Suvorov's entourage for being as 'cunning and treacherous as they are ignorant and brutal'.[15] He warned that with no 'increase of pay neither officers nor men can subsist in these countries but by pillage and plunder, by which they must infallibly in the end render the cause of the allies odious. Without a commissariat and without magazines, of which they are in total want, they can make no progress anywhere ... Without a staff composed entirely ... of foreign officers, and without foreign officers attached permanently to every corps, this army cannot possibly act by itself, but must be dispersed in separate bodies among the Austrians armies.' He anticipated that convincing the tsar to go along with all this would be a 'very delicate matter ... but truth must be spoken on this occasion, or all will be lost. Fortunately, the Russian officers ... seem now persuaded of their own ignorance and insufficiency and are themselves calling out for foreign officers to command them'. Wickham ended by quipping that although 'the Russians may be made great use in the conquest ... I would not trust them to guard the chateau of a bailiff'.[16]

The cabinet agreed on 26 October to underwrite a Russian army to join the Austrians but with greater British oversight. Grenville empowered Henry Phipps, Earl of Mulgrave, essentially to organise the campaign behind the scenes. He was to persuade Suvorov 'to reconcile the Emperor's mind to the appointment of a foreign staff and commissariat to that army, and of some foreign officers to serve in the line with it'. He was also 'to take the command of any Swiss force that may be raised in the King's pay'. Finally, he 'should select some English officers to be employed in both departments of the staff, and ... choose some Austrian and Conde officers for the same purpose, and that of the line', all the time reconciling Suvorov's 'mind to these arrangements'.[17]

By November 1799, the prevailing view in Whitehall was despair that the coalition would ever realise its promise. Dundas expressed that pessimism in a letter to Grenville: 'I confess myself totally at a loss to figure any speedy effects to arise from a Continental alliance.' With 'Vienna and Petersburg ... we had exhausted every endeavour ... in our power to unite them in any effectual or beneficial co-operation,' but 'jealousies and animosities' prevailed.

* * *

The coalition did win two campaigns in the eastern Mediterranean in 1799. A Russo–Turkish armada captured the Ionian Islands from France. Bonaparte invaded Palestine with 20,000 troops in February 1799. He defeated the Turkish army in a series of battles, then in mid-March opened a siege of Acre, Palestine's capital, whose governor was Pasha Achmet the 'Butcher' (Djezzar). Captain William Sydney Smith is among the era's most consequential and colourful naval commanders, and was critical to inflicting Bonaparte's first decisive defeat.[18] He then commanded two warships in the region. He aided Djezzar first by capturing the French siege guns as they were shipped along the coast, then landing 800 marines, gunners, and engineers at Acre to bolster its defence. The defenders repelled a series of French attacks. Bonaparte broke off the siege on 10 May, withdrew to Egypt, and entered Cairo on 14 June. A flotilla landed a Turkish army at Aboukir Bay on 11 July. Bonaparte quick-marched 10,000 troops to attack and slaughter the Turks on 25 July. With Egypt secure for now, Bonaparte devised his latest plan.

Bonaparte turned over his army's command to General Jean-Baptiste Kleber and sailed for France with his most trusted officers packed on two frigates on 22 August. They disembarked at Frejus on 9 October, and hurried to Paris, arriving on 16 October. Over the next three weeks, Bonaparte and a coterie plotted to overthrow the Directory. The coup unfolded over 9 and 10 November. Bonaparte got the legislature to appoint him First Consul along with two assistant consuls. Bonaparte sent a Christmas Day letter requesting peace to the British and Austrian monarchs.

Pitt assembled the cabinet to discuss Bonaparte's peace offering on 2 January 1800. True to stereotype, these very English ministers turned up their noses at what they considered the letter's bad form and dismissed the sincere call for peace. Richard Duke Buckingham, a cabinet advisor, described Bonaparte's offering as 'most curious, and, as a diplomatic piece is unique'. While Bonaparte's direct appeal to the king was offensive, far worse could be the political consequences if the public got wind of his olive branch. Buckingham warned of the 'danger ... from the pressure of the taxes, the tribe of those who, though well inclined to Government, will clamour for peace ... and that the opinion of the country will compel you to hear what Bonaparte has to propose'.[19]

Pitt and his ministers embraced Buckingham's views, along with the belief that Bonaparte's offer was a sign of weakness. Spies in Paris had reported 'the total want of money [and] ... the unsettled state of Bonaparte's authority'.[20] If so, then Britain should spurn peace for unrelenting war that toppled his regime and restored the Bourbons to power. Undersecretary of State George Canning was especially adamant that 'the whole game is our hands now, and that it wants little more than patience to play it well, to the end'.[21]

The question remained under what French concessions that Britain would accept peace. Here the cabinet split. War Secretary Dundas insisted that they keep pretty much everything they took, especially Martinique, Ceylon, and the Cape of Good Hope. Otherwise, if the French and Dutch got back their colonies, they will 'revive rapidly all their commercial and maritime resources, and proportionally rob us of all the means of strength and pre-eminence by which we have been enabled to perform those miracles of exertion which have distinguished Great Britain in the course of this arduous contest'.[22] Secretary of State Grenville favoured peace as long as the Bourbons once again ruled France. Home Secretary Portland believed that Egypt was the key: 'Until the fate of Egypt is decided, we can have no peace: till then Bonaparte will not and cannot be expected to negotiate. With Egypt clear, and the flower of French veterans beaten by English valour and prowess, consider how a negotiation will open.'[23]

Pitt concluded that: 'I think we can have nothing to do but to decline all negotiations at the present moment on the ground that the actual situation of France does not as yet hold out any solid security to be derived from negotiation ... This may be so expressed as to convey to the people of France that the shortest road to the peace is by effecting the restoration of royalty.'[24] In other words, Britain would war against France as long as it remained a republic. Pitt's policy soon became a classic case of be careful what you wish for. In 1804, Bonaparte had the Senate transform the republic into a monarchy with himself the emperor.

They dispatched their reply on 6 January, with copies sent to Vienna and St Petersburg. The reply was addressed from Grenville to French Foreign Minister Charles-Maurice Talleyrand-Périgord, or one foreign minister to another, deliberately snubbing Bonaparte's appeal to George III, as from one head of state to another, and implying that he was an illegitimate upstart. Indeed, Grenville chastised Bonaparte for daring to address the British monarch. He then accused the French revolutionaries for violating any treaties. This was hardly a fair critique since the only clear French violation was of the tenet of the 1648 Peace of Westphalia that closed the Scheldt River to sea commerce. Such historic and legal truths were irrelevant. Pitt and his cabinet wanted to continue the war and any excuses, however unfounded, were promoted.[25]

Before the House of Commons, Pitt justified the rejection of Bonaparte's peace offer as ideologically impossible: 'The all searching eye of the French revolution looks to every part of Europe, and every quarter of the world, in which can be found an object either of acquisition or plunder. Nothing is too great for the temerity of its ambition, nothing too small or insignificant for the grasp of its rapacity.' For Pitt, the French Revolution posed an unprecedented existential threat against not just Britain but all civilised countries. Britain must fight to the death for its 'security against a danger which never existed in any past period of society'.[26]

* * *

With his peace offers spurned, Bonaparte planned his latest campaign against Austria. General Jean Moreau would lead an army across the Rhine, through the Black Forest, and down the Danube River valley, while Bonaparte led an army over the Alps, into northern Italy, then north-east. Ideally, they would unite before Vienna. Both campaigns were eventually victorious. Bonaparte defeated Austrian General Michael von Melas at Marengo on 14 June and under the Convention of Alessandria signed the next day, Melas agreed to an armistice and withdrawal of all Austrian troops east of the Ticino River. Fearful of a coup, Bonaparte hurried back to Paris to govern France.

* * *

Whitehall beseeched Vienna to resume the war. Chancellor Thugut insisted that Whitehall pay Vienna £1,600,000 for its own army or £2,400,000 for that and 30,000 German troops that the Austrians would command. Grenville agreed to the subsidy for an Austrian army but would hire the German troops for its own army. Thugut then raised his demand to £2,000,000 and threatened negotiating a separate peace with France if Britain did not fork over that cash. Pitt and his cabinet felt they had no choice but to yield to the shakedown. In Vienna, Ambassador Gilbert Elliot, Earl of Minto, signed that treaty on 23 June 1800.

The war did indeed resume with disastrous consequences for the coalition. Moreau won a series of victories against Austrian forces down the Danube valley, decisively at Hohenlinden on 3 December. Vienna desperately asked for and received an armistice. A relentless French advance in north-east Italy led to an armistice there on 16 January.

Bonaparte tapped his brother to negotiate a generous peace with Austria. The Treaty of Luneville, signed on 9 February 1801, differed little from the previous Treaty of Campo Formio that the Austrians blatantly violated. Vienna recognised France's annexation of the Austrian Netherlands and other territories on the Rhine's west bank and parts of Switzerland, and the Cisalpine, Swiss, Ligurian, and Batavian republics; the Adige River was the boundary between the Italian Republic and Austrian empire's control of Venetia, Illyria, and Dalmatia; Tuscany's duke would cede his realm and Vienna would compensate him by granting him Salzburg and Berchtesgaden.

* * *

Once again, Bonaparte had defeated Austria, whose war effort Whitehall had expended vast sums to underwrite. Pitt and his ministers tried to fill that coalition void with small German states. Grenville sent Wickham to Germany to hire 30,000 troops from Bavaria, Baden, Württemberg, and Mainz for £1 million. Wickham got Bavarian Duke Maximilian Joseph to commit 12,000 troops in a treaty signed on 16 March 1800. By late April he had negotiated agreements with other German states for a total of 30,000 soldiers. That proved to be the easy part. The British never effectively deployed those mercenaries against the French.

While no amount of British money could purchase winning foreign generals who did not exist, other British policies undermined the coalition that cost so much effort and treasure to forge. The worst defection was Russia. Ambassador Charles Whitworth conspired with a faction that sought to overthrow Tsar Paul. Rumours of that prompted Paul to demand that Whitehall recall Whitworth on 31 March 1800. Word of Bonaparte's victory at Marengo on 14 June convinced Paul to switch to what appeared to be the invincible side. The excuse to do so was Britain's Orders in Council that loosened its Royal Navy and privateers to capture foreign merchants that traded with France along with its allies and conquests. That infuriated the governments of all the neutral states whose merchant ships were captured and auctioned off with the cargos in British prize courts.

In retaliation, Paul forged the League of Armed Neutrality among Russia, Sweden, Denmark, and Prussia in November and December 1800 to seize all British merchant ships and subjects in and deny the Royal Navy access to the Baltic Sea region. Over the next few weeks, they captured over 300 British vessels and thousands of Britons in the Baltic at sea or in port. Prussian and Danish troops overran Hanover. Atop that, Paul gave notice to Louis XVIII and his court on 15 January 1801 that they were no longer welcome at Mittau, in the Russian empire's north-west region, and withheld the annual 200,000 rouble subsidy. Louis and his followers hit the road on a search for another refuge, tarrying at Riga and Memel before residing in a Warsaw palace in Prussia's empire.

Whitehall retaliated by issuing an embargo against Russia, Prussia, Sweden, and Denmark on 15 January. Admiral Hyde Parker received command of sixteen ships of the line and a couple score smaller warships and transports with the mission of attacking the Danish fleet at Copenhagen. Fortunately for the campaign's fate, Nelson was second-in-command. On 2 April 1801, he led the attack of twelve ships of the line against nine Danish ships of the line supported by fortress batteries. During the battle three of his ships grounded in shallow water. Parker was aboard his flagship safely anchored several miles away. He had flags hoisted ordering Nelson to break off the action. It was then that Nelson brought his spyglass to his blind eye and truthfully claimed he saw no such order. Eventually, the British warships destroyed three Danish warships and inflicted 1,600 casualties while suffering 1,200.

Parker then assigned Nelson to negotiate with the Danish government. Word arrived that a cabal of officers had murdered tyrannical Paul and enthroned his son Alexander on 24 March 1801, and that the new tsar wanted peace. Under the armistice treaty signed on 9 April, Denmark withdrew from the League and surrendered its fleet to Britain. With that, the League of Armed Neutrality effectively no longer existed. Alexander signed a peace treaty with Britain in July 1801. He also signed peace treaties with France on 8 and 10 October 1801 whereby Russia recognised France's conquests, sister republics, and terms of the Franco–Austrian peace treaty.

* * *

Amidst the sporadic military campaigns, British spies across Europe and beyond ceaselessly sought to recruit agents, steal secrets, and influence politics. The Alien Office painstakingly rebuilt its espionage network in Paris after the 1797 purge. By 1801, the Philanthropic Institute and royalist newspaper *L'Invisible* were collecting intelligence, spreading propaganda, and plotting coups with links to the Chouan and Vendean rebels in north-western France. Paul Hyde de Neuville headed the Institute's English Committee directly linked with the Alien Office. Hyde was an active and creative agent. For instance, during the night of the anniversary of Louis XVI's death on 21 January 1800, he and nine men wrapped the Madeline Church's pillars in black and left a placard that read: 'In this detestable regime, only thieves or deputies can be happy in France.'[27]

The most audacious operations were attempts to assassinate First Consul Napoleon Bonaparte. The closest came on 24 December 1800. Seven

Chouan conspirators led by Georges Cadoudal packed gunpowder into a huge wine barrel atop a horse-drawn cart. Pierre Robinault de la Saint Regeant positioned the cart on Rue Saint Nicaise along the route that Bonaparte's coach would take to a concert that evening. He paid a girl to hold the horse while he went to the back of the cart. After another plotter signalled that the coach was approaching, he lit the fuse and hurried away. Bonaparte's driver spotted the cart partly blocking the road. Fearing a trap, he whipped the horses into a canter past. The cart exploded seconds later, killing the girl and six other people and wounding twenty-six. Bonaparte and several generals in his coach escaped harm. His wife Josephine, daughter-in-law Hortense, and sister Caroline were in a coach following his; the explosion shattered the windows of the approaching coach and cut Hortense's hand. Bonaparte suspected Jacobins and had 130 of them arrested and exiled. Police Chief Joseph Fouche arrested several of the Chouan plotters including Saint Regeant, who were tried, found guilty of attempted murder, and executed; Cadoudal evaded arrest and escaped.

That failed assassination disappointed Pitt and his colleagues. Atop that came another thwarted plan. In the autumn of 1799, Foreign Secretary Grenville helped organise a royalist rebellion in north-western France to divert French forces from other fronts. To Wickham, he explained: 'We are making quiet preparations for an immense effort next year against France itself in support of the Royalists. We are obliged to speak with reserve on this point both to Vienna and Petersburgh, that our schemes may not be known long before they are ripe for execution. You can much assist us by your activity and judgment in opening communications with Royalists in the middle, east, and south of France, and by giving them every degree of encouragement and aid.' He admitted that the 'insurrection broke out in the Vendee and Normandy sooner than we wished, but ... we must endeavour to support it. Our first disembarkation of money and arms has been very happily made. Our second is arrived off the coast and seems likely to be landed without any difficulty.' Grenville's optimism was most misplaced with his assessment of 'the situation of affairs in Paris' that 'appears to be in the highest degree favourable to the establishment and progress of the Royalist cause'. He dismissed Bonaparte's government as wobbly to the point of collapse with a good royalist shove.[28]

Pitt met with Charles, Comte d'Artois, on 21 December, and they concocted a plan to invade France. A British naval squadron would land 15,000 royalists on the Ruis peninsula in Quiberon Bay, which would be fortified to defy a republican attack. The next step was to march north 60 miles to Rennes, Brittany's largest city, and sever the main road from Brest to Paris. Charles confidently predicted that 25,000 insurgents would join forces with the liberating army. To reinforce this royalist army in Brittany, Pitt envisioned eventually sending 'from thirty to forty thousand men' with 'a reserve of about twenty thousand (exclusive of cavalry) to follow whenever it is thought expedient. On this plan our army, aided only by the Royalist force already in arms, would be clearly superior to any troops the enemy could collect without detaching from the frontiers.'[29]

Dundas was sceptical and warned Pitt not to be overly optimistic about any of the plan's succession of assumptions. General Charles Grey cross-examined one of d'Artois's officers who admitted that 'there are hardly any, or rather, no resources on the peninsula for such an army, and even on the quality of the water, he is silent ... In fact many of the queries remain unanswered' and, thus 'mitigates completely against such an enterprise.'[30] Pitt and his cabinet debated strategy on 21 March. Dundas led the opposition. Grenville defended. After a contentious debate, they agreed to suspend the operation.[31]

Typically, Whitehall did not get its money's worth from its coalition partners and covert operations. Alien Office Chief William Wickham expressed the universal exasperation: 'What a game have we not lost by the stupid obstinacy and misconduct of these allies?'[32] Grenville certainly shared that frustration, yet had nothing but praise for his intelligence chief: 'What you have done has been done in the same masterly style which distinguishes your work from that of all other artists in the same line.'[33]

* * *

Despite the failures of its allies, Britain's empire expanded with the war. Expeditions captured Spain's island province of Minorca in November 1798; the Dutch colonies of Surinam in 1799 and Curaçao in 1800; the French colony of Saint Martin in 1801; the Danish colonies of Saint Thomas and Saint Croix in 1801; and the Swedish colony of Saint Bartholomew in 1801. Each reaped profits for most British merchants who flocked there.

Whitehall policies also boosted the domestic economy. The 1799 West India Dock Act and 1803 East India Dock Act led the modernisation and expansion of wharf complexes and thus shipping on the Thames below London. Few people opposed developing infrastructure. Far more controversial were bills that stifled any labour unions or strikes. Pitt had Parliament pass the Combination Acts of 1799 and 1800 that outlawed any labourers uniting or even asking employers for higher wages and better conditions, which would be prosecuted by one magistrate in the former law and two under the second.

Astonishingly, amidst the war, Prime Minister Pitt fought a nearly deadly duel with parliamentarian George Tierney on 27 May 1798. Tierney had provoked Pitt's rage for demanding a longer debate on a bill the Prime Minister had introduced two days earlier. They met on Putney Heath at dawn. Each missed in the first round. With honour satisfied and anger cooled, each fired wide in the second round. King George III was appalled to hear about the duel and wrote to Pitt that: 'I trust what has happened will never happen repeated ... Public characters have no right to weigh alone what they owe themselves; they must consider also what is due to their country.'[34]

Of course, Pitt fought incessant political duels with his opponents, who at times included the king. Policy toward Ireland was a perennial source of contention. Pitt championed the political meshing of Ireland with Britain and had Irish Secretary of State Robert Stewart, Viscount Castlereagh, work with Irish parliamentarians to draft a union bill.[35] Castlereagh explained how union would boost the realm's power: 'By the incorporation of our legislature with that of Great Britain, it would not only consolidate the strength and glory of the empire, but it would change our internal and local government to a system of strength and calm security, instead of being a garrison in the island.'[36] Nonetheless, that bill passed by just one vote on 22 January 1799. What followed was a year and a half of negotiations between and within the British and Irish parliaments on the terms of union between them. The Union bills passed the London and Dublin parliaments on 1 July and 1 August 1800, respectively, to take effect in two steps: first on 1 January 1801, when Ireland's parliament dissolved itself, and second on 1 February, when Britain's Parliament opened with a hundred Irish members added to the House of Commons and twenty-four peers and four Anglican bishops added to the House of Lords.

Whitehall wielded £30,000 in secret service funds to promote Union in Ireland with parliamentary votes bought for an average 4,000 guineas each. Members of Ireland's parliament who lost seats received £7,500 in compensation. The total buyout bill for all expenses came to a stunning £1,260,000![37] For Castlereagh that was money well spent because of the benefits it conferred on virtually everyone: 'It bribes the whole community of Ireland by offering to embrace them within the pale of the British constitution, and to communicate to them all the advantage of British commerce. It is this kind of bribe which is held out to the Protestant, to the Catholic, to the Dissenter; it is this kind of bribe which is held out to the merchant, to the manufacturer, to the landowner.'[38]

That done, Pitt turned to Catholic emancipation. The 1798 Irish rebellion and French invasion, and the British army's mass atrocities in crushing them, profoundly shook him. He recognised that the threat of a foreign-aided Irish revolt would forever haunt Britain as long as Catholics suffered religious, economic, political, and social repression. He also knew well that George III opposed emancipation. He sought to convince the king that 'the admission of the Catholics and Dissenters to offices, and of the Catholics to Parliament (from which the Dissenters are now excluded), would, under certain circumstances ... be highly advisable, with a view to the tranquillity and improvement of Ireland, and to the general interest of the United Kingdom'. Pitt was 'convinced that the measure would be attended with no danger to the Established Church, or to the Protestant interest in Great Britain or Ireland'.[39]

King George remained adamantly opposed. He insisted that his position rested on 'religious as well as political duty ... from the moment I mounted the throne' and took 'the oath' to defend the supremacy of 'the Church of England'.[40] He warned that: 'I shall look upon every Man as my personal Enemy, who proposes that Question to me ... I hope all my Friends will not desert me.'[41] He wanted to replace Pitt as Prime Minister with Henry Addington, a parliamentarian since 1784 and speaker of the House of Commons since 1789, if he also rejected emancipation. He wrote Addington condemning those committed to 'placing the Roman Catholics of the kingdom in an equal state of right to sit in both houses of parliament and hold offices of trust and emolument, with those of the Established Church. It is suggested, by those best informed, that Mr. Pitt favours this opinion. That Lord Grenville and Mr. Dundas do, I have the fullest proof; they having intimated as much to me, who have certainly not disguised to them my abhorrence of the idea, and my feeling it is a duty, should it ever be brought forward, publicly to express my disapprobation of it, and that no consideration could ever make me give my consent to what I look upon as the destruction of the Established Church, which, by the wisdom of parliament, I, as well as my predecessors, have been obliged to take an oath at our coronation to support.'[42] Upon receiving Addington's promise of support, the king expressed his delight and invited him on 31 January, either to stop by that evening or at eight o'clock the next morning 'whichever may be most convenient'.[43] When they met, the king implored Addington to be his Prime Minister, ensuring these words that any loyal subject would find virtually impossible to refuse: 'Lay your hand upon your heart, and ask yourself where I am to turn for support if you do not stand by me.'[44]

Pitt offered to resign on 3 February 1801, after seventeen years heading the government. The king agreed and on 5 February appointed Addington to take his place. George's relapse of madness on 19 February delayed that transition but within a couple of weeks he recovered. Pitt officially resigned on 14 March.

Addington became Prime Minister on 17 March after Parliament elected him and the king handed him his seals of office. The new Prime Minister's character certainly contrasted with that of his predecessor. Addington was genial, soft-spoken, conciliatory, and willing to give peace a chance if both sides made serious concessions.[45] For the key posts, he named William Cavendish-Benedick, Duke of Portland, as Lord President of the Council and Home Secretary; Robert Hobart, Earl of Buckinghamshire, as the newly established Secretary of State for War and Colonies; Robert Jenkinson, then Lord Hawkesbury and later Liverpool as Foreign Secretary; Portland as Home Secretary, and John Jervis, Earl of Saint Vincent, as First Lord of the Admiralty. He frequently asked Pitt for his advice and support.

* * *

Meanwhile, Captain William Sydney Smith and his squadron blockaded Egypt for month after torpid month. He reasoned that if he could not starve out the French he might talk them out. He initiated negotiations with General Jean-Baptiste Kleber that culminated on 24 January 1800, when they signed a treaty at El Arish whereby the French surrendered Egypt in return for being shipped back to France with all their weapons and spoils. That would have spared Britain the sharp cost of time, treasure, and blood that Egypt's conquest eventually cost it. Whitehall, however, rejected the treaty as too lenient.

Meanwhile, after a two-year blockade and siege, the British captured Malta on 4 September 1800. Thereafter that island was as strategically vital for British operations in the central Mediterranean as Gibraltar was for the western Mediterranean. It was a stepping stone for the campaign to conquer Egypt.

The Egyptian-bound armada included 16,000 troops under General Ralph Abercromby packed in around sixty transports that were guarded by a dozen warships under Admiral George Keith. The first wave of 5,000 troops landed at Aboukir Bay on 2 March 1801. The French commander was now General Jacques Menou, who replaced Kleber after a Jihadist murdered him. Abercromby outflanked Menou's 4,000 troops drawn up before Alexandria and pushed them back into the city. A bullet killed Abercromby. General John Hely-Hutchinson replaced him and besieged the city. Menou held out for months as supplies dwindled before finally surrendering on 2 September 1801. He was a better diplomat than general. He got free passage of his army back to France, the same deal Smith had granted Kleber fourteen months earlier. Nonetheless, the British were now Egypt's latest masters. The question was what to do with that conquest.

* * *

Addington was pessimistic about the coalition's future, especially with Austria's latest defeat. He lamented that 'the battles of Marengo and Hohenlinden had crushed the efforts and annihilated the hopes of the Continent'.[46] He and his ministers forged a consensus that the key requirement for peace was that Britain had captured enough colonies from France and its allies to justify the war.[47] He had General Charles Cornwallis negotiate with Foreign Minister Charles-Maurice Talleyrand-Périgord.

Like virtually anyone who had to deal with Talleyrand, Cornwallis found his 'spirit of chicanery and intrigue' was the biggest hindrance to the swift conclusion of a peace treaty. In contrast, he encountered a different Bonaparte from the scary and absurd cartoon version prevalent in Britain. During their first meeting: 'Bonaparte was gracious to the highest degree; he inquired particularly after His Majesty and the state of his health, and spoke of the British nation in terms of great respect, intimating that as long as we remained friends there would be no interruption of the peace of Europe.' Cornwallis explained that 'the horrors of ... the French Revolution had created a general alarm; that all the neighbouring nations dreaded the contagion'. He then lauded Bonaparte for restoring 'good order and tranquillity' to France, that made us respect him as a statesman and a legislator, and had removed our apprehensions of having connexion and intercourse with France.[48] He longed to negotiate directly with Bonaparte so 'that the business would have been conducted in a more liberal, as well as a more expeditious manner than at a formal diplomatic assembly'. He was able to get Bonaparte to let him deal with his older brother Joseph, 'who has the character of being a well-meaning, but not very able man, and whose near connexion with the First Consul might perhaps be in some degree a check on' Talleyrand. To escape Talleyrand's shadow, Cornwallis and Joseph agreed to move their talks to Amiens.[49]

They signed the preliminary peace articles on 1 October 1801, and the formal Treaty of Amiens on 27 March 1802. Under the terms, France would withdraw from the Kingdom of Naples, the Papal States, and Egypt, while Britain would return all its foreign conquests except two – it retained Ceylon from the Netherlands and Trinidad from Spain. The British abandoned any meaningful presence in the Mediterranean by ceding Minora, Malta, Elba, and Egypt, and restored the West Indian power balance by restoring Martinique, Tobago, and Saint Lucia to France. Politically, Britain recognised France's 'fraternal republics' of Batavia (the Netherlands), Cisalpine (northern Italy),

Helvetia (Switzerland), and Liguria (Genoa). That represented a stunning shift in Europe's ideological and thus military power balance in France's favour.

Nonetheless, Britain's economic and naval might had strengthened steadily over the previous nine years. Leading the economy's expansion was trade whose volume doubled from 1793 to 1800. The share of British cargos shipped in foreign vessels to lessen the danger of French warships or privateers capturing them rose from 13 per cent to 43 per cent.[50]

Britain's navy and merchant fleets were already the world's largest when the war began. During the war, those fleet numbers soared both from constructing new ones and capturing those of enemy and neutral states. Warships and privateers seized an astonishing 5,600 vessels and 600,000 tons of shipping from 1793 to 1801 alone. Meanwhile, British shipping nearly doubled from 1,055,000 tons in 1785 to 1,924,000 tons in 1800. British fleets devastated French and its allied fleets at the battles of the First of June, Saint Vincent, Camperdown, Nile, and Copenhagen. During those battles, the British suffered 4,059 dead and wounded while inflicting 25,017 or five times more on the enemy fleets. By 1802, 70,000 French sailors were British prisoners of war. The Royal Navy had 135 ships of the line and 133 frigates in 1793 and 202 ships of the line and 277 frigates in 1802, while cutting in half France's navy from eighty ships of the line and sixty-six frigates to thirty-nine and thirty-five respectively. Indeed, Britain's intrepid captains and crews captured most of the warships that France lost, augmenting the Royal Navy at its enemy's expense.[51]

Despite all those gains, Addington and his ministers worried that many Britons would consider Ceylon and Trinidad measly pickings after seven years of war. Robert Jenkinson, Lord Hawkesbury, who had recently replaced Grenville as foreign secretary, assured him that 'nothing could have been reasonably expected from a continuance of the war which would have justified us, under present circumstances, in rejecting these terms'.[52] From the sidelines, former Prime Minister Pitt observed of the peace that: 'I know no more satisfactory arrangement that could have been made in the present moment ... as far as security ... The great object in my mind was that the ... peace should ... not ... appear in any degree dictated, and that we should reserve what is most essential for the security of our East and West Indian possessions ... Ceylon and Trinidad.'[53]

Addington triumphantly introduced bills that rescinded most of the wartime taxes and cut back the army and navy budgets. Britain's reprieve from death and most taxes did not last long. Cornwallis's parting words about the peace treaty he had negotiated were prescient: 'God knows how all will end, but I think Bonaparte's power will not easily be shaken.'[54]

Chapter 6

Third, 1803–05

Europe is not to be saved by a single man. England has saved herself by her exertions and will, as I trust, save Europe by her example.

[*William Pitt*]

Roll up that map. It will not be wanted these next ten years.

[*William Pitt's alleged last words*]

The peace of Amiens soon proved to be nothing more than a tense truce before war resumed.[1] A consensus emerged among British leaders that peace diminished rather than enhanced their nation's security. Their worries rose with reports that First Consul Napoleon Bonaparte exploited the ceasefire to strengthen France's economy and military while trying to reassert power in the Caribbean Basin.

Under the secret Treaty of San Ildefonso signed on 1 October 1800, Bonaparte swapped Tuscany with Spain for New Orleans and the Louisiana Territory. He intended eventually to transform the Caribbean into a French sea. The first step was to crush the rebellion on Saint-Domingue led by General Francois Toussaint Louverture, restore slavery and the sugar plantations, and reap revenues from that 'white gold'. The result was Bonaparte's second geopolitical defeat after Egypt. He dispatched a 20,000-man army led by his brother-in-law General Charles Leclerc, but yellow fever, malaria, typhoid, and black guerrillas devastated it and thousands of reinforcements.

By spring 1803, Bonaparte was ready to cut his losses, especially as renewal of war with Britain was increasingly likely. His worst fear was that Britain would capture New Orleans and thus the Louisiana Territory that included the entire Mississippi River watershed west to the Rocky Mountains. Meanwhile, President Thomas Jefferson learned that France had secretly taken title to that vast territory. To Paris, he dispatched James Monroe to purchase New Orleans and thus control of the Mississippi River. Bonaparte was happy to sell the entire Louisiana Territory for $15,000,000 on 2 May 1803. Thus did the United States double its size, although it would take generations before it began reaping the territory's full economic potential. The history of not just

Britain but the world would have been radically different had Whitehall somehow won that territory.

Meanwhile, elsewhere both France and Britain violated the Amiens treaty and condemned the other for doing the same. The French kept troops in the Kingdom of Naples. The British kept troops in Malta and Egypt. On 3 March 1803, Bonaparte blistered Ambassador Charles Whitworth for Britain's violations during a reception for the diplomatic community. On 23 April, Whitehall instructed Whitworth to return to Britain if Bonaparte refused to withdraw not just from the Kingdom of Naples, which was a treaty requirement, but also from the Batavian and Helvetian republics, which were not. After Bonaparte rejected that demand unless Britain also departed Malta, Whitworth left Paris on 12 May.

Whitehall declared war against France on 16 May 1803. The result for the next two and a half years was a very limited war. With France powerful on land and Britain at sea, neither could strike the other decisively. All Bonaparte could do was order the arrest of British subjects and confiscation of any ships and cargos in French ports and have General Edouard Mortier march an army into Hanover. Britain inflicted far more damage. British warships and privateers seized ever more French and neutral merchant ships trading with France and its colonies. British expeditions captured the French colonies of Tobago and Saint Lucia in 1803, and the Dutch colonies of Demerara, Essequibo, and Berbice in 1803, and Surinam in 1804.

* * *

The only other way that Whitehall could war against Bonaparte's government was with covert actions designed to topple it by murdering him. To that end, British warships separately conveyed counter-revolutionary leaders Jean-Charles Pichegru, Georges Cadoudal, and other agents to deserted beaches on the Normandy coast in August and December 1803 and January 1804. From there, each made his way to the underground in Paris, where they planned the coup. The key was to convince General Jean Moreau, who was deathly jealous of Bonaparte, to lead his overthrow and replacement. Pichegru met Moreau twice. Moreau hesitated to join the plot but also swore to keep it secret.

French police arrested a conspirator and, after interrogating him, arrested others who yielded new names; eventually they jailed 356 suspects. Police knabbed Moreau on 13 February, Pichegru on 19 February, and Cadoudal on 9 March. Pichegru cheated the hangman by committing suicide. Although the court sentenced Moreau to death, Bonaparte had him sent to foreign exile. Cadoudal went stoically to the gallows, his last words noting the likely ironic result of the failed coup: 'We have achieved more than we intended. We came to give France a king. We have given her an emperor.'[2]

The interrogations revealed other suspects. One was a prince residing in Germany who was likely the plot's mastermind. Louis Antoine de Bourbon, Duc d'Enghien, seemed to fit that profile. He inhabited a palace at Ettenheim, Baden, close to the Rhine River with Strasbourg on the west side. The Committee of Public Safety had already condemned him to death for fighting with the French émigré army against France. Bonaparte had a company of dragoons cross the river during the night of 14 March, capture d'Enghien, and bring him to Vincennes Palace just outside Paris. There on the night of 21 March, a military commission found him guilty of treason and had him shot.

D'Enghien's rendition and execution shocked many people across Europe. Tsar Alexander condemned that act. Bonaparte replied by taunting Alexander for being complicit in his own father's murder to seize the throne. That comparison enraged rather than humbled Alexander. He would seek vengeance by allying with Austria to war against France.

* * *

Bonaparte could only defeat Britain by invading it. To that end, he issued an order establishing the Army of England on 14 June 1803. By August 1805, he had massed 160,000 troops in camps centred at the port of Boulogne on the English Channel. He had constructed more than a thousand craft 60ft long and 16ft wide to be packed with troops and rowed to England. All he needed for a successful invasion was a couple of calm sea days and a powerful enough French fleet to defend his army's crossing. Although tranquil sea days came and went, the Royal Navy's domination of the English Channel remained unchallenged. That made First Lord of the Admiralty John Jervis, Earl of Saint Vincent, sanguine about Napoleon's invasion threat: 'I do not say the French cannot come. I only say they cannot come by water.'[3]

Meanwhile, Bonaparte transformed France from a republic into a monarchy. The Senate unanimously named him France's emperor on 18 May 1804. Pope Pius VII presided over his coronation in Notre Dame Cathedral on 2 December 1804, during which he crowned himself emperor. He engineered the Italian Republic's transformation into the Italian Kingdom, whose assembly asked him to be king. He was crowned Italy's king in Milan's cathedral on 26 May 1805.

* * *

In Britain, George III presented William Pitt his old offices of Chancellor of the Exchequer and First Lord of the Treasury on 18 May 1804. Ironically, Pitt resumed the Prime Ministership the same day that France's Senate declared Napoleon the emperor. Although Pitt was only forty-four years old, he was a shadow of his previous self. His alcoholism had bloated his body and dulled his mind, and the slightest exertions left him wheezing for breath.

Pitt did put together a talented cabinet. The key ministers were John Pratt, Marquess of Camden, as Secretary of State for War and the Colonies, until Robert Stewart, Viscount Castlereagh, replaced him; Henry Dundas, who had become Viscount Melville, as First Lord of the Admiralty; Dudley Ryder, Earl of Harrowby, then Henry Phipps, Earl of Mulgrave, as Foreign Secretary of State; Robert Jenkinson, Lord Hawkesbury, as Home Secretary; and Henry Addington, newly titled Viscount Sidmouth, as Lord President of the Council.

Ignoring the groans, Pitt boosted army and navy spending with the Additional Force Bill and partially paid for it by restoring the old taxes and new ones in a series of bills. The question was just how to fight and win the war. Pitt answered that with the 'Memorandum on the Deliverance and Security of Europe' issued on 1 January 1805. The primary goal was to liberate from 'France those Countries which it has subjected since the beginning of the Revolution, and to reduce France within its former limits'. Over the long term, Britain would contain France by two policies. One was to liberate Holland from France and erect a line of fortresses across the southern Netherlands to protect it from a future French attack. The other was to cooperate with other European states to ensure that international law, including non-interference in the domestic affairs of others, prevailed for all states including republican France.[4]

Britain's unfolding industrial revolution made such goals financially and thus politically and militarily feasible. For instance, a recent invention revolutionised production of a key part for any ship and saved the government enormous sums of money. At Portsmouth's Royal Dockyard, Marc Brunel invented a steam-powered machine that mass-produced blocks or pullies for a ship's rigging. Ships of the line needed a thousand or so blocks. With mass production, ten workers replaced 110 men and reduced costs by £24,400 the first year.[5]

* * *

Throughout the latter half of 1804, diplomats of Tsar Alexander and Emperor Francis negotiated a bilateral alliance. In November, they formally agreed that Austria and Russia would respectively commit 235,000 and

115,000 troops against France. The next step was getting the British to underwrite their campaigns.

Whitehall initially earmarked £5,000,000 with £2,500,000 to Austria, £1,000,000 each to Russia and, hopefully, Prussia, and £500,000 for other possible German allies. For Pitt and the cabinet, those subsidies seemed at once generous and prudent since government revenues in 1804 came to £46,000,000. Typically, each potential recipient dismissed its share as far below its needs. Pitt had the ambassadors in those capitals explain that Britain had no objections to any reasonable territorial gains that each ally took from France. Meanwhile, he got Parliament to allocate £6,250,000 in potential subsidies. Eventually the bill came to £7,000,000.[6]

Alexander initially insisted on a potential dealbreaker for Whitehall. Britain must give up Malta. Pitt replied by agreeing to do so only under four future conditions: Russia must garrison Malta; Spain must cede Majorca to Britain; Napoleon must restore Piedmont to Sardinia; and Napoleon must accept a land barrier controlled by Prussia between France and the Netherlands. The odds of all four being realised was so great that Pitt was willing theoretically to render Malta. Envoys signed Britain's treaty with Russia on 11 April 1805.

* * *

Napoleon negotiated a secret alliance with Spain that Charles IV intended to reveal as soon as four frigates packed with treasure sailing from Montevideo reached Cadiz. Learning of that secret alliance and treasure ships, Whitehall decided to jump the gun. Commodore Graham Moore received Admiralty orders to capture that fleet with his squadron's four frigates. On 5 October 1804, Moore intercepted the Spanish frigates off Cape Santa Maria. In the battle, the British suffered nine casualties while inflicting 349, and inadvertently sank one frigate but captured the other three packed with £900,000 worth of gold and silver. Charles IV declared war against Britain on 14 December 1804.

Napoleon sent a peace offer to George III on New Year's Day 1805 and was once again snubbed for his effort. In March, he devised and implemented a plan for the French and Spanish navies to win control over the Dover Straits long enough for his army to safely row across and invade England.[7] The French fleets from Brest, Rochefort, and Toulon, and Spanish fleets from Cadiz and Ferrol would break through their British blockades and sail west to unite in the Caribbean. Having drawn most British warships in pursuit, the united fleet would then sail for the English Channel, overwhelm that British fleet, and position itself to protect the army's passage.

Only the fleets of Admirals Pierre Villeneuve from Toulon and Edouard Missiessy's from Rochefort managed to break through the cordon of British warships for the open ocean. What followed was an extraordinary Odyssey that carried them to the West Indies, where they tarried for weeks then headed eastward but bound for Spanish ports rather than the English Channel.

* * *

By early August 1805, the coalition had forged two related campaign plans. The Austrians and Russians would launch an offensive up the Danube River valley to vanquish Bavaria and then defeat Napoleon's inevitable onslaught. General Karl von Mack with 80,000 troops would invade Bavaria as other Austrian troops along with 180,000 Russian troops marched to reinforce him. Meanwhile, an Austrian army led by Archduke Charles would invade the Italian kingdom from Venetia. In late November, 6,000 British soldiers under General James Craig and 7,350 Russian troops under General Peter von Lacy would land in Naples, join with the Neapolitan army and march north to join Charles.

Napoleon did not get definitive intelligence that Austria and Russia would soon war against him until 23 August. Within two days he devised a plan to march his Army of England, now called the Grand Army, south-east to destroy his enemies in the Danube valley. His troops began that long march on 25 August. To supplement his army, he signed alliance treaties with Bavaria's Elector Maximilian IV Joseph on 23 August, Baden's Elector Charles Frederick on 5 September, and Württemberg's Elector Frederic on 5 October. He thought he had secured his Italian kingdom by signing a neutrality treaty with Neapolitan King Ferdinand IV on 21 September. He would be enraged when the king grossly violated that treaty and openly joined the coalition.

Mack's 80,000 troops routed the Bavarian army, captured the capital Munich, then advanced west up the Danube valley as far as Ulm. Napoleon marched his corps on parallel roads with two straight at Ulm and three to cut the Austrian supply and escape line down the Danube valley. By mid-October, the French corps had routed Austrian forces in their way and isolated Mack in Ulm. Mack surrendered with 25,000 troops on 19 October.

Napoleon then quick-marched his corps down the Danube valley. Along the way the French routed Austrian and advanced Russian troops and marched unopposed into Vienna on 13 November. Emperor Francis fled with his court and army's remnants north-east into Moravia, eventually joining Tsar Alexander and the main Russian army at Olmutz.

After initial repulses, the French army led by General Andre Masséna in northern Italy also drove back the Austrian army led by Archduke Charles. General Laurent Gouvion Saint Cyr's army marching from southern Italy joined forces with Masséna in mid-October. Facing overwhelming odds, Charles fought delaying actions as he withdrew toward Raab.

* * *

First Lord of the Admiralty Charles Middleton, Baron Barham, named Horatio Nelson the French pursuit fleet commander. Nelson chased Villeneuve across the Atlantic, then, learning he had reversed course, back across. Villeneuve sailed first to Ferrol, then south to Cadiz, entering the bay on 22 August. Learning of his whereabouts, Napoleon sent new orders to Villeneuve on 16 September. The Franco–Spanish fleet should sail for the Mediterranean, join with the Cartagena fleet, then sail to Toulon. Fed-up with Villeneuve's timidity, he tapped Admiral Francois Rosily to replace him.

Nelson joined a fleet blockading Cadiz on 28 September. Eventually he massed twenty-seven ships of the line just beyond the horizon west of Cadiz and picketed four frigates to observe the port. The allied fleet sailed from Cadiz on 20 October, with Villeneuve commanding eighteen ships of the line and Frederico Gravina fifteen Spanish ships of the line. The next day, Nelson's fleet intercepted them south-west of Cape Trafalgar. As usual, the British warships were battered but none destroyed as they devastated the enemy fleet that day and the following days of pursuit, capturing twenty-one ships of the line, sinking one, inflicting 6,593 casualties and capturing around 8,000 sailors while suffering 448 dead and 1,241 wounded; Nelson was among the dead.[8] Trafalgar crippled French and Spanish sea power for the remaining Napoleonic era and long after.

* * *

Whitehall expanded the coalition. British and Swedish envoys signed a treaty on 31 August 1805, whereby King Gustavus supplied 12,000 troops for £150,000 annually for the war's duration. Pitt did what he could to entice Prussia into the coalition. On 10 September, Berlin received an offer of £1,250,000 for 100,000 Prussian troops and territorial gains at France's expense. Frederick William III's two closest advisors could not agree on policy, with Christian Graf von Haugwitz and Karl August von Hardenberg advocating continued neutrality and war, respectively.

Whitehall dispatched 11,000 British troops to the Elbe River mouth on 16 October, and eventually committed 60,000 troops there. They did not fire a shot as Napoleon's army was far away. Their purpose was to encourage

Frederick William to join the coalition. Pitt sent Dudley Ryder, Earl of Harrowby, to Berlin with the promise of £2,500,000 annually for 100,000 Prussian soldiers. The king succumbed to that temptation. On 3 November, he agreed to join the coalition if Napoleon rejected demands that he evacuate the Netherlands, Switzerland, and Naples; compensate with territory the King of Sardinia-Piedmont for his forced cession of Piedmont to France; and give up the Italian crown. He sent Foreign Minister Haugwitz to issue Napoleon that ultimatum, intended to be angrily spurned. Frederick William promised to launch the Prussian army toward Napoleon's supply line back to France on 15 December. Extraordinary events prevented him from fulfilling that pledge.

* * *

Napoleon's whirlwind campaign performed wonders by late November, having won nearly every battle, captured around 50,000 enemy troops, overrun the Danube valley as far as Vienna, and advanced north as far as Brno. The trouble was that he was overextended, having had to deploy tens of thousands of troops to guard against residual Austrian forces that threatened his long supply lines or against Archduke Charles at Raab. He had only about 65,000 troops at or within a couple of days march from Brno. Fifty miles away at Olmutz, the allied army numbered around 85,000 troops. That army marched toward Brno on 27 November. Learning of that advance, Napoleon concentrated his forces on the west bank of a small stream half a dozen miles east of Brno near a town called Austerlitz. On 2 December, the allied army attacked. Napoleon brilliantly directed his corps to repel the onslaught and then counter-attack. The French routed the allies, inflicting 15,500 dead and wounded and capturing 20,000 troops then and in the pursuit, while suffering around 8,500 casualties.

Francis sent word for an armistice and peace talks, which Napoleon granted on 4 December. Alexander withdrew his devastated army eastward. First Napoleon rewarded his allies with separate treaties that enhanced their territory at Austria's expense and promoted the respective electors of Bavaria and Württemberg to king and Baden to grand duke. With the Treaty of Schönbrunn signed on 15 December, he forged an alliance with Prussia against Britain that granted Hanover to Berlin in return for Cleves and Neuchatel to France and Ansbach to Bavaria. As for Austria, although this was Vienna's fourth aggressive war against France since 1792, Napoleon's terms were relatively lenient. He resisted the temptation to break up the Austrian empire into three sovereign states of Austria, Hungary, and Moravia. Instead, under the Treaty of Pressburg, signed on 26 December, Austria ceded Lucca

Bank of England, from *Microcosm of London*, c.1808 J. Hill, and Harraden. (*aquatint engravers*)

The 'Old Lady of Threadneedle Street', the Bank of England today. (*Courtesy Eluveitie*)

Bust of Nathan Rothschild.

Recruiting for the British Army, by Thomas Rowlandson.
(*Anne S.K. Brown Military Collection*)

Bond of the Russian Government, issued 1 March 1822, signed by Nathan Mayer Rothschild.
(Unbekannte Autoren und Grafiker)

Pitt the Younger in 1804, by John Hoppner.

Shot stacked up outside the Royal Laboratory gates and rows of guns arrayed in the background, Royal Arsenal. *(James Cockburn, 1795)*

East India Company soldiers at the Battle of Seringapatam, by Alexander Allan.
(*Anne S.K. Brown Military Collection*)

HMS *Shannon* leading the captured American frigate *Chesapeake* into Halifax, Nova Scotia, in June 1813, by John Christian Schetky.

Old Mill, built as a steam-powered mill in Ancoats in 1798, is the oldest-surviving cotton mill in Manchester. (*Courtesy, Pit-yacker*)

The Thirteen Factories, the area of Guangzhou to which China's Western trade was restricted in 1757–1842; painting by an unknown artist.

An old carronade, part of a now neglected display in the archway of the old clocktower of the Carron Works. By 1814, the Carron Company was the largest iron works in Europe. (*Kim Traynor*)

(*Left*) Prussia's Friedrich Wilhelm II, painting by Anton Graff. (*Right*) William Wyndham Grenville, 1st Baron Grenville, succeeded his cousin William Pitt as Prime Minister in 1806.

Portrait of Friedrich Wilhelm II of Prussia, by Anton Graf.

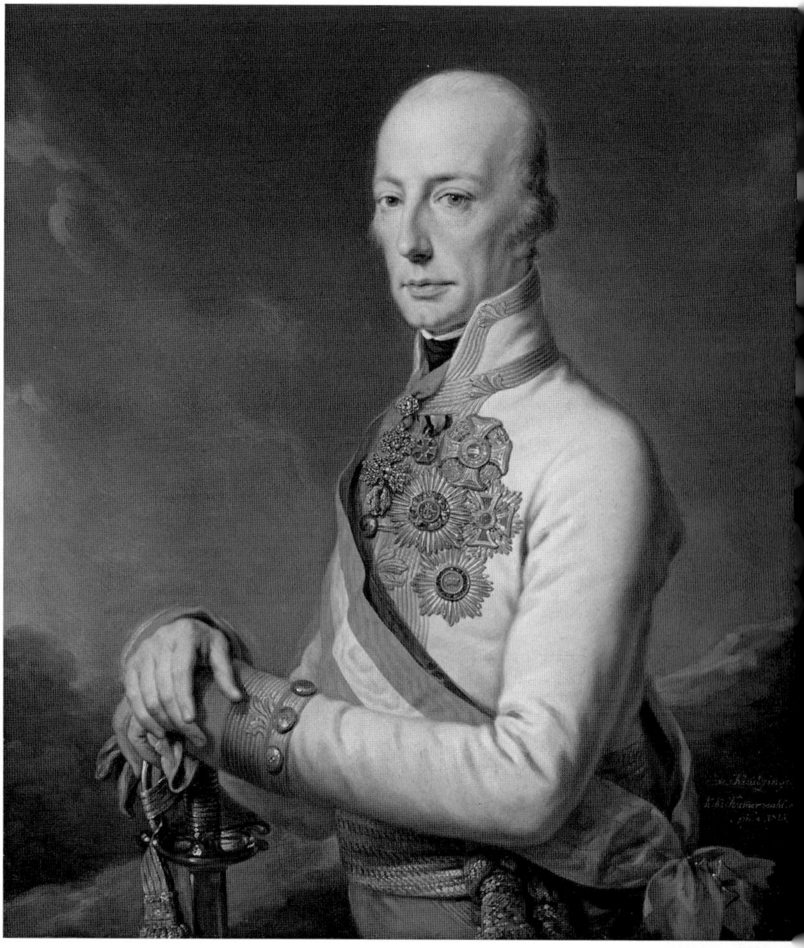

The signed Treaty of Amiens.
(Jerónimo Roure Pérez)

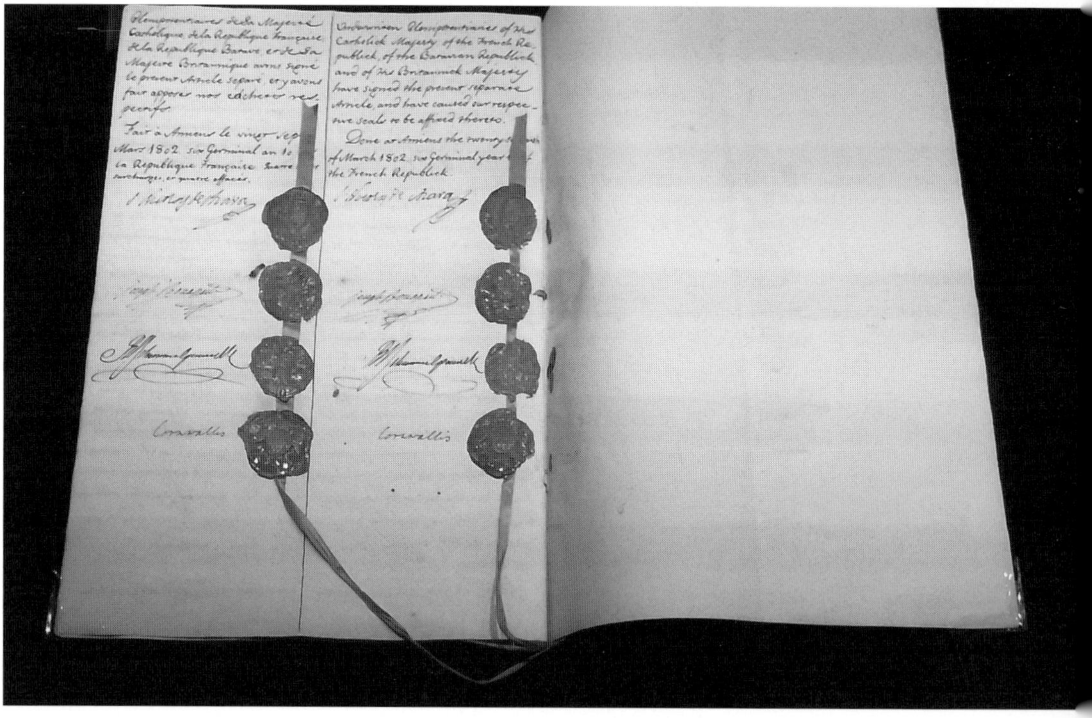
Catholick Majesty of the French Re-
publick, of the Batavian Republick
and of his Britannick Majesty
have signed the present separate
Article, and have caused our respective seals to be affixed thereto.

Done at Amiens the twenty
of March 1802 six Germinal year
the French Republick.

and Piombino to the Italian kingdom; Venetia, Dalmatia, Istria, and Cattaro to France; territories and higher aristocratic status to Bavaria, Württemberg, and Baden; recognition of the Batavian and Helvetian republics; and 40 million francs in reparations to France.

Upon hearing of Napoleon's crushing of the Austrians and Russians, Pitt allegedly said: 'Roll up that map. It will not be wanted these next ten years.'[9] What is certain is that a heart attack killed him on 23 January 1801, in his forty-sixth year.

Chapter 7

Fourth, 1806–07

Our interest is that till there can be a final settlement that shall last, every thing should remain as unsettled as possible; that no usurper should feel sure of acknowledgement; no people confident of their new masters; no kingdom sure of its existence; no spoliator sure of his spoil; and even the plundered not acquiescent in their loss. {*George Canning*}

George III replaced the deceased William Pitt with William Grenville as Prime Minister, First Lord of the Treasury, and Leader of the House of Lords. Grenville assembled a cabinet called the Ministry of All Talents including Charles Fox as Foreign Secretary and Leader of the House of Commons; George, Earl Spencer, as Home Office Secretary; William Windham as War and Colonies Secretary; Henry Petty-Fitzmaurice, Marquess of Lansdowne, as Chancellor of the Exchequer; and Charles Grey, Viscount Howick, as First Lord of the Admiralty.

With the latest coalition destroyed, Grenville and his colleagues agreed to peace talks with Napoleon. Negotiations opened and continued sporadically for half a year. During that time, Fox most fervently advocated peace; his death on 13 September 1806 knocked the political wind out of the talks. Four weeks later, the eruption of war between Prussia and France dealt those talks the death blow.

* * *

Meanwhile, Napoleon decisively punished King Ferdinand IV for his duplicity in signing a neutrality treaty with France, then letting Russian and British troops land in Naples to join forces with the Neapolitan army on 20 November. That allied army did not advance beyond Naples. Hearing of Austerlitz and the subsequent Pressburg treaty, the British and Russians withdrew their troops, leaving Ferdinand exposed to Napoleon's wrath. Napoleon dispatched Marshal Andre Masséna with 50,000 troops to capture Naples. Napoleon had his brother Joseph accompany Masséna and named him the king of Naples after the French occupied that capital on 14 February 1806.

Days earlier a British fleet conveyed the royal family from Naples to their latest exile at their palace in Palermo. Ambassador Hugh Elliot funnelled subsidies to the court that amounted to £424,657 from 1804 to 1807. That generosity did not prevent Maria Carolina from demanding more and criticising Elliot. Whitehall replaced Elliot with William Drummond and charged him with negotiating a new subsidy deal that included excluding the queen from the Council of State, subjecting the Neapolitan army to British command, cutting government bureaucracy and corruption, and ending tariffs on British goods sent to British forces in Sicily. Pressured by his wife, Ferdinand sheepishly rejected those demands. On 23 March 1807, Drummond reluctantly signed a treaty whereby Britain gave the Palermo court £300,000 annually for nothing more than an alliance. Canning did not submit the treaty to King George III for ratification. Instead, he offered £400,000 for those reforms. Ferdinand refused that deal. Nonetheless, the British supplied his army with £24,000 in 1807.[1]

From Messina, Sicily, the British conducted a large-scale raid on the Italian mainland that lifted the nation's spirits. On 1 July 1806, General Charles Stuart and 5,149 redcoats landed at Saint Euphemia, 60 miles up the coast from Reggio, the port on Italy's toe. Learning of the landing, the region's French commander, Jean Reynier, swiftly gathered 6,440 troops and quick-marched toward the invaders. On 4 July, Reynier launched his army against Stuart's army at Maida. The redcoats held steady, fired volleys into the attackers, then charged and routed them. The result was a lopsided victory that cost the French 490 killed, 870 wounded, and 722 captured, while the British suffered only forty-five killed and 282 wounded. Stuart led his men south-east along the coast to capture the fortresses of Tropea and Scilla, then march unopposed into Reggio on 23 July. A British flotilla evacuated the expedition back across the straits to Messina. That campaign had no important strategic result other than offering a war-weary British public a source of pride in a home victory and hope that other more even greater triumphs lay ahead.[2]

Elsewhere, Britain expanded its empire and suffered a humiliating defeat in 1806. An expedition of 6,000 troops packed aboard sixty-one transports guarded by nine warships dropped anchor before Cape Town on 4 January. Admiral Home Popham and General David Baird respectively headed the fleet and army. Baird led the troops ashore, where they drove the small Dutch army within the port. The Dutch surrendered Cape Town on 10 January.

Popham conceived a plan to weaken the Spanish empire and ideally reap a fortune in prize money. With 1,200 troops led by Colonel William Beresford, he sailed west on 14 April bound for Buenos Aires, Argentina, arriving on 25 June. Unprepared for war, Viceroy Marquis Rafael de Sobremonte fled with his entourage to Cordoba. The city surrendered on 27 June. Beresford led his troops into Buenos Aires. Then Colonel Santiago Liniers gathered scattered troops and militia and besieged the city. Beresford surrendered on 7 July.

* * *

Napoleon reorganised Germany into a French protectorate. Under a treaty signed on 12 July 1806, sixteen German states withdrew from the Holy Roman Empire to form the Rhine Confederation under French protection; eventually twenty other states joined. Napoleon pressured Francis to resign as the Holy Roman Emperor and declare himself Austria's emperor on 6 August.

Napoleon did not want a war with Prussia but inadvertently provoked one. The Prussians were outraged when he offered to restore Hanover to Britain after promising it to Berlin. That along with Napoleon's transformation of the Holy Roman Empire into a French-dominated Rhine Confederation convinced Prussian King Frederick William III to war against France. Berlin opened secret talks with the British, Saxons, and Russians for a coalition. Although the details, especially British subsidies, had not yet been decided, the Prussian king issued Napoleon an ultimatum on 1 October to withdraw west of the Rhine River.

Napoleon massed 160,000 troops in central Germany and invaded Prussia on 9 October. The result was a series of French victories, most decisively at the battles of Jena and Auerstadt on 14 October, and the conquest of most of Prussia, with Napoleon triumphantly entering Berlin on 21 October. In all, the French and their allied troops inflicted 65,000 dead and wounded and captured 150,000 Prussian and Saxon troops over six weeks. Frederick William, his court, and his army's shards withdrew to East Prussia, where a Russian army joined them in late November. On 21 November 1806 Napoleon issued what was called his Berlin Decree that outlawed all trade with Britain from France, its empire, and its allies, a boycott that came to be called the Continental System.[3] He hoped to defeat Britain by depriving it of its wealth reaped from trade with Europe. He then advanced his army east all the way to Warsaw, intending to decisively defeat the Prussians and Russians. His December offensive drove off but failed to crush the Russians and Prussians. After early 1807 offensive resulted in an indecisive slaughter for both armies at Eylau on 7 and 8 February 1807. Both sides withdrew into late winter quarters and rebuilt their ranks and supplies for a spring campaign.

* * *

An exhausted and dispirited Prime Minster Grenville resigned on 25 March 1807. George III asked William Cavendish-Bentinck, Duke of Portland, to replace him.[4] Portland's cabinet initially included George Canning as Foreign Secretary; Robert Stewart, Viscount Castlereagh, as Secretary of War and Colonies; Robert Jenkinson, Earl of Liverpool, as Home Secretary; and Spencer Percival as Chancellor of the Exchequer and Leader of the House of Commons.

Portland named Canning as Foreign Secretary on 28 March 1807, a post he retained for two and a half years, resigning on 11 October 1809. With a rags to riches early life, Canning was virtually unique among Britain's governing elite during this age.[5] His father died shortly after his birth, leaving his mother in poverty. She became an actress and swiftly achieved success for her talented performances on stage and off with a series of patrons. Canning's uncle underwrote his education through Fitch, Eton, Oxford, and Lincoln Inn. At Oxford, he was renowned as an orator, debater, and wit, which helped him forge friendships with several future political leaders, most importantly Robert Jenkinson, who would become Prime Minister and Earl of Liverpool. Like his mother, Canning was a skilled networker. He joined William Pitt's social and political circle in 1792 and won a House of Commons seat in 1793. He served as Foreign Undersecretary from 1795 to 1799, Paymaster of the Forces from 1800 to 1801 and Navy Treasurer from 1804 to 1806. Along the way, he acquired wealth through marriage.

Canning had a sophisticated understanding of British foreign policy's ends and means. One core tenet was: 'We can be but precariously safe as long as there is no safety for the rest of Europe.' British national security strengthened as British diplomats manipulated the insecurities of others. That was best achieved by fostering the enemies of one's worst enemy: 'Any nation in Europe that starts up with a determination to oppose a power which, whether professing insidious peace or declaring open war, is the common enemy of all nations ... becomes instantly our essential ally.' He boasted that: 'We have now what we have had once before and once only, a maritime war in our power – unfettered by any consideration of whom we may annoy – or whom we may offend – And we have ... determination to carry it through.' However, what Whitehall did instead was build and lead the latest coalition while bolstering its own armed forces: 'We have supplied by turns almost the whole continent with arms – Russia, Prussia, Sweden, Portugal, Sicily, and Spain – while at the same time our ... military establishments are sixfold what they formerly were.'[6]

* * *

Whitehall did what it could to aid the Russians and Prussians. During 1807's first half alone, 70,000 British muskets reached those allies.[7] The British also tried to bolster the Russians by attacking their enemy, the Ottoman Empire, which had declared war on 16 December 1806. Admiral John Duckworth received orders to lead a fleet of eight ships of the line, two frigates, and half a dozen support ships through the Dardanelles Straits, Marmara Sea, and Bosporus Strait to anchor off Constantinople. If Ottoman Sultan Selim III did not surrender, Duckworth was to bombard the city until he yielded. In February 1807, the expedition sailed a gauntlet of bombardments by batteries and forts just below Constantinople. Selim wisely anchored his fourteen ships of the line and nine frigates to reinforce the city's batteries, so Duckworth did not dare attack. Instead, he withdrew back to the Mediterranean, having lost a ship of the line and several hundred casualties without winning anything.

The British suffered a worse debacle in an invasion of Egypt. The plan was to join forces with Muhammad Bey Al-Alry, who led the Mamluk military caste, against the Ottoman governor, overthrow him, and place Al-Alry in power as a British protegé. But Al-Alry died shortly before 17 March, when General Alexander McKenzie-Fraser led 6,000 troops ashore east of Alexandria, Egypt, then over the next few days invested the city. Although the British captured Alexandria, the Mamluks joined the Ottomans in fighting the invaders. The Turks routed a British attempt to capture Rosetta and Al-Hammad, then besieged Alexandria. The Royal Navy evacuated the expedition's remnants on 25 September.

Frederick William sent a request that London help underwrite its war. On 27 June, Canning signed a treaty whereby Britain would pay Prussia £1,000,000 in three £333,333 payments every four months over the next year if Berlin mobilised all available resources against France and its allies. Canning then authorised Ambassador Granville Leveson Gower in St Petersburg to entice Tsar Alexander with a similar offer. Swedish King Gustavus agreed to join the coalition. Whitehall organised and dispatched the King's German Legion 10,000 troops led by William, Earl Cathcart, to Stralsund where it would join a Swedish contingent to threaten France's northern communication lines. The expedition dropped anchor at Stralsund on 8 July. Within a week, word arrived of the Tilsit treaties.

* * *

Napoleon crushed the allied army at Friedland on 14 June, inflicting as many as 40,000 casualties and captured then and over the next week of pursuit. Tsar Alexander and King Frederick William agreed to an armistice followed by peace talks at Tilsit. Under the Treaty of Tilsit signed between Napoleon and

Alexander on 7 July 1807, Russia would join the Continental System and with France pressure Denmark, Sweden, and Portugal to do the same. In addition, each leader pledged to act as a diplomatic intermediary for the other. Napoleon would try to convince the Turks to end their war with Russia; Alexander would try to convince the British to end their war against France. Should either fail by 1 December, he would openly ally with the other against his enemy. Napoleon was as harsh with Frederick William as he had been lenient with Alexander. After all, the Prussians were the aggressors in October 1806, starting a war that Napoleon had not wanted. Under the Treaty of Tilsit signed on 9 July, Prussia lost half of its territory; could have no more than a 42,000-man army; and had to pay reparations eventually assessed at 154,500,000 francs to France. Napoleon created two states from Prussia's territorial cessions. From the land west of the Elbe, he made the Kingdom of Westphalia with its capital at Cassel and his brother Jerome the king. From the Polish provinces, he made the Duchy of Warsaw with Saxon King Frederic Augustus its duke.

* * *

After Denmark joined the Continental System, Whitehall targeted it as the weak link to devastate.[8] The British would repeat the attack they made in 1801 after Denmark joined the League of Armed Neutrality. Admiral James Gambier commanded the armada, with General Arthur Wellesley heading the 20,000 troops. They were joined by General George Cathcart and the King's German Legion from Stralsund. The Danes had strengthened their seaward defences over the half dozen years since their previous defeat. The British plan now was for the fleet to support the army's landing on Zealand Island, then a siege of Copenhagen. Wellington got most of his men ashore on 16 August 1807, marched toward the capital, trounced the Danish army at Køge on 29 August, and drove the remnants into the city. On 3 September, the batteries opened fire and for three days demolished Copenhagen. On 9 September, the Danes surrendered, agreeing to give their fleet and naval stores to Britain. Thus was the Royal Navy augmented with eighteen ships of the line, fifteen frigates, two brigs, twenty gunboats and vast amounts of supplies for building and sustaining ships.

Foreign Secretary Canning explained how that brutal treatment of Denmark was crucial to Britain's grand strategy for decisively defeating rather than appeasing Napoleon: 'We are hated throughout Europe and that hate must be cured by fear ... We have now ... a maritime war, in our power – unfettered by any consideration of whom ... we may offend ... Could any peace settle Europe now ...? [T]hat is not our interest. Our interest is that till there can be a final settlement that shall last, everything should remain as unsettled as possible; that no usurper should feel sure of acknowledgement; no people confident of their new masters; no kingdom sure of its existence; no spoliator sure of his spoil; and even the plundered not acquiescent in their loss.'[9] That was why Whitehall rejected St Petersburg's offer to mediate peace with Napoleon.

* * *

Napoleon sought to subordinate Portugal within the Continental System.[10] On 19 July 1807, he had Foreign Minister Talleyrand demand that Lisbon sever all trade with Britain; confiscate all British ships and their cargos in port; and arrest all British subjects. If Portugal failed to comply before 1 September, France and Spain would war against Portugal. The French and Spanish ambassadors in Lisbon repeated that threat on 12 August. Crown Prince Joao was the regent for his mother, Queen Maria I, incapacitated by insanity. The British promised to ally with or war against Portugal depending on whether it resisted or joined Napoleon. British power terrified Joao more than French power. The French could only conquer Portugal but the British could sweep the seas of Portugal's navy and merchant ships, blockade and bombard Lisbon and other ports into rubble, and capture Brazil and other colonies. He rejected the French and Spanish demand. On 30 September, the French and Spanish ambassadors left Lisbon, severing relations.

General Jean Junot led 25,000 French troops from Bayonne on the long march west to Portugal on 12 October. Along the way, 16,000 Spanish troops commanded by General Juan Carraffa joined them. Joao grew increasingly alarmed. On 20 October, he sent word to Paris and Madrid that Portugal would join the Continental System. The diplomatic silence was the terse reply that he had missed the deadline and so must face the consequences. Under the Treaty of Fontainebleau, signed by French and Spanish envoys on 27 October, Portugal would be split in three parts, with the south given to Prime Minister Manuel Godoy, the north to the Etrurian Kingdom, whose Queen Maria Luisa was the Spanish king's daughter, and the centre to France.

The only British aid that arrived at Lisbon was Captain William Sydney Smith with six ships of the line on 6 November. That flotilla could do nothing to defend Portugal's borders against the enemy onslaught. Joao and the royal court packed into Smith's squadron as word arrived that Junot's army was a two days march away on 27 November. They sailed to Rio de Janeiro, where they remained until 1821 long after General Arthur Wellesley, Duke of

Wellington, commanding the British and Portuguese army, drove the French far from their country.

Whitehall underwrote Joao and his fellow exiles with £80,000 and a £20,000 credit line in London. In return, Joao opened Brazil to British trade on 28 January 1808. Ambassador Domingos de Sousa Coutinho invited interested merchants to a banquet on 25 June 1808, and 113 attended to form the Society of British Merchants Trading in Brazil. On 19 February 1810, Ambassador Percy Smythe, Viscount Strangford, signed with Joao a treaty that established 15 per cent tariffs for Britons, 25 per cent for all other foreign nations, and the extraterritorial privilege for Britons accused of committing crimes in Brazil to be tried in British courts. By 1811, seventy-five British firms had established offices in Rio de Janeiro alone. British merchants dominated the economy and reaped countless times more profits from Brazil than Whitehall paid for that privilege.[11]

* * *

Amidst a global war with no end in sight the British committed an extraordinary moral act. For a couple of centuries, slavery had enriched British traders and planters. Then Parliament passed the Act to Abolish the Slave Trade by 283 votes to 16 on 23 March, and George III approved it on 25 March 1807. Beginning on 1 January 1808, that act outlawed an important source of wealth for Britain.[12]

Several decades of political debate preceded that law. The first decisive step came when William Murray, Earl of Mansfield, Chief Justice for the Court of the King's Bench, issued a decision on 22 June 1772 that essentially outlawed slavery in Britain. William Paley presented powerful arguments against slavery in his 1785 *Principles of Moral and Political Philosophy*. William Wilberforce became Britain's leading abolitionist.[13] He and half a dozen like-minded associates founded the Society for Effecting the Abolition of the Slave Trade in 1787 and annually published more anti-slavery pamphlets and sent more petitions with longer lists of names to Parliament. The Society steadily massed allied followers and groups, most importantly the Clapham Sect. Abolitionists wielded powerful images alongside arguments such as William Cowper's poem, 'The Negro's Complaint', and Josiah Wedgewood's ceramic with a kneeling black imploring, 'Am I Not a Man and a Brother'.

The abolitionist strategy was first to end the international slave trade and later slavery. The logic was that masters would better treat their slaves the more limited the supply. British merchants accounted for half the eighteenth century's trafficking of Africans across the Atlantic. Those were a powerful interest group that abolitionists had to overcome. With time, Wilberforce inspired more adherents. One was Prime Minister William Pitt, who in 1788 established a Privy Council committee to examine the economic, political, and moral consequences for Britain of abolition. Parliament voted against the immediate abolition of the slave trade by 230 to 85 but for its gradual abolition by 193 to 125 in April 1792. That same month the eruption of war between France and an alliance of other European states forced Pitt to put the abolition question on the political backburner. During the 1790s, the mass death and destruction caused by West Indian slave revolts first in French and later British colonies provoked a fierce debate over whether to liberate slaves after crushing them. In the House of Commons, Wilberforce spearheaded that campaign as the first step toward complete abolition. The Slave Trade Act of 25 March 1807 prevented British traders from selling slaves in British and other European colonies. In Britain's colonies, most slaveowners actually supported that law because the value of their slaves would rise as the foreign supply dwindled. Britain would not abolish slavery partially until 1833 and completely until 1838.

Chapter 8

Fifth, 1808–11

However the conduct of the Spanish Government may increase the difficulties of co-operation, alienate the spirit of the English from their cause, and even apparently justify a total separation of the interest of the two nations, yet it must never be forgotten that in fighting the cause of Spain, we are struggling for the last hope of continental Europe.

[*Richard Wellesley*]

With its latest coalition wrecked, Whitehall did what it could to protect any remaining fragments. Eventually the British knit together what became the Fifth Coalition that joined Spain and Austria to Portugal and Sweden. The first step was to retain Sweden as an ally.

The Tilsit treaties gave Russia and Prussia a free hand against Sweden. That rendered Sweden's toehold in Stralsund vulnerable. Rather than lose a Swedish corps along with that seaport, King Gustavus withdrew those troops. That nullified the treaty whereby Britain subsidised that contingent. Foreign Secretary George Canning sent word to Gustavus that Britain would back Sweden with money and troops if he refused to join the Continental System and make peace with Napoleon and his allies. On 8 February 1808 envoys signed a treaty whereby Britain paid Sweden £100,000 monthly and sent 35,000 muskets worth £94,023. In May a flotilla carried General John Moore and 10,000 redcoats to Gothenburg, Sweden.[1] Learning of their unexpected arrival, Gustavus refused to let them land and arrested Moore when he came ashore to meet him. Although the king soon released Moore, Gustavus's bizarre behaviour stunned Whitehall. Portland soon had another vital mission for Moore and his men.

* * *

Meanwhile, Napoleon exploited a vicious rift in Spain's royal family. Charles IV was an incompetent king and cuckold. Queen Maria had talked him into elevating her lover, Manuel Godoy, a Royal Guard sergeant, to be his prime minister. Crown Prince Ferdinand despised his parents and sought to replace his father on the throne. His first coup attempt failed in November

1807. His parents warily forgave his feigned repentance. His second attempt forced Charles IV to abdicate on 19 March 1808.

Napoleon called Charles, Maria, Ferdinand, Godoy, their entourages, and Spain's parliament, the Cortes, to Bayonne, in south-western France, where he promised to resolve their differences. Once there, he pressured Charles and Ferdinand to transfer their conflicting royal claims to him in return for separate chateaux and annual generous pensions in France; by treaty, Charles and Ferdinand did so on 5 and 10 May, respectively. He then gave Spain's throne to his older brother Joseph, then the Neapolitan king. He had the Cortes acclaim Joseph as Spain's king in Madrid on 25 July. In Naples, he replaced Joseph with his brother-in-law and cavalry commander Joachim Murat, who had married his sister Caroline.

The constitution that Napoleon devised for Spain transformed the realm from a feudal absolute monarchy into a liberal constitutional monarchy. The king governed with a cabinet of ministers and a bicameral national assembly whose members were elected indirectly. The Constitution transformed the Spanish people from subjects into citizens who enjoyed equal protection; freedom of employment, residence, and movement; and freedom from torture, serfdom, and arbitrary arrest. State and church were separated, with the latter subjected to the former.

Taking title and designing a constitution for Spain was astonishingly easy. Governing Spain proved to be impossible. Only a tiny minority of Spaniards welcomed Joseph as king and his liberal constitution. Revolts erupted against the new regime across the country. Each region formed a Junta or ad hoc government to organise resistance. Napoleon dispatched ever more troops but never enough to smother the rebellion.

Foreign Secretary Canning received envoys from the Asturian and Galician Junta in June 1808. Each requested $5,000,000 in Spanish silver dollars, around £1,000,000. Canning promised to send as much as Britain could spare to those juntas and others that sought aid. He dispatched Charles Stuart to disperse money. In 1808 alone, Britain gave £500,000 to Galicia, £200,000 to Asturias, £200,000 to Seville, £100,000 to Leon, £100,000 to Cadiz, and £50,000 to General Pedro Carlo y Suredo, Marquis de la Romana, along with around 200,000 muskets and 100,000 uniforms. The Asturias Junta alone received £350,000 in cash, 26 cannon, 20,000 muskets, 12,000 swords, 14,000 pikes, 1,080 barrels of gunpowder, 18,600 artillery loads, 2,752,155 musket rounds, 2,500 kettles, 10,000 pairs of shoes, 9,000 shirts, and 6,000 packs.[2]

During the summer of 1808, the Spanish armies captured one French army and defeated others. Joseph and his entourage fled Madrid to Vitoria in northern Spain. The Spaniards established a Supreme Junta with delegates from each region and installed themselves at Aranjuez, 20 miles south of Madrid. The Supreme Junta sent Whitehall a request in September 1808 for £2,000,000, 300,000 muskets, and 300,000 uniforms. Canning assigned John Frere as ambassador to the Supreme Junta and gave him £650,000 to disperse.

The Spanish revolt was just the opportunity that Whitehall had hoped for to undermine Napoleon's empire. Frederick Augustus, Duke of York, explained: 'The Spaniards are the first people of Europe that have risen in one mass, and that have enthusiastically united in support of their own cause against the common enemy; they are the first nation upon the Continent that appear to have made their country's cause individually their own.'[3] Those appearances would eventually be exposed as grossly deceptive. The Spaniards were riddled with factions, corruption, and incompetence.

* * *

Meanwhile, Whitehall dispatched a 13,000-man army commanded by General Arthur Wellesley to Portugal to expel the French. Over the next half dozen years, Wellesley would lead that increasingly larger army to one brilliant victorious battle and campaign after another against a succession of French generals. Year by year, those victories steadily drove the French back across the Peninsula and then into south-west France all the way to Toulouse when the war ended in April 1814. To do that, Wellesley had to be as able a diplomat as a general, first in developing and subordinating Portugal's army to his own, then in trying to co-ordinate his campaigns with fickle and jealous Spanish allies. He also had to be a scrupulously honest and skilled financier as he wielded millions of pounds sterling in money and materials for his army and allies. For all that, a grateful Parliament titled him first the viscount then marquess and finally Duke of Wellington. The sixth coalition could never have defeated Napoleon when and how it did without Wellington. The same can be said about the seventh coalition that definitively defeated Napoleon at Waterloo. Wellington was Britain's greatest general, far above runners-up Oliver Cromwell and John Churchill, the Duke of Marlborough.[4]

That extraordinary legacy depended on Wellesley being a second son whose cruel mother deemed him 'food for powder and nothing more'.[5] Ironically, he received his military schooling not in Britain but at France's cavalry academy in Angers. His older brother Richard, Lord Mornington, bought him an ensign's commission in 1787 and then helped him up through the ranks to make him the 33rd Regiment of Foot's lieutenant colonel in 1793.[6] His first campaign was in Flanders from June 1794 until March 1795, when the defeated British expedition was evacuated back home. Whitehall sent his regiment to India in 1796. They reached Calcutta in February 1797.

That was a quiet posting until May 1798, when Mornington arrived as India's governor-general and gave Wellesley an army command. Over the next seven years, Wellesley defeated a series of threats to British rule that expanded the empire over much of India. In doing so, he mastered the military arts of strategy, tactics, logistics, finance, administration, diplomacy, and psychology. In September 1805, he returned to England rich and an Order of Bath awardee. His next victorious campaign was against Denmark from 30 July to 30 September 1807, during which his army defeated the Danish army at Køge, besieged Copenhagen, then received its surrender, ending the war.

Wellesley was Whitehall's obvious choice to head the Portugal expedition in 1808. He was confident of victory: 'I am thinking of the French I am going to fight ... They ... have a new system of strategy which has outmanoeuvred and overwhelmed all the armies of Europe ... they may overwhelm me, but I don't think they will outmanoeuvre me. First, because I am not afraid of them as everyone else seems to be; secondly, because, if what I hear of their system of manoeuvre be true, I think it is a false one as against steady troops. I suspect that all the Continental armies were more than half beaten before the battle was begun. I, at least, will not be frightened beforehand.'[7]

Wellesley led his men ashore at Mondego Bay on 1 August and marched toward Lisbon, 80 miles away, on 9 August. His troops trounced the French advance guard at Roliça on 17 August and General Jean Junot with most of his army at Vimeiro on 21 August. Unfortunately, Whitehall had assigned two other generals to supersede him in command after he opened the campaign, Hew Dalrymple and his deputy Harry Burrard. Junot asked for an armistice, which they granted as Wellesley planned a knockout blow. With Wellesley observing, Dalrymple and Burrard negotiated with Junot, who proved to be a wilier diplomat than general. Under the Convention of Sintra signed on 30 August, Junot could sail with his army and their loot back to France. Whitehall reluctantly accepted the Convention while recalling the three British generals for an investigation over whether they could have imprisoned rather than repatriated the French army. Fortunately, the Court of Inquiry exonerated Wellesley. Regardless, Wellesley's generalship had for now liberated Portugal from France and he would soon return to lead its defence.

Whitehall assigned General William Beresford to rebuild the Portuguese army. In late 1808, Beresford distributed 26,766 firearms and 17,000 pikes to the Portuguese troops.[8] Meanwhile, Britain sent £2,500,000 worth of cash, arms, uniforms, and equipment to the Spaniards from June 1808 to February 1809.[9] Two British generals landed with armies in the Peninsula in October,

John Moore with 20,000 troops at Lisbon and David Baird with 12,000 at Corunna.

Napoleon sought a knockout blow against the Spanish armies in November 1808. In the region surrounding his headquarters at Vitoria, he massed seven corps and a cavalry corps. He unleashed three corps in different directions while he led four toward Madrid. By early December, he and his marshals had routed the Spanish armies before them and overrun much of northern and north-eastern Spain. Napoleon reinstalled Joseph on the throne in Madrid on 4 December.

Moore devised a plan with Baird to join forces and attack Marshall Nicolas Soult's corps, which had reached Burgos. Getting word of those advancing British armies, Napoleon sought to trap and destroy them between two French armies. Learning of that danger, Moore and Baird withdrew toward Corunna and Vigo respectively, where each hoped a British fleet could evacuate them. Napoleon concentrated on running down and destroying Moore. In early January, he turned over the advance to Soult and hurried back to Paris after receiving an alarming intelligence report that Austria was massing its armies for its latest war against France and its allies.

Moore and his army's remnants reached Corunna on 12 January 1809, but the sea was empty of a British fleet. During Moore's retreat, he had lost thousands of his troops to battle and exhaustion. Three days later, the British fleet and Soult's corps arrived. On 16 January, the British repelled a massive French attack, although Moore was among the dead. That evening the fleet's longboats evacuated the army and the next day the fleet sailed away. That was a very close escape. Had Soult arrived a day earlier, he might have bagged Moore's entire army. Although the British lost over 7,000 troops during the campaign, most of Moore's and Baird's troops survived to form the core of the next British army to disembark on the Peninsula, this one commanded by Wellesley.

* * *

The Royal Navy's latest smashing victory over a French fleet came at Basque Roads near the Charente River mouth on Biscay Bay in western France from 11 to 24 April 1809. Admiral Zacharie Allemand commanded eleven ships of the line and two frigates that Admiral James Gambier's fleet had blockaded for months. The Admiralty sought to break that stand-off by ordering Captain Thomas Cochrane, as aggressive and skilled a commander as Horatio Nelson, to attack that fleet with a squadron of warships preceded by fireboats. Cochrane's attacks unfolded over a dozen days and eventually resulted in four destroyed French ships of the line and one frigate, while other French warships ran aground to avoid destruction. During these battles, Gambier remained anchored safely with his fleet far beyond cannon shot and rejected Cochrane's requests for reinforcements. At one point Cochrane with two ships of the line squared off with and battered four French ships of the line. Cochrane was later court-martialled for publicly condemning Gambier's inaction that led to a limited rather than total victory.

* * *

As a coalition partner, Whitehall found dealing with Sweden's erratic king nearly as frustrating as dealing with Spain's junta. Canning sent Anthony Merry to Stockholm to renew the subsidy treaty that would expire in December 1808. Gustavus demanded that the subsidy rise from £1,200,000 to £2,000,000, with £300,000 immediately due. He threatened to sever trade with Britain if he did not receive that money and treaty in six days. Merry felt he had no choice but to yield. Word of that blackmail infuriated Canning, who informed Merry that the 1809 subsidy would remain £2,000,000 with £300,000 the first quarterly payment. If the king rejected that offer, Merry was to sail for home. On 1 March 1809, Gustavus approved the treaty for that amount and schedule.

A cabal deposed Gustavus and replaced him with his uncle Charles as regent on 13 March 1809. The Riksdag of the Estates transformed the regent into King Charles XIII on 6 June. The relief in Whitehall at that favourable political change was fleeting. The Russians defeated Sweden and forced the new king to cede Finland to Russia, join the Continental System, and sever trade with Britain.

* * *

Meanwhile, the Austrians had indeed decided to launch their fourth war against France since 1792, determined to avenge their previous humiliating defeats. Thus, did hope once again trump harsh experience. Vienna sent envoys to London with its greatest request yet – £2,000,000 in preparation money and thereafter £400,000 monthly to field 443,000 troops. The cabinet debated that request for nearly a month. In April, Canning informed Vienna that Britain would send £200,000 directly to Austria and establish an account with £1,000,000. Beyond that, Whitehall would lend Vienna up to £4,000,000 at 5 per cent interest. Foreign Minister Georg Starhemberg rejected the loan and demanded cash. The British ended up giving Austria £1,187,500 by the time word of Wagram reached London.[10]

Napoleon inflicted as decisive a defeat on Austria for its latest aggression in 1809 as he had during the three previous wars. He led his army down the

Danube River valley, trouncing the enemy in a series of battles, and captured Vienna on 13 May. The Austrians defeated his initial attempt to cross the Danube on pontoon bridges and attack them at Aspern and Essling on 21 and 22 May. Meanwhile, General Eugene Beauharnais, his son-in-law and viceroy of Italy, led an army that invaded Austria from Italy. Napoleon built up his forces, recrossed the Danube, and decisively defeated the Austrians at Wagram on 5 and 6 July and then at Znaim on 10 and 11 July. He accepted an armistice, during which diplomats negotiated the latest peace treaty between France and Austria. Under the Treaty of Schönbrunn signed on 14 October, Vienna ceded Illyria to France, Salzburg to Bavaria, east Galicia to Russia, and west Galicia to the Duchy of Warsaw; recognised all of France's previous conquests; joined the Continental System; and paid an indemnity to France.

* * *

Whitehall tried to assist Vienna by mustering an expedition to attack part of the French empire and hopefully distract Napoleon from his assault against Austria. Walcheren is a huge island north of the Scheldt River's mouth on the North Sea. A combined Dutch and French fleet was anchored at Flushing on Walcheren's south side. The British sought to capture or destroy those warships by seizing Walcheren Island and besieging Flushing. Admiral Richard Strachan and General John Pitt, Earl of Chatham, respectively commanded the fleet and army. Neither was a distinguished choice. The 40,000 troops began to disembark on Walcheren's north shore in late July. Over the next couple of weeks, the redcoats occupied most of Walcheren and a corner of adjacent South Beveland Island, then stalled before French and Dutch fortifications and inundated lowlands after the dykes were opened. The allied fleet repelled a British naval attack on Flushing. Days of bombardment led the allies to surrender Flushing's 5,800 defenders on 5 August, although the fleet sailed up the Scheldt to anchor safely at Antwerp. The British army made no further headway against the Franco–Dutch defences. Instead, 'Walcheren fever', a mix of malaria and typhoid, devastated the redcoats by sickening 11,513 men and killing 3,960, or one of ten among them. Atop that, the expedition cost taxpayers £884,275.[11] On 9 December, the British evacuated their army from Walcheren.

* * *

Moore's campaign was a major defeat that narrowly missed being a catastrophe with the entire army captured. By spring 1809, French armies had overrun most of Spain, with Soult advancing as far as Oporto in northern

Portugal. General John Cradock commanded 16,000 British troops at Lisbon.

Whitehall dispatched Arthur Wellesley to replace Cradock as the army's commander. With 17,000 redcoats and 11,000 Portuguese, Wellesley advanced against Soult, outmanoeuvring and routing his army at Oporto on 12 May. Wellesley then learned that Marshal Claude Victor-Perrins's army threatened to invade Portugal from western Spain. A lack of money delayed Wellesley's offensive against Victor-Perrin for more than a month in early summer 1809 since he could not buy supplies and transport for his army.[12] By the time he received an infusion of coin in early July, reinforcements had swelled Victor-Perrins's army. What might have been an easy victory six weeks earlier ended in a bloodbath at Talavera on 27 and 28 July. Wellesley's British and Portuguese troops alongside General Gregorio de la Cuesta's Spanish troops repelled a series of French attacks and Victor-Perrin withdrew his battered army toward Madrid. For now, Portugal was secure. In gratitude, King George and Parliament rewarded Wellesley by naming him Viscount Wellington on 4 September.

Wellesley used that lull for Beresford to complete his transformation of Portugal's army. Beresford started with top-down reforms whereby over the next four months he cashiered 215 officers on various charges and forced another 107 to retire. For the enlisted men, he raised pay; forbade humiliating punishments; issued regulations for wearing proper uniforms, camp order and hygiene; and increased close order drill.[13] These reforms yielded increasingly positive effects. Staff officer William Warre proclaimed that: 'I am anxious that the campaign should begin, and to be able to judge of what our Portuguese will in reality do, I confess I have great hopes of them. Their discipline is most wonderfully improved ... Our cavalry is also getting into a very respectable state, and is now tolerably mounted.'[14] Wellington paid high tribute to his Portuguese troops: 'They have proved that the trouble which has been taken with them has not been thrown away, and that they are worthy of contending in the same ranks with British troops in this interesting cause, which they afford the best hopes of saving.'[15] However, attrition from disease and desertion was high. Of an authorised strength of 56,000 men, Portugal's army counted only 18,000 in September 1808, 42,000 in September 1809, and 47,000 in August 1810. More men deserted than died. For instance, from May 1809 to October 1810, a staggering 10,224 of 23,885 new recruits fled.[16]

To disperse subsidies to Portugal's army, the British Military Commission established the British Aid Office at Lisbon in April 1809. All money would first go to Wellesley's Military Chest and each month he would transfer the official amount to the Aid Office. On 12 April, the Aid Office made the first payment – £15,378 – to Portugal's Commissary General. On 21 April, Whitehall agreed to guarantee a £600,000 loan to Portugal's government in Rio de Janeiro, with one third of that earmarked for the Lisbon Council of Regency. Meanwhile, the British sent more subsidies and supplies to Portugal. By late July, the Portuguese received £270,538 in cash and £109,082 worth of 30,000 muskets along with uniforms, blankets, shoes, and other essentials.[17] Beresford wore two powerful hats, one as the Portuguese army's commander and the Kingdom's effective governor-general by Regent Joao's decree on 7 March 1809; he retained those posts until 1820.

Charles Stuart, the Aid Office chief in Lisbon, initially gave the Regency Council £980,000 to expand its army from 20,000 to 30,000 men in 1810, then made other disbursements that carried the year's total to £1,800,000. That included 51,200 muskets, 512,000 flints, 7,500,000 cartridges, 3,000 pistols, 6,000 swords, 30,000 sets of accoutrements, 30,000 uniforms, 40,000 shirts, 60,000 shoes, and 42,000 knapsacks.[18]

Despite all that aid, the Regency Council suffered a £1,000,000 budget deficit in 1810. That was exasperating enough for British officials, but the ingratitude of some Portuguese was especially rankling. Council Principal Jose de Souza e Coutinho was the haughtiest and most obstructionist. His family dominated Portuguese politics. One younger brother, Domingos Souza e Coutinho, was the ambassador in London and another, Rodrigo Souza e Coutinho, was Regent Joao's advisor in Rio de Janeiro.

Nonetheless, Stuart was eventually able to negotiate the 1810 Commercial Treaty whereby Portugal formally opened its imperial markets to British goods. Tariffs were high and the Portuguese retained some monopolies for some of their businesses like the Oporto Wine Company's over the wine trade.

* * *

Wellington's campaign was the only land victory of 1809 amidst the latest coalition's defeat and took place during more than two years of the British government's battering by a series of convulsions that included a scandal, duel, resignation, and madness.

The scandal erupted in January 1809, when a parliamentarian presented evidence that Commander-in-Chief Frederick, Duke of York, had sold commissions through his mistress, Mary Anne Clarke.[19] Mary Anne instigated the scandal by taking bribes from ambitious men for promotions to plumb positions that she sweet-talked the duke into granting. A parliamentary investigation found York guilty of naivete, not corruption. York resigned in deep embarrassment, if not outright disgrace. The humiliation worsened after he dumped Clarke and she printed and sold as a book all his torrid love letters to her. The crown finally bought her silence with an immediate payment of £7,000 and £400 annually thereafter.

Then there was the duel. Foreign Secretary George Canning hated Robert Stewart, Viscount Castlereagh, and sought to remove him from the War Department and replace him with Richard, Marquess Wellesley. To do so, he convinced Portland to ask the king to transfer Castlereagh to the largely ceremonial posts of Lord Presidency of the Council and the Privy Seal. Naturally, Castlereagh was enraged when he learned of the plot against him. His honour offended, he challenged Canning to a duel. They met at Putney Heath on 21 September 1809. Although Castlereagh was considered a good shot and Canning a novice, both missed. Castlereagh insisted on a second round. This time his ball cut through Canning's thigh, while the Foreign Secretary again shot wide. Word of the duel outraged the king, and he had both men resign. Thus did the cabinet lose two talented members in wartime.

Exhausted from his duties, William Cavendish-Bentinck, Duke of Portland, suffered a stroke on 11 August, resigned on 3 October 1809, and died on 30 October. Meanwhile, George III appointed Spencer Perceval Prime Minister on 4 October 1809.[20] The following day, Perceval named Richard Wellesley Foreign Secretary and his brother William Wellesley-Pole Ireland's Chief Secretary.

George III plunged into his latest madness, this time with no exit, after his daughter Amelia died on 2 November 1809. Prime Minister Perceval introduced the Regency Act on 10 December 1810, which Parliament passed on 5 February 1811. Crown Prince George would assume his father's royal duties until he resumed lucidity. For his debauchery, vulgarity, and spitefulness, most Britons despised him as regent from 1811 to 1820 and as King George IV from 1820 to 1830.[21]

* * *

Wellington's thin red line in Portugal faced its latest French onslaught in 1810. In May, Marshal André Masséna advanced with 65,000 troops from Salamanca. He besieged and captured the frontier fortress cities of Spain's Ciudad Rodrigo on 10 July and Portugal's Almeida on 28 August. Then he attacked Wellington's 35,000-man Anglo–Portuguese army deployed along a mountain ridge with a village named Bussaco on 27 September. The allies repelled that attack, inflicting twice as many casualties. Wellington withdrew his army to the Torres Vedas line of forts that stretched from the Tagus River above Lisbon north-west to the Atlantic coast. Wellington had prepared those fortifications as an impregnable fallback during the summer and, as

Masséna's army approached, had the countryside outside the lines stripped of all crops and livestock. In mid-October, Masséna's army was deployed before the lines but the marshal did not dare attack. In mid-November, he retreated to Santarem on the Tagus River and wintered there as disease, starvation, and desertion steadily devoured his army. In March 1811, Masséna withdrew toward Salamanca as Wellington warily shadowed him and inflicted several defeats on his rearguard. Wellington dispatched a force to besiege Almeida and positioned his army on a ridge line across the road that Masséna would have to take to relieve that fortress city. Masséna launched a series of attacks that Wellington's troops repelled from 3 to 5 May. Masséna withdrew his depleted army to Salamanca. The allies captured Almeida on 10 May. Wellington had General William Beresford join Spanish General Joaquin Blake to block an advance by Marshal Nicolas Soult. The Anglo–Spanish army defeated the French at Albuera on 16 May. Portugal was again secure until the next French campaign.

* * *

The French probably would have overrun the entire Peninsula if they only had to fight a conventional war against the Spanish, Portuguese, and British armies. But they faced a worsening guerrilla war that forced them to deploy ever more troops to guard hundreds of miles of supply lines, and replace thousands of killed or maimed soldiers.[22] André François de Miot de Mélito, King Joseph's friend and advisor, explained that threat: 'Spread out in parties in every part of the territory ... [the guerillas] did us more damage than the regular armies by intercepting all our commendations and forcing us never to send out a courier without an escort or leave isolated soldiers on the roads ... Large parties of guerillas often advanced to the gates of the capital ... This small-scale warfare undermined us. We only possessed the ground actually occupied by our armies, and our power did not extend beyond it. The business of administration ceased, and there was neither order, nor justice, nor taxation.'[23] In some regions, the guerillas grew so powerful that, 'it sometimes required entire battalions to carry an order of a battalion to another distant one. The soldiers, wounded, sick, or fatigued, who remained behind the French columns, were immediately murdered.'[24]

By preying on their enemy's rear, guerillas slowed French advances and hastened French retreats. Strategic consumption, or the need to detach troops to protect vital supply and communication lines, is ubiquitous to conventional warfare. Guerillas magnify that consumption. Obviously, the fewer troops and supplies that reach an army's front lines diminish its victories and worsen its defeats. As the years passed, the scale of guerilla operations grew through three stages of numbers, strategies, and tactics: hit and run, take and hold, circle and destroy. Nonetheless, guerrillas were of secondary importance in deciding the war's outcome. While the guerrillas did inflict a steady, worsening haemorrhage of French power, they were incapable of defeating the French on their own.

The transformation of ever more Spanish people from cowed peasants into guerrillas was not difficult since groups among them had in effect been doing it for centuries. Smuggling and banditry dominated the economies of many, perhaps most, provinces. The same organisation and skills necessary to, say, slip goods around a customs post, hold up a mail coach, or fight off pursuers could be applied to waylaying French couriers and wiping out guard posts. Surviving a life on the run demands being cunning, furtive, and light-footed. Compounding all that was a culture that extolled a prickly, hair-triggered sense of honour, and throat-slitting violence to uphold it. The notion of patriotic guerillas fighting to the death for Spain is a myth. Spain was as hazy a notion for most people living there as their livelihoods, clan, and church were rock-hard sources of identity, loyalty, and meaning. The bands fought not for the government nor even for Spain, but primarily to satisfy their cravings for vengeance and greed, and perhaps secondarily for their provincial interests and identity.

For reasons of culture and cover, guerillas were most deeply rooted in mountainous regions. Vengeance, hatred, honour, and loot motivated countless guerrillas, with the latter most important. Heinrich von Brandt, who fought against them, observed that the guerillas 'rushed for with the utmost rapidity upon their booty ... As soon as the enterprise was completed everyone went his way, and armed men were scattered in all directions.' This dispersal actually bolstered their strength as 'the communication on all roads was closed'.[25]

The Junta tried to assert control over the guerillas with a decree in December 1808. Henceforth, all guerilla bands would swear allegiance to the government, subordinate themselves to regional army commanders, and accept regular officers as their leaders. This decree provoked snorts of contempt among the guerillas. The Junta and generals found that, at best, by supplying them with arms and munitions, they could rent guerilla groups but not own them. The generals did what they could to assert themselves over the swelling bands and co-ordinate their operations. That was never easy and often impossible. The bands usually operated on their own. The most effective guerilla bands had military-style organisation, discipline, and leadership.

What was it like to fight guerilas? Their tactics were to conceal, swarm, overwhelm, then disperse: 'Thousands of enemies were on the spot, though not a single one could be discovered; no courier could be dispatched without being taken; no supplies could be set off without being attacked ... The French were ... obliged to be constantly on their guard against an enemy, who, while continually flying, and who, without actually being seen, was everywhere. It was neither battles nor engagements which exhausted their forces, but the incessant molestation of an invisible enemy who, if pursued, became lost among the people, out of which he reappeared immediately afterwards with renewed strength.'[26]

The French faced a classic 'hydra dilemma' of counter-insurgency, whereby the brutal methods they wielded to suppress guerrillas and their supporters pushed ever more survivors into the enemy's ranks. Thus, while the French might win tactically, they steadily lost strategically: 'Every victory produced only a new conflict, victories had become useless by the preserving and invincible character of the Spaniards, and the French armies were consuming themselves ... in continual fatigues, nightly watchings, and anxieties.'[27]

Relying on guerrillas proved to be a double-edged sword for the allies, especially Spain's government. Guerillas did not just diminish French army ranks. Guerilla bands drained regular Spanish regiments as soldiers deserted their miserable duties for all the loot and liberty they could reap as freebooters. It was far more safe, profitable, and enjoyable to be a guerilla than a soldier. The guerillas devastated the Spanish people nearly as rapaciously as the French. Spanish officer Luis de Villaba angrily insisted that 'guerillas that go by the name of Patriots should be exterminated; they are gangs of thieves ... [that] rob ... The disadvantages outweigh the benefits.'[28] After the French were driven out and the British went home, the government was left to put together a shattered country.

* * *

Despite his repeated defeats of the French, Wellington at times worried that: 'Britain has undertaken a larger concern in Portugal than she has the means of executing.'[29] Whitehall shared that fear. Prime Minister Robert Jenkinson, Earl of Liverpool, warned Wellington to expect the worst: 'The unanimous opinion of ... the government ... is that it is absolutely impossible to continue our exertion upon the present scale in the Peninsula for any considerable length of time.'[30]

That pessimism was especially acute for Spain. Bitter at the Supreme Junta's corruption, incompetence, and cowardice, Whitehall ended all aid in February 1809. That policy was fleeting. Whitehall resumed aiding the Junta after it fled to Seville, with the initial gift including £213,750, 10,000 muskets, and enough other equipment for 30,000 men by late summer. The Junta insisted that the British send enough muskets, uniforms, and equipment for 500,000 troops. Once again, Britain's leaders were aghast at the ingratitude at what they had already sacrificed and the stunning demand for more. Nonetheless, they did send more money, bringing the total to £517,919 for 1809.[31] The British Consul was charged with dispensing those funds.

Whitehall replaced John Frere with Richard Wellesley, Wellington's older brother, as ambassador to the Junta in 1809. Shortly after arriving at Seville, Wellesley proposed that the Supreme Junta create a five-man Regency Council that would act as Spain's executive and summon the Cortes, which would include representatives from Spain and its colonies.[32] He then sailed home in October to accept the post of Foreign Secretary. Whitehall replaced him with his younger brother, Henry Wellesley. The latest Wellesley stepped ashore at Cadiz on 28 February 1810. His most vital duty was funnelling money to the Council while imploring the members to coordinate strategy with Wellington. He paid out £445,000 in coin, £291,991 in supplies, and 12,000 muskets in 1810 but typically the Spaniard Council members dismissed that and insisted that their survival depended on much more. First, they demanded £2,000,000, then quintupled the amount to 10,000,000.[33]

Like all other British officials who had to deal with the Junta and other Spanish officials and officers, Wellesley was disgusted by their greed, incompetence, corruption, and ingratitude: 'If the authority of the government has not hitherto been respected in the country, it is solely to be ascribed to the neglect of all the measures necessary to assist the exertions of the people, and to the want of public confidence in the regular armies and the officers selected to command them.'[34]

Dealing with the Spaniards endlessly exasperated Wellington: 'What a pity it is that the Spaniards will not set to work seriously to discipline their troops. We do what we please now with the Portuguese troops, we manoeuvre them under fire equally with our own, and have some dependence on them; but these Spaniards can do nothing, but stand still, and we consider ourselves fortunate if they do not run away.'[35] At times he was scathing about the ally's deficiency of martial abilities and courage: 'I do not expect much from the exertions of the Spaniards ... They cry 'viva' ... but they are in general the most incapable of all the nations that I have known, the most vain, and at the same time the most ignorant ... I am afraid that the utmost we can hope for is to teach them how to avoid being beat.'[36] He was contemptuous of Spanish soldiers and guerrillas alike, but much more the former: 'I have never known the Spaniards do anything, much less do it well ... A few rascals called guerrillas attack one quarter of their numbers and sometimes succeed and sometimes not, but, as for any regular operations, I have not known of such a thing ... successful in the whole course of the war.'[37] He condemned the Supreme Junta as 'neither an adequate representation of the crown, nor of the aristocracy, nor of the people, nor does it comprise any useful quality as an executive council, or of a deliberative assembly, while it combines many defects which tend to disturb both deliberation and action ... It is not an instrument of sufficient power to ... bring into action the resources of the country and the spirit of the people ... which might ... repel a foreign invader.'[38]

One of Wellington's aides, Captain Thomas Sydenham, wrote that: 'Wellington declares that he has not yet met with any Spanish officer who can be made to comprehend the nature of a military operation. If the Spanish officers had knowledge and vanity like the French, or ignorance without vanity as our allies in India, something might be done with them. But they unite the greatest ignorance with the most insolent and intractable vanity. They can therefore be neither persuaded, nor instructed, nor forced to do their duty.'[39]

Yet Wellington insisted that the Peninsular War was worth every penny for diverting and draining Napoleon's power that otherwise would directly threaten Britain: 'I have no doubt that if the British army were for any reason to withdraw from the Peninsula, and the French Government were relieved from the pressure of military operations on the Continent, they would incur all risks to land an army in his Majesty's dominions. Then it indeed would commence an expensive contest.'[40]

Many politicians questioned the Peninsular War's soaring cost in treasure and lives. Opposition leader Samuel Whitbread summed up the general disgust: 'Spain has not done its duty – no matter from what cause – the people had, however, some excuse – they had been under the selfish sway of an aristocracy that only wanted to use them as an instrument to effect their own narrow purposes [and they were] abused by the blind bigotry of an intolerant priesthood.'[41] Alexander Gordon vented the pervasive disgust that: 'Everyone is indignant with the cowardice, stupidity, and presumptuous arrogance of the Spaniards. Following our immediate feelings, we might leave them to their fate, but unfortunately our own interest is too nearly connected with theirs, and we must learn to conquer them with patience and forbearance.' And for that, the flow of money and supplies from Whitehall to the Peninsula did not cease. By February 1811, the British had dispersed 336,000 muskets and 60,000,000 cartridges to Spain and Portugal.[42]

A handful of British were sympathetic to the Spanish and recognised their own faults as strangers in a strange land. One officer appealed to his comrades 'to reflect upon the effect of their conduct ... on the people of a different nation ... The British officer ... sticks to his national habits, struts about, and not only despises but lets it be seen that he despises, all he meets save those of his own nation.'[43] Private Atchison noted: 'I cannot say whether the people are happy at our entrance ... It is all the same to the poor man whether the enemy take by force or the British lay all the provisions under contribution for payment.'[44] The redcoats witnessed stomach-churning poverty: 'The poor are very numerous here, and many are most wretched ... In the ... streets you are stopped every five or six yards, and frequently by six or seven at once ... I have seen children five or six years old lying on the pavement with scarcely one once of flesh on their arms and making a piteous moaning. After dark they lie down against a door ... together ... some sleeping, others crying.'[45] Campaign demands inevitably undercut even well-supplied and well-behaved troops. For instance, during the 1813 campaign, the men revelled in being greeted at 'every town ... by the peasant girls, who were in the habit of meeting us with garlands of flowers'. The Spanish elation at their 'liberators' was short lived as 'it not infrequently happened that while they were so employed with one regiment, the preceding one was diligently engaged in pulling down some of the houses for firewood'.[46]

At times, British soldiers inflicted crimes on the people they were supposed to save from the French. General Robert Long grimly recalled 'our line of retreat as vandalic as any Frenchified Spaniards could wish, and it has distressed me not a little to witness it. The poor peasants have indeed abundant reason to be heartily sick of both friends and foes.'[47] The worst was the sack of Badajoz after capturing it on 6 April 1812, when soldiers committed mass murders, robberies, and rapes of Spanish civilians. Wellington warned his men that atrocities turn allies into enemies: 'The commander of the forces is sorry to observe that the outrages so frequently committed by the soldiers when absent from their regiments, and the disgraceful scenes which occurred during the storming of Badajoz, have had the effect of rendering the people of the country the enemies instead of being the friends of the army.'[48]

Nonetheless, the Spaniards were capable of some reforms. The Supreme Junta would not change its name to the Regency Council until 1812 but it did establish a national assembly or Cortes in several stages. The first step came with a decree issued on 28 October 1809 that a three-month election process for the Cortes would begin on 1 January 1810. The suffrage included all property owners aged twenty-five or older. They voted for parish deputies to district assemblies that voted for deputies to provincial assemblies that, finally, voted for deputies to the national assembly. Amidst this election the French advance forced the government to flee Seville for the nearby and nearly impregnable walled island city of Cadiz. The Cortes opened on 24 September 1810.

* * *

Spain's Supreme Junta faced not just a war against France, but from 1809, a worsening revolt across its American colonies. Those colonial subjects, called criollos, had accumulated centuries of animosities against the government in Madrid and aspirations for themselves. As in America, nationalism frayed imperial rule. Among the colonial elite, notions of being Mexican, Peruvian, Columbian, and so on steadily eroded a Spanish identity with each generation born in the empire. Spain's protectionist policies were self-defeating. They cramped rather than promoted economic development and, thus, fed the colonial frustrations that eventually provoked independence wars against Spain's inept, smothering rule. Despite censorship, word seeped into the Spanish empire of America's successful war for independence from Britain and establishment of a republic, as well as France's overthrow of its own king. Copies of America's Declaration of Independence and France's Declaration of the Rights of Man and the Citizens inspired countless criollos.

The rebellion's catalyst was Napoleon's dethroning of Charles IV and the enthroning of his brother, Joseph. That became the excuse for revolts that erupted in La Paz and Quito, Peru, in 1809, and cities and regions in Mexico, Venezuela, Argentina, Chile, and Columbia in 1810. Latin America's rebellions, however, lacked two crucial ingredients that enabled America's revolution to endure – mass nationalism and liberalism. Race and revolution were inseparable. Provinces with mostly white populations such as Argentina, Chile, Uruguay, and Venezuela were the first to shake off Spanish rule. Provinces where a white elite exploited a mostly Indian population like Peru or Guatemala were more loyal to Madrid.

Venezuela's revolutionary leaders issued a contradictory statement on 19 April 1810, when they declared themselves at once independent and loyal to Ferdinand VII. If that puzzled British observers, they were delighted by the accompanying declaration that henceforth opened Venezuela's markets to the world. The Venezuelans sent a request for military aid and reciprocal trade relations to the British governor of Curaçao. Word that the governor had agreed appalled Liverpool and the cabinet. Britain was now at once allied with and subsidising the Spanish Junta and aiding rebels trying to break free from the Junta! Liverpool tried to limit the diplomatic damage by publicly reprimanding the governor and offering to mediate the conflict between Cadiz and Caracas.[49]

Venezuelan envoys Simon Bolivar and Luis Mendez arrived in London on 11 July 1810. That posed a dilemma for Whitehall. If Foreign Secretary Wellesley officially welcomed them, he would alienate the Junta. If he refused to meet them, the rebels would certainly not open their markets to British merchants and would probably turn to Napoleon for financial and military aid. So, Wellesley split the difference. He met them privately and expressed his sympathy with their cause. He then explained to José María de la Cueva, Duke of Albuquerque, that he 'considered the arrival of these deputies as a circumstance of great advantage as it would enable H.M.'s Govt. to represent in the most expeditious manner to the authorities of the Province of Venezuela the erroneous view which they have taken of the state of Spain and to urge the expediency of reuniting that province to the authorities of the provincial Govt. established in the Mother Country.'[50]

The British certainly had mixed feelings about the independence movements.[51] The rebellions weakened the effort against Napoleon's empire as the Junta diverted scarce resources to eliminate that threat to their own empire. Colonial revenues plummeted as revolts spread across the Spanish empire. The last good year was 1810, when the government received 407,700,000 reales, then, in 1811, less than half that or 201,600,000, and a mere 136,000,000 in 1812.[52] Spain's national debt rose from 7,000,000,000 reales in 1808 to 12,000,000,000 in 1814.[53] Atop that, of course, was the hypocrisy of aiding colonial rebels against their imperial masters only a generation after losing thirteen of its American colonies when France decisively aided their struggle for independence.

Yet the rebellions also presented Whitehall with an opportunity. Henry Wellesley received instructions to tie Britain's soaring aid to Cadiz to the opening of the Spanish empire's markets to British merchants. The Junta was willing to discuss possibly opening markets in Spain and its empire to British merchants if Whitehall would guarantee a loan from £10,000,000 to £20,000,000 and forty vessels to transport their troops wherever they pleased. Obviously, the Spanish intended to wield that financial and shipping power to help crush the revolts in their empire. The sheer chutzpah of that demand flabbergasted the cabinet. Canning replied that he was 'for a long time in doubt whether there must not have been some mistake in the translation of the phrase. A loan of twenty, or ten millions could not be raised in the City of London for any Foreign Power whatsoever.'[54]

So, Secretary of State Eusebio de Bardají y Azara bluntly rejected Wellesley's latest appeal for open markets when they met on 5 July 1810. He insisted that any trade could only occur on Spanish vessels that first passed through Spanish ports. That, of course, was exactly the same imperial policy that the British imposed on their own colonies. The hypocrisy did not faze Wellesley from continuing to press Britain's national interests. He was willing to accept indirect trade with Spain's colonies via Spain's port, but only if British vessels carried it. Bardají then demanded that the Royal Navy help repress British smuggling in the empire. Wellesley was noncommittal. Bardají demanded a £1,500,000 loan. Wellesley spoke of Britain's financial difficulties and wondered how Spain might service the debt given its own financial straits. With time the difficulty of cutting deals lessened. In spring 1811, Bardají requested a $500,000 loan. Wellesley gently rebuffed the request, thought about it, then granted it the next day in return for the promise that the money would be allocated to Spanish armies operating in Extremadura, repayment from Cadiz's custom's house, and a licence to buy $5,000,000 of specie duty free from Mexico.[55]

They resolved one long-standing issue. Wellesley had requested that Britain's Exchequer be allowed to buy gold and silver bullion mined in Spanish America to mint coins, of which some would be sent as aid to Spain. In March 1810, they finally agreed to grant Britain a licence to buy $10,000,000 worth of specie, but only in return for a 17 per cent transaction fee. Wellesley got the Spaniards to lower their cut to 11 per cent.[56]

Ambassador Wellesley called the revolts in Spain's empire 'the principal cause of all the trouble and vexation I have met with in my different communications with the government'. He explained wearily to Foreign Secretary Castlereagh that the 'subject of America' influenced 'the conduct of this government ... in all their transactions with Great Britain. Even those who have given unequivocal proofs of their attachment to Great Britain ... consider it to be our policy to establish a commercial intercourse with the Spanish colonies, and they think that in the pursuit of this object we have given a degree of countenance to the insurgents, which by exciting jealousies here has considerably weakened our influence.' Those tensions were especially pronounced in Spain's current capital: 'The city of Cadiz is more connected with South America than all the rest of Spain put together, and the establishment of our interest here will greatly facilitate any arrangements we may wish to make hereafter with South America.' He recognised the contradictions and dilemmas facing Whitehall. Britain had to strengthen itself financially to underwrite its allies to war against the French, but to do so had to demand trade privileges that weakened its allies economically and thus militarily. Nowhere was that dilemma more glaring than with Spain: 'I am apprehensive that any measure likely to prove injurious to their mercantile interest would contribute toward the completion of the designs of the enemy upon Cadiz.' He noted with alarm 'the violent spirit against us here, and it is to be attributed entirely to our conduct in south America'. He complained that 'petty British objects of commerce suffered to interfere with the great and interesting work of releasing this country from the yoke of France, and, unless the British Government takes the decided line of discouraging the spirit which has broken forth in the colonies, and that too in the most open manner, it will create such a jealousy here as never can be got under and will probably be the ruin of the whole cause.'[57]

* * *

Whitehall suffered nearly as maddening frustrations dealing with the exiled king and queen of the Kingdom of Naples. Foreign Secretary Liverpool replaced Ambassador William Amherst with William Cavendish Bentinck as ambassador to Ferdinand IV and Maria Carolina at Palermo on 24 July 1811. Bentinck was empowered to command all British troops in Sicily. His first problem was how to handle Maria Carolina's recent dismissal from the Royal Council of five liberal members that the British had backed. The fear was that the queen's tyranny and the king's fecklessness could provoke a revolution. Bentinck submitted a full report to Foreign Secretary Wellesley. Meanwhile, Whitehall continued trying to bolster Sicily's army with officers who oversaw training and distribution of £40,058 worth of arms in 1811.[58]

Wellesley sent word to Bentinck to inform Ferdinand that on 7 October, Britain had suspended all subsidies to the kingdom until the king agreed to reforms that essentially would transform him from an absolute into a constitutional monarch. He must also name Bentinck his army's Captain General and the crown prince as the Vicar or effective regent. Finally, he must bar the queen permanently from politics. Ferdinand refused. Bentinck persisted. Eventually the king submitted in a treaty signed on 12 September 1812. Whitehall would annually grant the realm £400,000, with expenses deducted for various British services that brought the actual transfer to £170,000. Bentinck could deploy the 7,314-man Sicilian division that the British had trained and equipped to the Peninsula or elsewhere overseas.

Britain's global grabs continued. Expeditions captured France's West Indian colonies of Guadeloupe, Saint Martin, and Saint Eustatius in February 1810, and its East Indian colonies of Ile de Bourbon in July 1810 and Ile de France (Mauritius) in December 1810, and Dutch colony of Java in September 1811. Thus did Britain at once expand its empire, acquire more dependencies to defend, and more sources of revenue to help pay for it.

Chapter 9

Sixth, 1812–14

With respect to the Continent, we must sustain and animate those Powers through whose exertions we can alone hope to improve it, taking care, in aiming at too much, not to destroy our future means of connexion and resistance. [*Robert Stewart, Viscount Castlereagh*]

What distinguished the English Nation in the late war with France? It was not merely the greatness of her exertions, nor was it the skill of her generals ... It was the firmness and perseverance with which the country had maintained the contest and pertinacity with which it upheld the independence of the Peninsula. [*Henry, Earl of Bathurst*]

Napoleon ultimately self-destructed because he let his ambitions exceed his abilities on two decisive fronts. First was his obsession with conquering Portugal and Spain. That led to a chronic war that sapped his empire's troops and treasure from 1807 to 1814. Then came the spectacular catastrophe after he invaded Russia with half a million troops in June 1812; six months later, he fled to Paris after nearly losing nearly all his men to combat, capture, disease, starvation, frostbite, and desertion. He then rejected coalition demands that he give up most of his empire. Instead, he rebuilt an army and led it into central Germany in late April 1813. That led to another crushing defeat, this time at Leipzig in October. He still refused to accept any compromise. He rebuilt another army to defend eastern France against the coalition onslaught from January to April 1814. Once again, the allies overwhelmed him but this time he lost everything. He abdicated on 6 April after the coalition armies captured Paris, the Senate deposed him, and his marshals refused to fight.

Yet without Britain's relentless opposition, Napoleon might have retained not just his throne but his empire despite his blunders. It was British money, supplies, army, navy, and Wellington that prevented Napoleon from crushing all key opposition in the Peninsula. Likewise, had Whitehall not bankrolled and supplied seven coalitions, Napoleon would have defeated the sixth and seventh as decisively as he had the first five.

* * *

As 1812 dawned, no Briton could have rationally been optimistic about ultimately triumphing over Napoleon. Indeed, many feared that their nation was on the ropes. A worsening vicious economic cycle trapped Britain's economy by 1811. An abysmal harvest and widespread business failures because of Napoleon's Continental System caused food prices, hunger, poverty, joblessness, homelessness, and despair to soar. Inflation damaged the economy as most people could afford fewer goods and the poor struggled to pay for food and rent. Falling demand led to lay-offs or wage cuts in those industries, which led to more falling demand. Bankruptcies doubled from around 1,000 in 1809 to 2,000 in 1811.[1]

The Luddite movement violently opposed mechanisation that destroyed craftsmanship and dehumanised and alienated workers. Inspired by a weaver named Ned Ludd, who smashed a weaving machine in 1779, mobs in Yorkshire, Lancashire, Nottinghamshire, and Derbyshire surged into factories and destroyed their machines in 1811 and 1812. Whitehall deployed 12,000 troops across the Midlands to restore order.

A merchant who scapegoated the government for his bankruptcy shot Prime Minister Spencer Perceval dead in the House of Commons' lobby on 11 May 1812. Robert Banks Jenkinson, formerly Lord Hawkesbury and now Earl of Liverpool, became Prime Minister on 8 June 1812, and would hold that post until 9 April 1827. He kept as Foreign Secretary Robert Stewart, Viscount Castlereagh, who Perceval had appointed on 4 March 1812.

* * *

Castlereagh ranks among the greatest British statesmen.[2] He would become Britain's longest continuously serving Foreign Secretary from 1812 to 1822, while at the same time was Leader of the House of Commons, having previously been a member of Ireland's Parliament from 1790 to 1793 and Britain's parliament since 1794, Ireland's Chief Secretary from 1798 to 1800, Board of Control President from 1802 to 1805, and War and Colonial Secretary from 1806 to 1809. He was reserved, knowledgeable, articulate, and diplomatic. He understood the essence of British interests and strategy: 'With respect to the Continent, we must sustain and animate those Powers through whose exertions we can alone hope to improve it, taking care, in aiming at too much, not to destroy our future means of connexion and resistance.' He brilliantly expressed the challenges of defining, then asserting, British interests: 'The political arrangement of Europe ... is ... difficult to decide on. So much depends on events ... The main features we are agreed upon – that, to keep France in order, we require great masses – that Prussia, Austria, and Russia ought to be as great and powerful as they have ever been – and that the

inferior States must be summoned to assist, or pay the forfeit, of resistance.'
A critical related British interest involved restoring territory and rightful rule to secondary powers like the Netherlands, Portugal, Spain, the Two Sicilies, and Sweden to check the ambitions of Prussia, Austria, and Russia along with that of France.[3] In other words, Castlereagh adhered to the classic strategy of 'the enemy of my enemy is my friend', whereby Britain built coalitions of weaker powers against greater powers.

Castlereagh's strategy was imperative in 1812 as Napoleon massed 600,000 troops, half French and half from a score of other European states, to conquer Russia. His motive was the same that led him to the Peninsula – upholding the Continental System that boycotted trade with Britain. After defeating the Russian army at Friedland on 14 June 1807, Napoleon forced Alexander to sign on 8 July the Treaty of Tilsit, whereby the tsar allied with France and joined the Continental System. But four years later, Alexander withdrew from the System, raised barriers against French goods, and resumed trade with Britain. He did so emboldened by Napoleon's failure to vanquish the Peninsula and enraged by Napoleon's annexation of the Duchy of Oldenburg, whose heir his sister had married, along with the Baltic coast all the way to the Russian border.

Napoleon's power peaked at Dresden in May 1812, when he gathered nearly all of his subjected or allied leaders for a grand conference and celebration. Among the countries that contributed the most troops to the pending campaign were Austria's 30,000 and Prussia's 20,000. He sent word to Alexander that he preferred talking to fighting. The tsar replied that he would never negotiate as long as a single enemy soldier was on Russian soil.

Napoleon split his 600,000 troops among five armies, with three on the broad front and two in echelon rearward. He commanded the largest army, the centre with 250,000 men. The invasion began on 22 June by crossing the Neiman River, Russia's frontier. For several months, Napoleon and the two other front-line commanders tried to encircle and destroy the Russian armies before them, but the Russians always managed to evade. Daily thousands of men left the march through exhaustion, disease, desertion, and combat. Finally, General Mikhail Kutuzov stood his ground with 120,000 troops at Borodino, 80 miles west of Moscow, on 7 September. Napoleon attacked with his 125,000 troops and eventually bashed the Russians into retreat. The French marched unopposed into Moscow on 14 September. There Napoleon tarried with his army, now reduced to 95,000 troops, for the next month waiting for peace talks that Alexander had no intention of opening.

Meanwhile, Foreign Secretary Castlereagh did what he could to bolster Russia's power and entice other states into what became the sixth coalition.

152 *The Coalitions against Napoleon*

He sent William Schaw Cathcart, Earl Cathcart, to St Petersburg to negotiate. Cathcart was a career officer who had served in the American war, the Low Countries from 1794 to 1795, and the 1807 Copenhagen campaign, but lacked diplomatic skills. He had trouble finding Alexander, who spent much of early summer with the army at the receding front.

Sweden was eager to join the coalition for an ample price. Napoleon had enraged the Swedes by annexing its northern German province of Pomerania. Sweden's effective leader was now Jean-Baptiste Bernadotte, a former French marshal that Sweden's parliament had named the crown prince for childless King Charles XIII. Bernadotte was a mediocre general who hated Napoleon and now welcomed the chance to join the coalition against him. He also had ambitions to conquer Norway from Napoleon's ally, Denmark.

Bernadotte initially asked Ambassador Edward Thornton for £1,200,000 to underwrite Sweden's participation in the coalition. Thornton apologised that Whitehall could not afford to give any money to Stockholm. Bernadotte dropped his price to £1,000,000 but insisted that Sweden had to conquer Norway from Denmark before its army could operate against France. Whitehall finally agreed to provide £500,000 of war supplies, although by December had dispersed only £200,000 including 23,000 muskets and twenty-three cannon. A definitive deal would not emerge until March 1813.[4]

Meanwhile, in late August, Cathcart caught up to the tsar at Åbo, Finland, where he was summiting with Bernadotte. Thornton had accompanied Bernadotte from Stockholm and was already negotiating with Alexander. Thornton had rebuffed the tsar's opening request that Britain assume Russia's £4,500,000 debts to Dutch bankers. Alexander made the same request to Cathcart, who replied that he was authorised to offer no more than £500,000 in aid atop 50,000 muskets he had expedited earlier that summer. Frustrated with Thornton and Cathcart, Alexander sent Count Christoph Lieven to London to implore Castlereagh to grant Russia £4,000,000 annually for the war's duration.[5]

* * *

Napoleon finally accepted that Alexander would not negotiate and began his retreat from Moscow on 19 October. The weather then was warm days and cool nights but steadily morphed to ever colder temperatures and blizzards. Three Russian armies converged on his retreat. Thousands of Napoleon's troops died from freezing, starvation, combat, and suicide. Napoleon had only 8,000 troops at Smogorni in western Russia on 5 December, when he turned over command to Marshal Joachim Murat, packed into a sleigh with an aide, and the driver began the long journey to Paris 1,500 miles away.

On 18 December, he strode into the Tuileries Palace determined to rebuild his army and defend his central European empire from a likely Russian invasion in the spring.

* * *

Castlereagh understood Napoleon's debacle and Russia's triumph in a continent-wide geopolitical context. He sagely observed that: 'It is by the war in Spain that Russia has been preserved, and that Germany may be delivered.'[6] The year 1812 was the Peninsula's strategic turning point. From 1807 until then, the British and their allies were on the strategic defensive; thereafter, the strategic offensive. Napoleon unwittingly assisted that transformation by withdrawing troops from the Peninsula for his Russian campaign, dropping the total from 354,000 in July 1811 to 262,000 in October 1812.[7]

Arthur Wellesley, then Viscount Wellington, was eager to exploit his weakened enemy by taking the offensive with his combined British and Portuguese army. He began the year by besieging and capturing two fortress cities, Ciudad Rodrigo from 7 to 20 January, and Badajoz from 16 March to 6 April. Those were blood-drenched victories both for the allies and the Spanish inhabitants. Wellington turned a blind eye to his troops' sack of each town with three days of mass robbery, rape, and murder.

After replenishing his army's ranks and supplies, he marched toward Marshal Auguste Marmont and his army at Salamanca in early May. Outgunned, Marmont evacuated Salamanca to concentrate scattered French forces east of the city. Wellington led his troops – 30,000 British, 18,000 Portuguese, and 3,000 Spaniards – into Salamanca on 17 June. After massing 50,000 troops, Marmont marched toward then south around Salamanca to threaten Wellington's supply line to Portugal. On 22 July, Wellington launched his army against Marmont's as it was strung out across the plain, and routed it, inflicting 15,000 casualties while suffering 5,000.

Wellington followed up that victory by marching to Valladolid and capturing it on 29 June, then veering toward Madrid and entering unopposed on 12 August. That forced Marshal Nicolas Soult to break off his army's siege of Cadiz and hastily retreat eastward to Valencia. Soult sent messages for French forces to converge on Madrid. Learning of that plan, Wellington marched north to Burgos and besieged it. Soult's advance with overwhelming numbers of troops forced Wellington to abandon his siege and withdraw westward. By mid-November, Wellington and his weary men were back in Ciudad Rodrigo. There they could savour three great victories and an epic march as far east as Madrid. Wellington's triumphant year owed little to his Spanish allies.

The Junta Central formed a five-man Regency Council that took power on 21 January 1812. The Regency promulgated a constitution that established a constitutional monarchy with most power in the Cortes, Spain's parliament. The 1812 Constitution hardly expressed unsullied liberalism. A tenet declared Spain solely and forever Catholic. However, the Cortes did abolish the Inquisition on 22 January 1813.

The constitution did not fundamentally change Spain's political culture. Wellington, his officers, and British diplomats were generally dismayed no matter what Spanish leaders and institutions they had to deal with. The Junta's change into the Regency provoked one officer to quip that we now 'had only five blockheads to transact business with instead of thirty-five'.[8] Wellington was contemptuous of the government: 'The Spanish politicians have only one object in the measure, and that is to get hold of the resources of the country, as they are afraid of forcing the people of Spain themselves to submit to the privation and inconveniences to which they must submit, if ever they mean to form an army.'[9] Ambassador Henry Wellesley wearily noted 'the same defects which so strongly characters the proceedings of the Supreme Junta ... The same want of energy and firmness, the same system of procrastination ... prevails ... in the ... Council of Regency.'[10] Henry Wellesley cautioned that 'whatever defects may exist in the Cortes, we can look to no other source for the salvation of the country, and it is therefore necessary that every possible degree of support should be given to them'.[11] He was disgusted that the 'Cortes appears ... to suffer under the national disease to as great a degree as the other authorities; that is, boasting of the strength and power of the Spanish nation till they are seriously convinced they are in no danger, and then sitting down quietly and indulging in their national indolence.'[12]

The word of Wellington's victory at Salamanca and occupation of Madrid naturally electrified the government and people in Cadiz. Ambassador Henry Wellesley wrote to Wellington that: 'I wish you could have witnessed the effect it produced here ... A deputation of the Cortes came to congratulate me upon the victory, and the people assembled under my windows, hailing you as the saviour of Spain.'[13] That led the Supreme Junta to a dramatic policy shift. The Spanish were hypersensitive to anything that offended their notion of honour. On 15 March 1811, Wellesley formally asked the Cortes to grant Wellington authority over Spain's provinces in his domain of operations. Initially, the Spanish politicians angrily rejected the request.[14]

For Spain's government to confer such powers would simultaneously deprive the Cortes and war ministry of its powers of patronage, corruption, prestige, and oversight. Speaking for most Spaniards in and beyond the Regency, Florez Estrade, who edited the *Tribuno del Pueblo Espana*, issued this cutting reply: 'It is credible that Lord Wellington, who was born ... in a free country where such a union of authorities is entirely unknown ... could have made such a proposal? How could a general destined to have the glory of bringing liberty to a nation which esteems it so much ... have made so absurd a mistake? How could this illustrious soldier have persuaded himself that a plan so degrading to a nation that has sacrificed itself for its liberty ... could have been ... heard by the heroic Spanish people without the author of so impertinent an idea having aroused their anger? ... The Spaniards have not only shed their blood so as not to suffer the yoke of Napoleon, they have shed it so as not to suffer any yoke at all.'[15] That was a moderate voice compared to radical Juan Alpuente, whose words appeared in the *Diario Redactor de Sevilla*: 'Offering Wellington so great a dignity ... overlooks the Nation's sons and gives preference ... to a foreigner ... It is true that British blood has been shed in Spain, but ... for every drop ... that has been shed, a sea of Spanish blood has been poured out ... Pretending to be friends, the British have taken over the greatest fortresses that defend our coasts ... The French ... have stripped us of all the treasure that we did not manage to hide, and ... the British have stripped us of all the rest ... The French have murdered thousands of our brothers ... but in the midst of our shipwreck the British have cut off the very hands by which were clinging to the land.'[16]

Eventually, cooler Spanish heads prevailed and on 22 September 1812 the Cortes conferred upon Wellington the title of commander-in-chief. Nonetheless, Wellesley greeted the gesture with more cynicism than gratitude: 'After the experience of four years there is no one in Spain who believes that this country will be saved by the measures of this or any other government composed of Spaniards, and it is to the prevalence of this sentiment in the Cortes, as much as the increasing confidence of the nation in the British army and in its commander that we are indebted for the sacrifice of those prejudices which existed to placing a foreigner at the head of the Spanish armies.'[17]

Wellington wanted the title generalissimo only if it held genuine power: 'I am fully alive to the importance which has been attached ... to my having been entrusted with the command of the Spanish armies ... But I have a character to lose, and, in proportion as expectations have been raised by my appointment, will be the extent of the disappointment ... and unless some measures can be adopted to prevail upon the government to force the Minister of War to perform the engagements of the government with me, I must ... resign a situation ... which I should not have accepted if these engagements had not been entered into.'[18] He worried about commanding Spanish 'troops that are neither fed nor paid nor disciplined (and they cannot be disciplined ... unless they are paid and fed) to be dangerous only to themselves when collected in large bodies ... I never will voluntarily command troops who cannot and will not obey, and therefore I am not desirous of having anything to say to the command of the Spanish troops till I shall see the means provided for their food and pay, and till I shall be certain that the regular issue of these has been the effect of introducing among them a regular system of subordination and discipline.'[19]

He nicely captured the trade-offs and dilemmas of at once trying to govern and liberate Spain in a letter to War Minister Jose Maria de Carvajal: 'There is but little authority of any description whatever in the provinces, which have been occupied by the enemy, and even that little depends on the exercise of military power. It is vain to expect ... an Intendent [to] ... exercise the power to realise the resources of the country without the assistance of a military force, which military force to the existing in the existing state of the army will destroy more than its effects will produce ... I am aware that it is wrong in principle to invest military men with civil powers, but when the country is in danger that must be adopted which will tend most directly to save it ... whatever may be the constitutional principles invaded by these measures.'[20] He asked Carvajal to empower him to promote and dismiss officers, construct the military's budget, and consolidate the number of armies to increase efficiency and reduce costs, and, finally, to subject the provincial and local governments to the captain generals, and the captain generals to him.[21]

In the end, Wellington got exactly what he most feared – the title generalissimo without the power. This potentially made Wellington the scapegoat rather than commander-in-chief. Jealous Spaniards blamed him and his fellow Britons for their own incompetence, corruption, and insubordination. To this, Wellington erupted in wrath: 'Are we to blame if the Spanish armies are not in such a state that they can be opposed to the enemy? Or if the Cortes have neglected their duty, have usurped the power of the executive Govt. & have misspent their time in fruitless debates? Are we in fault because by the mismanagement of the American colonies, the world has been deprived of its usual supply of specie, & ... Britain in particular cannot find money to carry on her own operations or aid the allies?'[22]

The Regency decreed on 6 January 1813 that henceforth each army would have an intendent general who would command all captain generals in the region; theoretically that did bring the captain generals ultimately under the generalissimo's command. A cabal of Spanish generals and politicians conspired to undercut and ideally oust Wellington as generalissimo. When Wellington learned of the machinations, he fired off a letter to Ambassador Wellesley at Cadiz, to warn the government that 'if I have not some satisfaction for the insult offered me by these arrangements ... it will be impossible for me to continue to hold the command'.[23]

A cabal of pro-British Spanish officers sought Wellington's support for a coup to overthrow the Regency Council. Wellington sympathised but was not willing to take that drastic step without Whitehall's approval.[24] In a letter to Secretary at War Henry Bathurst, Earl Bathurst, he not only condemned Spain's government but advocated destroying it: 'We ... are interested in the success of the war in the Peninsula, but the creatures who govern at Cadiz ... feel no such interest. All that they care about is the praise of their foolish constitution ... It appears to me that as long as Spain shall be governed by the Cortes along republican principles, we cannot hope for any permanent amelioration ... I acknowledge that I do not believe that Spain can be a useful ally ... if the republican system is not put down.'[25]

Wellington faced his own problems with Whitehall. Troops were only as useful as the supplies and money that sustained them. He explained to Liverpool that: 'I do not care how many men ... the government send here provided they ... supply us with proportionate means to feed and pay them.'[26] In another letter, he issued this stark warning: 'Unless this army should be assisted with a very large sum of money at a very early period the distress felt by all the troops will be most severe ... and it will be impossible for me to do anything.'[27] He detailed just how deep the financial hole was: 'The troops are four months in arrears of pay; the Staff of the army six months; and the muleteers nearly twelve months; and we are in debt for every article of supply of every description.'[28] He warned Liverpool that their junior partners were reaching a breaking point: 'The people of Portugal and Spain are tired out by requisitions not paid for, of the British, Spanish, Portuguese, and French armies, and nothing can now be procured without ready money.[29]

Liverpool explained the worsening financial constraints: 'The expenditure of this country has become enormous, and if the war is to continue, we must look to economy. I do not believe so great a continued effort has ever been made by this country, combining the military and pecuniary aid together as his Majesty is making for Portugal and Spain. The respective governments of these countries should be made sensible of the truth of this position and should feel the necessity of making extraordinary exertions for their own support.'[30]

The British noticed a slackening of Portuguese enthusiasm, effort, and discipline after their country was secure. For most Portuguese, the feeling about the French apparently was 'out of sight, out of mind'. Commissary General Augustus von Schaumann noted: 'One hears no more patriotic sentiments from [the populace] than joy over the liberation of their precious selves

9.1. Portuguese Recipients of Subsidies and Supplies[34]

	Council	Field Forces	Commissary	Supplies	Total
1812	£595,079	£699,593	£511,348	£160,039	£2,276,839
1813	£637,159	£918,061	£634,791	£278,756	£2,486,012
1814	£98,472	£522,969	£649,946	£61,561	£1,345,082
1815	£50,908	£3,057	£950	n.a.	£54,915

from French molestation ... National freedom on a grand scale ... and the desire for a national constitution ... are matters in which they are not interested.'[31] Wellington urged Prince Joao to sail from Rio de Janeiro back to Lisbon and govern his country: 'I request permission to call the attention of Your Royal Highness to the state of your troops ... in consequence of the great arrear of pay which is due to them ... The serious consequences which may result from the backwardness of these payments ... and the uniform refusal of the governors of the Kingdom to attend to any one of the measures which I have recommended ... oblige me ... to express ... my very ardent wish that Your Royal Highness will be pleased to return to your kingdom to take charge of its government.'[32]

Wellington observed that: 'Britain has ruined Portugal by her free trade with the Brazils; not only the customs of Portugal, to the amount of a million sterling per annum are lost, but the fortunes of numerous individuals, who lived by this trade are ruined; and Cadiz will suffer in a similar manner, if this demand is agreed to. Portugal would be now in a very different situation as an ally if our trade with the Brazils was still carried on through Lisbon; and I would only ask, is it wise or liberal or just to destroy the power and resources, and absolutely to ruin our allies, in order to put into the pockets of our merchants the money which before went into their treasuries, and would be now employed in the maintenance of military establishments against the common enemy.'[33]

Portugal received £10,605,689 from 1808 to 1814. Those subsidies peaked in 1813, then declined steeply after Wellington invaded south-west France and only pockets of French troops remained in north-eastern Spain. Yet plenty was still in the pipelines and eventually delivered even after Napoleon's defeat and first abdication in April 1814, then revived for Napoleon's brief but harrowing return in 1815.[35]

* * *

Amidst Wellington's latest brilliant campaign in the Peninsula and the titanic struggle across the Russian steppes, Whitehall found itself in an unexpected and unwanted conflict. The United States Congress declared war against Britain on 18 June 1812.[36] No specific grave recent British offence provoked that declaration. It came instead from a quarter century of accumulating British depredations against American enterprise, security, and honour. The most egregious were Britain's violations of America's vital national interest of 'freedom of the seas'. British warships and privateers captured American merchant ships and their cargos and impressed American sailors to British service. America's State Department received 6,257 official appeals for help or compensation from citizens impressed by the British, while perhaps as many as 20,000 suffered that fate during the era.[37] Atop that, British agents instigated Native Americans in America's north-west and south-west to war against the frontier settlements.

Whitehall issued Orders in Council on 8 June and 6 November 1793 that authorised warships and privateers to capture any neutral ships sailing to or from ports in France and its colonies. That policy enraged all neutral powers, especially the United States. President George Washington dispatched to London John Jay to address that and other bilateral conflicts. After several months of talks, Foreign Secretary William Grenville and Jay signed on 18 November 1793 a treaty whereby the United States recognised Britain's right to seize war goods in neutral ships heading to enemy ports and promised to pay outstanding debts to Britain in return for Britain's promise to withdraw from eight forts on American territory, grant the United States most favoured nation status, and allow American ships to trade with its West Indian colonies.

American merchants capitalised on the new opportunities. The tonnage of American ships and foreign ships in American ports was 355,000 and 251,000 respectively in 1790 and 799,304 and 138,000 in 1801, while the tonnage of American ships in foreign ports rose from 363,100 in 1791 to 848,300 in 1807.[38] Meanwhile, United States relations with France deteriorated as French warships and privateers captured ever more American ships sailing to or from the ports of Britain and its colonies. In retaliation, President John Adams and Congress launched a so-called 'quasi-war' against France in July 1797. During that war, American frigates won virtually every combat against French warships. Napoleon finally ended that war with the Treaty of Mortefontaine, signed on 30 September 1800, whereby France agreed to stop seizing American ships, the American government agreed to compensate merchant claims against France, and each gave the other 'most favoured nation' trade status.

America's next war for freedom of the seas was against the sultanate of Tripoli, one of North Africa's Barbary States along with Morocco, Algiers, and Tunis. Each Barbary State shook down the United States for bribes by threatening to unleash its navy to seize American merchant ships. In May 1801, Tripoli went to war against the United States when it did not receive its tribute and began capturing American ships and enslaving the crews. President Thomas Jefferson and Congress authorised a retaliatory war against Tripoli. The result was a draw in which each side won limited victories but ended in June 1805 with the United States resuming its tribute, although at a much lower price. The Americans emerged from the war with a stronger, more experienced navy and the determination to defend their international commerce and national honour against all odds.

Britain resumed its policy of capturing neutral ships with contraband bound for enemy ports after declaring war against France on 18 May 1803. The British not only confiscated American ships and their cargos but impressed any sailors who could not prove they were Americans. Then, on 22 June 1807, Captain Salusbury Humphreys of the frigate HMS *Leopard* committed a vicious attack on the frigate USS *Chesapeake* commanded by Commodore James Barron. The British warship intercepted the American warship in American waters as it sailed from Norfolk, Virginia, toward the Atlantic. Humphreys demanded that Barron let marines aboard to determine whether any of his crew were British deserters. When Barron refused, Humphreys ordered his gunners to fire three broadsides into the *Chesapeake*. Unprepared for battle and with six of his men dead and twenty-three wounded, Barron struck his colours. The marines boarded, interrogated each crew member, and hauled away four sailors.

Jefferson and his cabinet debated how to respond for six weeks. Finally, on 2 July, Jefferson publicly ordered all British warships to leave American waters and sent to London a demand for reparations. Whitehall ignored the demand and instead, on 16 October, reiterated its right to search neutral ships bound to or from enemy ports for contraband and British subjects; and ordered all British sailors in foreign service to return home. On 22 December 1807, Congress imposed an embargo that forbade Americans from international trade or foreigners from trading with the United States. The result was a self-inflicted disaster for America's economy as the embargo turned flourishing ports into ghost towns with high unemployment, poverty, and despair.

Atop the chronic worsening economic losses, the Americans bristled at British snobbery and arrogance toward them. In a report to Foreign Minister Grenville, diplomat Thomas McDonald expressed the common condescending view of Americans: 'Conceive to yourself a set of grown boys broke loose from school, and playing the various parts of men ... you will have ... a just impression of the American community ... most of them may be supposed to have been ... sharply schooled in an attorney's office ... The business of printing is much followed in America ... The consequence is that the opinions of all classes arise entirely from what they read in their newspapers, so that by newspapers the country is governed. But Britain (for they studiously avoid in general saying Great Britain) makes a very poor figure in the greater part of the ... newspapers.'[39]

Ironically, President James Madison had no sooner got his country into the war when he tried to get out. The day that he signed the war declaration, Secretary of State James Monroe summoned Augustus Foster, Britain's minister, and urged him to work for peace. Monroe sent instructions to Jonathan Russell, the charge d'affaires in London, to explain to Whitehall that the United States would bar British seamen from American ships if the British agreed to stop confiscating American ships, cargos, and sailors. Whitehall actually repealed the Orders in Council on 23 June, although it upheld the principle and practice of impressment. Castlereagh explained that political as well as military necessity demanded that the policy continue: 'No administration could expect to remain in power that should consent to renounce of the right of impressment, or to suspend the practice.'[40] Rather than grab half a diplomatic loaf and call off the war, the Madison administration persisted in demanding that the British give up impressment. And so, the war continued.

* * *

Wellington devised a plan for 1813 that would expel the French from most of Spain. King Joseph and Marshal Jean-Baptiste Jourdan had concentrated 55,000 French troops west of Valladolid. In the region around Almeida on Portugal's frontier, Wellington had 52,000 British, 29,000 Portuguese, and 21,000 Spanish troops. The Royal Navy had captured Santander on Spain's north coast. Wellington shifted his main supply base from Lisbon to Santander, then marched toward it in mid-May. As he crossed the frontier, Wellington raised his hat and proclaimed: 'Farewell Portugal! I shall never see you again.'[41]

His troops captured lightly defended Salamanca on 25 May and crossed the Douro River on 4 June. Joseph abandoned first Valladolid then Burgos before halting before Vitoria. On 21 June, Wellington launched his troops in a double envelopment of the French that routed them. As Joseph retreated toward Bayonne, Wellington began twin sieges of the fortress cities of San Sebastian and Pamplona. Learning of Vitoria, Napoleon replaced Joseph and Jourdan with Marshal Nicola Soult.

After reinforcing his army, Soult led it over the Pyrenees toward Pamplona. Wellington left a covering force at Pamplona and marched with most of his army to block Soult's advance in the foothills. After several days of fierce fighting, the allies drove back the French. San Sebastian and Pamplona surrendered respectively on 8 September and 31 October. Wellington then readied his army to march toward Bayonne.

Wellington's triumphs electrified Britain's war-weary leaders and people alike. In a rousing speech before Parliament, Secretary at War Bathurst explained why, after five years of war, Wellington's army had driven nearly all the French from the Iberian Peninsula and had now invaded France itself: 'What distinguished the English Nation in the late war with France? It was not merely the greatness of her exertions, nor was it the skill of her generals ... It was the firmness and perseverance with which the country had maintained the contest and pertinacity with which it upheld the independence of the Peninsula ... [Britain represented] a pillar of fire amidst the surrounding darkness which marked out to other nations the path to the Promised Land – to the haven of safety and independence.'[42]

Before crossing the frontier, Wellington left behind most of his Spanish troops and submitted his resignation as generalissimo on 5 October 1813. He feared what the Spanish would do to civilians after they invaded France: 'I despair of the Spaniards. They are in so miserable a state that it is really hardly fair to expect that they will refrain from plundering a beautiful country into which they enter as conquerors, particularly adverting to the miseries which their own country has suffered from its invaders. I cannot, therefore, venture to bring them into France ... Without pay and food, they must plunder, and if they plunder, they will ruin us all.'[43]

Indeed, the only problem in his otherwise brilliant campaign was the behaviour of the Spanish army. Co-ordinating strategy among the Spanish generals was like trying to herd as many cats. Indeed, they seemed deliberately to do the opposite of what Wellington and other British commanders encouraged. The Spanish lagged or stalled when the British urged advance, and often advanced recklessly when the British urged restraint. In utter exasperation, Wellington excoriated the Spaniards as allies: 'The Spanish troops will not fight; they are indisciplined, they have no officers, no provisions, no magazines, no means of any description. If we enter into a co-operation with them the burthern of the war must fall upon us, and with us will rest of the disgrace of its certain and unavoidable failure. This is not an exaggerated picture. I was slow as every man is to believe all the bad I had heard of the Spaniards, but I assure you there is nothing so bad.'[44] In sum, the Spanish officers could 'be neither instructed nor persuaded nor forced to do their duty'.[45] Nonetheless, during the Peninsular War, Spain's army underwent a revolution in class if not effectiveness. The proportion of nobles among the officers declined from 23 per cent in 1808 to 14 per cent in 1814, with 285 of 458 generals coming from the ranks of commoners.[46]

Wellington's army crossed the frontier and defeated Soult's army in the battles of the Nivelle River on 10 November and the Nive River from 9 to 13 December. He then massed reinforcements and supplies for what he intended would be a decisive spring campaign.

* * *

The coalition expanded when Prussia defected. General Johann Yorck von Wartenburg, the Prussian commander in the Russian invasion, took the first step on 30 December 1812 by signing with Russian General Hans von Diebitsch the Convention of Tauroggen that declared his army neutral and let Russian troops march through Prussia. Frederick William III publicly rebuked Yorck's act while preparing his court to join Alexander, which they did at his headquarters at Kalisch in late February. On 28 February 1813, Prussia and Russia formally allied with the Treaty of Kalisch, with each pledging to field at least 150,000 and 80,000 troops respectively to fight Napoleon until he was defeated with no separate peace; they warned the Rhine Confederation that any members who fought with Napoleon risked losing their sovereignty. Even then, Frederick William did not formally declare war against France until 16 March after most French troops had evacuated his territory and he had begun mobilising the Prussian army. Learning of the Russian–Prussian alliance, Foreign Secretary Castlereagh dispatched his half-brother Charles Stewart as ambassador to Prussia.

Meanwhile, General Karl Philipp, Prince of Schwarzenberg, withdrew his corps into neutrality with the Convention of Zeyes, signed with Russian envoys on 30 January 1813. The British, Prussians, and Russians sent envoys to Vienna to entice Austria into the coalition. For now, Chancellor Klemens von Metternich sought an intermediary role for Austria. He sent Count Ferdinand Bubna von Littitz and Baron Ludwig Lebzeltern respectively to Paris and Kalisch, with offers to help negotiate peace among the belligerents.

Whitehall had provided Russia with 100,000 muskets in 1812, and in February 1813 sent Russia another 50,000 muskets and fifty-four cannon and Prussia 100,000 muskets, 116 cannon, and 1,200 tons of munitions. The British also underwrote a 10,000-man German legion that the Russians organised and led. Meanwhile, in London Ambassador Lieven continued to press Foreign Secretary Castlereagh for £4,000,000 and another £500,000 as compensation for a Russian squadron that the British had captured at

Lisbon in 1808. Rounds of negotiations followed that would not be finalised until June.

Castlereagh repeatedly asserted that 'the cause of the Allies is the cause of all nations'. He recognised the ongoing war as historically unprecedented: 'The present Confederacy,' he insisted, 'may be considered as the union of nearly the whole of Europe against the unbounded and faithless ambition of an individual.' If former wars were struggles of sovereign powers against each other or their people, this war was 'dictated by the feelings of the people of all ranks as well as by the necessity of the cause. The sovereigns of Europe have at last confederated together for their common safety, having in vain sought that safety in detached and insulated compromises with the enemy. They have found that no extent of submission could procure for them either safety or repose, and that they no sooner ceased to be objects of hostility themselves, than they were compelled to become instruments in the hands of France for effectuating the conquest of other unoffending states ... It is this common danger which ought always to be kept on view as the true basis of the alliance, and which ought to preclude defection from the common cause. It must be represented to the Allies that having determined to deliver themselves from the vengeance of the conqueror by their collective strength, if collectively they fail, they are separately lost ... their own rational policy then is inseparable union.'[47]

As for the French army's remnants in East Prussia, Marshal Joachim Murat gave its command to Eugene Beauharnais at Posen on 11 January 1813 and hurried back to his Neapolitan kingdom. Beauharnais was Napoleon's son-in-law and viceroy for his Italian kingdom. He withdrew westward gathering garrisons as the Russian army approached and the Prussians first became neutral then allied with Russia. In mid-February he reached relative safety at Wittenberg on the Elbe River.

Whitehall's first diplomatic offensive of 1813 aimed to cement Sweden into the coalition. Castlereagh worried that Ambassador Thornton was too acquiescent to Crown Prince Bernadotte, so he sent General Alexander Hope to take over the negotiations. Under the treaty signed on 3 March 1813, Whitehall would provide Sweden with £1,000,000 for a 30,000-man army and another £1,000,000 for a German corps that the Swedes would form and command over the next eight months. The first shipment was 40,000 muskets to a depot established by Sweden at Stralsund in northern Germany. For nearly half a year, Whitehall experienced the same frustrations with Bernadotte that Napoleon had suffered over the years. Bernadotte promised much yet refused to march, claiming he needed more money. Castlereagh reluctantly authorised Thornton to yield to the demand. Under a treaty signed on 29 September, Britain would pay Sweden £1,200,000.[48]

A titanic struggle for central Germany would rage from late April to late October 1813. The Russians and Prussians massed their troops and slowly advanced westward until Alexander and Frederick William established their latest headquarters at Dresden. Their combined armies numbered 96,000 troops, nearly all veterans. Napoleon mustered more troops – 145,000 – but they were nearly all poorly trained, equipped, motivated, and led conscripts. His worst deficiency was cavalry vital for gathering intelligence, encircling, pursuing, and overrunning the enemy. He had only about 10,000 cavalry or 7 per cent of his total force, when he normally sought at least 20 per cent.

Napoleon defeated the allied army at Lützen on 2 May, captured Dresden, then won again at Bautzen on 20 and 21 May. However, those victories were pyrrhic as he suffered thousands more casualties than he inflicted, and without enough cavalry failed to follow up those victories by capturing thousands of fleeing demoralised enemy troops. Instead, the allies covered their retreats with overwhelming numbers of cavalry and replenished their ranks with ever more reinforcements.

Napoleon agreed to the Armistice of Pläswitz on 4 June, followed by peace negotiations at Prague. The time limit for negotiations was first 20 July, then extended to 10 August. Napoleon had no intention of negotiating seriously, buying time while he brought up more reinforcements, especially desperately needed horsemen. But the allies also used the armistice for the same purpose and their reinforcements far outgunned his. Amidst the armistice word arrived of Wellington's rout of Joseph's army at Vitoria on 21 June.

The British understood Napoleon's motives for the armistice. Cathcart cautioned that if 'Napoleon will wish to enter into negotiations ... it will be for the purpose of gaining time of paralysing exertions, and, if possible, of exciting disunion somewhere, even in the British Parliament.'[49] Restraint was often a superior diplomatic strategy to interference. One's credibility was critical. Castlereagh worried that Austria and Russia might cut a separate peace with Napoleon under Austrian mediation. To dissuade Alexander from doing so, he instructed Cathcart to inform the tsar 'how fatal it would be to all were he to separate his cause from that of the other Powers. Neutrality must exhaust his resources as much as war, and, if Buonaparte should triumph over the others, his own fate is sealed.'[50] After encouraging Cathcart to lay low and not interfere, he added: 'The risk of treating with France is great, but the risk of losing our Continental Allies and the confidence of our own nation is great. We must preserve our own faith inviolate to Spain, Portugal, Sicily, and Sweden. We must maintain our most important conquests.'[51]

Castlereagh drew up a draft treaty of alliance for Cathcart to negotiate with the other powers. The first clause asserted the coalition's cause as achieving 'for Europe a general Peace ... delivered from the rapacity and oppression of France'. To this end, each member pledged to fight ceaselessly and resist the temptation of a separate peace. Once won, peace would be maintained by 'a perpetual defensive alliance' in which an attack on one member would be considered an attack on all. To this public treaty, Castlereagh would annex a secret treaty with specific goals, including the restoration of Austria and Prussia to their respective borders of 1805 and 1806; the dissolution of the Rhine Confederation and Duchy of Warsaw; the restitution of the Netherlands and its expansion to a defensive frontier with France; the restoration of Spain, Naples, and Brunswick-Lüneburg; the liberation of Italy from France; and Sweden's annexation of Norway.[52]

At Reichenbach, Stewart and Cathcart respectively signed treaties with Prussia and Russia on 14 and 15 June. The final deal had Whitehall split £2,000,000 between St Petersburg and Berlin for 1813 proportional to the number of troops each fielded, with £1,333,333 for 200,000 Russian and £666,666 for 100,000 Prussian troops. In addition, the British would redeem £2,500,000 of Russia's Dutch debt. Stewart immediately gave financially strapped Frederick William £100,000.[53] Both monarchs fell short of their promises as only about 160,000 Russian and 80,000 Prussian troops fielded in central Germany. Atop that, Alexander and Frederick William forbade the British from any negotiations that they conducted with Napoleon.

With that done, Castlereagh sought to entice Austria into the coalition. To that end, he authorised Cathcart 'to place at the disposal of that Government the £500,000 which was entrusted to your Lordship on leaving England for extraordinary purpose. You will concert as to the best mode of rendering this credit available without interfering with the pecuniary operations of the other Allied Powers: with this view it ought to be drawn for gradually, and ostensibly on commercial account.' Should the Austrians complain that 'the resources of Great Britain have been preferably directed to other Powers,' Cathcart should explain 'that has alone risen from those Powers being already committed in exertions on the success of which Austria had repeatedly declared her own ability to interfere must mainly depend. Under these circumstances it was for Austria first to open herself to Great Britain ... to push her exertions to the utmost, and to distribute her means as might serve the common cause.'[54] Cathcart should assure Metternich that Whitehall would pay another £1,000,000 once Austria's army warred against Napoleon.

Stewart reported that Austria's leadership was split over what to do: 'It seems now that Metternich is valiant, and the Emperor is the timid person.

To wind him up to a proper key, to pat him on the back and to commit him, decidedly, is the present aim. To accomplish this, it is necessary to hold the stoutest language: to declare that even without him the war will be carried on.'[55] Yet Metternich also demanded special handling. Cathcart became close to Metternich and believed that he understood him. Stroking his ego would yield the best results: 'He has been roughly handled by them who did not know or trust his sentiments. I think some public applause would be well bestowed.'[56] Castlereagh eventually concurred. In noting Metternich's 'great spirits and apparent self-satisfaction,' he recommended making 'a hero of him, and, by giving him a reputation, to excite him to sustain it'.[57] Yet, to that, Castlereagh would appeal to a different dimension of Metternich's overweening ego and pride: 'Metternich is fond of negotiating, but the best remedy is to convince him that England is as tired of the war as he can be, and as ready to negotiate at a proper moment. The British Government only deprecates ineffectual negotiations as relaxing the tone and spirit of the Allies, and as enabling the enemy to call forth new resources ... How could Metternich hope to invigorate his own nation, to rouse them to exertion, or to animate them to great pecuniary sacrifices whilst the white flag was flying.'[58]

Francis Jackson reported two forces pushing Austria off the fence into the coalition's arms: 'In looking for the cause of this change, and apparently sudden maturity of the Austrian Councils ... the late brilliant and glorious successes of Field Marshal Wellington have had a very great share in producing them. Bonaparte's own conduct has happily in aid of this.' He went on to cite Napoleon's 'obstinate silence; his delay in sending a plenipotentiary; the chicane which, on his part, marked the discussions relative to the prolongation of the Armistice ... everything he has done, or, rather, everything he has not done, has, at last, forced Austria to open her eyes to his real designs, and ... finally convinced her that it is in vain to hope to bring him to reason but by force of arms.'[59]

Metternich met twice with Napoleon at Dresden in July but failed to talk him into accepting peace. That enabled Metternich to convince Francis to join the coalition. The pressing question then became how much the Austrians could extract in subsidies from Britain to underwrite their campaign. Castlereagh sent George Hamilton-Gordon, Earl of Aberdeen, as his special envoy to Metternich. Hamilton-Gordon joined Metternich at Teplitz in mid-September. Metternich expressed his disappointment that Whitehall could only immediately provide Austria £500,000. On 3 October, after weeks of talks, Hamilton-Gordon and Metternich signed a treaty whereby Britain gave Austria £1,000,000 or £100,000 each month for ten months for 150,000

Austrian troops in the field, to expire in April 1814 unless the war persisted. That time limit proved to be exactly right.

At Trachenberg from 9 to 12 July, the Russians, Prussians, and Swedes devised a strategy for the pending campaign. Bernadotte would command a northern army of Swedes, Russians, and Prussians, while Mikhail Barclay de Tolly would command an eastern army of Russians and Prussians. After Vienna joined the coalition, General Karl von Schwarzenberg would command the Austrian army southward. Those three armies with 450,000 troops would converge and crush Napoleon's 250,000 troops among them.

Napoleon dispatched armies against Bernadotte and Barclay while he squared off against Schwarzenberg, who he routed at Dresden from 26 to 27 August. The allies then adopted a strategy of withdrawing from Napoleon while attacking his autonomous marshals. That resulted in a series of allied victories that hemmed in Napoleon. Under the Treaty of Reid, signed on 8 October, Bavarian King Maximilian Joseph joined the coalition and began mobilising his army to march against Napoleon's rear. Napoleon concentrated his army at Leipzig for what he gambled would be a decisive victory. It was, but it was the allies who devastated him from 16 to 19 October, inflicting 73,000 casualties while suffering 54,000 out of their respective armies of 175,000 and 325,000 troops. Napoleon retreated westward, routed the Bavarian army at Hanau on 30 October, and withdrew across the Rhine into France in early December. The allied armies pursued, then paused at the Rhine to replenish their ranks and supplies.

At Frankfurt, Metternich talked the allied leaders into a peace whereby Napoleon could remain emperor of a France reduced to its 1791 boundaries. On 9 November, they gave this proposal to a captured French diplomat, Baron Auguste de Saint Aignan, to carry to Napoleon in Paris.[60] Napoleon eventually agreed to the terms but missed a 5 December deadline formally accepting them. The allied leaders then concentrated on planning their military strategy for the new year. Two massive armies – Gebhard von Blücher's mostly Prussian and Russian troops marching from the middle-Rhine and Karl von Schwarzenberg's mostly Austrians and Russians from Basel – would converge on Napoleon and throttle him between them.

Prime Minister Liverpool asked Castlereagh on 26 December to journey to allied headquarters and take over negotiations. Castlereagh drew up his instructions and got the cabinet to approve them. For the final campaign, he would promise the Russian, Austrian, and Prussian monarchs to split £5,000,000 among them. Before leaving, Castlereagh negotiated a treaty with Hanover to field 15,000 troops for £600,000.[61]

* * *

Napoleon cut a deal with once and would-be future Spanish King Ferdinand VII, then living at a French chateau. He would release that deposed monarch to return and rule Spain if he immediately withdrew Spain from the war, signed a peace treaty with France, expelled all British and Portuguese troops from Spain, released all French prisoners, and pardoned any Spaniards who collaborated with the French. Ferdinand eagerly signed the Treaty of Valençay on 11 December 1813.[62]

Ferdinand dispatched as envoys the Jose Miquel Duque de San Carlos and Jose Palafox to the Cortes to ratify the treaty and prepare for his return. Foreign Minister Jose Lujando refused to see them until after he consulted with British Ambassador Henry Wellesley. Lujando assured Wellesley that Spain would never sign a separate peace with Napoleon but remained dedicated to his destruction. He wrote to Ferdinand that the Cortes automatically rejected anything he did in Napoleon's gilded cage as from duress. On 2 February, the Cortes issued a decree that would grant Ferdinand the throne only if he ratified the 1812 Constitution.

Word of Ferdinand's pending return posed potential threats to British interests, especially Wellington's campaign. Wellington feared that the Cortes might just ratify the treaty and thus expel his supply lines in Spain before he could establish new ones from a French port.[63] He presented Wellesley a penetrating analysis of Spain's politics and likely future: 'The mob of Madrid will be just as bad as the mob in Cadiz ... Both are set in motion by the same machine, the press, in the hands ... of the same people. The mercantile class will not have quite so much influence at Madrid, although they will not want partisans when they desire to carry a question by violence. The grandees had formerly a great deal of influence at Madrid, but they are too poor at present, and their situation is too degraded for them to be able to do much under the circumstances.'[64] Wellesley was more optimistic.

To Castlereagh, he explained that: 'The only safe line for the King is to accept the Constitution and to declare his determination to govern according to its regulations and without showing any particular partiality to either of the leading Parties in the Cortes, and to select his ministers and advisors from among the ablest men on both sides. By adopting this line of conduct he will insure the good will and support of the Nation and may, by degrees, be enabled to effect such changes in the Constitution as are necessary.'[65]

Unfortunately, Ferdinand was immune to such sensible behaviour. He sent word that he would uphold the Constitution, even though he had no intention of doing so. After returning triumphantly to Madrid in May 1814, he suspended the Constitution and had liberals arrested. Most people were so elated at his return that they were initially indifferent to his transformation of

Spain from a constitutional into an absolute monarchy. Spain had suffered wrenching changes since Ferdinand last saw the capital six years earlier. The worst were the devastating effects of a war without mercy in which perhaps as many as a million Spanish people died. Although Spain was now free of the French, it was not free of violence. The line between guerillas and brigands was always fuzzy. Without a common foreign enemy, many bands fought each other to keep or take lucrative occupations like smuggling. From a liberal perspective, if anything positive emerged from the war, it was the 1812 Constitution that transformed Spain from an absolute into a constitutional monarchy. And now Ferdinand had suspended that Constitution.

Nonetheless, in 1814 Henry Wellesley signed a treaty with Madrid that established an alliance and trade between Britain and Spain. The Spanish requested that Britain guarantee a £10,000,000 loan. Liverpool rejected that but did agree to pay Madrid £800,000 if Spain abolished the slave trade within five years.

* * *

Britain's first diplomatic triumph of 1814 came on 7 January. British diplomats had assisted talks between Denmark and Sweden that led to the Treaty of Kiel whereby they swapped territory – Danish Norway for Swedish Pomerania. On 14 January, Ambassador Thornton signed a treaty that gave Denmark £400,000 and returned its colonies in return for 10,000 Danish troops to join the coalition.

The fate of the Low Countries remained a key British security interest. Castlereagh entreated Ambassador Hamilton-Gordon 'to keep your attention upon Antwerp. The destruction of that arsenal is essential to our safety. To leave it in the hands of France is little short of imposing upon Great Britain the charge of a perpetual war establishment.'[66] To that end, Whitehall dispatched General Thomas Graham with 20,000 troops to invade the Low Countries in co-ordination with Bernadotte's army.

Castlereagh reached the Hague on 7 January. He spent several days with Prince William of Orange discussing the bilateral alliance; the extent of Dutch territory in a comprehensive peace treaty; the cession of the Cape of Good Hope colony to Britain in return for money to strengthen frontier fortresses; and the prince's possible marriage to Prince Regent George's daughter Princess Charlotte. That done, he journeyed to join Metternich and Prussian Foreign Minister Charles von Hardenburg at Basel on 18 January. They then headed to the allied headquarters at Langres.

Britain's subsidies to its allies were £10,000,000 in 1814, just £1,000,000 less than in 1813. This time, the British finally got their money's worth.

Front-line and rear echelon troops included 278,000 Russians, 230,000 Austrians, and 162,000 Prussians.[67] Yet, all that hard power did not guarantee victory. Castlereagh feared that worsening animosities could unravel the alliance. In late February, he wearily noted that the 'temper here is very embarrassing, if not alarming. The criminations and recriminations between the Austrians and Russians are at their height, and my patience is worn out combating both. Austria both in Army and Government is a timid Power ... Russia could have enormous influence to correct the faults of Austria, if her Emperor was more measured in his projects, more accessible in Council, and more intelligible as to his own views.'[68]

Peace talks opened at Chatillon, France, on 5 February. Castlereagh oversaw Stewart, Cathcart, and Jackson, who together represented Britain. The allies first had to forge a consensus on the terms before they would meet with French envoy Armand de Caulaincourt. They initially differed over how much to reduce France's territory; whether an indemnity should be imposed and if so, how much; or if the Bourbons or some other claimant like Bernadotte should take the throne. Along with most of the allies, the British reluctantly backed the restoration of Bourbon rule, while Alexander leaned toward Bernadotte. For weeks, they passionately debated these issues without agreeing. Eventually they agreed to reduce France to its 'ancient limits' and restore the Bourbons without imposing an indemnity.

Castlereagh got the allied sovereigns to sublimate their differences with a treaty that bound Britain, Russia, Austria, and Prussia beyond any peace treaty with France. Under the Treaty of Chaumont signed on 9 March but dated 1 March, each state would maintain 150,000 troops for at least another year, which Britain would subsidise by splitting £5,000,000 equally among the other three in monthly payments. Their alliance would last twenty years, with each immediately to field 60,000 if France attacked any one of them; Britain could either annually maintain 60,000 troops or split £1,300,000 among the other three.

Russian Foreign Minister Charles von Nesselrode asked Castlereagh to assume Russia's debt to Dutch bankers, which was now £6,000,000. Initially Castlereagh bluntly rejected the request but then reconsidered. He proposed equally splitting the debt among Britain, Holland, and Russia, in return for which the Netherlands would be territorially expanded to more defensible borders that included Belgium. Nesselrode agreed but Prime Minister Liverpool rejected the notion, arguing that Parliament would refuse to add any more foreign debt to Britain's soaring national debt.

Yet another contentious issue arose – the fate of the kingdom of Naples. Napoleon had made Joachim and Caroline Murat, respectively his dashing cavalry commander and sister, the king and queen of Naples, whose territory included the Italian peninsula's southern third and Sicily. The royal couple controlled only the mainland, while the royal couple that Napoleon had displaced ruled Sicily with their capital at Palermo. Murat had accompanied Napoleon on his disastrous 1812 and 1813 campaigns but remained at Naples for the 1814 campaign. Knowing that the allies would eventually crush Napoleon, he decided to join rather than fight the coalition. Murat signed a peace treaty with Austria on 11 January 1814. He then asked for a similar treaty with Britain and promised to march with the coalition against Eugene Beauharnais, the viceroy for Napoleon's Italian kingdom.

Whitehall had always backed Ferdinand IV and Maria Carolina as the legitimate rulers for the entire realm and rejected what they condemned as parvenu usurpers in Naples. Austria's treaty with Murat prompted Liverpool and Castlereagh to reassess British policy. They authorised William Bentinck, the ambassador in Palermo, to forge a deal with Murat. On 3 February, Murat and Bentinck agreed to a ceasefire, alliance, and campaign plan. Murat would lead his army north to join forces with Bentinck after he landed at Livorno with the Sicilian army. Bentinck led his men ashore at Livorno on 8 March, and on 15 March called on all Italians to unite in defence of their rights, a seemingly revolutionary appeal against Murat, Ferdinand, and other monarchs that violated his instructions from Castlereagh. That alienated Bentinck from Murat, Ferdinand, and Austrian Emperor Francis. Nonetheless, the Austrians and Neapolitans defeated Eugene, who fled to exile on 16 April. Bentinck sailed with his men to Genoa and there proclaimed the Genoan Republic's restoration on 26 April. Castlereagh condemned his behaviour and ordered him to return to Palermo, which he did by mid-July.

Meanwhile, Napoleon fought a brilliant campaign against the invaders, quick-marching his small army to trounce repeatedly the converging allied armies of Generals Karl von Schwarzenberg and Gebhard von Blücher in two of three battles from 28 January to 31 March, when the allies captured Paris. Napoleon was at Fontainebleau Palace 40 miles south when Paris fell.

During those same two months in south-west France, Wellington routed Soult at Bayonne's outskirts, then besieged the city as Soult withdrew eastward. Leaving part of his army at Bayonne, Wellington pursued Soult with most of his troops. He defeated Soult at Orthez on 27 February and at Toulouse on 10 April. At Toulouse, Wellington received triumphant news on 14 April.

After the allies captured Paris, former foreign minister Charles-Maurice de Talleyrand-Périgord got the Senate to name himself interim president on 1 April and to depose Napoleon on 2 April. The provisional government convinced several marshals to pressure Napoleon to abdicate. Napoleon did so unconditionally on 6 April. That same day, the Senate proclaimed a constitution it called the Charter and invited Louis XVIII to return to the throne as a constitutional monarch.

Having toppled Napoleon, the key question for the allies now was what to do with him. Alexander pushed for making Napoleon the emperor of the small island of Elba off Italy's central west coast. Britain had never recognised Napoleon as French emperor and Castlereagh had no intention of acknowledging that status, even over a tiny realm. He 'wished to substitute another position in lieu of Elba for the seat of Napoleon's retirement, but none having the quality of security, on which [Alexander] insisted, seemed disposable'.[69] He reluctantly accepted Elba for Napoleon but British officials never addressed him by title other than 'general'. A four-man commission with one from each of the four key allies – Britain, Russia, Austria, and Prussia – would accompany and keep an eye on Napoleon. In the Treaty of Fontainebleau that Napoleon signed on 11 April, he agreed to forsake the French throne forever in return for receiving Elba and an annual French pension of 2,000,000 francs, while Marie Louise received the duchy of Parma and his other family members split 1,000,000 francs annually. On 20 April, Napoleon and his escort set forth on the long road then sail to Elba.

Louis XVIII and his entourage arrived in Paris on 3 May. Castlereagh and most other leaders favoured a soft peace with France to ensure the Bourbon dynasty got off to a relatively financially unburdened start. The Prussians demanded a harsh peace and 169,785,895 francs in reparations just for themselves. Castlereagh explained patiently that Britain had expended £700,000,000 on the war, yet opposed reparations. Eventually, the Prussians yielded. Under the Treaty of Paris that the allies signed with Louis XVIII on 30 May, they recognised the Bourbons as France's ruling family; reduced France to its 1792 borders and returned all its colonies except Saint Lucia, Tobago and Mauritius, which Britain kept from France and the Cape of Good Hope from Holland, while Santo Domingo reverted to Spain; required France annually to subsidise Napoleon with 2 million francs and the rest of the Bonaparte clan with 1 million francs; and called on all European nations to convene for a general peace congress at Vienna that autumn.[70]

Chapter 10

Seventh, 1815

The cause of the Allies is the cause of all nations.
[Robert Castlereagh, Viscount Castlereagh]

God be praised! I have set my foot upon the land which has saved us all.
[Alexander I]

The Congress of Vienna was not assembled for the discussion of moral principles, but for great practical purposes, to establish effectual provisions for the general security. *[Robert Castlereagh, Viscount Castlereagh]*

Mounted on a white horse and accompanied by his staff, General Arthur Wellesley, Duke of Wellington, rode into Paris on 4 May. He did not stay long. He and his officers left Paris on the 17th, bound for Spain on a critical diplomatic mission. Henry Wellesley offered this tease to his older brother: 'After all you have come through, you will find diplomacy a very pretty amusement.'[1] From 24 May to 8 June, Wellington did what he could to prevent Ferdinand VII from reversing the liberal reforms and 1812 Constitution of the Cortes. Wellington damned the king with faint praise, describing him as 'by no means the idiot he is represented'.[2] Nonetheless, Wellington's first diplomatic foray failed. The king established a tyranny.

Wellington returned to Paris as Britain's ambassador on 22 August 1814. Three weeks after arriving, he informed Foreign Secretary Robert Stewart, Viscount Castlereagh, that all 'goes well here. I think we are getting a little unpopular in the town, but I don't think that circumstance is of much importance.'[3] This sojourn's most lasting contribution to British interests involved real estate rather than diplomacy. On 1 November, Wellington bought the Hotel de Charon, also known as the Hotel Borghese, on the Rue du Faubourg Saint-Honoré. The seller was Pauline Borghese, Napoleon's beautiful, promiscuous sister. Pauline sweet-talked Wellington into paying 861,500 francs, twice what she had paid for it. Lost to history is just what array of her irresistible feminine charm Pauline wielded to sweeten the deal. Wellington paid Pauline out of his own pocket, bulging with Parliament's £400,000 gift to assist the duke's housing needs.[4] That magnificent building has housed Britain's embassy ever since.

Meanwhile, Russian Tsar Alexander I, Prussian King Frederick III, Klemens von Metternich, and their entourages journeyed to England on 6 June and sojourned in London for several weeks of official celebrations and diplomacy. Of them the tsar received the most public acclaim. Britons understood that no land power and its leader was more responsible for Napoleon's defeat than Russia and its tsar. For his part, Alexander was generous in ascribing salvation powers to Britain. Upon disembarking at Dover, he joyfully declared, 'God be praised! I have set my foot upon the land which has saved us all.'[5]

* * *

Whitehall still had another war to end.[6] Two years earlier, the United States had declared war against Britain. Since then that war had been an expensive sideshow. The number of troops, warships, treasure, and lost merchant ships and trade strained but did not break Britain's relentless war against Napoleon. The British won more land battles than they lost. Perhaps the best general was Isaac Brock, who captured an American army at Detroit on 16 August 1812, and repelled an American invasion across the Niagara River on 13 October; Brock was among the dead. The most humiliating defeat the British inflicted on the Americans was General Robert Ross's army capturing and burning Washington City on 24 August 1814. Yet, the Americans did score some decisive land victories. On 5 October 1813, General William Harrison defeated a British and Indian army at the battle of the Thames that captured a region of western Ontario and crushed the Northwest Indian Confederation. An American army led by General Samuel Smith repelled an attempted siege of Baltimore on 15 September 1814. American warships and troops led respectively by Captain Thomas Macdonough and General Alexander Macomb blunted attacks by British warships and troops led by Commodore George Downie and General George Prevost at Plattsburg on Lake Champlain on 13 September 1814.

The Americans proved far more formidable enemies at sea than the French. Indeed, American captains won two of three sea battles against the British. The greatest victory was the Battle of Put-in-Bay on Lake Erie, when Captain Oliver Perry's fleet battered and captured Captain Robert Barclay's entire fleet of two frigates, one brig, two schooners, and a sloop. These were all combats between frigates or brigs because the Americans had no ships of the line. After surrendering to Captain Stephen Decatur, Captain John Carden exclaimed: 'I am an undone man. I am the first British naval officer that has struck his flag to an American.' Decatur replied: 'You are mistaken, sir; our

Guerriere has been taken by us, and the flag of a frigate was struck before ours.'[7]

Tragically, America's greatest victory occurred after the peace treaty was signed. General Andrew Jackson devastated the British-backed Creek Confederacy in central Alabama in 1814, then marched to New Orleans after learning of a British expedition dispatched to capture it. Admiral Alexander Cochrane explained how capturing New Orleans could advance Britain's war goals and expand the empire: 'I have it much at heart to give them a complete drubbing before peace is made, when I trust their northern limits will be circumscribed and the command of the Mississippi be wrested from them.'[8] Jackson massed his men in redoubts behind a shallow quarter mile-long canal between a swamp and the Mississippi River a dozen miles south of the city. The Americans inflicted 2,034 casualties while suffering just sixty-two when General Edward Pakenham launched a massive assault on 8 January 1815.

Nonetheless, the Americans were often their own worst enemies, especially in the economic warfare that Whitehall had mastered. For instance, Jefferson's 1807 embargo devastated America's economy, not Britain's. In 1791, Treasury Secretary Alexander Hamilton established the Bank of the United States, modelled after Britain's Bank of England. President Madison and a Republican Party congressional majority eliminated that bank in 1811, citing their minimalist federal government philosophy. That cost America's economy $7 million worth of gold, which returned to European investors. During the 1812 War, prices soared for goods that could not be made in the United States and became less available as the Royal Navy scoured the seas of American ships and blockaded American ports.

Among the many ways the Madison administration figuratively shot itself in the foot during the 1812 War was letting some American trade persist with the enemy. Britain's Achilles heel was food. Feeding steadily climbing numbers of soldiers and sailors, most enlisted from farming or fishing communities, became more difficult. Britain's soils, pastures, and surrounding seas could not produce enough to fill all its civilian and military stomachs. Napoleon's Continental System that outlawed trade with Britain reduced European imports to high-priced smuggled goods that rarely included food. Whitehall had to close its food gap with imports from the United States. That gave America's government a powerful card to play against Whitehall's policy of confiscating its merchant ships, cargos, and sailors. Indeed, the British army could not have fought the Peninsular War for five years without American grain and other provisions. American grain shipments rose from 80,000 bushels in 1807 to 900,000 in 1812, 940,000 in 1813, and 970,000 in 1814.[9] By tolerating this trade, the White House tossed away perhaps its strongest economic card in pressuring Whitehall on its confiscation and impressment policy.

Canada also depended on American grain, cattle, and other provisions to survive the 1812 War. Although the White House and Congress forbade this trade, smuggling persisted and was crucial in helping keep Canada in the fight against the United States. In 1814 and 1815, the Americans paid $3,800,000 to Canadians for desperately needed, mostly manufactured products.[10] General George Izard complained to War Secretary John Armstrong that the roads to Canada are 'covered with Droves of Cattle and the River with Rafts destined for the enemy ... Were it not for these supplies the British forces in Canada would be suffering from famine, or their government subject to enormous expense for their maintenance.'[11] That was no exaggeration. General George Prevost wrote to Secretary at War Henry Bathurst that: 'Two thirds of the British Army in Canada are, at this Moment, eating beef provided by American contractors drawn principally from the States of Vermont and New York.'[12]

The Americans were not alone in aiding their enemy. Whitehall did nothing to shut off loans by British bankers and investors to the American government. The largest loan was $7 million, by Baring Brothers.[13] All along, the British welcomed the gold and silver with which Americans paid for products, thus enriching the treasury of the country that they warred against. They also welcomed the grain, cattle, and other provisions for British soldiers and subjects alike. To encourage this flow along with the region's anti-war sentiments, the Admiralty did not extend its blockade of America's Gulf and Atlantic coasts to New England until April 1814.

Perhaps Britain's most important victory of the 1812 War was bloodless, between trappers rather than soldiers, and eventually immensely profitable. On 12 November 1813, the New York-based Pacific Fur Company officers agreed to sell Fort Astoria, their trading post at the Columbia River mouth, to John McTavish, the Montreal-based Northwest Fur Company's field leader. On 30 November, the HMS *Racoon* dropped anchor and Captain William Black stepped ashore to rename Fort Astoria Fort George. The Americans and British would struggle for control of the Columbia River watershed for another four decades, and the result would have enormous consequences for the national power of both countries.

Prime Minister Liverpool found himself glancing back and forth from across the Channel to across the Atlantic. He worried that 'our war with America will probably now be of some duration. We owe it ... not to make enemies in other quarters if we can avoid it, for I cannot but feel apprehensive that some of our European allies will not be indisposed to favour the

Americans.'[14] In November 1813, Foreign Secretary Castlereagh wrote to Secretary of State Monroe of his willingness 'to enter upon a direct negotiation for the restoration of Peace ... upon principles of perfect reciprocity not inconsistent with the established maxims of Public Law, and with the maritime rights of the British Empire'.[15] They agreed to send peace talk envoys to Ghent. The American team included Henry Clay, the Speaker of the House of Representatives; Jonathan Russell the minister in London; John Quincy Adams, the minister in St Petersburg; treasury secretary Albert Gallatin; and senator James Bayard. In contrast to America's diplomatic A-team, Whitehall designated the decidedly lacklustre trio of William Adams, Henry Goulburn, and James Gambier, a doctor, politician, and admiral, respectively, to represent Britain. Castlereagh tried to micromanage the negotiations from London. That was almost immediately obvious to the frustrated Americans. Adams characterised the three envoys as 'little more than a medium of communication between us and the British Privy Council'.[16]

The negotiations proceeded in two stages broken by a long recess. The Americans and British first met on 8 August 1814. Three British demands were deal breakers – the Americans must accept impressment; the transfer to Britain of half of Maine's coast; and a swath of inviolable Indians territory south of the Great Lakes to buffer Canada from the United States. When the Americans rejected all three demands, the talks deadlocked.

Resolve in Whitehall for a tough peace was softening. Most minds widened at the Treasury's estimate that another year's military operations in North America would cost £10 million. The ministers also recognised that negotiations in Ghent and Vienna subtly influenced each other, with the Europeans, especially the Russians, seeing the David versus Goliath war between America and Britain as unjustified on practical or moral grounds. A breakthrough in Ghent might make deals easier to reach in Vienna. Liverpool explained that 'the negotiations are not proceeding in the way we could wish, and this consideration itself was deserving of some weight in deciding the question of peace with America'.[17]

The Americans had an unexpected ally in Arthur, Duke of Wellington. Liverpool tried to talk him into going to North America and take command of British forces. Wellington did not want to do so but packaged his reluctance in a way that at once made his appointment unlikely and did not jeopardise any future military, diplomatic, or political plums. He explained that: 'I feel no objection in going to America though I don't promise myself much success there.' He then insisted that 'you have no right ... to demand any concession of territory from America'.[18]

That was enough for Liverpool, who on 18 November, informed Castlereagh that: 'We have determined, if all other points can be satisfactorily settled, not to continue the war for the purpose of obtaining or securing any acquisition of territory.'[19] This gave the British delegation the leeway for the horse-trading vital for a breakthrough. The negotiations reopened on 1 December, after being suspended for nearly three and a half months since 19 August. It still took three weeks of tough bargaining before they settled all issues. Appropriately, the envoys bequeathed their nations the best of gifts when they signed the Treaty of Ghent on Christmas Eve 1814, then celebrated peace with a banquet.

The Treaty of Ghent's essence was status quo ante bellum, or the restoration of the pre-war borders. Each side would evacuate the other's territory and leave any spoils behind. All prisoners would be returned as soon as possible. Any prizes taken twelve days after ratification off America's coast to three months in distant seas would be released. Each side pledged to negotiate a just peace with its Indian tribes. Commissions would be formed to negotiate lingering border and debt disputes. Finally, both sides agreed to co-operate against the international slave trade. There was no mention of impressment.

Prince Regent George signed the treaty on Christmas Day 1814. After receiving the treaty, Madison sent it to the Senate on 15 February 1815. The following day, all thirty-five senators voted for ratification. Secretary of State Monroe exchanged ratified versions of the treaty with British minister Anthony Baker on 17 February.

That exchange officially re-established peace after two years and eight months of a war that was virtually impossible to justify on any rational grounds. The only concrete gains that the Americans got was crushing the north-west and south-west Indian tribes alliances and occupying West Florida. The British could not point to any concrete gains beyond Astoria, only losses in devastated lives, property, and forgone economic opportunities. Indeed, Whitehall did not want war with the United States. Washington's declaration forced Whitehall to divert ever more financial, army, and navy assets from warring against Napoleon's empire to warring against the United States. Typically, the only clear winners on either side were contractors who enriched themselves, but virtually everyone else was worse off.

If militarily the war was a draw, Britain inflicted far more economic damage on the United States than it sustained by capturing its trade and burning its towns. The war officially cost the United States $158 million, including $93 million for the army and navy, $16 million in interest payments on loans, and $49 million in veteran benefits. America's national debt skyrocketed from

$45 million in 1812 to $127 million in 1815. To fight its war, the Republicans raised virtually all the money from loans rather than taxes. And for that the Madison administration paid a Shylock's price for those loans figuratively and literally – of the $80 million borrowed, Washington received only $34 million in hard coin, with the rest covered by discounts and paper money.[20]

Ironically, Thomas Jefferson himself, whose principles and policies marched the United States toward the precipice, admitted that the 1812 War 'arrested the course of the most remarkable tide of prosperity any nation ever experienced'. Typically, that was an exaggeration. America's economy actually prospered more during the 1790s when Hamiltonism prevailed, than from 1801 to 1812, when Jeffersonism determined policies. Less inaccurate was his next assertion that the war 'has closed such prospects of future improvement ... Farewell all hopes of extinguishing public debt! Farewell all visions of applying surpluses of revenue to the improvements of peace rather than the ravages of war.'[21]

Despite, or likely because of the economic losses, the war did boost national pride. American propagandists papered over all the humiliating disasters, deaths, destruction, and debt by absurdly insisting that the United States had won a second war of independence. Canadians, typically, were more modest; they took quiet pride in defeating virtually every American invasion of their territory. As for British public opinion, relief was undoubtedly the prevailing sentiment.

* * *

Delegates to the Congress of Vienna began arriving in September.[22] Foreign Secretary Castlereagh appeared on 11 September. Eventually, the official attendees peaked with 215 heads of state and around 1,400 others, although the numbers varied over time as people came and went. The Congress was no mere conference but a virtually non-stop party of balls, banquets, concerts, teas, seductions, and espionage.

Castlereagh later explained that: 'The Congress of Vienna was not assembled for the discussion of moral principles, but for great practical purposes, to establish effectual provisions for the general security.'[23] The four great powers – Britain, Russia, Austria, and Prussia represented respectively by Castlereagh, State Secretary Karl von Nesselrode, Chancellor Klemons von Metternich, and Foreign Minister Karl von Hardenberg – agreed on 20 September that they would make all the key decisions as a Council of Four and draft them into a treaty that they and all the other delegations would ratify. Foreign Minister Charles-Maurice Talleyrand-Périgord arrived on 23 September and met with the Council of Four on 30 September, during which he demanded that France be equally represented as a fellow great power and ally. Castlereagh observed that Talleyrand's assertive attitude excited 'distrust and alarm with respect to the views of France; and ... the effect of this had been to deprive him of his just and natural influence for the purposes of moderating excessive pretentions, whilst it united all to preserve the general system'.[24]

The Council of Four initially rejected that demand, eventually accepted it on 31 December but even then Talleyrand did not join them as the Council of Five until 12 January. Meanwhile, the issues were split among ten committees dominated by the Council of Four but with members from other states with an interest in the issues that committee addressed. Supplementing the Council of Four was the Council of Eight that included them along with France, Spain, Sweden, and Portugal.

Early in the Congress, Castlereagh formed a good working relationship with Talleyrand and Metternich. Indeed, the five powers soon split in interests between Britain, France, and Austria on one side and Russia and Prussia on the other. For Castlereagh, Alexander proved to be the most formidable foreign leader. He was just twenty-three years old when a cabal murdered his father and crowned him tsar on 23 March 1801. The British welcomed that coup for deposing mercurial, despotic Paul and replacing him with an initially pliable Alexander. He was bright, idealistic, gentle, shy, and unprepared to rule an empire but over the next dozen years gradually matured as a statesman. As a coalition partner, Whitehall viewed Russia as the equivalent power on land that Britain was at sea.[25] Russia failed to realise that hope as Napoleon inflicted humiliating defeats in 1805 and 1807. The Tilsit treaty that Alexander signed in July 1807 made him Napoleon's junior partner. Napoleon's massive invasion and subsequent devastating defeat in 1812 transformed Alexander. He had presided over that stunning victory that cost hundreds of thousands of dead, crippled, and displaced Russians. He saw Russia and himself as Europe's saviours, a vision that swelled with the victories of 1813 and 1814.

Whitehall now viewed Alexander and Russia as a threat that demanded a shift in British foreign policy. In late November, Prime Minister Liverpool wrote to Castlereagh of his worry that 'the course the negotiations were taking with Russia might unintentionally lead us further than we had any idea of going, and eventually produce a renewal of the war in Europe. It may be quite true that if the Emperor of Russia does not relax his present demands, the peace of Europe may not be of long continuance.'[26] In assessing 'the different courts of Europe,' he concluded that 'the King of France is ... the only Sovereign in whom we can have any real confidence. The Emperor of

Russia is profligate from vanity and self-sufficiency, if not from principle. This King of Prussia may be a well-meaning man, but he is the dupe of the Emperor of Russia. The Emperor of Austria I believe to be an honest man, but he has a Minister [Metternich] in whom no one can trust, who considers all policy as consisting in finesse and trick, and who has got his government and himself into more difficulties by his devices than could have occurred from a plain course of dealing.'[27]

Alexander and Frederick William backed each other's demands respectively to take over all of Poland and Saxony. Castlereagh, Talleyrand, and Metternich heatedly opposed that vast expansion of Russian and Prussian power.[28] To prevent that, they formed the Triple Alliance on 3 January 1815, with each committing 150,000 troops against Russia and Prussia, and inviting Bavaria, Hanover, and the Netherlands to join them, which they did respectively on 13, 19, and 23 January. Although the alliance was secret, they ensured that word of it reached Nesselrode and Hardenberg. The brinksmanship worked. Alexander and Frederick William backed down and made concessions. Poland would become a constitutional monarchy with the tsar its king. Prussia settled for two fifths of Saxony rather than all of it. With enormous relief, Castlereagh wrote to Liverpool on 5 January that, 'The alarm of war is over.'[29]

Liverpool believed that Castlereagh had resolved most of the Congress's major issues and needed his political support in London. In mid-January, he recalled Castlereagh and instructed Wellington to replace him in Vienna. Castlereagh resented being replaced before finishing his work. He urged Liverpool that: 'I should not be withdrawn from hence at least till the important discussions now pending are closed. With every deference to the Duke of Wellington's ability and great personal authority, he cannot at once replace me in the habits of confidential intercourse which a long residence with the principal actors has established, and which gives facilities to my intervention to bring them together ... whereas the fate of Europe may depend on the conclusions of the ensuring month.'[30]

Liverpool explained that Castlereagh's talents were urgently needed back home: 'You can have no idea how much ground the Government lost in the House of Commons ... I can assure you that I feel ... the greatest reluctance in proposing to you to withdraw at this moment from Vienna. Last year we could spare you, everything was quiet in Parliament.'[31] Wellington left Paris on 24 January and reached Vienna on 3 February. Castlereagh departed Vienna on 15 February.

Wellington largely shared Castlereagh's views on British foreign policy's ends and means. He saw 'England and France as arbitrators at the Congress, if those Powers understand each other; and such an understanding may preserve the general peace.'[32] He favoured a monarchy over a republic: 'Revolutionary France is more likely to distress the world than France, however strong in her frontier, under a regular Government; and that is the situation in which we ought to endeavour to place her.'[33] He insisted that: 'The establishment of any other government than the King's in France [would] inevitably lead to new and endless wars.'[34] Wellington's candor, unpretentiousness, and, vitally, view of monarchial France as a natural British ally impressed Talleyrand, relieved that he 'never indulged in that parade of mystification which is generally employed by ambassadors: watchfulness, prudence, and experience of human nature were the only means he employed; and it is not surprising that, by the use of these simple agencies, he acquired great influence.'[35]

Among the more perplexing problems was what to do about Joachim Murat, the brother-in-law that Napoleon installed atop the Neapolitan throne. With Murat the British were caught between two conflicting interests, honouring a treaty and deposing a pest. British ambassador William Bentinck and Murat had signed an alliance treaty on 3 February 1814. Liverpool explained that to legally 'discharge us from all our obligations toward him,' Murat had blatantly to display 'treachery or willful and culpable inactivity' in fulfilling his treaty duties. Then, the next question was: 'How are we to get rid of him?' Liverpool and his inner cabinet finally decided that 'it would be more safe and prudent for the Powers of Europe to tolerate Murat than for any of them to undertake hostilities for the purpose of expelling him'.[36] Castlereagh and Wellington leaned toward dethroning him, ideally with a generous pension, but if necessary, through violence. Wellington pointed out that if Murat 'were gone, Buonaparte in Elba would not be an object of great dread'.[37] To Castlereagh's latest nudging in that direction, Liverpool insisted on the 'absolute impracticability of Great Britain engaging in war for the purpose of driving Murat from Naples. England is at this moment peace mad and thinking only of the reduction of taxes.' It was 'impossible after so long a contest to expect them to be sensible of all the inconveniences of leaving Murat on the throne of Naples'.[38]

A less contentious issue was abolition of the international slave trade. Castlereagh had placed that on the agenda in conformity with Parliament's unanimous resolution on 2 May 1814 that the European powers join Britain in ending the trade. With Talleyrand backing Castlereagh, the Council of Eight established a committee to study the issue on 10 December 1814. That committee issued a declaration that condemned the international slave trade on 8 February 1815.

* * *

Bombshell news that Napoleon had escaped Elba reached Vienna on 7 March. Napoleon had indeed decided to return to France and retake the throne. He did so believing that he had nothing to lose. After reaching Elba on 6 May 1814, he typically engaged in a flurry of administrative, financial, economic, military, and infrastructure reforms but soon ran out of money to finish them. Louis XVIII's government refused to send him or his family pensions required by the Treaty of Paris. He was soon bored and depressed to be ruling a petty island after having conquered and run an empire that spanned most of Europe. Austrian Emperor Francis I severed any communication between Napoleon and his wife Marie Louise and their son, whom he kept in Vienna. Rumours reached him that Marie Louise was enjoying a torrid affair with dashing Count Alfred von Neipperg and that the allies were considering transferring him to remote Saint Helena in the south Atlantic Ocean. He learned of worsening discontent with Louis XVIII's regime. On 26 February, he packed around 1,000 troops and officials into a small flotilla and set sail for France. On 1 March, he disembarked with his men near Antibes and marched north. Louis XVIII ordered his army to crush Napoleon but instead every regiment that Napoleon encountered on his route joined him. Louis XVIII and his court fled on 19 March and Napoleon triumphantly entered Paris the next day. His charisma, audacity, and luck had won back his throne without a shot fired.

The initial reaction among the delegates mingled dread and disbelief, followed by decisive acts. Castlereagh instructed Wellington on British policy and the diplomacy to follow: 'The re-establishment of Buonaparte's authority is deemed incompatible with the peace and security of Europe; and he trusts that the Powers, who have so gloriously conquered the peace will concur with him such efforts to restore it.' The first step was that the sovereigns at Vienna 'should publish a joint declaration, announcing their determination to maintain inviolable the Peace of Paris'.[39] Wellington conveyed those views to the coalition leaders. On 13 March, the Council of Eight issued a declaration that condemned Napoleon as an international outlaw for violating his abdication agreement and the Treaty of Paris. Under a treaty signed on 25 March, Britain, Russia, Austria, and Prussia each pledged to field 150,000 troops until Napoleon was defeated, while Whitehall would subsidise its allies with £5,000,000 split equally among them. Soon, the British promised its allies another £4,000,000.[40] Wellington was assigned to command an army of British and Dutch troops in Flanders, where Marshal Gerhard von Blücher would join him with a Prussian army. Meanwhile, the Austrians, Russians, and German states would mobilise their armies and march toward France.

Bonaparte's escape naturally provoked the coalition leaders to worry whether Murat might aid him. Whitehall now decided that Murat had to go.[41] Murat aided his own demise by declaring war against Austria on 15 March, and marching north to announce at Rimini on 30 March, Italy's unification under his rule. On 3 May, the Austrians routed Murat's army at Tolentino, pursued relentlessly, marched into Naples on 23 May, and returned Ferdinand IV to power. Murat sailed to exile to Corsica, tarried, then returned with a handful of followers. He was caught and executed by firing squad at Pizzo on 13 October.

Napoleon's last military campaign was his shortest and most inept. His plan was to drive his 125,000-man army between the armies of Wellington and Blücher, then defeat each separately, capture Brussels, then call for negotiations with the coalition. He launched his offensive on 14 June. Two days later, one wing routed the Prussians at Ligny while Wellington blunted the other at Quatre Bras. Wellington withdrew his army to a low ridge a mile south of Waterloo, a village 15 miles from Brussels, as Blücher marched his battered army to join him. Heavy rains on 17 June slowed Napoleon's pursuit. It was not until early afternoon on 18 June that he launched a series of attacks against Wellington's army, with each repelled. In late afternoon, Blücher's lead corps attacked Napoleon's right flank as Wellington attacked his front. The allies routed the French army, inflicting 42,000 casualties while the armies of Wellington and Blücher suffered 17,000 and 7,000 respective casualties.

Napoleon fled the battlefield for Paris, arriving on 21 June. Led by Joseph Fouche, the Senate forced him to sign an abdication declaration on 22 June. He lingered for several days at Malmaison, the chateau of his first wife and empress Josephine, who had died the previous year. On 29 June, he headed to Rochefort, hoping to board a ship bound for exile in America. Behind him in Paris, the French government capitulated on 3 July, allied troops marched into Paris on 7 July, and the next day, Louis XVIII entered Paris once again in the baggage train of a victorious allied army that he did nothing to aid. Napoleon surrendered to Captain Frederick Maitland of the HMS *Bellerophon* on 15 July. Maitland sailed for Plymouth and there awaited Whitehall's instructions for what to do with his prisoner. On 28 July, Whitehall announced that Napoleon would be exiled under guard at Saint Helena.

Napoleon's 'hundred days campaign' had little effect on the Congress of Vienna. On 9 June, nearly all the delegates signed the concluding 121-article treaty, called the Final Act. British diplomacy triumphed as the treaty restored Europe's dynamic balance of power and enhanced Low Country security. Not surprisingly, the biggest winners were the great powers with restored or expanded territory as Russia took Poland as an autonomous kingdom under the tsar; Prussia took two fifths of Saxony; Austria directly took Lombardy and Venetia, and indirectly as the Habsburgs took Parma and Tuscany; and the Netherlands took Belgium and the stadholder became king. The treaty recognised the restoration of former ruling families to the kingdoms of Piedmont-Sardinia and the Two Sicilies. The thirty-eight-state Rhine Confederation was transformed into a German Diet with Prussia and Austria as members. Switzerland received permanent neutrality status. A clause condemned the international slave trade and required signatories to end their participation within five years. Britain restored all its captured colonies except Saint Lucia and Tobago, which it retained from France, Trinidad from Spain, and Berbice, Demerara, and Essequibo from the Netherlands. Hanover became a kingdom and Britain's George III became the monarch of his ancestral realm. The signing of the Final Act was the only time that all the delegations actually convened together.

Tsar Alexander coped with the horrors of war, duties of office, and affronts of liberalism and nationalism with a deepening spiritual messianism. He sought to transform the coalition with its pragmatic goals of destroying Napoleon and restoring Europe's power balance into a Holy Alliance committed to crushing any revolutionary movements that challenged the divine right of absolute rule for himself and others who claimed it. To that end, he got Frederick William and Francis to agree to lead such a Holy Alliance as the respective upholders of the Orthodox, Protestant, and Catholic versions of Christianity. Louis XVIII enthusiastically accepted the tsar's invitation to join them.

Alexander's pitch to Castlereagh and Wellington provoked a very different response. Castlereagh admitted to Liverpool that he and the duke had struggled 'not without difficulty ... through the interview with becoming gravity'. He explained that Alexander had recently 'taken a deeply religious tinge' and his 'mind is not completely sound'. Although Castlereagh scorned the Holy Alliance as 'a piece of sublime mysticism and nonsense,' he committed Britain to it.[42] He agreed with Metternich's assessment that 'good may come of indulging the Emperor, and that real danger might result to the Alliance from a refusal'.[43] Those who signed the Treaty of Paris on 26 September 1815 committed themselves to: 'Regulation of their internal and external relations by the respective Sovereigns upon the Principle of the Christian Religion – mutual assistance, aid, and succours as Brothers.'

As the antidote to the Holy Alliance, Castlereagh spearheaded negotiations that led to two very pragmatic treaties signed at Paris on 20 November 1815.

Under the Treaty of Paris, France had to pay an indemnity of 700,000,000 francs over five years and underwrite a coalition occupation force of 150,000 troops during that time. Under the Quadruple Alliance Treaty, Britain, Austria, Prussia, and Russia reaffirmed their alliance established at Chaumont on 1 March 1814, amended by the new commitment to a 'restoration of confidence between France and neighbouring states'. With these two treaties Britain and the other great powers imposed and pledged to uphold peace with France.

The military alliance that Britain expended so much diplomacy, treasure, and military might to build and sustain was supposed to last two decades but slowly unravelled over the next decade. However, the security system of shared values and co-operation established by the Congress of Vienna and soon called the concert of Europe prevented a war between great powers for a generation and a continental-wide war for nearly another century.[44]

Chapter 11

Legacies

> England is not to be saved by any single man. England has saved herself by her exertions, and will, as I trust, save Europe by her example.
> [*William Pitt*]

Britain built and led seven coalitions against France from 1783 to 1793. Napoleon defeated the first five, but the sixth briefly and seventh permanently defeated and removed him from power. None of those coalitions would have been established or endured as long as they did without Britain's dynamic mix of hard or physical power – financial, commercial, manufacturing, naval, and geographic – and soft or psychological power, namely that of outstanding statesmen and generals. Both forms of power were crucial. Napoleon might well have lived out his life as France's emperor without the military brilliance of Wellington on land and Nelson on sea, along with the political brilliance of Pitt in Whitehall devising policies that developed and asserted Britain's hard power from 1783 to 1801 and 1804 to 1806.

Transforming Europe's traditional shifting imbalance of contending powers into a concert of co-operating powers imposed its own share of challenges for British policymakers. Britain and the other great powers managed a series of political crises that threatened the peace during Congresses at Aix-la-Chapelle (Aachen) in 1818, Troppau in 1820, and Laibach (Ljubljana) in 1821. William Grenville complained in 1822 that: 'We are mixed up in the affairs of the Continent in a manner we have never been before, which entails upon us endless negotiations and enormous expenses. We have associated ourselves with the members of the Holy Alliance, and countenanced acts of ambition and despotism in such a manner as to have drawn upon us the detestation of the nations of the Continent, and our conduct toward them at the close of the war has brought a stain upon our character for bad faith and desertion which no time will wipe away and the recollection of which will never be effaced from their minds.'[1]

British policymakers expended vast amounts of treasure and blood struggling to build and lead those seven coalitions because it served their national interests. Much as America did from the Second World War, Britain emerged from the revolutionary and Napoleonic era with its government, military, economy, and nation far stronger than a generation earlier.[2] The gap in economic power between Britain and all its rivals widened steadily. To varying degrees, war devastated the economies of Russia, Austria, Prussia, France, and the United States. England, Scotland, and Wales were spared invasion, although war devastated Ireland in 1798 and several West Indian colonies.

Ideally, war paid for itself. Although Whitehall never pulled that off, its attempts to do so certainly lowered the costs. Capturing enemy and neutral warships, merchant ships, markets, and colonies yielded the most profits and savings. The sharp rise in government spending during the revolutionary and Napoleonic wars at once expanded and distorted the economy. Whitehall helped develop the nation's economic infrastructure, especially with new canals and docks. In London, engineers built three state-of-the-art wharf and warehouse complexes: the West India Dock in 1802, the London Dock in 1805, and the East India Dock in 1806. Manufacturing's scale, efficiency, productivity, and profits climbed. For instance, musket production rose from 40,000 in 1803 to 270,000 in 1809.[3]

War was mostly good for business, especially for buying and selling in foreign markets. Trade is a zero-sum game in which one nation's gain is another's loss. With the Royal Navy dominating the seas, British trade soared from the war's eve of 1788–92, with £18,862,000 of imports, £15,315,000 of exports, and £5,600,000 of re-exports to 1798–1802, when, after a decade of war, there were £29,901,000 of imports, £24,145,000 exports, and £16,083,000 of re-exports.[4] The British also reaped vast profits from their conquests. For instance, in 1808, Britain imported from the West Indies goods worth £7,067,626, including £3,867,704 of sugar, £2,123,288 of coffee, and £349,467 of cotton; of that, vanquished colonies accounted for £2,479,251, including £1,170,858 of sugar, £861,018 of coffee, and £244,188 of cotton.[5]

Being the arsenal of monarchies threatened or conquered by France was an enormous assertion of economic power. The government's budget soared from £38,956,917, including £10,211,376 for the navy and £8,935,753 for the army in 1803, to peak at £117,587,079, including £33,795,556 for the army, £21,961,566 for the navy, £10,024,618 in subsidies to allies, £4,480,729 for ordnance, and £138,494 for militia and deserters' warrants in 1814.[6] Nowhere was that more sustained and expensive than in the Peninsula, where Portugal and Spain respectively received more than £10,000,000 and £6,000,000 in subsidies from 1808 to 1814. Conveying all the supplies needed to sustain British, Portuguese, and Spanish forces required 13,500 individual ship voyages among 400 convoys.[7] Yet, all that spending stimulated the economy.

Revenues rose with the economy, thus helping Whitehall pay for the war. The rest was borrowed from the Bank of England and an array of financiers. Two financiers were critical – Alexander Baring and Nathan Rothschild; both had international networks of agents who changed money profitably, gathered intelligence, and shared both with Whitehall.

After Waterloo, Whitehall steadily reduced spending, bureaucrats, soldiers, and sailors. The military accounted for £72,000,000 of £112,900,000 total government spending in 1815, bottomed out at £15,700,000 of £57,600,000 in 1819, then rose slightly to £16,700,000 of £57,500,000 in 1820, and remained £16,700,000 of a slightly larger budget of £58,400,000 in 1822.[8] Whitehall gradually reduced the army from 234,000 troops or 2.5 per cent of the population in 1815 to 115,000 or 1.1 per cent in 1820.[9]

The short-term effect of demobilising most of the army and fleet along with cutting back government procurement sharply caused joblessness to soar and prices to plummet. Compounding that was the 1815 Corn Law that protected farmers by imposing high tariffs on low-priced foreign imports. A disastrous harvest in 1815 led to worsening food shortages and inflation. The number of poor, homeless, jobless, and criminals soared. All that provoked food riots in London and other cities. Yet by 1816, the economy recovered and expanded steadily again and the lives of most people improved.

As for naval power, only three nations ended the era with more warships than they began, Britain, its ally Portugal, and its enemy the United States. The wars depleted, often drastically, the naval power of the other states. The Royal Navy was invariably responsible for those decimations. Intrepid captains accounted for scores of warships that swelled the Royal Navy. They battered, captured, and towed enemy and mostly French warships to ports, where the vessels were repaired, rechristened, reflagged, and recrewed.

Likewise, the British empire expanded at the expense of its rivals. The number of British colonies nearly doubled from twenty-six in 1792 to forty-three in 1815. During the war's second decade, the British retook and kept

11.1. Comparison of Naval Power by Tonnage of Ships over 550 Tons[10]

	1790	1815		1790	1815
Britain	458,900	609,300	Sweden	44,800	36,500
France	314,300	228,300	Portugal	40,600	44,400
Spain	242,200	59,900	Naples	21,200	14,900
Russia	181,700	167,300	Venice	20,600	n.a.
Netherlands	117,400	71,400	United States	n.a.	28,500
Denmark	86,000	7,800			

11.2. Population of Britain's West Indian Colonies, 1815[11]

	White	Slave	Free Coloured	Total
Barbados	15,500	75,300	3,000	93,800
Leeward Islands	5,300	72,200	6,200	83,700
Jamaica	27,900	339,800	35,000	402,700
Ceded Islands	5,200	105,200	10,000	120,400
Trinidad	2,500	25,600	7,600	35,700
Demerara	2,800	103,800	4,800	111,400
Marginal Colonies	4,300	21,200	3,800	29,300
Total	63,500	743,100	70,300	877,000

Leeward Islands: Antigua, St Martin, Nevis, St Kitts
Ceded Islands: Tobago, St Lucia, Essequibo, Demerara, Berbice
Marginal Islands: Virgin Islands, Belize, Cayman Islands, Bahamas

11.3. The Expansion of the East India Company's Army, 1793–1815[12]

		1793	1798	1805	1815
Bengal Army	European	5,440	7,389	7,811	12,617
	Native	29,482	40,105	81,257	116,915
Madras Army	European	9,881	11,283	12,990	13,903
	Native	29,914	36,501	68,842	57,741
Bombay Army	European	3,347	3,494	4,090	5,031
	Native	10,265	14,541	17,575	23,906
Total	European	18,768	22,166	24,891	31,611
	Native	69,661	91,147	167,674	195,752
Grand Total		88,429	113,313	192,565	227,183

many of the foreign colonies that they had returned during the first decade, including St Lucia, Essequibo, and Berbice in 1803; Surinam and the Deccan in 1804; Cape of Good Horn in 1806; Curaçao, St Thomas, St Croix, and St John in 1807; Sierra Leone in 1808; Guadeloupe in 1810; Tobago, Demerara, and the Seychelles in 1814; and Tristan da Cunha in 1815. Of course, the takings varied considerably in their relative strategic and economic value. Malta and the Cape of Good Hope were Britain's greatest strategic gains. And when the British did not directly take a colony they, often won the freedom to trade there, as in Portugal's Brazil and Spain's Latin America empire.[13]

In India, the British ruled 40 million people, from whom they annually reaped around £18 million to pay for governing, defending, and suppressing them. The British army included 31,000 regular and 140,000 native troops.

Whitehall ended the East India Company's trade monopoly in 1813. That freed an ever more diverse and dynamic array of businesses to emerge, compete, and expand wealth's creation and distribution.

Leaders struggle to protect or enhance their nation's interests amidst shifting threats and opportunities. Whether they succeed depends on how they mobilise and assert power that overwhelms that of their enemies. The outcome is rarely certain. Prime Minister William Pitt made this prediction in a speech before the House of Commons on 9 November 1805: 'England is not to be saved by any single man. England has saved herself by her exertions, and will, as I trust, save Europe by her example.'[14] Pitt was prescient, although another decade of mass death and destruction would pass before his vision came true. He was confident that Britain ultimately would prevail because he and his colleagues understood his nation's array of geographic, mercantile, naval, manufacturing, and financial powers, and how to assert them.

Notes

Abbreviations

Addington Correspondence – G. Pellew, ed., *The Life and Correspondence of the Right Hon. Henry Addington, 1st Viscount Sidmouth*, 3 vols (London: John Murray, 1897).
ASPFR – American State Papers, Foreign Relations.
Auckland Correspondence – Bishop of Bath and Wells, ed., *The Journal and Correspondence of William, Lord Auckland*, 4 vols (London: R. Bentley, 1861–62).
BL – British Library.
British Diplomacy – C.K. Webster, ed., *British Diplomacy: Select Documents Dealing with the Reconstruction of Europe, 1813–15* (London: G. Bell, 1921).
British Foreign Policy – Harold Temperley and Lillian Penson, eds., *The Foundations of British Foreign Policy* (London: Frank Cass and Company, 1966).
British Statistics – B.R. Mitchell and Phyllis Deane, *Abstract of British Historical Statistics* (Cambridge: Cambridge University Press, 1962).
Castlereagh Correspondence – Charles William Vane, Marquis of Londonderry, ed., *The Correspondence, Despatches, and Other Papers of Viscount Castlereagh, Second Marquis of Londonderry*, 12 vols (London: John Murray, 1848–53).
Chad Conversations – Gerald Wellington, ed., *The Conversations of the First Duke of Wellington with George William Chad* (Cambridge: Cambridge University Press, 1956).
Cornwallis Correspondence – Charles Ross, ed., *The Correspondence of Charles, First Marquis, Cornwallis*, 3 vols (London: John Murray, 1859).
Creevey Papers – John Gore, ed., *The Thomas Creevey Papers* (New York: Macmillan, 1904).
Croker Papers – Louis J. Jennings, ed., *The Croker Papers: The Correspondence and Diaries of John Wilson Croker, Secretary to the Admiralty from 1809 to 1830*, 3 vols (London: John Murray, 1885).
Farington Diary – James Greig, ed., *The Farington Diary*, 8 vols, (London: Hutchinson, 1922).
Fortescue Manuscripts – *Report on the Manuscripts of J.B. Fortescue, esq., preserved at Dropmore*, vols 1–10 (London: *Historical Manuscripts Commission*, 1890–1927).
FO – Foreign Office Home Office.
George III Correspondence – Arthur Aspinall, ed., *The Later Correspondence of George III*, 5 vols (Cambridge: Cambridge University Press, 1962–70).
George, Prince Correspondence – Arthur Aspinall, ed., *The Correspondence of George Prince of Wales, 1770–1812*, 8 vols, (London: Cassell, 1963–71).
George IV Letters – Arthur Aspinall, ed., *The Letters of George IV, 1812–30* (Cambridge: Cambridge University Press, 1938).
Leeds Political Memoranda – Oscar Browning, ed., *The Political Memoranda of Francis Fifth Duke of Leeds* (London: Nicolas and Sons, 1884).

Malmesbury Correspondence – James Harris, Earl Malmesbury, *The Diaries and Correspondence of James Harris, the First Earl of Malmesbury*, 4 vols (London: Richard Bentley, 1845).

Memoirs of the Courts – Duke of Buckingham and Chandos, ed., *Memoirs of the Courts and Cabinets of George the Third*, 2 vols (London: Hurst & Blackett, 1853–55).

Napoleon Correspondence – Thierry Lentz et al., ed., *Napoleon Bonaparte Correspondance Generale*, vols 1–9 (Paris: Fayard, 2004–12).

Nelson Dispatches – Nicolas Harris, ed., *The Dispatches and Letters of Vice-Admiral Lord Viscount Nelson*, 7 vols (Cambridge: Cambridge University Press, 2011).

NYPL – New York Public Library.

Parliamentary Debates – William Cobbett, ed., *Parliamentary Debates*, 22 vols (London: R. Bagshaw, 1804–1812).

Parliamentary Debates from 1803 – T.C. Hansard, ed., *The Parliamentary Debates from the Year 1803*, London: T.C. Hansard, 1812).

Parliamentary History William Cobbett, ed., *The Parliamentary History of England from the Earliest Times to 1803*, 36 vols (London: R. Bagshaw, 1806–20).

Parliamentary Register – John Debrett, ed., *The Parliamentary Register, or, History of the Proceedings and Debates of the House of Commons*, 45 vols 2nd ser. (London: R. Spottiswoode, 1781–96); 3rd ser. 18 vols (London: R. Spottiswoode, 1797–1802).

Pitt-Rutland Correspondence – Rutland, Duke of, *Correspondence between the Right Hon. William Pitt and Charles, Duke of Rutland* (London: R. Spottiswoode, 1842).

Pitt Speeches – *The Speeches of the Right Hon. William Pitt in the House of Commons*, 3 vols (London: Longman, Hurst, and Orne, 1817).

Pitt War Speeches – Richard Copeland, ed., *The War Speeches of William Pitt the Younger* (Oxford: Clarendon, 1918).

PRO – Public Record Office, National Archives.

Rose Correspondence – L.V. Harcourt, ed., *The Diaries and Correspondence of the Right Hon. George Rose* (London: Richard Bentley, 1860).

Smith Correspondence – J. Barrow, ed., *The Life and Correspondence of Admiral Sir William Sidney Smith*, 2 vols (London: Richard Bentley, 1848).

Stanhope Conversations – Philip Henry, fifth earl of Stanhope, *Notes of Conversations with the Duke of Wellington, 1831–1851* (London: John Murray, 1885).

Stanhope, Life of Pitt Philip Henry, fifth earl of Stanhope, Life of the Right Honorable William Pitt, 4 vols (London: John Murray, 1867).

Stanhope Miscellanies – Philip Henry, first earl of Stanhope, *Miscellanies: Collected and Edited by Earl Stanhope* (London: John Murray, 1872).

Spencer Papers – Julian Corbett, ed., *The Private Papers of George, 2nd Earl Spencer*, 2 vols (London: Navy Record Society, 1924).

WO – War Office.

Wellesley-Pole – Charles Webster, ed., *Some Letters of the Duke of Wellington to his Brother, William Wellesley Pole*, Camden Miscellany, Royal Historical Society, vol. 18, 1948.

Wellington Dispatches – Colonel Gurwood, ed., *The Dispatches of Field Marshall the Duke of Wellington*, 8 vols (London: Park, Furnivall, and Parker, 1944).

Wellington Supplements Duke of Wellington, *The Supplementary Despatches, Correspondence, and Memoranda of Field Marshall Arthur, Duke of Wellington*, 15 vols (London: John Murray, 1858–72).

Wraxall Memoir – Nathaniel Wraxall, ed., *The Historical and Posthumous Memoirs of Sir Nathaniel William Wraxall, 1772–1784* (London: Bickers & Sons, 1884).

Introduction

1. For explorations of the nature and application of both general and American national power, see: William Nester, *Globalization: A Short History of the Modern World* (New York: Palgrave Macmillan, 2010); William Nester, *Globalization, Wealth, and Power in the Twenty-First Century* (New York: Palgrave Macmillan, 2010); William Nester, *Globalization, War, and Peace in the Twenty-First Century* (New York: Palgrave Macmillan, 2010). William Nester, *The Revolutionary Years: The Art of American Power During the Early Republic, 1775–1789* (Washington D.C.: Potomac Books, 2011); William Nester, *The Hamiltonian Vision, 1789–1800: The Art of Power in the Early Republic* (Washington D.C.: Potomac Books, 2012); William Nester, *The Jeffersonian Vision, 1800–1815* (Washington D.C.: Potomac Books, 2013).
2. Michael Duffy, *Soldiers, Sugar, and Seapower: The British Expeditions to the West Indies and the War against Revolutionary France* (Oxford: Clarendon Press, 1987), 210.
3. William Wickham to Grenville, 15 April 1800, Fortescue Manuscripts, 6:196.
4. For overviews of British foreign policy that precede or embrace this era, see: Paul Langford, *Modern British Foreign Policy: The Eighteenth Century, 1688–1815* (New York: Vintage, 1976); Jeremy Black, *Natural and Necessary Enemies: Anglo-French Relations in the Eighteenth Century* (Athens: University of Georgia Press, 1986); Jeremy Black, ed., *Knight Errant and True Englishmen: British Foreign Policy, 1660–1800* (Edinburgh: University of Edinburgh Press, 1989); John Clarke, *British Diplomacy and Foreign Policy, 1782–1865: The National Interest* (Boston: Unwin, Hymen, 1989); H.M. Scott, *British Foreign Policy in the Age of the American Revolution* (Oxford: Oxford University Press, 1990); Jeremy Black, *A System of Ambition: British Foreign Policy, 1660–1793* (New York: Longmans, 1993); Jeremy Black, *British Foreign Policy in an Age of Revolution, 1783–1793* (New York: Cambridge University Press, 1994); Jeremy Black, *A System of Ambition?: British Foreign Policy, 1660–1793* (London: Longman, 2000); Linda Colley, *Captives: Britain, Europe, and the World, 1600–1850* (London: Pantheon, 2002); Niall Ferguson, *Empire: How Britain Made the Modern World* (New York: Basic Book, 2004); Brendan Sims, *Three Victories and a Defeat: The Rise and Fall of the First British Empire* (New York: Basic Books, 2007).
For in-depth, diverse analyses of the complexities of early modern British and European relations and power, see: Alfred Thayer Mahan, *The Influence of Sea Power Upon History, 1660–1783* (New York: Barnes and Noble, 2004); Derek McKay and Hamish Scott, *The Rise of the Great Powers, 1648–1815* (London: Longman, 1982); Paul Kennedy, *The Rise and Fall of the Great Powers: Economic Change and Military Conflict from 1500 to 2000* (New York: Vintage, 1989); Paul Schroeder, *The Transformation of European Politics, 1763–1848* (New York: Oxford University Press, 1994).
5. Schroeder, *Transformation of European Politics*, 330.
6. For the assertion of British financial power during this era, see: John Sherwig, *Guineas and Gunpowder: British Foreign Aid in the Wars with France, 1793–1815* (Cambridge, Mass.: Harvard University Press, 1969); Michael Bordo and Eugene White, *A Tale of Two Currencies: British and French Finance During the Napoleonic War* (Cambridge; Cambridge University Press, 1990).
7. Paul Kennedy, *The Rise and Fall of the Great Powers: Economic Change and Military Conflict from 1500 to 2000* (New York: Vintage, 1988), 105; Eckhart Hellmuth, 'The British State', in H.T. Dickinson, ed., *A Companion to Eighteenth-Century Britain* (New York: Blackwell Publishing, 2006), 21; John Sherwig, *Guineas & Gunpowder: British Foreign Aid in the Wars*

with France, 1793–1815 (Cambridge, Mass.: Harvard University Press, 1969), 288, 309–10, 345, 365–68.
8. Memorandum of Lord Richard Wellesley, 4 November 1809, *Wellesley Papers*, BL, add. mss. 37288.
9. For overviews of Britain's agrarian revolution, see: J.D. Chambers and G.E. Mingay, *The Agricultural Revolution, 1750–1880* (London: Batsford, 1966); Eric Kerridge, *The Agricultural Revolution* (New York: A.M. Kelly, 1967); Mark Overton, *Agricultural Revolution in England: The Transformation of the Agrarian Economy, 1500–1850* (Cambridge: Cambridge University Press, 1996); G.E. Mingay, *Parliamentary Enclosure in England: An Introduction to Its Causes, Incidence, and Improvements, 1750–1850* (London: Longman, 1997).
For overviews of Britain's financial power that transcend the era, see: Ralph Hidy, *The House of Baring in American Trade and Finance: English Merchant Bankers at Work, 1763–1861* (Cambridge, Mass.: Harvard University Press, 1949); L.S. Pressnell, *Country Banking in the Industrial Revolution* (Oxford: Oxford University Press, 1956); Frank Fetter, *The Development of British Monetary Orthodoxy, 1797–1875* (Cambridge, Mass.: Harvard University Press, 1965); Karl Hellene, *The Imperial Loans: A Study in Financial and Diplomatic History* (Oxford: Oxford University Press, 1965); Alice Carter, *The English Public Debt in the Eighteenth Century* (London: Historical Association, 1968); Patrick O'Brien, 'The Political Economy of British Taxation, 1660–1815', *Economic History Review*, vol. 41 (1988), 1–32; Patrick O'Brien and Philip Hunt, 'The Rise of a Fiscal State in England, 1485–1815', *Historical Research*, vol. 96 (1993), 129–76; John Brewer, *The Sinews of Power: War, Money, and the English State, 1688–1783* (New York: Alfred A. Knopf, 1989); Patrick O'Brien, *Power with Profit: The State and Economy, 1688–1815* (London: Weidenfeld and Nicolson, 1991); P.G.M. Dickson, *The Financial Revolution in England: A Study in the Development of Public Credit, 1699–1756* (New York: Routledge, 1993); Lawrence Stone, ed., *An Imperial State at War: Britain from 1689 to 1815* (London: Routledge, 1994); M.J. Braddick, *The Nerves of State: Taxation and the Financing of the English State, 1558–1714* (Manchester: Manchester University Press, 1996); Niall Ferguson, *The World's Banker: The History of the House of Rothschild* (London: Weidenfeld and Nicolson, 1998); Martin Daunton, *Taxing Leviathan: The Politics of Taxation in Britain, 1799–1914* (Cambridge: Cambridge University Press, 2001).
For overviews of Britain's related trade and industrial revolutions, see: C.N. Parkinson, *The Trade Winds: A Study of British Overseas Trade During the French Wars, 1793–1815* (London: Allen and Unwin, 1948); Bernard Semmel, *The Rise of Free Trade Imperialism: Classical Political Economy, the Empire of Free Trade, and Imperialism, 1750–1850* (Cambridge: Cambridge University Press, 1970); Judith Williams, *British Commercial Policy and Trade Expansion, 1750–1850* (Oxford: Oxford University Press, 1972); Ralph Davis, *The Industrial Revolution and British Overseas Trade* (Leicester: Leicester University Press, 1979); Eric Hobsbawm, *Industry and Empire: The Economic History of Britain since 1750* (New York: W.W. Norton, 1999).
For overviews of Britain's industrial revolution, see: Peter Mathias, *The First Industrial Nation: An Economic History of Britain, 1700–1914* (New York: Routledge, 1983); Francis Crouzet, *The First Industrialists: The Problem of Origins* (Cambridge: Cambridge University Press, 1985); L.A. Clarkson, *Proto-Industrialization: The First Phase of Industrialization?* (London: Macmillan, 1985); N.F.N. Crafts, *British Economic Growth During the Industrial Revolution* (Oxford: Oxford University Press, 1985); Maxine Berg, *The Age of Manufactures: Industry, Innovation, and Work in Britain, 1700–1820* (Totowa, N.J.: Barnes and Noble

Books, 1985); A. Wrighley, *Continuity, Chance, and Change: The Character of the Industrial Revolution in England* (Cambridge: Cambridge University Press, 1988); Pat Hudson, ed., *Regions and Industries: A Perspective on the Industrial Revolution in Britain* (Cambridge: Cambridge University Press, 1989); Pat Hudson, *The Industrial Revolution* (London: Macmillan, 1992); Patrick O'Brien and Roland Quinault, eds., *The Industrial Revolution and British Society* (Cambridge: Cambridge University Press, 1993); Joel Mokyr, ed., *The British Industrial Revolution* (Boulder, Colo.: Westview Press, 1993); Eric Evans, *The Forging of the Modern State: Early Industrial Britain, 1780–1870* (London: Longman, 1996); Roderick Floud and Paul Johnson, eds., *The Cambridge Economic History of Modern Britain: Industrialization, 1700–1860* (New York: Cambridge University Press, 2004); Robert Allen, *The British Industrial Revolution in Global Perspective* (New York: Cambridge University Press, 2009).

For Britain's related cultural and entrepreneurial revolutions, see: Sidney Pollack, *The Genesis of Modern Management: A Study of the Industrial Revolution in Great Britain* (New York: Penguin, 1965); Neil McKendrick, John Brewer, and J.H. Plumb, *The Birth of a Consumer Society: The Commercialization of Eighteenth Century England* (Bloomington: University of Indiana Press, 1982); Julian Hoppit, *The Rise and Failures of English Business, 1700–1800* (Cambridge: Cambridge University Press, 1987); Janet Wolfe and John Seed, eds., *The Culture of Capital: Art, Power, and the Nineteenth Century Middle Class* (Manchester: Manchester University Press, 1988); Peter Earle, *The Making of the English Middle Class: Business, Society, and Family Life in London, 1660–1730* (Berkeley: University of California Press, 1989); Paul Langford, *A Polite and Commercial People: England, 1727–1783* (Oxford: Oxford University Press, 1989); Martin Daunton, *Progress and Poverty: An Economic and Social History of Britain, 1700–1850* (Oxford: Oxford University Press, 1995); Alan Kidd and David Nicolls, eds., *The Making of the British Middle Class?: Studies of Regional and Cultural Diversity since the Eighteenth Century* (Stroud: Sutton, 1998); Penelope Corfield, *Power and the Professions in Britain, 1700–1850* (New York: Routledge, 2000); F.M.L. Thompson, *Gentrification and the Enterprise Culture: Britain, 1780–1980* (Oxford: Oxford University Press, 2001); William Ashworth, *Customs and Excise: Trade, Production, and Consumption in England, 1640–1845* (Oxford: Oxford University Press, 2003).

10. For comparative studies, see: François Crouzet, *Britain Ascendant: Comparative Studies in Franco-British Economic History* (New York: University of Cambridge Press, 1985); N.F.R. Crafts, *British Economic Growth During the Industrial Revolution* (Oxford: Oxford University Press, 1985); Kenneth Pomeranz, *The Great Divergence: China, Europe, and the Making of the Modern World* (Princeton, N.J.: Princeton University Press, 2000).
11. Dundas to Grenville, 24 November 1799, *Fortescue Manuscripts*, 6:39.
12. Nancy Koehn, *The Power of Commerce: Economy and Governance in the First British Empire*, (Ithaca, N.Y.: Cornell University Press, 1994), 49.
13. Koehn, *Power of Commerce*, 62, 72.
14. For overviews of British imperial power that precede, embrace, or transcend the era, see: Vincent Harlow, *The Founding of the Second British Empire, 1763–1793*, 2 vols (London: Longman, 1952, 1964); P.J. Cain and A.G. Hopkins, *British Imperialism: Innovation and Expansion, 1688–1914* (New York: Longman, 1993); Christopher Bayly, *Imperial Meridian: The British Empire and the World, 1780–1830* (New York: Longman, 1989); Paul Johnson, *The Birth of the Modern: World Society, 1815–1830* (New York: HarperCollins, 1991); Ronald Hyam, *Britain's Imperial Century, 1815–1914: A Study of Empire and Expansion* (Basingstoke: Palgrave Macmillan, 1993); Lawrence James, *The Rise and Fall of the British*

Empire (New York: St Martin's Griffith Press, 1994); Lawrence Stone, ed., *An Imperial State at War: Britain from 1689 to 1815* (London: Routledge, 1994); Nancy Koehn, *The Power of Commerce: Economy and Governance in the First British Empire* (Ithaca, N.Y.: Cornell University Press, 1994); Kathleen Wilson, *The Sense of the People: Politics, Culture, and Imperialism in England, 1715 to 1785* (Cambridge: Cambridge University Press, 1995); H.V. Bowen, Elites, *Enterprise, and the Making of British Overseas Empire, 1688–1775* (London: Palgrave Macmillan, 1996); P.J. Marshall, ed., *The Oxford History of the British Empire: The Eighteenth Century* (Oxford: Oxford University Press, 1998); David Armitage, *The Ideological Origins of the British Empire* (Cambridge: Cambridge University Press, 2000); Jennifer Mori, *Britain in the Age of the French Revolution, 1785–1820* (London: Longman, 2000); C.A. Bayly, *The Birth of the Modern World, 1780–1914: Global Connections and Comparisons* (Oxford: Oxford University Press, 2004); Bernard Porter, *The Absent-Minded Imperialists: Empire, Society, and Culture in Britain* (Oxford: Oxford University Press, 2004); Brendan Simms, *Three Victories and a Defeat: The Rise and Fall of the First British Empire* (New York: Basic Books, 2009).

15. Observations on the Island of Malta Communicated to Lord Grenville, 16 June 1800, *Fortescue Manuscripts*, 16 June 1800, *Fortescue Manuscripts*, 6:249.
16. For the relationship between Britain's naval and national power, see: Robert Albion, *Forests and Seapower: The Timber Problem of the Royal Navy, 1652–1862* (Cambridge, Mass.: Harvard University Press, 1926); Patrick Crowhurst, *The Defense of British Trade, 1689–1815* (Folkstone: Dawson, 1977); Richard Harding, *The Evolution of the Sailing Navy, 1509–1815* (Basingstoke: Palgrave Macmillan, 1995); Jeremy Black and Philip Woodfine, eds., *The British Navy and the Use of Naval Power in the Eighteenth Century* (Leicester: Leicester University Press, 1998); Richard Harding, *Seapower and Naval Warfare, 1650–1830* (Annapolis, Maryland: Naval University Press, 1999); Margarette Lincoln, *Representing the Royal Navy: British Sea Power, 1750–1815* (Burlington, Vermont: Ashgate, 2002); Peter Padfield, *Maritime Power and the Struggle for Freedom: Naval Campaigns that Shaped the Modern World, 1788–1851* (London: John Murray, 2003); Clive Wilkinson, *The British Navy and the State in the Eighteenth Century* (London: Boydell Press, 2004); N.A.M. Rodger, *The Command of the Ocean: A Naval History of Britain, 1649–1815* (New York: W.W. Norton, 2006).
17. John Brewer, *The Sinews of Power: War, Money, and the English State, 1688–1783* (New York: Alfred Knopf, 1989), 10–11.
18. C. Northcote Parkinson, *The Trade Winds: A Study of British Overseas Trade During the French Wars, 1793–1815* (London: George Allen, 1948), 72–73.
19. William Nester, *Napoleon and the Art of Diplomacy: How War and Hubris Determined the Rise and Fall of the French Empire* (New York: Savas Beattie, 2012); William Nester, *Napoleon and the Art of Leadership: How a Flawed Genius Change the History of Europe and the World* (London: Frontline Books, 2021).
20. Dundas Memorandum for the Consideration of His Majesty's Ministers, 31 March 1800, PRO, 30/8/243.
21. Dundas to Grenville, 2 September 1800, *Fortescue Manuscripts*, 6:213.
22. Duffy, *Soldiers, Sugar, and Seapower*, 371.
23. Dundas to Grenville, 24 November 1799, *Fortescue Manuscripts*, 6:38–39.
24. Michael Duffy, *Soldiers, Sugar, and Seapower: The British Expeditions to the West Indies and the War against Revolutionary France* (Oxford: Clarendon Press, 1987), 387.
25. Duffy, *Soldiers, Sugar, and Seapower*, 328–33.

26. Harold Nicolson, *The Congress of Vienna: A Study of Allied Unity, 1812–1822* (New York: Harcourt, Brace, and Company, 1946), 19.
27. This is the third and final volume of a trilogy on British power during that era that also includes William Nester, *Titan: The Art of British Power in the Age of Revolution and Napoleon* (Norman: University of Oklahoma Press, 2016); William Nester, *Britain's Rise to Global Superpower in the Age of Napoleon* (London: Frontline Books, 2020). *Titan* emphasises grand strategy and diplomacy while *Britain's Rise* explores the military campaigns.

Chapter 1: Political

1. For good studies of the origin and development of the modern and especially European state-nation, see: Charles Tilley, ed., *The Formation of Nation States in Western Europe* (Princeton, N.J.: Princeton University Press, 1975); Peter Evans, Dietrich Rusechemeyer, and Theda Skocpol, eds., *Bringing the State Back In* (Cambridge: Cambridge University Press, 1985); Eckhart Hellmuth, *The Transformation of Political Culture: England and Germany in the Late Eighteenth Century* (Oxford: Clarendon Press, 1990); Brian Downing, *The Military Revolution and Political Change: The Origins of Democracy and Aristocracy in Early Modern Europe* (Princeton, N.J.: Princeton University Press, 1992); Thomas Erbman, *The Birth of the Leviathan: Building States and Regimes in Medieval and Early Modern Europe* (Cambridge: Cambridge University Press, 1997); Richard Bonney, ed., *The Rise of the Fiscal State in Europe, 1200–1815* (Oxford: Clarendon Press, 1999); John Brewer and Eckhart Hellmuth, eds., *Rethinking Leviathan: The Eighteenth Century State in Britain and Germany* (Oxford: Clarendon Press, 1999); T.C.W. Blanning, *The Culture of Power and the Power of Culture: Old Regime Europe, 1660–1789* (New York: Oxford University Press, 2003).
2. For good studies on the development of modern and especially European nationalism, see: Anthony Smith, *Theories of Nationalism* (London: Holmes and Mier, 1983); Ernest Gellner, *Nations and Nationalism* (Oxford: Clarendon, 1985); Peter Boerner, ed., *Concepts of National Identity: An Interdisciplinary Dialogue* (Baden-Baden: Nomos, 1986); Benedict Anderson, *Imagined Communities: Reflections on the Origins and Spread of Nationalism* (New York: Verso Press, 1991); Liah Greenfeld, *Nationalism: Five Roads to Modernity* (Cambridge, Mass.: Harvard University Press, 1992); Eric Hobsbawm, *Nations and Nationalism Since 1780: Program, Myth, Reality* (New York: Cambridge University Press, 1995); Hegan Schulze, *States, Nations, and Nationalism from the Middle Ages to the Present* (Oxford: Clarendon Press, 1996); Adrian Hastings, *The Construction of Nationhood: Ethnicity, Religion, and Nationalism* (Cambridge: Cambridge University Press, 1997).
3. William Gibson, *The Church of England, 1688–1832, Unity and Accord* (London: Routledge, 2001).
4. For good studies on the origins and development of the British state, see: John Brewer, *The Sinews of Power: War, Money, and the English State, 1688–1783* (New York: Alfred A. Knopf, 1989); M.J. Braddick, *The Nerves of State: Taxation and the Financing of the English State, 1558–1714* (Manchester: Manchester University Press, 1996); J.C.D. Clark, *English Society, 1688–1832: Ideology, Social Structure, and Political Practice During the Ancien Regime* (Cambridge: Cambridge: Cambridge University Press, 2000); Michael Turner, *The Age of Unease: Government and Reform in Britain, 1782–1832* (London: Longman, 2000); Philip Harling, *The Modern British State: An Historical Introduction* (Oxford: Clarendon, 2001).
5. Gerald Newman, *The Rise of English Nationalism: A Cultural History, 1740–1830* (New York: St Martin's Press, 1987); Kathleen Wilson, *The Sense of the People: Politics, Culture, and Imperialism in England, 1715–1785* (Cambridge: Cambridge University Press, 1995);

Laurence Brockliss and David Eastwood, eds., *A Union of Multiple Identities: The British Isles 1750–1850* (Manchester: Manchester University Press, 1997); Tony Claydon and Ian McBride, eds., *Protestantism and National Identity: Britain and Ireland, 1650–1850* (Cambridge: Cambridge University Press, 1998); Brendan Bradshaw and Peter Roberts, ed., *British Consciousness and Identity: The Making of Britain, 1533–1707* (Cambridge: Cambridge University Press, 1998); Colin Kidd, *British Identities before Nationalism: Ethnicity and Nationhood in the Atlantic World, 1600–1800* (Cambridge: Cambridge University Press, 1999); Paul Langford, *Englishness Identified: Manners and Character, 1650–1850* (Oxford: Oxford University Press, 2000); Julian Hoppit, ed., *Parliaments, Nations, and Identities in Britain and Ireland, 1660–1850* (Manchester: Manchester University Press, 2003); Colin Kidd, *British Identities before Nationalism: Ethnicity and Nationhood in the Atlantic World, 1600–1800* (Cambridge: Cambridge University Press, 1999); Krisham Kumar, *The Making of English National Identity* (Cambridge: Cambridge University Press, 2003); Stuart Semmel, *Napoleon and the British* (New Haven, Conn.: Yale University Press, 2004); Linda Colley, *Britons: Forging the Nation, 1707–1837* (New Haven, Conn.: Yale University Press, 2007).

6. For the dynamic between war and British nationalism, see: Clive Emsley, *British Society and the French Wars, 1793–1815* (Basingstoke: Macmillan, 1979); Kathleen Wilson, *The Sense of the People: Politics, Culture, and Imperialism in England, 1715–1785* (Cambridge: Cambridge University Press, 1995); Emma Macleod, *A War of Ideas? British Attitudes to the Wars against Revolutionary France* (New Haven, Conn.: Yale University Press, 1998).

7. For the links between politics and civil society, see: E.P. Thompson, *Making of the English Working Class* (New York: Penguin, 1969); Harold Perkins, *The Origins of Modern English Society* (New York: Routledge, 1969); Clive Emsley, *British Society and the French Wars, 1793–1815* (Totowa, N.J.: Rowman and Littlefield, 1979); Roy Porter, *English Society in the Eighteenth Century* (New York: Penguin, 1982); J.C.D. Clark, *English Society, 1688–1832: Ideology, Social Structure, and Political Practice During the Ancien Regime* (New York: Cambridge University Press, 1984); Isaac Kramnick, *Republicanism and Bourgeois Radicalism: Political Ideology in Late Eighteenth Century England and America* (Ithaca, N.Y.: Cornell University Press, 1990); J.C.D. Clark, *The Language of Liberty, 1660–1832: Political Discourse and Social Dynamics in the Anglo-American World* (New York: Cambridge University Press, 1994); M.J. Daunton, *Progress and Poverty: An Economic and Social History of Britain, 1700–1850* (Oxford: Oxford University Press, 1995); H.T. Dickinson, *The Politics of the People in Eighteenth Century Britain* (Basingstoke: Palgrave Macmillan, 1995); Kathleen Wilson, *The Sense of the People: Politics, Culture, and Imperialism in England, 1715–1785* (Cambridge: Cambridge University Press, 1995); Charles Tilly, *Popular Contention in Great Britain, 1758–1834* (Cambridge, Mass.: Harvard University Press, 1995); Dror Wahrman, *Imagining the Middle Class: The Political Representation of Class in Britain, 1780–1840* (New York: Cambridge University Press, 1995); Philip Harling, *The Waning of 'Old Corruption': The Politics of Economical Reform in Britain, 1779–1846* (Oxford: Clarendon Press, 1996); John Rule, *Albion's People: English Society, 1714–1815* (London: Longman, 1997); Nicolas Rogers, *Crowds, Culture, and Politics in Georgian Britain* (Oxford: Oxford University Press, 1998); M.J.D. Roberts, *Making English Morals: Voluntary Associations and Moral Reform in England, 1787–1886* (New York: Cambridge University Press, 2004); Dror Wahrman, *The Making of the Modern Self: Identity and Culture in Eighteenth Century England* (New Haven, Conn.: Yale University Press, 2004); Boyd Hinton, *A Mad, Bad, & Dangerous People: England, 1783–1846* (New York: Oxford University Press, 2008); Jenny Uglow, *In These*

Times: Living in Britain through Napoleon's War's, 1793–1815 (London: Faber and Faber, 2014).

8. P.J. Marshall and Glyndwr Williams, *The Great Map of Mankind: British Perceptions of the World in the Age of Enlightenment* (London: Dent and Son, 1982); J.A.W. Gunn, *Beyond Liberty and Property: The Process of Self-Recognition in Eighteenth Century Political Thought* (Kingston, Ont.: McGill University Press, 1983); J.C.D. Clark, *The Language of Liberty, 1660–1832: Political Discourse and Social Dynamics in the Anglo-American World* (Cambridge: Cambridge University Press, 1994); Roy Porter, *Enlightenment: Britain and the Creation of the Modern World* (New York: Penguin, 2000).

9. For the power of the press, see: Arthur Aspinall, *Politics and the Press, 1780–1850* (New York: Barnes and Noble, 1973); Dorothy George, *English Political Caricature, 1793–1832: A Study of Opinion and Propaganda* (Oxford: Oxford University Press, 1959); James Bolton, *The Language of Politics in the Age of Wilkes and Burke* (Westport, Conn.: Greenwood, 1975); Colin Jones, ed., *Britain and Revolutionary France: Conflict, Subversion, and Propaganda* (Exeter: University of Exeter press, 1983); Olivia Smith, *The Politics of Language, 1791–1819* (Oxford: Oxford University Press, 1984); Michael Duffy, *The English Satirical Print, 1660–1832: The Englishman and the Foreigner* (Cambridge: Cambridge University Press, 1986); Jeremy Black, *The English Press in the Eighteenth Century* (London: Croom Helm, 1987); Lucyle Werkmeister, *A Newspaper History of England* (Lincoln: University of Nebraska Press, 1988); Vincent Carretta, *George III and the Satirists: From Hogarth to Byron* (Athens: University of Ohio Press, 1990); Bob Harris, *Politics and the Rise of the Press: Britain and France, 1620–1800* (London: Routledge, 1996); Diana Donald, *English Political Caricature: Satirical Prints in the Reign of George III* (New Haven, Conn.: Yale University Press, 1996); Hannah Barker, *Newspapers, Politics, and Public Opinion in Late Eighteenth Century England* (Oxford: Oxford University Press, 1998); Joad Raymond, ed., *News, Newspapers in Early Modern Britain* (London: Routledge, 1999); Hannah Barker, *Newspapers, Politics, and English Society, 1695–1855* (New York: Routledge, 2002); Hannah Barker and S. Burrows, eds., *Press, Politics, and the Public Sphere in Europe and North America, 1760–1820* (New York: Cambridge University Press, 2002).

10. John Bew, *Castlereagh: Enlightenment, War, and Tyranny* (London: Quercus, 2011), 397.

11. Philip Harling, *The Waning of 'Old Corruption': The Politics of Economical Reform in Britain, 1779–1846* (Oxford: Clarendon, 1996), 117.

12. For the best political biography, see: Jeremy Black, *George III: America's Last King* (New Haven, Conn.: Yale University Press, 2006). For the quote, see p. 44.

13. For the best political biography of George III, see Jeremy Black, *George III: America's Last King* (New Haven, Conn.: Yale University Press, 2006). For an excellent literature review on how historians have evaluated George III, see chapters 19 and 20. See also, Richard Pares, *King George III and the Politicians* (Oxford: Oxford University Press, 1953). For the king's 'madness', see: J.C.G. Rohl, M. Warren, and D. Warren, *Purple Secret, Genes, 'Madness,' and the Royal House of Europe* (London: Corgi Books, 1999). For the initial regency crisis, see: John Derry, *The Regency Crisis and the Whigs, 1788–89* (Cambridge: Cambridge University Press, 1963). For the king's role during the war against revolutionary France, see: Marilyn Morris, *The British Monarch and the French Revolution* (New Haven, Conn.: Yale University Press, 1998).

14. For the Prince of Wales, see: Christopher Hibbert, *George IV: Regent and King, 1811–1830* (New York: Penguin, 1973); E.A. Smith, *George IV* (New Haven, Conn.: Yale University

Press, 1999); Steven Parissien, *George IV: Inspiration of the Regency* (New York: St Martin's Press, 2001).
15. Brewer, *Sinews of Power*, 66.
16. Grenville to Minto, 20 May 1800, Fortescue Manuscripts, 6:283.
17. For political parties, see: Lewis Namier, *The Structure of Politics at the Accession of George III* (London: Macmillan, 1957); Archibald Ford, *His Majesty's Opposition, 1714–1830* (Oxford: Clarendon Press, 1964); L.G. Mitchell, *Charles James Fox and the Disintegration of the Whig Party, 1782–1794* (Oxford: Clarendon Press, 1971); Frank O'Gorman, *The Emergence of the Two Party System, 1760–1832* (London: E. Arnold, 1982); B.W. Hill, *British Parliamentary Parties, 1742–1832: From the Fall of Walpole to the First Reform Act* (London: Allen and Unwin, 1985); J.W. Burrow, *Whigs and Liberals: Continuity and Change in England Political Thought* (Oxford: Clarendon Press, 1988).

For opposition parties and politics, see: John Cannon, *The Fox-North Coalition: Crisis of the Constitution, 1782–84* (Cambridge: Cambridge University Press, 1969); L.G. Mitchell, *Charles James Fox and the Disintegration of the Whig Party, 1782–1794* (New York: Oxford, 1971).
18. For political clubs, see: Peter Clark, *British Clubs and Societies, 1580–1800: The Origins of an Associational World* (Oxford: Clarendon Press, 2000).
19. For the House of Commons, see: Lewis Namier and John Brooke, eds., *The House of Commons, 1754–1790*, 3 vols (New York: Oxford University Press, 1964); R.G. Thorne, ed., *The History of Parliament: The House of Commons, 1790–1820*, 5 vols (London: Haynes Publishing, 1986).
20. For the electoral system, see: J.A. Phillips, *Electoral Behavior in Unreformed England, 1761–1802* (Princeton, N.J.: Princeton University Press, 1982); Frank O'Gorman, *Voters, Patrons, and Parties: The Unreformed Electoral System of Hanoverian England, 1734–1832* (Oxford: Clarendon Press, 1989).
21. H.T. Dickinson, 'Popular Politics and Radical Ideas', in H.T. Dickinson, *A Companion to Eighteenth Century Britain* (New York: Blackwell Publishing, 2006), 98; James Sacks, 'The House of Lords and Parliamentary Patronage in Great Britain, 1802–1832', *Historical Journal*, vol. 23, no. 4 (1980), 919, 913–37.
22. Brewer, *Sinews of Power*, 44–45.
23. For the House of Lords, see: A.S. Turberville, *The House of Lords in the Age of Reform, 1784–1837* (London: Faber and Faber, 1958); Clive Jones and David Jones, ed., *Politics and Power: The House of Lords, 1603–1911* (London: Secker and Warburg, 1986); Michael McCahill, *Order and Equipoise: The Peerage and the House of Lords, 1783–1806* (London: Royal Historical Society, 1978).
24. John Cannon, *Aristocratic Century: The Peerage of Eighteenth Century England* (Cambridge: Cambridge University Press, 1984), 33.
25. Eric Evans, *The Forging of the Modern State: Early Industrial Britain, 1780–1870* (London: Longman, 1996), 9.
26. For the British aristocracy, see: G.E. Mingay, *English Landed Society in the Eighteenth Century* (London: Routledge, 1963); John Cannon, *The Aristocratic Century: the Peerage of Eighteenth Century England* (Cambridge: University of Cambridge Press, 1984); J.V. Beckett, *The Aristocracy in England, 1660–1914* (Oxford: Oxford University Press, 1986); Paul Langford, *Public Life and the Propertied Englishman, 1689–1798* (Oxford: Oxford University Press, 1991); J.W.C. Lowe, 'George III, Peerage Creations and Politics, 1760–1784', *Historical Journal*, vol. 35 (1992), 587–609; John Habakkuk, *Marriage, Debt,*

and the Estates System: English Land Ownership, 1650–1950 (Oxford: Oxford University Press, 1994); J.C. Sainty, *Peerage Creations, 1649–1800* (London: Whitey Blackwell, 1998); H.T. Dickinson, ed., *A Companion to Eighteenth Century Britain* (Oxford: Blackwell Publishing, 2006).
27. Ian Christie, *Wilkes, Wyvill, and Reform: The Parliamentary Reform Movement in British Politics, 1760–1785* (London: Macmillan, 1962); E.C. Black, *The Association: British Extra-Parliamentary Organization, 1769–1793* (Cambridge, Mass.: Harvard University Press, 1963).
28. For patronage and corruption, see: J.M. Bourne, *Patronage and Society in Nineteenth Century England* (London: E. Arnold, 1986); Philip Harling, *The Waning of 'Old Corruption': The Politics of Economical Reform in Britain, 1779–1840* (Oxford: Oxford University Press, 1996).
29. Philip Harling, *The Waning of 'Old Corruption': The Politics of Economical Reform in Britain, 1779–1846* (Oxford: Clarendon Press, 1996), 110.

Chapter 2: Economic

1. For overviews of Britain's industrial revolution, see: Peter Mathias, *The First Industrial Nation: An Economic History of Britain, 1700–1914* (New York: Routledge, 1983); Francis Crouzet, *The First Industrialists: The Problem of Origins* (Cambridge: Cambridge University Press, 1985); L.A. Clarkson, *Proto-Industrialization: The First Phase of Industrialization?* (London: Macmillan, 1985); N.F.N. Crafts, *British Economic Growth During the Industrial Revolution* (Oxford: Oxford University Press, 1985); Maxine Berg, *The Age of Manufactures: Industry, Innovation, and Work in Britain, 1700–1820* (Totowa, N.J.: Barnes and Noble Books, 1985); A. Wrighley, *Continuity, Chance, and Change: The Character of the Industrial Revolution in England* (Cambridge: Cambridge University Press, 1988); Pat Hudson, ed., *Regions and Industries: A Perspective on the Industrial Revolution in Britain* (Cambridge: Cambridge University Press, 1989); Pat Hudson, *The Industrial Revolution* (London: Macmillan, 1992); Patrick O'Brien and Roland Quinault, eds., *The Industrial Revolution and British Society* (Cambridge: Cambridge University Press, 1993); Joel Mokyr, ed., *The British Industrial Revolution* (Boulder, Colo.: Westview Press, 1993); Eric Evans, *The Forging of the Modern State: Early Industrial Britain, 1780–1870* (London: Longman, 1996); Roderick Floud and Paul Johnson, eds., *The Cambridge Economic History of Modern Britain: Industrialization, 1700–1860* (New York: Cambridge University Press, 2004); Robert Allen, *The British Industrial Revolution in Global Perspective* (New York: Cambridge University Press, 2009).
2. Jan de Vries, 'The Industrial Revolution and the Industrious Revolution', *Journal of Economic History*, vol. 54 (1994), 250–70.
3. N.F.R. Crafts, *British Economic Growth During the Industrial Revolution* (Oxford: Clarendon Press, 1985), 32, 37, 42.
4. N.F.R. Crafts, *British Economic Growth During the Industrial Revolution* (Oxford: Clarendon Press, 1985), 103.
5. S.W.S. Pack, *Admiral Lord Anson: The Story of Anson's Voyage and Naval Events of His Day* (London: Cassel, 1960); Richard Hough, *Captain James Cook* (New York: W.W. Norton, 1997); Dava Sobel, *Longitude: The True Story of a Lone Genius Who Solved the Greatest Scientific Problem of His Time* (New York: Penguin, 1995).
6. For Britain's related cultural and entrepreneurial revolutions, see: Sidney Pollack, *The Genesis of Modern Management: A Study of the Industrial Revolution in Great Britain* (New York: Penguin, 1965); Neil McKendrick, John Brewer, and J.H. Plumb, *The Birth of a*

Consumer Society: The Commercialization of Eighteenth Century England (Bloomington: University of Indiana Press, 1982); Julian Hoppit, *The Rise and Failures of English Business, 1700–1800* (Cambridge: Cambridge University Press, 1987); Janet Wolfe and John Seed, eds., *The Culture of Capital: Art, Power, and the Nineteenth Century Middle Class* (Manchester: Manchester University Press, 1988); Peter Earle, *The Making of the English Middle Class: Business, Society, and Family Life in London, 1660–1730* (Berkeley: University of California Press, 1989); Paul Langford, *A Polite and Commercial People: England, 1727–1783* (Oxford: Oxford University Press, 1989); Martin Daunton, *Progress and Poverty: An Economic and Social History of Britain, 1700–1850* (Oxford: Oxford University Press, 1995); Alan Kidd and David Nicolls, eds., *The Making of the British Middle Class?: Studies of Regional and Cultural Diversity since the Eighteenth Century* (Stroud: Sutton, 1998); Penelope Corfield, *Power and the Professions in Britain, 1700–1850* (New York: Routledge, 2000); F.M.L. Thompson, *Gentrification and the Enterprise Culture: Britain, 1780–1980* (Oxford: Oxford University Press, 2001); William Ashworth, *Customs and Excise: Trade, Production, and Consumption in England, 1640–1845* (Oxford: Oxford University Press, 2003).

7. Robert Allen, *The British Industrial Revolution in Global Perspective* (New York: Cambridge University Press, 2009), 53.
8. For Britain's agrarian revolution, see: J.D. Chambers and G.E. Mingay, *The Agricultural Revolution, 1750–1880* (London: Batsford, 1966); Eric Kerridge, *The Agricultural Revolution* (New York: A.M. Kelly, 1967); Mark Overton, *Agricultural Revolution in England: The Transformation of the Agrarian Economy, 1500–1850* (Cambridge: Cambridge University Press, 1996); G.E. Mingay, *Parliamentary Enclosure in England: An Introduction to Its Causes, Incidence, and Improvements, 1750–1850* (London: Longman, 1997).
9. Roderick Floud, Kenneth Wachter, and Annabel, Gregory, *Height, Health, and History: Nutritional Status in the United Kingdom, 1750–1890* (Cambridge: Cambridge University Press, 1990), 140–49.
10. Gordon Mingay, 'Agriculture and Rural Life', Dickinson, *Eighteenth Century*, 150, 141; Patrick O'Brien, 'Introduction: Modern Conceptions of the Industrial Revolution', Patrick O'Brien and Robert Quinault, eds., *The Industrial Revolution and British Society* (Cambridge: Cambridge University Press, 1993); 23; M.J. Daunton, *Progress and Poverty: An Economic and Social History of Britain, 1700–1850* (New York: Oxford University Press, 1995), 102.
11. Robert Allen, *The British Industrial Revolution in Global Perspective* (New York: Cambridge University Press, 2009), 17.
12. Eric Evans, *The Forging of the Modern State: Early Industrial Britain, 1783–1870* (London: Longman, 1996), 142.
13. For overviews of Britain's financial power that transcend the era, see: Ralph Hidy, *The House of Baring in American Trade and Finance: English Merchant Bankers at Work, 1763–1861* (Cambridge, Mass.: Harvard University Press, 1949); L.S. Pressnell, *Country Banking in the Industrial Revolution* (Oxford: Oxford University Press, 1956); Frank Fetter, *The Development of British Monetary Orthodoxy, 1797–1875* (Cambridge, Mass.: Harvard University Press, 1965); Karl Hellene, *The Imperial Loans: A Study in Financial and Diplomatic History* (Oxford: Oxford University Press, 1965); Alice Carter, *The English Public Debt in the Eighteenth Century* (London: Historical Association, 1968); Patrick O'Brien, 'The Political Economy of British Taxation, 1660–1815', *Economic History Review*, vol. 41 (1988), 1–32; Patrick O'Brien and Philip Hunt, 'The Rise of a Fiscal State in England, 1485–1815', *Historical Research*, vol. 96 (1993), 129–76; John Brewer, *The Sinews of Power: War, Money, and the English State, 1688–1783* (New York: Alfred A. Knopf, 1989); Patrick O'Brien,

Power with Profit: The State and Economy, 1688–1815 (London: Weidenfeld and Nicolson, 1991); P.G.M. Dickson, The Financial Revolution in England: A Study in the Development of Public Credit, 1699–1756 (New York: Routledge, 1993); Lawrence Stone, ed., An Imperial State at War: Britain from 1689 to 1815 (London: Routledge, 1994); M.J. Braddick, The Nerves of State: Taxation and the Financing of the English State, 1558–1714 (Manchester: Manchester University Press, 1996); Niall Ferguson, The World's Banker: The History of the House of Rothschild (London: Weidenfeld and Nicolson, 1998); Martin Daunton, Taxing Leviathan: The Politics of Taxation in Britain, 1799–1914 (Cambridge: Cambridge University Press, 2001).
14. John Clapham, The Bank of England: A History, 2 vols (New York: Cambridge University Press, 2008).
15. Mathias, First Industrial Nation, 151; Rule, 'Manufacturing and Commerce', Dickinson, Eighteenth Century, 136.
16. Berg, Age of Manufactures, 36.
17. For the transportation revolution, see: J.R. Ward, The Finance of Canal Building in Eighteenth Century England (London: Oxford University Press, 1974); Eric Pawson, Transport and Economy: The Turnpike Roads of Eighteenth Century Britain (New York: Academic Press, 1977).
18. Roger Knight, Britain Against Napoleon: The Organization of Victory, 1793–1815 (New York: Allen Lane, 2013), 54; Jenny Uglow, In These Times: Living in Britain through Napoleon's Wars, 1793–1815 (London: Faber and Faber, 2014), 202, Nancy Koehn, The Power of Commerce: Economy and Governance in the First British Empire (Ithaca, N.Y.: Cornell University Press, 1994), 41–42; M.J. Daunton, Progress and Poverty: An Economic and Social History of Britain, 1700–1850 (New York: Oxford University Press, 1995), 306.
19. For the technological and scientific revolutions, see: A.E. Munsen, and Eric Robinson, Science and Technology in the Industrial Revolution (Manchester: University of Manchester Press, 1969); G.N. Tunzelman, Steam Power and British Industrialization to 1860 (Oxford: Oxford University Press, 1978); Maxine Berg, The Age of Manufacturers: Industry, Innovation, and Work in Britain, 1700–1820 (Oxford: Oxford University Press, 1985).
20. N.F.R. Crafts, 'Steam as a General Purpose Technology: A Growth Accounting Perspective', Economic Journal, vol. 114 (2004), 342, 338–51.
21. Mathias, First Industrial Nation, 166–69.
22. Peter Lindert and Jeffrey Williamson, 'Revising England's Social Tables, 1688–1812', Explorations in Economic History, vol. 19, (1982), 385–408.
23. M.D. George, London Life in the Eighteenth Century (Harmondsworth: Penguin, 1966); Penelope Corfield, The Impact of English Towns, 1700–1800 (Oxford: Oxford University Press, 1982); Jan de Vries, European Urbanization, 1500–1800 (Cambridge, Mass.: Harvard University Press, 1984); Peter Borsay, The English Urban Renaissance: Culture and Society in the Provincial, 1660–1770 (Oxford: Oxford University Press, 1989); F.A. Wrigley and R.S. Schofield, The Population History of England, 1541–1871 (New York: Cambridge University Press, 1989); Jeffrey Williamson, Coping with City Growth During the British Industrial Revolution (New York: Cambridge University Press, 1990); Peter Clark, ed., The Cambridge Urban History of Britain, 1540–1840 (New York: Cambridge University Press, 2000).
24. H.T. Dickinson, 'Popular Politics and Radical Ideas', John Rule, 'Manufacturing and Commerce', in H.T. Dickinson, A Companion to Eighteenth Century Britain (New York: Blackwell Publishing, 2006), 103, 128.

25. Neil McKendrick, John Brewer, and J. H. Plumb, *The Birth of a Consumer Society: The Commercialization of Eighteenth Century England* (Bloomington: University of Indiana Press, 1982), 24.

Chapter 3: Imperial

1. For overviews of British imperial power that precede, embrace, or transcend the era, see: Vincent Harlow, *The Founding of the Second British Empire, 1763–1793*, 2 vols (London: Longman, 1952, 1964); P.J. Cain and A.G. Hopkins, *British Imperialism: Innovation and Expansion, 1688–1914* (New York: Longman, 1993); Christopher Bayly, *Imperial Meridian: The British Empire and the World, 1780–1830* (New York: Longman, 1989); Paul Johnson, *The Birth of the Modern: World Society, 1815–1830* (New York: HarperCollins, 1991); Ronald Hyam, *Britain's Imperial Century, 1815–1914: A Study of Empire and Expansion* (Basingstoke: Palgrave Macmillan, 1993); Lawrence James, *The Rise and Fall of the British Empire* (New York: St Martin's Griffith Press, 1994); Lawrence Stone, ed., *An Imperial State at War: Britain from 1689 to 1815* (London: Routledge, 1994); Nancy Koehn, *The Power of Commerce: Economy and Governance in the First British Empire* (Ithaca, N.Y.: Cornell University Press, 1994); Kathleen Wilson, *The Sense of the People: Politics, Culture, and Imperialism in England, 1715 to 1785* (Cambridge: Cambridge University Press, 1995); H.V. Bowen, Elites, *Enterprise, and the Making of British Overseas Empire, 1688–1775* (London: Palgrave Macmillan, 1996); P.J. Marshall, ed., *The Oxford History of the British Empire: The Eighteenth Century* (Oxford: Oxford University Press, 1998); David Armitage, *The Ideological Origins of the British Empire* (Cambridge: Cambridge University Press, 2000); Jennifer Mori, *Britain in the Age of the French Revolution, 1785–1820* (London: Longman, 2000); C.A. Bayly, *The Birth of the Modern World, 1780–1914: Global Connections and Comparisons* (Oxford: Oxford University Press, 2004); Bernard Porter, *The Absent-Minded Imperialists: Empire, Society, and Culture in Britain* (Oxford: Oxford University Press, 2004); Brendan Simms, *Three Victories and a Defeat: The Rise and Fall of the First British Empire* (New York: Basic Books, 2009).
2. For overviews of Britain's West Indian colonies that precede, embrace, or transcend the era, see: Frances Armytage, *The Free Port System in the British West Indies* (London: Longmans, 1953); Richard Dunn, *Sugar and Slaves: The Rise of the Planter Class in the English West Indies, 1624–1723* (Chapel Hill: University of North Carolina Press, 1972); Richard Sheridan, *Sugar and Slavery: An Economic History of the West Indies, 1623–1775* (Barbados: Caribbean University Press, 1974); E.L. Cox, *The Free Coloreds in the Slave Societies of St Kitts and Grenada, 1763–1833* (Knoxville: University of Tennessee, 1984).
3. Stephen Drescher, *Econocide: British Slavery in the Era of Abolition* (Pittsburgh: University of Pittsburgh Press, 1977), 48.
4. Jacob Price, 'Imperial Economy, 1700–1776', Marshall, *British Empire Eighteenth Century*, 90; Michael Duffy, *Soldiers, Sugar, and Seapower: The British Expeditions to the West Indies and the War against Revolutionary France* (Oxford: Clarendon Press, 1987), 10, 17, 21; Sheridan, *Sugar and Slavery*, 22, 489.
5. David Richardson, 'The British Empire and the Atlantic Slave Trade, 1660–1807', P.J. Marshall, ed., *The Oxford History of the British Empire: The Eighteenth Century* (New York: Oxford University Press, 1998), 440–64. See also: Roger Anstey, *The Atlantic Slave Trade and British Abolition, 1760–1810* (New York: Humanities Press, 1975).
6. C. Northcote Parkinson, *The Trade Winds: A Study of British Overseas Trade During the French Wars, 1793–1815* (London: Allen and Unwin, 1948), 268, 275–76.

7. Duffy, Soldiers, Sugar, and Seapower, 18.
8. Michael Craton, *Testing the Chains: Resistance to Slavery in the British West Indies* (Ithaca, N.Y.: Cornell University Press, 1982).
9. For overviews of British India that precede, embrace, or transcend the era, see: P.J. Marshall, ed., *The Problems of Empire: Britain and India, 1757–1813* (London: Allen and Unwin, 1968); M.E. Yapp, *Strategies of British India: Britain, Iran, and Afghanistan, 1798–1850* (Oxford: Oxford University Press, 1980); Edward Ingram, *Commitment to Empire: Prophecies of the Great Game for Asia, 1797–1800* (Oxford: Oxford University Press, 1981); P.J. Marshall, *The New Cambridge History of Indian: Bengal, the British Bridgehead, Eastern India, 1740–1828* (Cambridge: Cambridge University Press, 1987); Christopher Bayly, *The New Cambridge History of India: Indian Society and the Making of the British Empire* (Cambridge: Cambridge University Press, 1988).
10. John Keay, *The Honourable Company: A History of the English East India Company* (New York: Macmillan, 1991); Philip Lawson, *The East India Company: A History* (London: Routledge, 1993).
11. James Lawford, *Britain's Army in India from Its Origins to the Conquest of Bengal* (London: Unwin Hyman, 1978).
12. Jacob Price, 'The Imperial Economy, 1700–1776, Marshall, *British Empire Eighteenth Century*, 83.
13. C. Northcote Parkinson, *The Trade Winds: A Study of British Overseas Trade During the French Wars, 1793–1815* (London: Allen and Unwin, 1948), 144–56.
14. Patrick O'Brien, 'Inseparable Connections: Trade, Economy, Fiscal State, and the Expansion of Empire, 1688–1815, P.J. Marshall, ed., *British Empire Eighteenth Century*, (New York: Oxford University Press, 1998), 53–77.
15. For overviews of Britain's related trade and industrial revolutions, see: C.N. Parkinson, *The Trade Winds: A Study of British Overseas Trade During the French Wars, 1793–1815* (London: Allen and Unwin, 1948); Bernard Semmel, *The Rise of Free Trade Imperialism: Classical Political Economy, the Empire of Free Trade, and Imperialism, 1750–1850* (Cambridge: Cambridge University Press, 1970); Judith Williams, *British Commercial Policy and Trade Expansion, 1750–1850* (Oxford: Oxford University Press, 1972); Ralph Davis, *The Industrial Revolution and British Overseas Trade* (Leicester: Leicester University Press, 1979); Eric Hobsbawm, *Industry and Empire: The Economic History of Britain since 1750* (New York: W.W. Norton, 1999).
16. Phyllis Deane and W.A. Cole, *British Economic Growth, 1688–1959: Trends and Structure* (Cambridge: Cambridge University Press, 1969), 87.
17. Anton Howes, *Arts and Minds: How the Royal Society of Arts Changed a Nation* (Princeton, N.J.: Princeton University Press, 2020).
18. James Horn, 'British Diaspora: Emigration from Britain, 160–1815, in Marshall, *British Empire Eighteenth Century*, 28–52.
19. Brendan Simms, *Three Victories and a Defeat: The Rise and Fall of the First British Empire* (New York: Basic Books, 2009), 207.
20. Lawrence Stone, ed., *An Imperial State at War: Britain from 1689 to 1815* (London: Routledge, 1994).
21. Brewer, *Sinews of War*, 30.
22. Brewer, *Sinews of War*, 30.
23. Nancy Koehn, *The Power of Commerce: Economy and Governance in the First British Empire*, (Ithaca, N.Y.: Cornell University Press, 1994), 6–7.

24. Brewer, *Sinews of War*, 40.
25. P.J. Marshall, 'introduction', P.J Marshall, ed., *The Oxford History of the British Empire: The Eighteenth Century* (New York: Oxford University Press, 1998), 8.
26. Simms, *Three Victories*, 532.
27. Nancy Koehn, *The Power of Commerce: Economy and Governance in the First British Empire* (Ithaca, N.Y.: Cornell University Press, 1994), 96.
28. Nancy Koehn, *The Power of Commerce: Economy and Governance in the First British Empire* (Ithaca, N.Y.: Cornell University Press, 1994), 142.
29. Mostert, *Line Upon A Wind*, 45.
30. For nineteenth century accounts by people who either themselves or their descendants knew Pitt, see: George Pretyman, *Memoirs of the Life of the Right Hon. William Pitt*, 3 vols (London: John Murray, 1821); Philip Henry, lord Stanhope, *Life of the Right Honorable William Pitt*, 4 vols (London: John Murray, 1867).

    For the most detailed and wordy biography, see the trilogy: John Ehrman, *The Younger Pitt: The Years of Acclaim* (Stanford, Calif.: Stanford University Press, 1969); John Ehrman, *The Younger Pitt: The Reluctant Transition* (Stanford, Calif.: Stanford University Press, 1983); John Ehrman, *The Younger Pitt: The Consuming Struggle* (Stanford, Calif.: Stanford University Press, 1996).

    For good one volume biographies, see Robin Reilly, *William Pitt the Younger: A Biography* (New York: G.P. Putnam's Sons, 1978); William Hague, *William Pitt the Young* (New York: Harper Perennial, 2004).

    For Pitt the financial wizard, see: Patrick O'Brien, 'Political Biography and Pitt the Younger as Chancellor of the Exchequer', *History*, vol. 83 (1998), 225–33; John Torrance, 'Social Class and Bureaucratic Innovation: The Commissioners for Examining the Public Accounts, 1780–1787', *Past and Present*, 56–81; John Breihan, 'William Pitt and the Commission on Fees, 1785–1801', History Journal, vol. 27 (1984), 58–81; J.E.D. Binney, *British Public Finance and Administration, 1774–92* (Oxford: Oxford University Press, 1958). For aspects of Pitt's foreign policy, see: Jennifer Mori, *William Pitt and the French Revolution, 1785–1795* (New York: St Martin's Press, 1997).
31. John Ehrman, *The British Government and Commercial Negotiations with Europe, 1783–1793* (Cambridge: Cambridge University Press, 1963).
32. Jeremy Black, *British Foreign Policy in an Age of Revolution, 1783–1793* (Cambridge: Cambridge University Press, 1994), 35, 136; John Ehrman, *The Younger Pitt: The Years of Acclaim* (Stanford, Calif.: Stanford University Press, 1969), 311.

Chapter 4: First, 1793–97

1. William Doyle, *The Oxford History of the French Revolution* (New York: Oxford University Press, 1989); Ferenc Feher, *The French Revolution and the Birth of Modernity* (Berkeley: University of California Press, 1990); Simon Schama, *Citizens: A Chronicle of the French Revolution* (New York: Vintage, 1990); Florin Altalion, *The French Revolution: An Economic Explanation* (Cambridge: Cambridge University Press, 1990); Bailey, Stone, *Reinterpreting the French Revolution: A Global Historical Perspective* (New York: Cambridge University Press, 2002); Dylan Rees and Duncan Townson, *France in Revolution* (London: Hodder Education, 2008); David Andress, *The Oxford Handbook of the French Revolution* (New York: Oxford University Press, 2019).
2. T.C.W. Blanning, *The French Revolutionary Wars, 1787–1802* (New York: Arnold, 1996), 49.

3. Alfred Cobban, ed., *The Debate on the French Revolution* (London: N. Kaye, 1950); Frank O'Gorman, *The Whig Party and the French Revolution* (Basingstoke: Macmillan, 1967); Marilyn Butler, ed., *Burke, Paine, Godwin, and the Revolution Controversy* (Cambridge: Cambridge University Press, 1984); Robert Hole, *Pulpits, Politics, and Public Order in England, 1760–1832* (Cambridge: Cambridge University press, 1989); H.T. Dickinson, *Britain and the French Revolution* (Basingstoke: Macmillan, 1989); Mark Philp, ed., The French Revolution and *British Popular Politics* (Cambridge: Cambridge University Press, 1991); James Sack, *From Jacobite to Conservative: Reaction and Orthodoxy in Britain, 1760–1832* (New York: Cambridge University Press, 1993); Marilyn Morris, *The British Monarchy and the French Revolution* (New Haven, Conn.: Yale University Press, 1998).
4. Jenny Uglow, *In These Times: Living in Britain through Napoleon's Wars, 1793–1815* (London: Faber and Faber, 2014), 13.
5. Edmund Burke, *Reflections on the Revolution in France* (Mineola, N.Y.: Dover Publications, 2006). For an excellent overview of Burke's political philosophy, see: William Byrne, *Edmund Burke for Our Time: Moral Imagination, Meaning, and Politics* (DeKalb: Northern Illinois Press, 2011).
6. William Cobbett, ed., *The Parliamentary History of England, From the Earliest Period to the Year 1803*, 36 vols (London: R. Bagshaw, 1806–20), 28:332, 334; Edmund Burke, *Reflections on the Revolution in France* (Mineola, N.Y.: Dover Publications, 2006).
7. Michael Foot and Isaac Kramnick, eds., *The Thomas Paine Reader* (New York: Penguin, 1987), 201–364. See also: Gregory Claeys, *Thomas Paine: Social and Political Thought* (Boston: Unwin Hyman, 1989); John Keane, *Thomas Paine: A Political Life* (New York: Grove Press, 1989); Jack Fruchtman, *Thomas Paine: Apostle of Freedom* (New York: Four Walls, Eight Windows, 1994).
8. Albert Goodwin, *The French Revolution* (New York: Routledge, 2016), 204.
9. John Ehrman, *The Younger Pitt: The Reluctant Transition* (London: Constable, 1996), 49.
10. Alexander Mikaberidze, *The Napoleonic Wars: A Global History* (New York: Oxford University Press, 2020), 3.
11. Blanning, *French Revolutionary Wars*, 78.
12. Blanning, *French Revolutionary Wars*, 88.
13. William Grenville to Francois Bernard Chauvelin, 31 December 1792, *British Foreign Policy*, 7, 3–8.
14. *Parliamentary History*, 30: 283.
15. *Parliamentary Register*, 34: 459.
16. James Sack, *The Grenvillites, 1801–1829: Party Politics and Factionalism in the Age of Pitt and Liverpool* (Urbana: University of Illinois Press, 1979); Peter Jupp, *Lord Grenville, 1759–1834*, (Oxford: Clarendon Press, 1985).
17. Holden Furber, *Henry Dundas, First Viscount Melville: Political Manager of Scotland, Statesman, and Administrator of British India* (London: Oxford University Press, 1931).
18. Joel Mokyr, 'Introduction', Joel Mokyr, ed., *The British Industrial Revolution* (Cambridge: Cambridge University Press, 1993), 45.
19. Paul Kennedy, *The Rise and Fall of the Great Powers: Economic Change and Military Conflict from 1500 to 2000* (New York: Vintage, 1988), 105; Eckhart Hellmuth, 'The British State', in H.T. Dickinson, ed., *A Companion to Eighteenth-Century Britain* (New York: Blackwell Publishing, 2006), 21.
20. Hilton, *Mad, Bad, & Dangerous People*, 115.

21. Patrick O'Brien, 'Political Preconditions for the Industrial Revolution', Patrick O'Brien and Roland Quinault, eds., *The Industrial Revolution and British Society* (Cambridge: Cambridge University Press, 1993), 126.
22. Boyd Hilton, *A Mad, Bad, & Dangerous People?: England, 1783–1846* (Oxford: Clarendon, 2008), 22.
23. Haythornthwaite, *Armies of Wellington*, 9–10.
24. John Ehrman, *The Younger Pitt: The Years of Acclaim* (Stanford, Calif.: Stanford University Press, 1969), 311, 313.
25. For the public's mobilisation for taxes, recruits, and self-defence,, see: J.E. Cookson, *The British Armed Nation, 1793–1815* (New York: Oxford University Press, 1997); For the army, see: Philip Haythornthwaite, *The Armies of Wellington* (London: Brockhampton Press, 1996).
26. No good biography exists for Amherst or Dundas. For York, see: Alfred Burne, *The Noble, Duke of York* (London: Staples Press, 1949); Derek Winterbottom, *The Grand Old Duke of York: A Life of Frederick Augustus, Duke of York and Albany* (London: Pen and Sword, 2016).
27. Haythornthwaite, *Armies of Wellington*, 21.
28. Linda Colley, *Britons: Forging the Nation, 1707–1837* (New Haven, Conn.: Yale University Press, 2009), 316–17.
29. John Fortescue, *The County Lieutenants and the Army, 1803–1814* (London: Macmillan, 1909), 291–93.
30. Haythornthwaite, *Armies of Wellington*, 43.
31. For overviews of British naval strategy during this era, see: C. Northcote Parkinson, *Britannia Rules: The Classic Age of Naval History, 1793–1815* (London: Allan Sutton Publishing, 1994); Richard Woodman, *The Victory of Sea Power: Winning the Napoleonic War* (London: Caxton, 1998); Nicolas Tracy, ed., *The Naval Chronicle: The Contemporary Record of the Royal Navy at War, 1793–1815*, 5 vols (Mechanicsburg, Penn.: Stackpole Books, 1999); Peter Padfield, *Maritime Power and the Struggle for Freedom: Naval Campaigns that Shaped the Modern World, 1788–1851* (Woodstock, N.Y.: Overlook Press, 2003); Richard Harding, *British Admirals of the Napoleonic Wars: The Contemporaries of Nelson* (London: Chatham, 2005); Roy Adkins and Lesley Adkins, *The War for all the Oceans: From Nelson at the Nile to Napoleon at Waterloo* (New York: Viking, 2006); Noel Mostert, *The Line Upon the Wind: The Great War at Sea, 1793–1815* (New York: W.W. Norton, 2007).
32. Parkinson, *Britannia Rules*, 9.
33. Duffy, *Soldiers, Sugar, and Seapower*, 387.
34. Roger Morriss, *The Royal Dockyards During the Revolutionary and Napoleonic Wars* (Leicester: Leicester University Press, 1983), 106; Jean Claude Gillet, *La Marine Imperiale: La Grand Reve de Napoleon* (Paris: Bernard Giovanangeli Editeur, 2010), 68.
35. Geoffrey Bennet, *Nelson the Commander* (New York: Charles Scribner's, 1972); Terry Coleman, *The Nelson Touch: The Life and Legend of Horatio Nelson* (New York: Oxford University Press, 2002); David Cannadine, ed., *Admiral Lord Nelson: Context and Legacy* (Houndmills, Basingstoke, England: Palgrave Macmillan, 2005).
36. Adkins, *War of All the Oceans: From Nelson at the Nile to Napoleon at Waterloo* (New York: Viking, 2006), 68, 82.
37. Robert Albion, *Forests and Seapower: The Timber Problem of the Royal Navy, 1652–1862* (Cambridge, Mass.: Harvard University Press, 1926).
38. Mostert, *Line Upon A Wind*, 64.

39. Roger Knight, *Britain Against Napoleon: The Organization of Victory, 1793–1815* (New York: Allen Lane, 2013), 180–81.
40. Patrick Crowhurst, *The Defense of British Trade, 1689–1815* (Folkstone: Dawson, 1977); Patrick Crowhurst, *The French War on Trade: Privateering, 1793–1815* (London: Loughborough, 1985).
41. For the best account, see: Elizabeth Sparrow, *Secret Service: British Agents in France, 1792–1815* (London: Boydell Press, 1999). See also, Harvey Mitchell, *The Underground War against Revolutionary France: The Missions of William Wickham, 1794–1800* (Oxford: Oxford University Press, 1965); R.R. Nelson, *The Home Office, 1782–1801* (Durham, N.C.: Duke University Press, 1969); Mark Urban, *The Man Who Broke Napoleon's Codes: The True Story of a Forgotten Hero in Wellington's Army* (New York: HarperCollins, 2001); Tom Pocock, *The Terror Before Trafalgar: Nelson, Napoleon, and the Secret War* (Annapolis, Maryland: Naval Institute Press, 2005).
42. *Spencer Papers*, 2:305.
43. John Clapham, *The Bank of England: A History*, 2 vols (New York: Cambridge University Press, 2008), 1: 297.
44. Sherwig, *Guineas & Gunpowder*, 18–19.
45. Andrew Limm, *Walcheren to Waterloo: The British Army in the Low Countries During the French Revolutionary and Napoleonic Wars* (London: Pen and Sword, 2018), chapters 1–2.
46. Bernard Ireland, *The Fall of Toulon: The Last Opportunity to Defeat Revolutionary France* (London: Cassel, 2005); Robert Forczyk, *Toulon 1793: Napoleon's First Great Victory* (London: Osprey, 2005).
47. Blanning, *French Revolutionary Wars*, 200.
48. Wolfgang Kruse, 'Revolutionary France and the Meaning of Levee en Masse', in Roger Chickering and Stig Forster, eds., *War in an Age of Revolution, 1775–1815* (New York: Cambridge University Press, 2010), 308.
49. Ehrman, *Younger Pitt*, 2: 311.
50. Linda Colley, *Britons: Forging the Nation, 1707–1837* (New Haven, Conn.: Yale University Press, 2009), 318.
51. Sherwig, *Guineas & Gunpowder*, 40–41.
52. Grenville to William Wickham, 11 February 1800, *Fortescue Manuscripts*, 6:123.
53. William Wickham to Grenville, 13 December 1799, *Fortescue Manuscripts*, 6:73.
54. For British campaigns in the West Indies, see: Richard Pares, *War and Trade in the West Indies, 1739–1763* (London: Routledge, 1963); David Geggus, *Slavery, War, and Revolution: The British Occupation of Saint Dominque, 1793–1798* (New York: Oxford University Press, 1982); Michael Duffy, *Soldiers, Sugar, and Seapower: The British Expeditions to the West Indies and the War against Revolutionary France* (New York: Oxford University Press, 1989); Martin Howard, *Death before Glory!: The British Soldier in the West Indies in the French Revolution and Napoleonic Wars* (London: Pen and Sword, 2015).
55. Jean Claude Gillet, *La Marine Imperiale: Le Grand Reve de Napoleon* (Paris: Bernard Giovanagneli, 2010), 132–33.
56. David Geggus, *Slavery, War, and Revolution: The British Occupation of Saint Domingue, 1793–1798* (Oxford: Clarendon Press, 1982).
57. Duffy, *Soldiers, Sugar, and Seapower*, 110, 113.
58. Duffy, *Soldiers, Sugar, and Seapower*, 156.
59. For overviews of British dissidents that preceded, embrace, or transcend the era, see: George Rude, *The Crowd in History: A Study of Popular Disturbances in France and England,*

1730–1848 (New York: Wiley, 1964); E.P. Thompson, *The Making of the English Working Class* (London: Penguin, 1968); Simon Maccoby, *The English Radical Tradition, 1763–1783* (Westport, Conn.: Greenwood, 1978); Albert Goodwin, *The Friends of Liberty: The English Democratic Movement in the Age of the French Revolution* (Cambridge, Mass.: Harvard University Press, 1979); J.E. Cookson, *The Friends of Peace: Anti-War Liberalism in England, 1793–1815* (Cambridge: Cambridge University Press, 1982); Ann Hone, *For the Cause of Truth: Radicalism in London, 1796–1821* (Oxford: Oxford University Press, 1982); Michael Kennedy, *The Jacobin Clubs in the French Revolution: The First Years* (Princeton, N.J.: Princeton University Press, 1982); Roger Wells, *Insurrection: The British Experience, 1795–1803* (Oxford: Oxford University Press, 1983); John Bohstedt, *Riots and Community Politics in England and Wales, 1790–1810* (Cambridge, Mass.: Harvard University Press, 1983); H.T. Dickinson, *British Radicalism and the French Revolution, 1789–1815* (Oxford: Oxford University Press, 1985); William Stafford, *Socialism, Radicalism, and Nostalgia: Social Criticism in Britain, 1775–1830* (New York: Cambridge University Press, 1987); Roger Wells, *Wretched Faces: Famine in Wartime England, 1793–1801* (Gloucester: Sutton, 1988); Seamus Deane, *The French Revolution and Enlightenment in England, 1789–1832* (Cambridge, Mass.: Harvard University Press, 1988); Gwyn Williams, *Artisans and Sans Culottes: Popular Movements in France and Britain During the French Revolution* (London: Edward Arnold, 1989); Derek Jarrett, *Three Faces of Revolution: Paris, London, New York in 1789* (London: G. Philip, 1989); David Bindman, *The Shadow of the Guillotine: Britain and the French Revolution* (London: British Museum Publications, 1989); Bernard Porter, *Plots and Paranoia: A History of Political Espionage in Britain, 1790–1988* (New York: Routledge, 1992); Alan Wharam, *The Treason Trials, 1794* (Leicester: Leicester University Press, 1992); David Worrall, *Radical Culture: Discourse, Resistance, and Surveillance, 1790–1820* (Detroit: Wayne State University Press, 1992); Martin Credel, *The Origins of War Prevention: The British Peace Movement and International Relations, 1730–1854* (Oxford: Oxford University Press, 1996); Peter Spence, *The Birth of Romantic Radicalism: War, Popular Politics, and English Radical Reformism, 1800–1815* (Aldershot: Scholar Press, 1996); Jenny Graham, *The Nation, the Law, and the King: Reform Politics in England, 1789–1799* (Lanham, Maryland: University Press of America, 2000); Edward Royle, *Revolutionary Britain?: Reflections on the Threat of Revolution in Britain, 1789–1848* (Manchester: Manchester University Press, 2000); John Barrell, *Imagining the King's Death: Figurative Treason, Fantasies of Regicide, 1793–1796* (Oxford: Oxford University Press, 2000); Robert Shoemaker, *The London Mob: Violence and Disorder in Eighteenth Century England* (London: Hambledon, 2004).

60. Robert Dozier, *For King, Constitution, and Country: The English Loyalists and the French Revolution* (Lexington: University of Kentucky Press, 1983).
61. Boyd Hinton, *A Mad, Bad, & Dangerous People?: England 1783–1846* (Oxford: Clarendon Press, 2008), 65.
62. Sparrow, *Secret Service*, 3.
63. John Ehrman, *The Younger Pitt: The Reluctant Transition* (London: Constable, 1996), 136–37 Mitchell, *Underground War*, 256–60.
64. Mitchell, *Underground War*, 103–05.
65. Mitchell, *Underground War*, 51–68, 118–19.
66. Jean Gallet, *Les Paysans en Guerre* (Paris: Editions Ouest-France, 1988), 104–33; Nicolas Tracy, ed., *The Naval Chronicle: The Contemporary Record of the Royal Navy at War, 1793–1815*, 5 vols (Mechanicsburg, Penn.: Stackpole Books, 1999), 1:133–38.
67. Mitchell, *Underground War*, 132, 135–36.

68. Jenny Uglow, *In These Times: Living in Britain through Napoleon's Wars* (New York: Faber and Faber, 2015), 163.
69. Sherwig, *Guineas & Gunpowder*, 99.
70. Sherwig, *Guineas & Gunpowder*, 137.
71. Duffy, *Soldiers, Sugar, and Seapower*, 257.
72. Duffy, *Soldiers, Sugar, and Seapower*, 309.
73. Roger Buckley, *Slaves in Red Coats: The British West Indian Regiments, 1795–1815* (New Haven, Conn.: Yale University Press, 1979).
74. Howard, *Death Before Glory!*, 13, 200.
75. William Nester, *Napoleon and the Art of Diplomacy: How War and Hubris Determined the Rise and Fall of the French Empire* (New York: Savas Beattie, 2012); William Nester, *Napoleon and the Art of Leadership: How a Flawed Genius Changed the History of Europe and the World* (London: Frontline Books, 2021).
76. Mitchell, *Underground War*, 119–124.
77. Mitchell, *Underground War*, 140–47, 157.
78. Mitchell, *Underground War*, 182–83.
79. Mitchell, *Underground War*, 212–13.
80. Mostert, *Line Upon a Wind*, 194.
81. Parkinson, *Britannia Rules*, 44.
82. Sherwig, *Guineas & Gunpowder*, 87–88, 95.
83. Mitchell, *Underground War*, 163.
84. *British Statistics*, 402.
85. Grenville to Starhemberg, 4 July 1797, *Fortescue Manuscripts*, 3:332.

Chapter 5: Second 1798–1802

1. *Nelson's Dispatches*, 3:24.
2. Mackesy, *War without Victory*, 150.
3. William Wickham to Grenville, 13 December 1799, *Fortescue Manuscripts*, 6:74.
4. William Wickham to Grenville, 15 April 1800, *Fortescue Manuscripts*, 6:196.
5. William Grenville to William Wickham, 30 November 1799, *Fortescue Manuscripts*, 6:52–53.
6. For the best overview, see: Thomas Pakenham, *The Year of Liberty: The Great Irish Rebellion of 1798* (New York: Abacus 2004).
    For the broader political situation, see: Edith Johnston, *Ireland in the Eighteenth Century* (Dublin: Gill and Macmillan, 1974); M.R. O'Connell, *Irish Politics and Social Conflict in the Age of the American Revolution* (Westport, Conn.: Greenwood, 1976); R.B. McDowell, *Ireland in the Age of Imperialism and Revolution, 1760–1801* (Oxford: Oxford University Press, 1979); T.W. Moody and W.E. Vaughan, *A New History of Ireland: Eighteenth Century Ireland, 1691–1800* (Oxford: Oxford University Press, 1986); Gerard O'Brien, *Anglo-Irish Politics in the Age of Grattan and Pitt* (Dublin: Irish Academic Press, 1987); James Kelly, *Prelude to Union: Anglo-Irish Politics in the 1780s* (Cork: Cork University Press, 1992); Thomas Bartlett, *The Fall and Rise of the Irish Nation: The Catholic Question, 1691–1830* (New York: Barnes and Noble Books, 1992).
7. For the United Irishmen and the revolutionary movement, see: Marianne Elliot, *Partners in Revolution: The United Irishman and France* (New Haven, Conn.: Yale University Press, 1982); Marianne Eliot, *Wolf Tone: The Prophet of Irish Independence* (New Haven, Conn.: Yale University Press, 1989); Hugh Gough and David Dickson, eds., *Ireland and the French*

Revolution (Dublin: Irish Academic Press, 1990); Jim Smyth, *The Men of No Property: Irish Radicals and Popular Politics in the Late Eighteenth Century* (Basingstoke: Palgrave Macmillan, 1992); David Dickson, Daire Keogh, and Kevin Whelan, eds., *The United Irishmen: Republicanism, Radicalism, and Rebellion* (Dublin: Irish Academic Press, 1993); Daire Keogh, *The French Disease: The Catholic Church and Irish Radicalism, 1790–1800* (Dublin: Irish Academic Press, 1993); Nancy Curtin, *The United Irishmen: Popular* Politics in Ulster and *Dublin, 1791–1798* (Oxford: Oxford University Press, 1994); John Gibney, *The United Irishmen, Rebellion, and the Act of Union, 1798–1803* (New York: Palgrave Macmillan, 2019).

8. E.H. Jones, *An Invasion that Failed: The French Expedition to Ireland, 1796* (Oxford: Oxford University Press, 1950).
9. Pakenham, *Year of Liberty*, 342, 281, 265.
10. Horatio Nelson to John Jervis, 4 October 1798, *Nelson Dispatches*, (??????????????).
11. John Davis, *Nelson and Naples: Revolution and Retribution in 1799* (London: Amberley Publishing, 2018).
12. Grenville to Mulgrave, 29 October 1799, *Fortescue Manuscripts*, 5:506.
13. Grenville to Mito, 1 November 1799, *Fortescue Manuscripts*, 6:1.
14. Dundas to Grenville, 8 November 1799, *Fortescue Manuscripts*, 6:12–13.
15. William Wickham to Grenville, 19 October 1799, *Fortescue Manuscripts*, 5:485.
16. William Wickham to Grenville, 7 October 1799, *Fortescue Manuscripts*, 5:456.
17. Grenville to Mulgrave, 29 October 1799, *Fortescue Manuscripts*, 5:505–06.
18. Tom Pocock, *A Thirst for Glory: The Life of Admiral Sir Sidney Smith* (London: Thistle, 2013).
19. Buckingham to Grenville, 2 January 1800, *Fortescue Manuscripts*, 6:95.
20. George Hammond to Grenville, December [n.d], 1799, *Fortescue Manuscripts*, 6:72.
21. Piers Mackesy, *War without Victory: The Downfall of Pitt, 1799–1802* (Oxford: Clarendon Press, 1984), 43.
22. Dundas to Grenville, 24 November 1799, *Fortescue Manuscripts*, 6:38.
23. Portland to Henry Addington, 16 May 1801, *Addington Correspondence*, 1:404.
24. Stanhope, *Life of Pitt*, 3:207.
25. Pitt to Grenville, 3 January 1800, *Fortescue Manuscripts*, 6:96.
26. William Hague, *William Pitt the Younger* (New York: Harper Perennial, 2004), 252.
27. Elizabeth Sparrow, *Secret Service: British Agents in France, 1792–1815* (London: Boydell Press, 1999), 209.
28. Grenville to William Wickham, 30 November 1799, *Fortescue Manuscripts*, 6:53.
29. William Pitt to Grenville, 22 December 1799, *Fortescue Manuscripts*, 6:84.
30. Charles Grey to William Pitt, 16 January 1800, *Fortescue Manuscripts*, 6:98. See also the report, 'Royalist Insurrection in Brittany', [n.d.], *Fortescue Manuscripts*, 6:99–104.
31. Dundas Memorandum for the Consideration of His Majesty's Ministers, 31 March 1800, PRO, 30/8/243.
32. William Wickham to Grenville, 13 December 1799, *Fortescue Manuscripts*, 6:74.
33. William Grenville to William Wickham, 28 March 1800, *Fortescue Manuscripts*, 6:186.
34. Stanhope, *Life of Pitt*, 3:XIV, appendix.
35. G.C. Bolton, *The Passing of the Act of Union: A Study in Parliamentary Politics* (Oxford: Clarendon Press, 1966); Patrick Geoghegan, *The Irish Act of Union: A Study in High Politics, 1798–1801* (Dublin: Irish Academic Press, 1999).
36. John Bew, *Castlereagh: Enlightenment, War, and Tyranny* (London: Quercus, 2011), 132.

37. John Gibney, *The United Irishmen, Rebellion, and the Act of Union, 1798–1803* (New York: Palgrave Macmillan, 2019); David Wilkinson, *The Duke of Portland: Politics and Party in the Age of George III* (New York: Palgrave Macmillan, 2003), 152; C.F. McGleenon, *A Very Independent County: Parliamentary Elections and Politics in County Armagh, 1750–1800* (Belfast: Ulster Historical Foundation, 2011), 265–66.
38. Bew, *Castlereagh*, 143.
39. William Pitt to King George III, 31 January 1801, *Addington Correspondence*, 1:290.
40. King George III to William Pitt, 31 January 1801, *Addington Correspondence*, 1:291.
41. William Hague, *William Pitt the Younger* (New York: Harper Perennial, 2004), 468.
42. King George III to Henry Addington, 29 January 1801, *Addington Correspondence*, 1:285.
43. King George III to Henry Addington, 29 January 1801, *Addington Correspondence*, 1:285.
44. Mr Abbot's Diary, 31 January 1801, *Addington Correspondence*, 1:287
45. Philip Ziegler, *Addington: A Life of Henry Addington, First Viscount Sidmouth* (New York: John Day Company, 1965); Charles Fedorak, *Henry Addington, Prime Minister, 1801–1804: Peace, War, and Parliamentary Politics* (Akron, Ohio: Akron University Press, 2002).
46. Henry Addington quoted by Lord Spencer, February [n.d.] 1801, *Addington Correspondence*, 1:356.
47. Sketch of a Plan of Peace, [n.d.] 1800, Settled at the Cabinet at the Time of the Discussions with Otto', *Addington Correspondence*, 1:257–60.
48. Cornwallis to Hawkesbury, 10 November 1801, *Cornwallis Correspondence*, 3:390.
49. Cornwallis to Hawkesbury, 20 November 1801, *Cornwallis Correspondence*, 3:394–95.
50. Mostert, *Line Upon a Wind*, 294.
51. Blanning, *French Revolutionary Wars*, 203, 211; Mostert, *Line Upon the Wind*, 421.
52. Hawkesbury to Grenville, 1 October 1801, *Fortescue Manuscripts*, 7:45.
53. William Pitt to Grenville, 5 October 1801, *Fortescue Manuscripts*, 7:49.
54. Cornwallis to Hawkesbury, 7 December 1801, *Cornwallis Correspondence*, 3:406.

Chapter 6: Third, 1803–05

1. For the best book on the Third Coalition, see Frederick Kagan, *The End of the Old Order: Napoleon and Europe, 1801–1805* (New York: Da Capo Press, 2006).
2. Andrew Roberts, *Napoleon: A Life* (New York: Viking, 2014), 347.
3. Stephen Taylor, *Commander: The Life of and Exploits of Britain's Greatest Frigate Commander* (New York: W.W. Norton, 2012), 176.
4. William Pitt memorandum on the Deliverance and Security of Europe, 19 January 1805, *British Foreign Policy*, 10–21.
5. Jonathan Coad, *The Portsmouth Block Mills: Bentham, Brunel, and the Start of the Royal Navy's Industrial Revolution* (London: English Heritage, 2005).
6. Sherwig, *Guineas & Gunpowder*, 148–49, 153, 165.
7. For the best overview of the years of plans and campaigns that ended with Trafalgar, see: Alan Schom, *Trafalgar: Countdown to Battle, 1803–1805* (New York: Oxford University Press, 1990).
8. Schom, *Trafalgar*, 354–55.
9. William Hague, *William Pitt the Younger* (New York: Harper Perennial, 2004), 572.

Chapter 7: Fourth, 1806–07

1. Sherwig, *Guineas & Gunpowder*, 186.
2. Richard Hopton, *The Battle of Maida, 1806* (London: Leo Cooper, 2002).

3. Eli Heckscher, *The Continental System, an Economic Interpretation* (Oxford: Clarendon Press, 1922).
4. Wilkinson, David, *The Duke of Portland: Politics and Party in the Age of George III* (New York: Palgrave Macmillan, 2003).
5. Dixon, Peter, *George Canning: Politician and Statesman* (New York: Mason and Charter, 1976).
6. Dixon, *Canning*, 56, 126, 115, 123–24.
7. Sherwig, *Guineas & Gunpowder*, 186.
8. Thomas Munch-Petersen, *Defying Napoleon: How Britain Bombarded Copenhagen and Seized the Danish Fleet in 1807* (London: Sutton Mill, 2007).
9. Paul Schroeder, *The Transformation of European Politics, 1763–1848* (New York: Oxford University Press, 1994), 330.
10. For a good overview of the subsequent French campaign and results for Portugal, Brazil, and Britain, see: Laurentino Gomes, *1808, The Flight of the Emperor: How A Weak Prince, A Mad Queen, and the British Navy Tricked Napoleon and Changed the World* (Guilford, Conn.: Lyons Press, 2013).
11. Sherwig, *Guineas & Gunpowder*, 191.
12. For overviews of Britain's abolitionist movement, see: Roger Anstey, *The Atlantic Slave Trade and British Abolition, 1760–1810* (London: Verso, 1975); Seymour Drescher, *Econocide: British Slavery in the Era of Abolition* (Pittsburgh: University of Pittsburgh, 1977); Seymour Drescher, *Capitalism and Antislavery: British Mobilization in Comparative Perspective* (Basingstoke: Palgrave Macmillan, 1986); David Eltis, *Economic Growth and the Ending of the Trans-Atlantic Slave Trade* (Oxford: Oxford University Press, 1987); David Turley, *The Culture of English Antislavery, 1780* (London: Routledge, 1991); David Davis, *The Problem of Slavery in the Age of Revolution, 1770–1823* (Ithaca, N.Y.: Cornell University Press, 1997); Robin Blackburn, *The Overthrow of Colonial Slavery, 1776–1848* (London: Verso, 1993); J.R. Oldfield, *Popular Politics and British Anti-Slavery: The Mobilization of Public Opinion against the Slave Trade, 1787–1807* (Manchester: Manchester University Press, 1995); Judith Jennings, *The Business of Abolishing the British Slave Trade* (New York: Routledge, 1997).
13. John Pollock, *Wilberforce* (New York: St Martin's Press, 1977).

Chapter 8: Fifth, 1808–11

1. Sherwig, *Guineas & Gunpowder*, 192–93.
2. Sherwig, *Guineas & Gunpowder*, 198–200.
3. Mostert, *Line Upon a Wind*, 558.
4. For Wellington's best biographies, see: Elizabeth Longford, *Wellington: Years of the Sword* (New York: Harper and Row, 1969); Arthur Bryant, *The Great Duke or the Invincible General* (New York: William Morrow and Company, 1972); Jac Weller, *Wellington in the Peninsula* (Mechanicsburg, Penn.: Stackpole Books, 1992); Christopher Hibbert, *Wellington: A Personal History* (Reading, Mass.: Perseus Books, 1997); Michael Glover, *Wellington as Military Commander* (New York: Penguin, 2001).
5. Longford, *Wellington*, 19.
6. For the importance of Wellington's family to his success and their own political achievements, see: Iris Butler, *The Eldest Brother: The Marquess Wellesley, 1760–1842* (London: Hodder and Stoughton, 1972); John Severn, *Architects of Victory: The Duke of Wellington and His Brothers* (Norman: University of Oklahoma Press, 2007).
7. *Croker Papers*, I:12–13.

8. Sherwig, *Guineas & Gunpowder*, 199.
9. Sherwig, *Guineas & Gunpowder*, 203.
10. Sherwig, *Guineas & Gunpowder*, 210–12.
11. Roger Knight, *Britain against Napoleon: The Organization of Victory, 1793–1815* (New York: Allen Lane, 2013), 408; Andrew Lim, *Walcheren to Waterloo: The British Army in the Low Countries During the French Revolutionary and Napoleonic Wars, 1793–1815* (London: Pen and Sword, 2018), 127.
12. Arthur Wellesley to William Huskisson, 5 May 1809; Arthur Wellesley to John Villiers, 31 May and 1 June 1809; Arthur Wellesley to Castlereagh, 11 June 1809; *Wellington Dispatches*, 4:302; 374 and 382–83; 413–14; Castlereagh to Arthur Wellesley, 11 July 1809, *Castlereagh Correspondence*, 7:95–96.
13. Esdaile, *Peninsular War*, 314.
14. Frederick Ware, ed., *Letters from the Peninsula, 1808–1812, by Lieutenant General Sir William Ware* (London: John Murray, 1909), 115–16.
15. Wellington to Liverpool, 30 September 1810, *Wellington Dispatches*, 6:444.
16. Esdaile, *Peninsular War*, 316.
17. Sherwig, *Guineas & Gunpowder*, 219.
18. Sherwig, *Guineas & Gunpowder*, 226, 229–30.
19. Paul Berry, *By Royal Appointment: A Biography of Mary Ann Clark, Mistress of the Duke of York* (London: Femina, 1970); Philip Harling, 'The Duke of York Affair (1809) and the Complexities of War Time Patriotism', *History Journal*, vol. 39 (1996), 963–84.
20. Denis Gray, *Spencer Perceval: The Evangelical Prime Minister, 1762–1812* (Manchester: Manchester University, 1963).
21. Steven Parissien, *George IV: Inspiration of the Regency* (New York: St Martin's Press, 2001).
22. Ronald Fraser, *Napoleon's Cursed War: Popular Resistance in the Spanish Peninsular War* (New York: Verso, 2008).
23. Andre Miot, *Memoires du Comte Miot de Melito*, 3 vols, Ancien Ministre, Ambassadeur, Conseilleur d'Etat et Membre de l'Institut (Paris: Michael Levy Freres, 1858), 3:56–58.
24. Philip Haythornthwaite, *Memoirs of the War in the Peninsula* (London: Greenhill, 1990), 89.
25. Heinrich von Brandt, *The Two Minas and the Spanish Guerillas* (London: T. Egerton, 1825), 54–55.
26. Brandt, *Spanish Guerillas*, 57–58.
27. Haythornthwaite, *Memoirs of the War in the Peninsula*, 89.
28. Esdaile, *Peninsular War*, 260.
29. *Wellington Dispatches*, 5:411–15.
30. *Wellington Supplements*, 7:69.
31. Sherwig, *Guineas & Gunpowder*, 219, 221, 223.
32. Richard Wellesley to George Canning, 15 September 1809, PRO, FO, 72/76; Plan for the Future of the Peninsula, September [n.d], 1809, Wellesley Papers, BL add. mss 37287.
33. Sherwig, *Guineas & Gunpowder*, 227–28.
34. *Henry Wellesley Diary*, 64.
35. Wellington to Henry Wellesley, 12 May 1811, *Wellington Dispatches*, 7:568.
36. Wellington to Bathurst, 5 October 1812, Esdaile, *Peninsular War*, 410.
37. Wellington to William Cooke, 25 November 1812, Esdaile, *Peninsular War*, 420.
38. Arthur Wellesley to Richard Wellesley, 24 August 1809, BL Add. Mss. 37289, ff. 41–70.
39. Thomas Sydenham to Henry Wellesley, 12 September 1812, Esdaile, *Peninsular War*, 410.
40. Wellington to Liverpool, 23 March 1811, *Wellington Dispatches*, 7:380.

41. Samuel Whitbread, 22 February 1810, *Parliamentary Debates*, 1st series, 16:10–11.
42. Alexander Gordon to Aberdeen, 30 April 1811, *Gordon Letters*, 197.
43. William Grattan, *The Adventures of the Connaught Rangers from 1808 to 1814* (London: Edward Arnold, 1902), 2:95–96.
44. William Thompson, ed., *An Ensign in the Peninsular War: The Letters of John Aichison* (London: Michael Joseph, 1981), 162.
45. Michael Glover, ed., *A Gentleman Volunteer: The Letters of George Hennell from the Peninsular War* (London: Heineman, 1979), 52.
46. John Kincaid, Adventures in the Rifle Brigade (London: (), 1909), 103.
47. T.H. McGuffie, ed., *Peninsula Cavalry General: The Correspondence of Lieutenant General Robert Ballard Long* (London: George C. Harrap, 1951), 231.
48. General Order, 10 June 1812, *Wellington Supplements*, 7:345.
49. Liverpool to Layard, July [n.d.], 1810, PRO, FO 185/18; Richard Wellesley to Henry Wellesley, 13 July 1810, PRO, FO, 185/18.
50. Richard Wellesley to Henry Wellesley, 13 July 1810, *Wellesley Papers*, BL, add. mss. 49979. Quote from John Severn, *Architects of Empire: The Duke of Wellington and His Brothers* (Norman: University of Oklahoma Press, 2007), 317.
51. William Kaufman, *British Policy and the Independence of Latin America, 1804–1828* (New Haven, Conn.: Yale University Press, 1951).
52. Esdaile, *Peninsular War*, 406.
53. Esdaile, *Peninsular War*, 438.
54. Sherwig, *Guineas & Gunpowder*, 204.
55. Henry Wellesley to Richard Wellesley, 15 April 1811, PRO, FO, 72/110.
56. Henry Wellesley to Richard Wellesley, 31 March 1810, Wellesley Papers, BL, add. mss. 49981; Henry Wellesley to Bardají, 5 July 1810; Henry Wellesley to Richard Wellesley, 11 July 1810, PRO, FO 72/96.
57. Charles Esdaile, *The Peninsular War: A New History* (New York: Palgrave Macmillan, 2003), 290; Henry Wellesley to Castlereagh, 25 May 1813, PRO FO 72/144, ff. 196–200; Henry Wellesley to Wellington, 2 April 1810, *Cowley Papers*, PRO FO, 519/34; Henry Wellesley to Richard Wellesley, 13 July 1810, PRO, FO 72/96; Henry Wellesley to Wellington, 4 February 1813, *Wellington Supplements*, 7:546. 72/96; Henry Wellesley to Wellington, 31 August 1810, *Wellesley Supplements*, 6:583–84.
58. Sherwig, *Guineas & Gunpowder*, 266.

Chapter 9: Sixth, 1812–14

1. Muir, *Defeat of Napoleon*, 158.
2. For the best biography, see: John Bew, *Castlereagh: Enlightenment, War, and Tyranny* (London: Quercus, 2011). See also: C.J. Bartlett, *Castlereagh* (New York: Charles Scribners' Sons, 1966) and C.K. Webster, *The Foreign Policy of Castlereagh, 1812–1815: Britain and the Reconstruction of Europe* (London: G. Bell and Sons, 1931).
3. Castlereagh to Cathcart, 6 July 1813, *British Diplomacy*, 11; Castlereagh to Cathcart, 8 April 1812, *British Diplomacy*, 1.
4. Sherwig, *Guineas & Gunpowder*, 274–79.
5. Sherwig, *Guineas & Gunpowder*, 277–81.
6. Castlereagh to Cathcart, 18 September 1813, *British Diplomacy*, 20.
7. Rory Muir, *Britain and the Defeat of Napoleon, 1807–1815* (New Haven, Conn.: Yale University Press, 1996), 198–99.

8. Philip Roche to Wellington, 6 March 1810, PRO WO 1/243, ff. 490–94.
9. Wellington to Henry Wellesley, 3 October 1810, *Wellington Dispatches*, 6:456.
10. Henry Wellesley to William Wellesley, 12 March 1801, *Henry Wellesley Diary*, 54.
11. Henry Wellesley to Richard Wellesley, 10 November 1810, PRO, FO, 72/98.
12. Esdaile, *Peninsular War*, 307.
13. Henry Wellesley to Wellington, 6 August 1812, Esdaile, *Peninsular War*, 401.
14. Henry Wellesley to Richard Wellesley, 5 April 1811, *Wellesley Papers*, BL, add. mss. 49983.
15. Esdaile, *Peninsular War*, 424.
16. Esdaile, *Peninsular War*, 426.
17. Henry Wellesley to Castlereagh, 1 October 1812, PRO FO 72/132, ff. 105–07.
18. Wellington to Angel de la Vega, 3 April 1813, Esdaile, *Peninsular War*, 438.
19. Wellington to Henry Wellesley, 3 May 1812, Esdaile, *Peninsular War*, 409.
20. Wellington to Jose Maria de Carvajal, 4 December 1812, Esdaile, *Peninsular War*, 423.
21. Wellington to Jose Maria de Carvajal, 4 December 1812, Esdaile, *Peninsular War*, 423.
22. Wellington to Henry Wellesley, 2 August 1811, *Wellington Dispatches*, 8:159.
23. Wellington to Henry Wellesley, 2 July 1813, Esdaile, *Peninsular War*, 465.
24. Esdaile, *Peninsular War*, 495.
25. Wellington to Bathurst, 29 June 1813, Esdaile, *Peninsular War*, 466.
26. Wellington to Liverpool, *Wellington Dispatches*, 5:536.
27. Jenny Uglow, *In These Time: Living in Britain through Napoleon's War, 1793–1815* (London: Faber and Faber, 2014), 571.
28. Wellington to Liverpool, *Wellington Supplements*, 9:266.
29. Wellington to Liverpool, *Wellington Dispatches*, 5:434.
30. Liverpool to Wellington, 15 December 1809, *Liverpool Papers*, BL, add. mss. 38244.
31. Schaumann, *Diary*, 162.
32. Wellington to Prince Joao, 12 April 1813, *Wellington Dispatches*, 6:417–20.
33. Wellington to Henry Wellesley, 20 August 1810, *Wellington Dispatches*, 6:351.
34. Sherwig, *Guineas & Gunpowder*, 246.
35. Sherwig, *Guineas and Gunpowder*, 365–68.
36. For the best overview, see: Donald Hickey, *The War of 1812: A Forgotten Conflict* (Urbana: University of Illinois Press, 1990).
37. C. Northcote Parkinson, *Britannia Rules: The Classic Age of Naval History, 1793–1815* (London: Allan Sutton, 1994), 149.
38. Mostert, *Line Upon a Wind*, 294.
39. Thomas MacDonald to Grenville, 25 October 1800, *Fortescue Manuscripts*, 6:359.
40. Jonathan Russell to James Monroe, 17 September 1812, ASPFR, 3:394–95.
41. Elizabeth Longford, *Wellington: Years of the Sword* (New York: Harper and Row, 1969), 307.
42. Henry, Earl Bathurst speech, 8 November 1813, *Parliamentary Debates*, 26:47.
43. Wellington to Bathurst, 27 November 1813, BL Add. Mss. 38255, ff. 55–58.
44. Arthur Wellesley to William Wellesley-Pole, 29 August 1809, *Wellesley-Pole Letters*, 22.
45. Wellington's words recorded by Sydenham to Henry Wellesley, 12 September 1812, quoted in Huw J. Davies, *Wellington's Wars: The Making of Military Genius* (New Haven, Conn.: Yale University Press, 2012), 167.
46. Esdaile, *Peninsular War*, 488.
47. Castlereagh to Aberdeen, 28 September 1813, *British Diplomacy*, 99; Castlereagh to Cathcart, 18 September 1813, *British Diplomacy*, 20.
48. Sherwig, *Guineas & Gunpowder*, 284–87.

222 The Coalitions against Napoleon

49. Cathcart to Castlereagh, private [November 1813], *British Diplomacy*, 42.
50. Castlereagh to Cathcart, 7 August 1813, *British Diplomacy*, 17.
51. Castlereagh to Cathcart, 6 July 1813, *British Diplomacy*, 11.
52. Project of a Treaty of Alliance Offensive and Defensive against France, 18 September 1813, Project of Secret Articles, *British Diplomacy*, 24–25, 26–27.
53. Sherwig, *Guineas & Gunpowder*, 287–92, 296.
54. Castlereagh to Cathcart, 30 June 1813, *British Diplomacy*, 5–6.
55. Stewart to Castlereagh, 16 June 1813, *British Diplomacy*, 69.
56. Cathcart to Castlereagh, private [November 1813], *British Diplomacy*, 42.
57. Castlereagh to Aberdeen, 21 September 1813, *British Diplomacy*, 97.
58. Castlereagh to Cathcart, 21 September 1813, *British Diplomacy*, 30.
59. Francis Jackson to Charles Stewart, 27 July 1813, *British Diplomacy*, 73.
60. Aberdeen to Castlereagh, 8, 9, November 1813; *British Diplomacy*, 107–08, 109–11.
61. Memorandum of Cabinet, 26 December 1813; Memorandum on the Maritime Peace, *British Diplomacy*, 123–26; 12628.
62. Traite de Valencay avec Ferdinand VII, Michel Kerautret, ed., *Les Grand Traites de L'Empire* (Paris: Nouvelle Monde Editions, 2004), 2:100–03.
63. Wellington to (), (), *Wellington Dispatches*, 11:306–07.
64. Wellington to Henry Wellesley, 26 January 1814, Esdaile, *Peninsular War*, 488.
65. Quoted in Severn, *Architects of Empire*, 373.
66. Castlereagh to Aberdeen, 13 November 1813, *British Diplomacy*, 112.
67. Sherwig, *Guineas & Gunpowder*, 317.
68. Castlereagh to Liverpool, 26 February 1814, *British Diplomacy*, 160.
69. Castlereagh to Liverpool, 13 April 1814, *British Diplomacy*, 176.
70. Zamoyski, *Rites of Peace*, 194–203.

Chapter 10: Seventh, 1815

1. Henry Wellesley to Wellington, 16 May 1814, *Wellington Supplements*, 9:74.
2. *Stanhope Conversations*, 79.
3. Wellington to Castlereagh, 15 September 1814, Longford, *Wellington: Years of the Sword*, 378.
4. Hibbert, *Wellington*, 159.
5. Philip Haythornthwaite, *The Armies of Wellington* (London: Brockhampton Press, 1996), 8.
6. For overviews, see: Fred Engelman, *The Peace of Christmas Eve* (New York: Harcourt, Brace, 1962); Bradford Perkins, *Castlereagh and Adams: England and the United States, 1812–1823* (Berkeley: University of California Press, 1964); Frank Updyke, *The Diplomacy of the War of 1812* (Gloucester, Mass.: P. Smith, 1965).
7. Adkins, *War of the Oceans*, 383.
8. Noel Mostert, *The Line Upon A Wind: The Great War at Sea, 1793–1815* (New York: W.W. Norton, 2007), 670.
9. W.F. Galpin, 'The American Grain Trade to the Spanish Peninsula, 1810–1814, *American History Review*, vol. 28 (October 1922), 25; Muir, *Britain and the Defeat of Napoleon*, 237.
10. J. Van Fenstermaker, *The Development of American Commercial Banking, 1782–1837* (Kent, Ohio: Kent State University Press, 1965), 111; Bray Hammond, *Banks and Politics in America from the Revolution to the Civil War* (Princeton, N.J.: Princeton University Press, 1991), 182–83.

11. George Izard to John Armstrong, 31 July 1814, Allen S. Everest, ed., *The War of 1812 in the Champlain Valley* (Syracuse, N.Y.: Syracuse University Press, 1981), 150–52.
12. George Prevost to Henry, Earl Bathurst, 27 August 1814, PRO CO42/157.
13. Ralph Hidy, *The House of Baring in American Trade and Finance: English Merchants Bankers at Work, 1763–1861* (Cambridge, Mass.: Harvard University Press, 1949).
14. Liverpool to Castlereagh, 28 October 1814, *British Diplomacy*, 220.
15. Castlereagh to Monroe, 4 November 1813, (), Hickey, *War of 1812*, 285.
16. F.L. Engelman, *The Peace of Christmas Eve* (London: Rupert Hart-Davis, 1962), 297.
17. Liverpool to Canning, 28 December 1814, in Charles D. Yonge, *The Life and Administration of Robert Banks, Second Earl of Liverpool, K.G., Late First Lord of the Treasury*, 3 vols (London: Macmillan, 1868), 2:76.
18. Wellington to Liverpool, 9 November 1814, *Wellington Dispatches*, 9:425–26.
19. Liverpool to Castlereagh, 18 November 1814, *Wellington Dispatches*, 9:438.
20. *United States Bureau of the Census: Historical Statistics of the United States*, 2:1140; Hickey, *War of 1812*, 303.
21. Thomas Jefferson to William Short, 28 November 1814, Adrienne Koch and William Peden, eds., *The Life and Selected Writings of Thomas Jefferson* (New York: Modern Library, 1998), 587–98.
22. Harold Nicolson, *The Congress of Vienna: A Study in Allied Unity, 1812–1822* (New York: Harcourt, Brace, and Company, 1946); Gregor Dallas, *The Final Act: The Roads to Waterloo* (New York: Henry Holt, 1997); Henry Kissinger, *A World Restored: Metternich, Castlereagh, and the Problems of Peace, 1812–1822* (London: Weidenfeld and Nicolson, 1999); Adam Zamoyski, *Rites of Peace: The fall of Napoleon and the Congress of Vienna* (New York: Harper Press, 2007).
23. Nicolson, *Congress of Vienna*, 187.
24. Castlereagh to Liverpool, 9 October 1814, *British Diplomacy*, 204.
25. Castlereagh to Cathcart, 18 December 1813, *British Diplomacy*, 56.
26. Liverpool to Castlereagh, 25 November 1814, *British Diplomacy*, 244–45.
27. Liverpool to Wellington, 23 December 1814, *British Diplomacy*, 268.
28. For Castlereagh's reports on the developing crisis, see: Castlereagh to Liverpool, 24, 25 December 1814, 1 January 1815 (4 letters), 2, 3, 4, 5, 8, 11, *British Diplomacy*, 268–71, 272–73, 274–75, 276–77, 277–78, 279, 280, 280–81, 281–82, 282–83, 283–85, 285–86.
29. Nicolson, *Congress of Vienna*, 178.
30. Castlereagh to Liverpool, 4 January 1815, *British Diplomacy*, 281.
31. Liverpool to Castlereagh, 16 January 1815, *British Diplomacy*, 290.
32. Wellington to Castlereagh, 18 August 1814, *British Diplomacy*, 191.
33. Wellington to Castlereagh, 11 August 1815, *Wellington Dispatches*, 12:596.
34. Wellington to (), (), *Wellington Dispatches*, 12:534.
35. John Raymond, ed., *The Reminiscences and Recollections of Captain Gronow* (London: Bodley Head, 1964), 374.
36. Liverpool to Castlereagh, 23 December 1814, *British Diplomacy*, 264–65.
37. Wellington to Liverpool, 25 December 1814, *British Diplomacy*, 273.
38. Liverpool to Castlereagh, 20 February 1815, *British Diplomacy*, 307.
39. Castlereagh to Wellington, 12 March 1815, *British Diplomacy*, 309.
40. Sherwig, *Guineas & Gunpowder*, 33438.
41. Castlereagh to Wellington, 12, 24 March 1815, *British Diplomacy*, 31011, 314–16.
42. Kissinger, *World Restored*, 189.

43. Castlereagh to Liverpool, 28 September 1815, *British Diplomacy*, 382–84.
44. Carsten Holbraad, *The Concert of Europe: A Study in German and British International Theory, 1815–1914* (New York: Barnes and Noble, 1971); Roy Bridge and Roger Bullen, *The Great Powers and the European State System, 1815–1914* (London: Longman, 2004); Paul Schroeder, 'Did the Vienna Settlement Rest on a Balance of Power?' *The American Historical Review*, vol. 97, no. 3, June 1992, 683–70.

Chapter 11: Legacies

1. Philip Whitwell, ed., *The Grenville Diaries: Volume 1 and 2* (London: William Heinemann, 1927), 1:154–55.
2. For the expansion of British hard power, see: Christopher Bayly, *Imperial Meridian: The British Empire and the World, 1780–1830* (New York: Longman, 1989); Paul Johnson, *The Birth of the Modern: World Society, 1815–1830* (New York: HarperCollins, 1991); Ronald Hyam, *Britain's Imperial Century, 1815–1914: A Study of Empire and Expansion* (Basingstoke: Palgrave Macmillan, 1993); Jennifer Mori, *Britain in the Age of the French Revolution, 1785–1820* (London: Longman, 2000); Linda Colley, *Captives: Britain, Empire, and the World, 1600–1850* (New York: Pantheon, 2002); Christopher Bayly, *The Birth of the Modern World, 1780–1914: Global Connections and Comparisons* (Oxford: Oxford University Press, 2004); Bernard Porter, *The Absent-Minded Imperialists: Empire, Society, and Culture in Britain* (Oxford: Oxford University Press, 2004).

   For the expansion of British soft power, see: Gerald Newman, *The Rise of English Nationalism: A Cultural History, 1740–1830* (Houndmills, Basingstoke: Palgrave Macmillan, 1987); Tony Claydon and Ian McBride, eds., *Protestantism and National Identity: Britain and Ireland, 1650–1850* (Cambridge: Cambridge University Press, 1998); Julian Hoppit, ed., *Parliaments, Nations, and Identities in Britain and Ireland, 1660–1850* (Manchester: Manchester University Press, 2003); Colin Kidd, *British Identities before Nationalism: Ethnicity and Nationhood in the Atlantic World, 1600–1800* (Cambridge: Cambridge University Press, 1999); Krisham Kumar, *The Making of English National Identity* (Cambridge: Cambridge University Press, 2003); Stuart Semmel, *Napoleon and the British* (New Haven, Conn.: Yale University Press, 2004); Linda Colley, *Britons: Forging the Nation, 1707–1837* (New Haven, Conn.: Yale University Press, 2007).
3. Roger Knight, *Britain Against Napoleon: The Organization of Victory, 1793–1815* (New York: Allen Lane, 2013), 372.
4. British Statistics, 281.
5. C. Northcote Parkinson, *The Trade Winds: A Study of British Overseas Trade During the French Wars, 1793–1815* (London: Allen and Unwin, 1948), 165–66.
6. Haythornthwaite, Armies of Wellington, 9–10.
7. Christopher Hall, *Wellington's Navy: Sea Power and the Peninsular War, 1807–1814* (London: Greenhill, 2006), 112.
8. Philip Harling, *The Waning of 'Old Corruption': The Politics of Economical Reform in Britain, 1779–1846* (Oxford: Clarendon, 1996), 170.
9. Boyd Hilton, *A Mad, Bad, & Dangerous People: England, 1783–1846* (New York: Oxford University Press, 2008), 143.
10. Michael Duffy, 'World-Wide War and British Expansion, 1793–1815', P.J. Marshall, ed., *The Oxford History of the British Empire: The Eighteenth Century* (New York: Oxford University Press, 1998), 204.

11. J.R. Ward, 'The British West Indies in the Age of Abolition, 1748–1815', P.J. Marshall, ed., *The Oxford History of the British Empire: The Eighteenth Century* (New York: Oxford University Press, 1998), 433.
12. Michael Duffy, 'World-Wide War and British Expansion, 1793–1815, in P.J. Marshall, ed., *The Oxford History of the British Empire: The Eighteenth Century* (New York: Oxford University Press, 1998), 202.
13. Martin Robson, *Britain, Portugal, and South America in the Napoleonic Wars: Alliance and Diplomacy in Economic Maritime Conflict* (London: I.B. Tauris, 2010).
14. Peter Ackroyd, *Revolution: The History of England from the Battle of the Boyne to the Battle of Waterloo* (New York: Thomas Dunne Books, 2017), 352.

Bibliography

Books

Ackroyd, Peter, *Revolution: The History of England from the Battle of the Boyne to the Battle of Waterloo* (New York: Thomas Dunne Books, 2017).
Adkins, Roy, and Lesley Adkins, *The War for all the Oceans: From Nelson at the Nile to Napoleon at Waterloo* (New York: Viking, 2006).
Albion, Robert, *Forests and Seapower: The Timber Problem of the Royal Navy, 1652–1862* (Cambridge, Mass.: Harvard University Press, 1926).
Allen, Robert, *The British Industrial Revolution in Global Perspective* (New York: Cambridge University Press, 2009).
Altalion, Florin, *The French Revolution: An Economic Explanation* (Cambridge: Cambridge University Press, 1990).
Anderson, Benedict, *Imagined Communities: Reflections on the Origins and Spread of Nationalism* (New York: Verso Press, 1991).
Andress, David, *The Oxford Handbook of the French Revolution* (New York: Oxford University Press, 2019).
Anstey, Roger, *The Atlantic Slave Trade and British Abolition, 1760–1810* (New York: Humanities Press, 1975).
Armitage, David, *The Ideological Origins of the British Empire* (Cambridge: Cambridge University Press, 2000).
Armytage, Frances, *The Free Port System in the British West Indies* (London: Longmans, 1953).
Ashworth, William, *Customs and Excise: Trade, Production, and Consumption in England, 1640–1845* (Oxford: Oxford University Press, 2003).
Aspinall, Arthur, *Politics and the Press, 1780–1850* (New York: Barnes and Noble, 1973).
Barker, Hannah, *Newspapers, Politics, and Public Opinion in Late Eighteenth Century England*, Oxford: Oxford University Press, 1998).
Barker, Hannah, *Newspapers, Politics, and English Society 1695–1855* (New York: Routledge, 2002).
Barker, Hannah, and S. Burrows, eds., *Press, Politics, and the Public Sphere in Europe and North America, 1760–1820* (New York: Cambridge University Press, 2002).
Barrell, John, *Imagining the King's Death: Figurative Treason, Fantasies of Regicide, 1793–1796* (Oxford: Oxford University Press, 2000).
Bartlett, C.J., *Castlereagh* (New York: Charles Scribners' Sons, 1966).
Bartlett, Thomas, *The Fall and Rise of the Irish Nation: The Catholic Question, 1691–1830* (New York: Barnes and Noble Books, 1992).
Bayly, Christopher, *The New Cambridge History of India: Indian Society and the Making of the British Empire* (Cambridge: Cambridge University Press, 1988).
Bayly, Christopher, *Imperial Meridian: The British Empire and the World, 1780–1830* (New York: Longman, 1989).

Bayly, Christopher, *The Birth of the Modern World, 1780–1914: Global Connections and Comparisons* (Oxford: Oxford University Press, 2004).
Beckett, J.V., *The Aristocracy in England, 1660–1914* (Oxford: Oxford University Press, 1986).
Bennet, Geoffrey, *Nelson the Commander* (New York: Charles Scribner's, 1972).
Berg, Maxine, *The Age of Manufacturers: Industry, Innovation, and Work in Britain, 1700–1820* (Oxford: Oxford University Press, 1985).
Berry, Paul, *By Royal Appointment: A Biography of Mary Ann Clark, Mistress of the Duke of York* (London: Femina, 1970).
Bew, John, *Castlereagh: Enlightenment, War, and Tyranny* (London: Quercus, 2011).
Bindman, David, *The Shadow of the Guillotine: Britain and the French Revolution* (London: British Museum Publications, 1989).
Binney, J.E.D., *British Public Finance and Administration, 1774–92* (Oxford: Oxford University Press, 1958).
Black, E.C., *The Association: British Extra-Parliamentary Organisation, 1769–1793* (Cambridge, Mass.: Harvard University Press, 1963).
Black, Jeremy, *The English Press in the Eighteenth Century* (London: Croom Helm, 1987).
Black, Jeremy, *Natural and Necessary Enemies: Anglo-French Relations in the Eighteenth Century* (Athens: University of Georgia Press, 1986).
Black, Jeremy, ed., *Knight Errant and True Englishmen: British Foreign Policy, 1660–1800* (Edinburgh: University of Edinburgh Press, 1989).
Black, Jeremy, *A System of Ambition: British Foreign Policy, 1660–1793* (New York: Longmans, 2000).
Black, Jeremy, *British Foreign Policy in an Age of Revolution, 1783–1793* (New York: Cambridge University Press, 1994).
Black, Jeremy, *George III: America's Last King* (New Haven, Conn.: Yale University Press, 2006).
Black, Jeremy, and Philip Woodfine, eds., *The British Navy and the Use of Naval Power in the Eighteenth Century* (Leicester: Leicester University Press, 1998).
Blackburn, Robin, *The Overthrow of Colonial Slavery, 1776–1848* (London: Verso, 1988).
Blanning, T.C.W., *The French Revolutionary Wars, 1787–1802* (New York: Arnold, 1996).
Blanning, T.C.W., *The Culture of Power and the Power of Culture: Old Regime Europe, 1660–1789* (New York: Oxford University Press, 2003).
Boerner, Peter, ed., *Concepts of National Identity: An Interdisciplinary Dialogue* (Baden-Baden: Nomos, 1986).
Bohstedt, John, *Riots and Community Politics in England and Wales, 1790–1810* (Cambridge, Mass.: Harvard University Press, 1983).
Bolton, G.C., *The Passing of the Act of Union: A Study in Parliamentary Politics* (Oxford: Clarendon Press, 1966).
Bolton, James, *The Language of Politics in the Age of Wilkes and Burke* (Westport, Conn.: Greenwood, 1975).
Bonney, Richard, ed., *The Rise of the Fiscal State in Europe, 1200–1815* (Oxford: Clarendon Press, 1999).
Bordo, Michael, and Eugene White, *A Tale of Two Currencies: British and French Finance During the Napoleonic War* (Cambridge: Cambridge University Press, 1990).
Borsay, Peter, *The English Urban Renaissance: Culture and Society in the Provincial, 1660–1770* (Oxford: Oxford University Press, 1989).
Bourne, J.M., *Patronage and Society in Nineteenth Century England* (London: E. Arnold, 1986).
Bowen, H.V., *Elites, Enterprise, and the Making of British Overseas Empire, 1688–1775* (London: Palgrave Macmillan, 1996).

Braddick, M.J., *The Nerves of State: Taxation and the Financing of the English State, 1558–1714* (Manchester: Manchester University Press, 1996).
Bradshaw, Brendan, and Peter Roberts, ed., *British Consciousness and Identity: The Making of Britain, 1533–1707* (Cambridge: Cambridge University Press, 1998).
Brewer, John, *The Sinews of Power: War, Money, and the English State, 1688–1783* (New York: Alfred A. Knopf, 1989).
Brewer, John, and Eckhart Hellmuth, eds., *Rethinking Leviathan: The Eighteenth-Century State in Britain and Germany* (Oxford: Clarendon Press, 1999).
Bridge, Roy, and Roger Bullen, *The Great Powers and the European State System, 1815–1914* (London: Longman, 2004).
Brockliss, Lawrence, and David Eastwood, eds., *A Union of Multiple Identities: The British Isles 1750–1850* (Manchester: Manchester University Press, 1997).
Bryant, Arthur, *The Great Duke or the Invincible General* (New York: William Morrow and Company, 1972).
Buckley, Roger, *Slaves in Red Coats: The British West Indian Regiments, 1795–1815* (New Haven, Conn.: Yale University Press, 1979).
Burke, Edmund, *Reflections on the Revolution in France*, Mineola, N.Y.: Dover Publications, 2006).
Burne, Alfred, *The Noble, Duke of York* (London: Staples Press, 1949).
Burrow, J.W., *Whigs and Liberals: Continuity and Change in England Political Thought* (Oxford: Clarendon Press, 1988).
Butler, Iris, *The Eldest Brother: The Marquess Wellesley, 1760–1842* (London: Hodder and Stoughton, 1972).
Butler, Marilyn, ed., *Burke, Paine, Godwin, and the Revolution Controversy* (Cambridge: Cambridge University Press, 1984).
Byrne, William, *Edmund Burke for Our Time: Moral Imagination, Meaning, and Politics* (DeKalb: Northern Illinois Press, 2011).
Cain, P.J., and A.G. Hopkins, *British Imperialism: Innovation and Expansion, 1688–1914* (New York: Longman, 1993).
Cannadine, David, ed., *Admiral Lord Nelson: Context and Legacy* (Houndmills, Basingstoke, England: Palgrave Macmillan, 2005).
Cannon, John, *The Fox-North Coalition: Crisis of the Constitution, 1782–84* (Cambridge: Cambridge University Press, 1969).
Cannon, John, *The Aristocratic Century: The Peerage of Eighteenth Century England* (Cambridge: University of Cambridge Press, 1984).
Carretta, Vincent, *George III and the Satirists: From Hogarth to Byron* (Athens: University of Ohio Press, 1990).
Carter, Alice, *The English Public Debt in the Eighteenth Century* (London: Historical Association, 1968).
Chambers, J.D., and G.E. Mingay, *The Agricultural Revolution, 1750–1880* (London: Batsford, 1966).
Chickering, Roger, and Stig Forster, eds., *War in an Age of Revolution, 1775–1815* (New York: Cambridge University Press, 2010).
Christie, Ian, *Wilkes, Wyvill, and Reform: The Parliamentary Reform Movement in British Politics, 1760–1785* (London: Macmillan, 1962).
Claeys, Gregory, *Thomas Paine: Social and Political Thought* (Boston: Unwin Hyman, 1989.
Clapham, John, *The Bank of England: A History*, 2 vols (New York: Cambridge University Press, 2008).

Clark, J.C.D., *English Society, 1688–1832: Ideology, Social Structure, and Political Practice During the Ancien Regime* (New York: Cambridge University Press, 2000).
Clark, J.C.D., *The Language of Liberty, 1660–1832: Political Discourse and Social Dynamics in the Anglo-American World* (New York: Cambridge University Press, 1994).
Clark, Peter, *British Clubs and Societies, 1580–1800: The Origins of an Associational World* (Oxford: Clarendon Press, 2000).
Clark, Peter, ed., *The Cambridge Urban History of Britain, 1540–1840* (New York: Cambridge University Press, 2000).
Clarke, John, *British Diplomacy and Foreign Policy, 1782–1865: The National Interest* (Boston: Unwin, Hymen, 1989).
Clarkson, L.A., *Proto-Industrialisation: The First Phase of Industrialisation?* (London: Macmillan, 1985).
Claydon, Tony, and Ian McBride, eds., *Protestantism and National Identity: Britain and Ireland, 1650–1850* (Cambridge: Cambridge University Press, 1998).
Coad, Jonathan, *The Portsmouth Block Mills: Bentham, Brunel, and the Start of the Royal Navy's Industrial Revolution* (London: English Heritage, 2005).
Cobban, Alfred, ed., *The Debate on the French Revolution* (London: N. Kaye, 1950).
Coleman, Terry, *The Nelson Touch: The Life and Legend of Horatio Nelson* (New York: Oxford University Press, 2002).
Colley, Linda, *Captives: Britain, Empire, and the World, 1600–1850* (New York: Pantheon, 2002).
Colley, Linda, *Britons: Forging the Nation, 1707–1837* (New Haven, Conn.: Yale University Press, 2007).
Cookson, J.E., *The Friends of Peace: Anti-War Liberalism in England, 1793–1815* (Cambridge: Cambridge University Press, 1982).
Cookson, J.E., *The British Armed Nation, 1793–1815* (New York: Oxford University Press, 1997).
Corbett, Julian, ed., *The Private Papers of George, 2nd Earl Spencer*, 2 vols (London: Navy Record Society, 1924).
Corfield, Penelope, *The Impact of English Towns, 1700–1800* (Oxford: Oxford University Press, 1982).
Corfield, Penelope, *Power and the Professions in Britain, 1700–1850* (New York: Routledge, 2000).
Cox, Edward, *The Free Coloreds in the Slave Societies of St Kitts and Grenada, 1763–1833* (Knoxville: University of Tennessee, 1984).
Crafts, N.F.N., *British Economic Growth During the Industrial Revolution* (Oxford: Oxford University Press, 1985).
Craton, Michael, *Testing the Chains: Resistance to Slavery in the British West Indies* (Ithaca, N.Y.: Cornell University Press, 1982).
Credel, Martin, *The Origins of War Prevention: The British Peace Movement and International Relations, 1730–1854* (Oxford: Oxford University Press, 1996).
Crouzet, François, *The First Industrialists: The Problem of Origins* (Cambridge: Cambridge University Press, 1985).
Crouzet, François, *Britain Ascendant: Comparative Studies in Franco-British Economic History* (New York: University of Cambridge Press, 1985).
Crowhurst, Patrick, *The Defence of British Trade, 1689–1815* (Folkstone: Dawson, 1977).
Crowhurst, Patrick, *The French War on Trade: Privateering, 1793–1815* (London: Loughborough, 1985).

Curtin, Nancy, *The United Irishmen: Popular* Politics in Ulster and *Dublin, 1791–1798* (Oxford: Oxford University Press, 1994).
Dallas, Gregor, *The Final Act: The Roads to Waterloo* (New York: Henry Holt, 1996).
Daunton, Martin, *Progress and Poverty: An Economic and Social History of Britain, 1700–1850* (Oxford: Oxford University Press, 1995).
Daunton, Martin, *Taxing Leviathan: The Politics of Taxation in Britain, 1799–1914* (Cambridge: Cambridge University Press, 2001).
Davis, David, *The Problem of Slavery in the Age of Revolution, 1770–1823* (Ithaca, N.Y.: Cornell University Press, 1997).
Davis, John, *Nelson and Naples: Revolution and Retribution in 1799* (London: Amberley Publishing, 2018).
Davis, Ralph, *The Industrial Revolution and British Overseas Trade* (Leicester: University of Leicester Press, 1979).
Derry, John, *The Regency Crisis and the Whigs, 1788–89* (Cambridge: Cambridge University Press, 1963).
Dickson, David, Daire Keogh, and Kevin Whelan, eds., *The United Irishmen: Republicanism, Radicalism, and Rebellion* (Dublin: Irish Academic Press, 1993).
Dickinson, H.T., *British Radicalism and the French Revolution, 1789–1815* (Oxford: Oxford University Press, 1985).
Dickinson, H.T., *Britain and the French Revolution* (Basingstoke: Macmillan, 1989).
Dickinson, H.T., *The Politics of the People in Eighteenth Century Britain* (Basingstoke: Palgrave Macmillan, 1995).
Dickinson, H.T., ed., *A Companion to Eighteenth Century Britain* (Oxford: Blackwell Publishing, 2006).
Dickson, P.G.M., *The Financial Revolution in England: A Study in the Development of Public Credit, 1699–1756* (New York: Routledge, 1993).
Dixon, Peter, *George Canning: Politician and Statesman* (New York: Mason and Charter, 1976).
Donald, Diana, *English Political Caricature: Satirical Prints in the Reign of George III* (New Haven, Conn.: Yale University Press, 1996).
Downing, Brian, *The Military Revolution and Political Change: The Origins of Democracy and Aristocracy in Early Modern Europe* (Princeton, N.J.: Princeton University Press, 1992).
Doyle, William, *The Oxford History of the French Revolution* (New York: Oxford University Press, 1989).
Dozier, Robert, *For King, Constitution, and Country: The English Loyalists and the French Revolution* (Lexington: University of Kentucky Press, 1983).
Drescher, Seymour, *Econocide: British Slavery in the Era of Abolition* (Pittsburgh: University of Pittsburgh, 1977).
Drescher, Seymour, *Capitalism and Antislavery: British Mobilisation in Comparative Perspective* (Basingstoke: Palgrave Macmillan, 1986).
Duane, Seamus, *The French Revolution and Enlightenment in England, 1789–1832* (Cambridge, Mass.: Harvard University Press, 1988).
Duffy, Michael, *The English Satirical Print, 1660–1832: The Englishman and the Foreigner* (Cambridge: Cambridge University Press, 1986).
Duffy, Michael, *Soldiers, Sugar, and Seapower: The British Expeditions to the West Indies and the War against Revolutionary France* (New York: Oxford University Press, 1989).
Dunn, Richard, *Sugar and Slaves: The Rise of the Planter Class in the English West Indies, 1624–1723* (Chapel Hill: University of North Carolina Press, 1972).

Earle, Peter, *The Making of the English Middle Class: Business, Society, and Family Life in London, 1660–1730* (Berkeley: University of California Press, 1989).
Ehrman, John, *The British Government and Commercial Negotiations with Europe, 1783–1793* (Cambridge: Cambridge University Press, 1963).
Ehrman, John, *The Younger Pitt: The Years of Acclaim* (Stanford, Calif.: Stanford University Press, 1969).
Ehrman, John, *The Younger Pitt: The Reluctant Transition* (Stanford, Calif.: Stanford University Press, 1983).
Ehrman, John, *The Younger Pitt: The Consuming Struggle* (Stanford, Calif.: Stanford University Press, 1996).
Elliot, Marianne, *Partners in Revolution: The United Irishman and France* (New Haven, Conn.: Yale University Press, 1982).
Elliot, Marianne, *Wolf Tone: The Prophet of Irish Independence* (New Haven, Conn.: Yale University Press, 1989).
Eltis, David, *Economic Growth and the Ending of the Trans-Atlantic Slave Trade* (Oxford: Oxford University Press, 1987).
Emsley, Clive, *British Society and the French Wars, 1793–1815* (Totowa, N.J.: Rowman and Littlefield, 1979).
Engelman, Fred, *The Peace of Christmas Eve* (New York: Harcourt, Brace, 1962).
Erbman, Thomas, *The Birth of the Leviathan: Building States and Regimes in Medieval and Early Modern Europe* (Cambridge: Cambridge University Press, 1997).
Esdaile, Charles, *The Peninsular War: A New History* (New York: Palgrave Macmillan, 2003).
Evans, Eric, *The Forging of the Modern State: Early Industrial Britain, 1783–1870* (New York: Pearson, 1996).
Evans, Peter, Dietrich Rusechemeyer, and Theda Skocpol, eds., *Bringing the State Back In* (Cambridge: Cambridge University Press, 1985).
Fedorak, Charles, *Henry Addington, Prime Minister, 1801–1804: Peace, War, and Parliamentary Politics* (Akron, Ohio: Akron University Press, 2002).
Feher, Ferenc, *The French Revolution and the Birth of Modernity* (Berkeley: University of California Press, 1990).
Fenstermaker, Joseph Van *The Development of American Commercial Banking, 1782–1837* (Kent, Ohio: Kent State University Press, 1965).
Ferguson, Niall, *The World's Banker: The History of the House of Rothschild* (London: Weidenfeld and Nicolson, 1998).
Ferguson, Niall, *Empire: How Britain Made the Modern World* (New York: Basic Book, 2004).
Fetter, Frank, *The Development of British Monetary Orthodoxy, 1797–1875* (Cambridge, Mass.: Harvard University Press, 1965).
Floud, Roderick, Kenneth Wachter, and Annabel, Gregory, *Height, Health, and History: Nutritional Status in the United Kingdom, 1750–1890* (Cambridge: Cambridge University Press, 1990).
Floud, Roderick, and Paul Johnson, eds., *The Cambridge Economic History of Modern Britain: Industrialisation, 1700–1860* (New York: Cambridge University Press, 2004).
Foot, Michael, and Isaac Kramnick, eds., *The Thomas Paine Reader* (New York: Penguin Books, 1987).
Forczyk, Robert, *Toulon 1793: Napoleon's First Great Victory* (London: Osprey, 2005).
Ford, Archibald, *His Majesty's Opposition, 1714–1830* (Oxford: Clarendon Press, 1964).
Fortescue, John, *The County Lieutenants and the Army, 1803–1814* (London: Macmillan, 1909).

Fraser, Ronald, *Napoleon's Cursed War: Popular Resistance in the Spanish Peninsular War* (New York: Verso, 2008).
Fruchtman, Jack, *Thomas Paine: Apostle of Freedom* (New York: Four Walls, Eight Windows, 1994).
Furber, Holden, *Henry Dundas, First Viscount Melville: Political Manager of Scotland, Statesman, and Administrator of British India* (London: Oxford University Press, 1931).
Gallet, Jean, *Les Paysans en Guerre* (Paris: Editions Ouest-France, 1988).
Gates, David, *The Napoleonic Wars, 1803–1815* (New York: Arnold, 1997).
Geggus, David, *Slavery, War, and Revolution: The British Occupation of Saint Dominque, 1793–1798* (Oxford: Clarendon Press, 1982).
Gellner, Ernest, *Nations and Nationalism* (Oxford: Clarendon, 1985).
Geoghegan, Patrick, *The Irish Act of Union: A Study in High Politics, 1798–1801* (Dublin: Irish Academic Press, 1999).
George, Dorothy, *English Political Caricature, 1793–1832: A Study of Opinion and Propaganda* (Oxford: Oxford University Press, 1959).
George, M.D., *London Life in the Eighteenth Century* (Harmondsworth: Penguin, 1966).
Gibney, John, *The United Irishmen, Rebellion, and the Act of Union, 1798–1803* (New York: Palgrave Macmillan, 2019).
Gibson, William, *The Church of England, 1688–1832, Unity and Accord* (London: Routledge, 2001).
Glover, Gareth, *The Forgotten War: Conflict in the Mediterranean, 1793–1815* (London: Pen and Sword, 2017).
Glover, Michael, ed., *A Gentleman Volunteer: The Letters of George Hennell from the Peninsular War* (London: Heineman, 1979).
Glover, Michael, *Wellington as Military Commander* (New York: Penguin, 2001).
Gomes, Laurentino, *1808, The Flight of the Emperor: How A Weak Prince, A Mad Queen, and the British Navy Tricked Napoleon and Changed the World* (Guilford, Conn.: Lyons Press, 2013).
Goodwin, Albert, *The Friends of Liberty: The English Democratic Movement in the Age of the French Revolution* (Cambridge, Mass.: Harvard University Press, 1979).
Goodwin, Albert, *The French Revolution* (New York: Routledge, 2016).
Gough, Hough, and David Dickson, eds., *Ireland and the French Revolution* (Dublin: Irish Academic Press, 1990).
Graham, Jenny, *The Nation, the Law, and the King: Reform Politics in England, 1789–1799* (Lanham, Maryland: University Press of America, 2000).
Grattan, William, *The Adventures of the Connaught Rangers from 1808 to 1814* (London: Edward Arnold, 1902).
Gray, Denis, *Spencer Perceval: The Evangelical Prime Minister, 1762–1812* (Manchester: Manchester University, 1963).
Greenfeld, Liah, *Nationalism: Five Roads to Modernity* (Cambridge, Mass.: Harvard University Press, 1992).
Gunn, J.A.W. Gunn, *Beyond Liberty and Property: The Process of Self-Recognition in Eighteenth Century Political Thought* (Kingston, Ont.: McGill University Press, 1983).
Habakkuk, John, *Marriage, Debt, and the Estates System: English Land Ownership, 1650–1950* (Oxford: Oxford University Press, 1994).
Hague, William, *William Pitt the Young* (New York: Harper Perennial, 2004).
Hall, Christopher, *Wellington's Navy: Sea Power and the Peninsular War, 1807–1814* (London: Greenhill, 2006).

Hammond, Bray, *Banks and Politics in America from the Revolution to the Civil War* (Princeton, N.J.: Princeton University Press, 1991).
Harding, Richard, *The Evolution of the Sailing Navy, 1509–1815* (Basingstoke: Palgrave Macmillan, 1995).
Harding, Richard, *Seapower and Naval Warfare, 1650–1830* (Annapolis, Maryland: Naval University Press, 1999).
Harding, Richard, *British Admirals of the Napoleonic Wars: The Contemporaries of Nelson* (London: Chatham, 2005).
Harling, Philip, *The Waning of the 'Old Corruption': The Politics of Economic Reform in Britain, 1779–1840* (Oxford: Oxford University Press, 1996).
Harling, Philip, *The Modern British State: An Historical Introduction* (Oxford: Clarendon, 2001).
Harlow, Vincent, *The Founding of the Second British Empire, 1763–1793*, 2 vols (London: Longman, 1952, 1964).
Harris, Bob, *Politics and the Rise of the Press: Britain and France, 1620–1800* (London: Routledge, 1996).
Hastings, Adrian, *The Construction of Nationhood: Ethnicity, Religion, and Nationalism* (Cambridge: Cambridge University Press, 1997).
Haythornthwaite, Philip, *Memoirs of the War in the Peninsula* (London: Greenhill, 1990).
Haythornthwaite, Philip, *The Armies of Wellington* (London: Brockhampton Press, 1996).
Hecksher, Eli, *The Continental System, an Economic Interpretation* (Oxford: Clarendon Press, 1922).
Helleiner, Karl, *The Imperial Loans: A Study in Financial and Diplomatic History* (Oxford: Oxford University Press, 1965).
Hellmuth, Eckhart, *The Transformation of Political Culture: England and Germany in the Late Eighteenth Century* (Oxford: Clarendon Press, 1990).
Hibbert, Christopher, *George IV: Regent and King, 1811–1830* (New York: Penguin, 1973).
Hibbert, Christopher, *Wellington: A Personal History* (Reading, Mass.: Perseus Books, 1997).
Hickey, Donald, *The War of 1812: A Forgotten* (Urbana: University of Illinois Press, 1990).
Hidy, Ralph, *The House of Baring in American Trade and Finance: English Merchant Bankers at Work, 1763–1861* (Cambridge, Mass.: Harvard University Press, 1949).
Hill, B.W., *British Parliamentary Parties, 1742–1832: From the Fall of Walpole to the First Reform Act* (London: Allen and Unwin, 1985).
Hilton, Boyd, *A Mad, Bad, & Dangerous People?: England, 1783–1846* (Oxford: Clarendon, 2008).
Hinton, Boyd, *A Mad, Bad, & Dangerous People: England, 1783–1846* (New York: Oxford University Press, 2008).
Hobsbawm, Eric, *Nations and Nationalism Since 1780: Program, Myth, Reality* (New York: Cambridge University Press, 1995).
Hobsbawm, Eric, *Industry and Empire: The Economic History of Britain since 1750* (New York: W.W. Norton, 1999).
Holbraad, Carsten, *The Concert of Europe: A Study in German and British International Theory, 1815–1914* (New York: Barnes and Noble, 1971).
Hole, Robert, *Pulpits, Politics, and Public Order in England, 1760–1832* (Cambridge: Cambridge University press, 1989).
Hone, Ann, *For the Cause of Truth: Radicalism in London, 1796–1821* (Oxford: Oxford University Press, 1982).
Hoppit, Julian, *The Rise and Failures of English Business, 1700–1800* (Cambridge: Cambridge University Press, 1987).

Hoppit, Julian, ed., *Parliaments, Nations, and Identities in Britain and Ireland, 1660–1850* (Manchester: Manchester University Press, 2003).
Hopton, Richard, *The Battle of Maida, 1806: Fifteen Minutes of Glory* (London: Leo Cooper, 2002).
Hough, Richard, *Captain James Cook* (New York: W.W. Norton, 1997).
Howard, Martin, *Death Before Glory!: The British Soldier in the West Indies in the French Revolution and Napoleonic Wars* (London: Pen and Sword, 2015).
Howes, Anton, *Arts and Minds: How the Royal Society of Arts Changed a Nation* (Princeton, N.J.: Princeton University Press, 2020).
Hudson, Pat, ed., *Regions and Industries: A Perspective on the Industrial Revolution in Britain* (Cambridge: Cambridge University Press, 1989).
Hudson, Pat, *The Industrial Revolution* (London: Macmillan, 1992).
Hyam, Ronald, *Britain's Imperial Century, 1815–1914: A Study of Empire and Expansion* (Basingstoke: Palgrave Macmillan, 1993).
Ingram, Edward, *Commitment to Empire: Prophecies of the Great Game for Asia, 1797–1800* (Oxford: Oxford University Press, 1981).
Ireland, Bernard, *The Fall of Toulon: The Last Opportunity to Defeat Revolutionary France* (London: Cassel, 2005).
James, Lawrence, *The Rise and Fall of the British Empire* (New York: St Martin's Griffith Press, 1994).
Jarrett, Derek, *Three Faces of Revolution: Paris, London, New York in 1789* (London: G. Philip, 1989).
Jennings, Judith, *The Business of Abolishing the British Slave Trade* (New York: Routledge, 1997).
Johnson, Paul, *The Birth of the Modern: World Society, 1815–1830* (New York: HarperCollins, 1991).
Johnston, Edith, *Ireland in the Eighteenth Century* (Dublin: Gill and Macmillan, 1974).
Jones, Clive, and David Jones, ed., *Politics and Power: The House of Lords, 1603–1911* (London: Secker and Warburg, 1986).
Jones, Colin, ed., *Britain and Revolutionary France: Conflict, Subversion, and Propaganda* (Exeter: University of Exeter press, 1983).
Jones, E.H., *An Invasion that Failed: The French Expedition to Ireland, 1796* (Oxford: Oxford University Press, 1950).
Jupp, Peter, *Lord Grenville, 1759–1834* (Oxford: Clarendon Press, 1985).
Kagan, Frederick, *The End of the Old Order: Napoleon and Europe, 1801–1805* (New York: Da Capo, 2006).
Kaufman, William, *British Policy and the Independence of Latin America, 1804–1828* (New Haven, Conn.: Yale University Press, 1951).
Keane, John, *Thomas Paine: A Political Life* (New York: Grove Press, 1989).
Keay, John, *The Honourable Company: A History of the English East India Company* (New York: Macmillan, 1991).
Kennedy, Michael, *The Jacobin Clubs in the French Revolution: The First Years* (Princeton, N.J.: Princeton University Press, 1982).
Kennedy, Paul, *The Rise and Fall of the Great Powers: Economic Change and Military Conflict from 1500 to 2000* (New York: Vintage, 1988).
Keogh, Daire, *The French Disease: The Catholic Church and Irish Radicalism, 1790–1800* (Dublin: Irish Academic Press, 1993).
Kelly, James, *Prelude to Union: Anglo-Irish Politics in the 1780s* (Cork: Cork University Press, 1992).

Kerridge, Eric, *The Agricultural Revolution* (New York: A.M. Kelly, 1967).
Kidd, Alan, and David Nicolls, eds., *The Making of the British Middle Class? Studies of Regional and Cultural Diversity since the Eighteenth Century* (Stroud: Sutton, 1998).
Kidd, Colin, *British Identities before Nationalism: Ethnicity and Nationhood in the Atlantic World, 1600–1800* (Cambridge: Cambridge University Press, 1999).
Kissinger, Henry, *A World Restored: Metternich, Castlereagh, and the Problems of Peace, 1812–1822* (London: Weidenfeld and Nicolson, 1999).
Knight, Roger, *Britain Against Napoleon: The Organisation of Victory, 1793–1815* (New York: Allen Lane, 2013).
Koehn, Nancy, *The Power of Commerce: Economy and Governance in the First British Empire* (Ithaca, N.Y.: Cornell University Press, 1994).
Kramnick, Isaac, *Republicanism and Bourgeois Radicalism: Political Ideology in Late Eighteenth Century England and America* (Ithaca, N.Y.: Cornell University Press, 1990).
Kumar, Krisham, *Making of English National Identity* (Cambridge: Cambridge University Press, 2003).
Langford, Paul, *Modern British Foreign Policy: The Eighteenth Century, 1688–1815* (New York: Vintage, 1976).
Langford, Paul, *A Polite and Commercial People: England, 1727–1783* (Oxford: Oxford University Press, 1989).
Langford, Paul, *Public Life and the Propertied Englishman, 1689–1798* (Oxford: Oxford University Press, 1991).
Langford, Paul, *Englishness Identified: Manners and Character, 1650–1850* (Oxford: Oxford University Press, 2000).
Lawford, James, *Britain's Army in India from Its Origins to the Conquest of Bengal* (London: Unwin Hyman, 1978).
Lawson, Philip, *The East India Company: A History* (London: Routledge, 1993).
Limm, Andrew, *Walcheren to Waterloo: The British Army in the Low Countries During the French Revolutionary and Napoleonic Wars, 1793–1815* (London: Pen and Sword, 2018).
Lincoln, Margarette, *Representing the Royal Navy: British Sea Power, 1750–1815* (Burlington, Vermont: Ashgate, 2002).
Longford, Elizabeth, *Wellington: Years of the Sword* (New York: Harper and Row, 1969).
Maccoby, Simon, *The English Radical Tradition, 1763–1783* (Westport, Conn.: Greenwood, 1978).
Macleod, Emma, *A War of Ideas? British Attitudes to the Wars against Revolutionary France* (New Haven, Conn.: Yale University Press, 1998).
Marshall, P.J., ed., *The Problems of Empire: Britain and India, 1757–1813* (London: Allen and Unwin, 1968).
Marshall, P.J., and Glyndwr Williams, *The Great Map of Mankind: British Perceptions of the World in the Age of Enlightenment* (London: Dent and Son, 1982).
Marshall, P.J., *The New Cambridge History of India: Bengal, the British Bridgehead, Eastern India, 1740–1828* (Cambridge: Cambridge University Press, 1987).
Marshall, P.J., ed., *The Oxford History of the British Empire: The Eighteenth Century* (Oxford: Oxford University Press, 1998).
Mathias, Peter, *The First Industrial Nation: An Economic History of Britain, 1700–1914* (New York: Routledge, 1983).
McCahill, Michael, *Order and Equipoise: The Peerage and the House of Lords, 1783–1806* (London: Royal Historical Society, 1978).

McDowell, R.B., *Ireland in the Age of Imperialism and Revolution, 1760–1801* (Oxford: Oxford University Press, 1979).
McGleenon, C.F., *A Very Independent County: Parliamentary Elections and Politics in County Armagh, 1750–1800* (Belfast: Ulster Historical Foundation, 2011).
McKendrick, Neil, John Brewer, and J.H. Plumb, *The Birth of a Consumer Society: The Commercialization of Eighteenth Century England* (Bloomington: University of Indiana Press, 1982).
Mikaberidze, Alexander, *The Napoleonic Wars: A Global History* (New York: Oxford University Press, 2020).
Mingay, G.E., *English Landed Society in the Eighteenth Century* (London: Routledge, 1963).
Mingay, G.E., *Parliamentary Enclosure in England: An Introduction to Its Causes, Incidence, and Improvements, 1750–1850* (London: Longman, 1997).
Miot, Andre, *Memoires du Comte Miot de Melito*, 3 vols (Ancien Ministre, Ambassadeur, Conseilleur d'Etat et Membre de l'Institut, Paris: Michael Levy Freres, 1858).
Mitchell, Harvey, *The Underground War against Revolutionary France: The Missions of William Wickham, 1794–1800* (Oxford: Oxford University Press, 1965).
Mitchell, L.G., *Charles James Fox and the Disintegration of the Whig Party, 1782–1794* (New York: Oxford, 1971).
Mokyr, Joel, ed., *The British Industrial Revolution* (Boulder, Colo.: Westview Press, 1993).
Moody, T.W., and W.E. Vaughan, *A New History of Ireland: Eighteenth Century Ireland, 1691–1800* (Oxford: Oxford University Press, 1986).
Mori, Jennifer, *William Pitt and the French Revolution, 1785–1795* (New York: St Martin's Press, 1997).
Mori, Jennifer, *Britain in the Age of the French Revolution, 1785–1820* (London: Longman, 2000).
Morris, Marilyn, *The British Monarchy and the French Revolution* (New Haven, Conn.: Yale University Press, 1998).
Morriss, Roger, *The Royal Dockyards During the Revolutionary and Napoleonic Wars* (Leicester: Leicester University Press, 1983).
Mostert, Noel, *The Line Upon the Wind: The Great War at Sea, 1793–1815* (New York: W.W. Norton, 2007).
Muir, Rory, *Britain and the Defeat of Napoleon, 1807–1815* (New Haven, Conn.: Yale University Press, 1996).
Munch-Petersen, Thomas, *Defying Napoleon: How Britain Bombarded Copenhagen and Seized the Danish Fleet in 1807* (London: Sutton Mill, 2007).
Munsen, A.E., and Eric Robinson, *Science and Technology in the Industrial Revolution* (Manchester: University of Manchester Press, 1969).
Namier, Lewis, *The Structure of Politics at the Accession of George III* (London: Macmillan, 1957).
Namier, Lewis, and John Brooke, eds., *The House of Commons, 1754–1790*, 3 vols (New York: Oxford University Press, 1964).
Nelson, R.R., *The Home Office, 1782–1801* (Durham, N.C.: Duke University Press, 1969).
Nester, William, *Globalization: A Short History of the Modern World* (New York: Palgrave Macmillan, 2010).
Nester, William, *Globalization, Wealth, and Power in the Twenty-First Century* (New York: Palgrave Macmillan, 2010).
Nester, William, *Globalization, War, and Peace in the Twenty-First Century* (New York: Palgrave Macmillan, 2010).
Nester, William, *The Revolutionary Years: The Art of American Power During the Early Republic, 1775–1789* (Washington D.C.: Potomac Books, 2011).

Nester, William, *The Hamiltonian Vision, 1789–1800: The Art of Power in the Early Republic* (Washington D.C.: Potomac Books, 2012).
Nester, William, *Napoleon and the Art of Diplomacy: How War and Hubris Determined the Rise and Fall of the French Empire* (New York: Savas Beattie, 2012).
Nester, William, *The Jeffersonian Vision, 1800–1815* (Washington D.C.: Potomac Books, 2013).
Nester, William, *Titan: The Art of British Power in the Age of Revolution and Napoleon* (Norman: University of Oklahoma Press, 2016).
Nester, William, *Britain's Rise to Global Superpower in the Age of Napoleon* (London: Frontline Books, 2020).
Nester, William, *Napoleon and the Art of Leadership: How a Flawed Genius Changed the History of Europe and the World* (London: Frontline Books, 2021).
Newman, Gerald, *The Rise of English Nationalism: A Cultural History, 1740–1830* (New York: St Martin's Press, 1987).
Nicolson, Harold, *The Congress of Vienna: A Study in Allied Unity, 1812–1822* (New York: Harcourt, Brace, and Company, 1946).
O'Brien, Gerard, *Anglo-Irish Politics in the Age of Grattan and Pitt* (Dublin: Irish Academic Press, 1987).
O'Brien, Patrick, *Power with Profit: The State and Economy, 1688–1815* (London: Weidenfeld and Nicolson, 1991).
O'Brien, Patrick, and Roland Quinault, eds., *The Industrial Revolution and British Society* (Cambridge: Cambridge University Press, 1993).
O'Connell, M.R., *Irish Politics and Social Conflict in the Age of the American Revolution* (Westport, Conn.: Greenwood, 1976).
O'Gorman, Frank, *The Whig Party and the French Revolution* (Basingstoke: Macmillan, 1967).
O'Gorman, Frank, *The Emergence of the Two-Party System, 1760–1832* (London: E. Arnold, 1982).
O'Gorman, Frank, *Voters, Patrons, and Parties: The Unreformed Electoral System of Hanoverian England, 1734–1832* (Oxford: Clarendon Press, 1989).
Oldfield, J.R., *Popular Politics and British Anti-Slavery: The Mobilisation of Public Opinion against the Slave Trade, 1787–1807* (Manchester: Manchester University Press, 1995).
Overton, Mark, *The Agricultural Revolution in England: The Transformation of the Agrarian Economy, 1500–1850* (Cambridge: Cambridge University Press, 1996).
Pack, S.W.S., *Admiral Lord Anson: The Story of Anson's Voyage and Naval Events of His Day* (London: Cassel, 1960).
Padfield, Peter, *Maritime Power and the Struggle for Freedom: Naval Campaigns that Shaped the Modern World, 1788–1851* (London: John Murray, 2003).
Pakenham, Thomas, *The Year of Liberty: The Story of the Great Irish Rebellion of 1798* (New York: Abacus, 1969).
Pares, Richard, *King George III and the Politicians* (Oxford: Oxford University Press, 1953).
Pares, Richard, *War and Trade in the West Indies, 1739–1763* (London: Routledge, 1963).
Parissien, Steven, *George IV: Inspiration of the Regency* (New York: St Martin's Press, 2001).
Parkinson, C. Northcote, *The Trade Winds: A Study of British Overseas Trade During the French Wars, 1793–1815* (London: Allen and Unwin, 1948).
Parkinson, C. Northcote, *Britannia Rules: The Classic Age of Naval History, 1793–1815* (London: Allan Sutton Publishing, 1994).
Pawson, Eric, *Transport and Economy: The Turnpike Roads of Eighteenth Century Britain* (New York: Academic Press, 1977).

Perkins, Bradford, *Castlereagh and Adams: England and the United States, 1812–1823* (Berkeley: University of California Press, 1964).
Perkins, Harold, *The Origins of Modern English Society* (New York: Routledge, 1969).
Phillips, J.A., *Electoral Behaviour in Unreformed England, 1761–1802* (Princeton, N.J.: Princeton University Press, 1982).
Philp, Mark, ed., The French Revolution and *British Popular Politics* (Cambridge: Cambridge University Press, 1991).
Pocock, Tom, *The Terror Before Trafalgar: Nelson, Napoleon, and the Secret War* (Annapolis, Maryland: Naval Institute Press, 2005).
Pocock, Tom, *A Thirst for Glory: The Life of Admiral Sir Sidney Smith* (London: Thistle, 2013).
Pollock, John, *Wilberforce*, New York: St Martin's Press, 1977).
Pollack, Sidney, *The Genesis of Modern Management: A Study of the Industrial Revolution in Great Britain* (New York: Penguin, 1965).
Pomeranz, Kenneth, *The Great Divergence: China, Europe, and the Making of the Modern World* (Princeton, N.J.: Princeton University Press, 2000).
Porter, Bernard, *The Absent-Minded Imperialists: Empire, Society, and Culture in Britain* (Oxford: Oxford University Press, 2004).
Porter, Bernard, *Plots and Paranoia: A History of Political Espionage in Britain, 1790–1988* (New York: Routledge, 1992).
Porter, Roy, *English Society in the Eighteenth Century* (New York: Penguin, 1982).
Porter, Roy, *Enlightenment: Britain and the Creation of the Modern World* (New York: Penguin, 2000).
Pressnell, L.S., *Country Banking in the Industrial Revolution* (Oxford: Oxford University Press, 1956).
Pretyman, George, *Memoirs of the Life of the Right Hon. William Pitt*, 3 vols (London: John Murray, 1821).
Raymond, John, ed., *The Reminiscences and Recollections of Captain Gronow* (London: Bodley Head, 1964).
Raymond, Joad, ed., *News, Newspapers in Early Modern Britain* (London: Routledge, 1999).
Reilly, Robin, *William Pitt the Younger: A Biography* (New York: G.P. Putnam's Sons, 1978).
Rees, Dylan, and Duncan Townson, *France in Revolution* (London: Hodder Education, 2008).
Roberts, Andrew, *Napoleon: A Life* (New York: Viking, 2014).
Roberts, M.J.D., *Making English Morals: Voluntary Associations and Moral Reform in England, 1787–1886* (New York: Cambridge University Press, 2004).
Rodger, N.A.M., *The Command of the Ocean: A Naval History of Britain, 1649–1815* (New York: W.W. Norton, 2006).
Rogers, Nicolas, *Crowds, Culture, and Politics in Georgian Britain* (Oxford: Oxford University Press, 1998).
Rohl, J.C.G., M. Warren, and D. Warren, *Purple Secret, Genes, 'Madness', and the Royal House of Europe* (London: Corgi Books, 1999).
Royle, Edward, *Revolutionary Britain? Reflections on the Threat of Revolution in Britain, 1789–1848* (Manchester: Manchester University Press, 2000).
Rude, George, *The Crowd in History: A Study of Popular Disturbances in France and England, 1730–1848* (New York: Wiley, 1964).
Rule, John, *Albion's People: English Society, 1714–1815* (London: Longman, 1997).
Sack, James, *The Grenvillites, 1801–1829: Party Politics and Factionalism in the Age of Pitt and Liverpool* (Urbana: University of Illinois Press, 1979).

Sack, James, *From Jacobite to Conservative: Reaction and Orthodoxy in Britain, 1760–1832* (New York: Cambridge University Press, 1993).
Sainty, J.C., *Peerage Creations, 1649–1800* (London: Whitey Blackwell, 1998).
Schama, Simon, *Citizens: A Chronicle of the French Revolution* (New York: Vintage, 1990).
Schom, Alan, *Trafalgar: Countdown to Battle, 1803–1805* (New York: Oxford University Press, 1990).
Schroeder, Paul, *The Transformation of European Politics, 1763–1848* (New York: Oxford University Press, 1994).
Schulze, Hegan, *States, Nations, and Nationalism from the Middle Ages to the Present* (Oxford: Clarendon Press, 1996).
Scott, H.M., *British Foreign Policy in the Age of the American Revolution* (Oxford: Oxford University Press, 1990).
Semmel, Bernard, *The Rise of Free Trade Imperialism: Classical Political Economy, the Empire of Free Trade, and Imperialism, 1750–1850* (Cambridge: Cambridge University Press, 1970).
Semmel, Stuart, *Napoleon and the British* (New Haven, Conn.: Yale University Press, 2004).
Severn, John, *Architects of Victory: The Duke of Wellington and His Brothers* (Norman: University of Oklahoma Press, 2007).
Sheridan, Richard, *Sugar and Slavery: An Economic History of the West Indies, 1623–1775* (Barbados: Caribbean University Press, 1974).
Sherwig, John, *Guineas and Gunpowder: British Foreign Aid in the Wars with France, 1793–1815* (Cambridge, Mass.: Harvard University Press, 1969).
Shoemaker, Robert, *The London Mob: Violence and Disorder in Eighteenth Century England* (London: Hambledon, 2004).
Simms, Brendan, *Three Victories and a Defeat: The Rise and Fall of the First British Empire* (New York: Basic Books, 2009).
Smith, Anthony, *Theories of Nationalism* (London: Holmes and Mier, 1983).
Smith, E.A., *George IV* (New Haven, Conn.: Yale University Press, 1999).
Smith, Olivia, *The Politics of Language, 1791–1819* (Oxford: Oxford University Press, 1984).
Smyth, Jim, *The Men of No Property: Irish Radicals and Popular Politics in the Late Eighteenth Century* (Basingstoke: Palgrave Macmillan, 1992).
Sobel, Dava, *Longitude: The True Story of a Lone Genius Who Solved the Greatest Scientific Problem of His Time* (New York: Penguin, 1995).
Sparrow, Elizabeth, *Secret Service: British Agents in France, 1792–1815* (London: Boydell Press, 1999).
Spence, Peter, *The Birth of Romantic Radicalism: War, Popular Politics, and English Radical Reformism, 1800–1815* (Aldershot: Scholar Press, 1996).
Stafford, William, *Socialism, Radicalism, and Nostalgia: Social Criticism in Britain, 1775–1830* (New York: Cambridge University Press, 1987).
Stanhope, Philip Henry, Lord, *Life of the Right Honorable William Pitt*, 4 vols (London: John Murray, 1867).
Stone, Lawrence, ed., *An Imperial State at War: Britain from 1689 to 1815* (London: Routledge, 1994).
Stone, Bailey, Stone, *Reinterpreting the French Revolution: A Global Historical Perspective* (New York: Cambridge University Press, 2002).
Sun Tzu, *The Art of War* (Oxford: Clarendon Press, 1963).
Taylor, Stephen, *Commander: The Life of and Exploits of Britain's Greatest Frigate Commander* (New York: W.W. Norton, 2012).
Thompson, E.P., *The Making of the English Working Class* (London: Penguin, 1968).

Thompson, F. M. L., *Gentrification and the Enterprise Culture: Britain, 1780–1980* (Oxford: Oxford University Press, 2001).
Thompson, William, ed., *An Ensign in the Peninsular War: The Letters of John Aichison* (London: Michael Joseph, 1981).
Thorne, R.G., ed., *The History of Parliament: The House of Commons, 1790–1820*, 5 vols (London: Haynes Publishing, 1986).
Tilley, Charles, ed., *The Formation of Nation States in Western Europe* (Princeton, N.J.: Princeton University Press, 1975).
Tilly, Charles, *Popular Contention in Great Britain, 1758–1834* (Cambridge, Mass.: Harvard University Press, 1995).
Tracy, Nicolas, ed., *The Naval Chronicle: The Contemporary Record of the Royal Navy at War, 1793–1815*, 5 vols (Mechanicsburg, Penn.: Stackpole Books, 1999).
Turberville, A.S., *The House of Lords in the Age of Reform, 1784–1837* (London: Faber and Faber, 1958).
Tunzelman, G.N., *Steam Power and British Industrialisation to 1860* (Oxford: Oxford University Press, 1978).
Turley, David, *The Culture of English Antislavery, 1780* (London: Routledge, 1991).
Turner, Michael, *The Age of Unease: Government and Reform in Britain, 1782–1832* (London: Longman, 2000).
Uglow, Jenny, *In These Times: Living in Britain through Napoleon's Wars* (New York: Faber and Faber, 2014).
Updyke, Frank, *The Diplomacy of the War of 1812* (Gloucester, Mass.: P. Smith, 1965).
Urban, Mark, *The Man Who Broke Napoleon's Codes: The True Story of a Forgotten Hero in Wellington's Army* (New York: HarperCollins, 2001).
Von Brandt, Heinrich, *The Two Minas and the Spanish Guerillas* (London: T. Egerton, 1825).
Vries, Jan de, *European Urbanisation, 1500–1800* (Cambridge, Mass.: Harvard University Press, 1984).
Wahrman, Dror, *Imagining the Middle Class: The Political Representation of Class in Britain, 1780–1840* (New York: Cambridge University Press, 1995).
Wahrman, Dror, *The Making of the Modern Self: Identity and Culture in Eighteenth Century England* (New Haven, Conn.: Yale University Press, 2004).
Ward, J.R., *The Finance of Canal Building in Eighteenth Century England* (London: Oxford University Press, 1974).
Ware, Frederick, ed., *Letters from the Peninsula, 1808–1812, by Lieutenant General Sir William Ware* (London: John Murray, 1909).
Webster, C.K., *The Foreign Policy of Castlereagh, 1812–1815: Britain and the Reconstruction of Europe* (London: G. Bell and Sons, 1931).
Wells, Roger, *Insurrection: The British Experience, 1795–1803* (Gloucester: Sutton, 1983).
Wells, Roger, *Wretched Faces: Famine in Wartime England, 1793–1801* (Gloucester: Sutton, 1988).
Weller, Jac, *Wellington in the Peninsula* (Mechanicsburg, Penn.: Stackpole Books, 1992).
Werkmeister, Lucyle, *A Newspaper History of England* (Lincoln: University of Nebraska Press, 1988).
Wharam, Alan, *The Treason Trials, 1794* (Leicester: Leicester University Press, 1992).
Whitwell, Philip, ed., *The Grenville Diaries: Volume 1 and 2* (London: William Heinemann, 1927).
Wilkinson, Clive, *The British Navy and the State in the Eighteenth Century* (London: Boydell Press, 2004).

Wilkinson, David, *The Duke of Portland: Politics and Party in the Age of George III* (New York: Palgrave Macmillan, 2003).
Williams, Gwyn, *Artisans and Sans Culottes: Popular Movements in France and Britain During the French Revolution* (London: Edward Arnold, 1989).
Williams, Judith, *British Commercial Policy and Trade Expansion, 1750–1850* (Oxford: Clarendon Press, 1972).
Williamson, Jeffrey, *Coping with City Growth During the British Industrial Revolution* (New York: Cambridge University Press, 1990).
Wilson, Kathleen, *The Sense of the People: Politics, Culture, and Imperialism in England, 1715–1785* (Cambridge: Cambridge University Press, 1995).
Winterbottom, Derek, *The Grand Old Duke of York: A Life of Frederick Augustus, Duke of York and Albany* (London: Pen and Sword, 2016).
Wolfe, Janet, and John Seed, eds., *The Culture of Capital: Art, Power, and the Nineteenth Century Middle Class* (Manchester: Manchester University Press, 1988).
Woodman, Richard, *The Victory of Sea Power: Winning the Napoleonic War* (London: Caxton, 1998).
Worrall, David, *Radical Culture: Discourse, Resistance, and Surveillance, 1790–1820* (Detroit: Wayne State University Press, 1992).
Wrigley, E.A., *Continuity, Chance, and Change: The Character of the Industrial Revolution in England* (Cambridge: Cambridge University Press, 1988).
Wrigley, E.A., and R.S. Schofield, *The Population History of England, 1541–1871* (New York: Cambridge University Press, 1989).
Yapp, M.E., *Strategies of British India: Britain, Iran, and Afghanistan, 1798–1850* (Oxford: Oxford University Press, 1980).
Zamoyski, Adam, *Rites of Peace: The fall of Napoleon and the Congress of Vienna* (New York: Harper Press, 2007).
Ziegler, Philip, *Addington: A Life of Henry Addington, First Viscount Sidmouth* (New York: John Day Company, 1965).
Articles
Breihan, John, 'William Pitt and the Commission on Fees, 1785–1801', History Journal, vol. 27 (1984), 58–81.
Crafts, N.F.R., 'Steam as a General Purpose Technology: A Growth Accounting Perspective', *Economic Journal*, vol. 114 (2004), 338–51.
De Vries, Jan, 'The Industrial Revolution and the Industrious Revolution', *Journal of Economic History*, vol. 54 (1994), 250–70.
Harling, Philip, 'The Duke of York Affair (1809) and the Complexities of War Time Patriotism', *History Journal*, vol. 39 (1996), 963–84.
Lindert, Peter, and Jeffrey Williamson, 'Revising England's Social Tables, 1688–1812', *Explorations in Economic History*, vol. 19, (1982), 385–408.
Lowe, J.W.C., 'George III, Peerage Creations and Politics, 1760–1784', *Historical Journal*, vol. 35 (1992), 587–609.
O'Brien, Patrick, 'The Political Economy of British Taxation, 1660–1815', *Economic History Review*, vol. 41 (1988), 1–32.
O'Brien, Patrick, and Philip Hunt, 'The Rise of a Fiscal State in England, 1485–1815', *Historical Research*, vol. 96 (1993), 129–76.
O'Brien, Patrick, 'Political Biography and Pitt the Younger as Chancellor of the Exchequer', *History*, vol. 83 (1998), 225–33.

Sacks, James, 'The House of Lords and Parliamentary Patronage in Great Britain, 1802–1832', *Historical Journal*, vol. 23, no. 4 (1980), 913–37.

Schroeder, Paul, 'Did the Vienna Settlement Rest on a Balance of Power?' *The American Historical Review*, vol. 97, no. 3, June 1992, 683–70.

Torrance, John, 'Social Class and Bureaucratic Innovation: The Commissioners for Examining the Public Accounts, 1780–1787', *Past and Present*, vol. 78, no. 1 (February 1978), 56–81.

Index

Abercromby, Ralph 80, 93, 105
Aberdeen, George Hamilton-Gordon, Earl 167–68
Acton, John 92
Adams, John 159
Adams, John Quincy 179
Adams, William 179
Addington, Henry (Viscount Sidmouth) 104–05, 106, 107, 112
Addison, Joseph 15
Africa 31, 33–34, 40
Al-Alry, Muhammed Bey 123
Albuquerque, Jose de la Cueva 146
Alfred I 12
Alexander I 100, 111, 112–13, 123–24, 151, 152, 171, 173, 175, 176, 182, 183, 187
Al-Hamad 123
Allemand, Zacharie 133
Alpuente, Juan 155
Amherst, Jeffrey 58
Amherst, William 148
Andrews, John 15
Anne Queen 40
Anson, George 23
Antraigues, Louis de Launay, Comte d' 76, 83
Argentina 145
Arkwright, Richard 27
Armstrong, John 178
Artez, Louis Gabriel Chevalier d' 77
Asia 31–32, 36
Augereau, Pierre 83
Austen, Jane 29
Austria 2, 18, 32, 40, 41, 51–52, 53, 66, 70, 71, 77–78, 78–79, 81–82, 84–85, 88, 89, 93, 95, 96, 97, 98–99, 100, 101, 106, 111, 112–13, 114–15, 116–17, 129, 134–35, 151, 159, 163–68, 171–73, 181–84, 185, 187, 188, 190

Bacon, Francis 23
Baden 67, 99, 111, 114, 116
Baird, David 120, 133
Baker, Anthony 180
Barclay, Robert 176
Barclay de Tolly, Mikhail 168
Bardaji y Azara, Eusebio 146–47
Barham, Charles Middletown, Baron 62, 115
Baring, Alexander 191
Barra, Paul 81
Barron, James 160
Bathurst, Henry, Earl 149, 157, 162, 178
Battles and Sieges
 Aboukir Bay 96
 Acre 96
 Albuera 139
 Alexandria 105, 123
 Alkmaar 94
 Almeida 138, 139
 Aspern-Essling 135
 Auerstadt 121
 Aughrim 14
 Austerlitz 116
 Badajoz 153
 Ballynahinch 91
 Baltimore 176
 Basque Roads 133–34
 Bastia 71
 Bastille 50, 52, 74
 Bautzen 165
 Bayonne 172
 Bergin 94
 Blenheim 40, 50

246 *The Coalitions against Napoleon*

Borodino 151
Boston 44
Boyne 14
Buenos Aires 120–21
Burgos 153
Bussaco 138
Camperdown 84, 107
Cape Town 81, 120
Cape Vincent 83–84
Capes 44
Castricum 94
Ciudad Rodrigo 138, 153
Ciutadella 91
Copenhagen 64, 100, 107, 124, 132
Corunna 133
Curragh 91
Dardanelles 123
Demerara 80
Detroit 176
Dominica 63
Dresden 168
Dunkirk 67
Eylau 121
Fleurus 71
Flushing 135
Friedland 12, 121, 141
Glorious First of June 72
Guadeloupe 73
Hanau 168
Helder 93
Hohenlinden 98, 106
Hondschoote 67
Jena 121
Koge 124, 132
Krabbendam 94
Leipzig 149, 168
Lexington and Concord 44
Ligny 186
Lough Swilly 91
Lutzen 165
Maida 120
Mainz 67
Malplaquet 40
Martinique 73
Marengo 98, 106
New Orleans 177
New Ross 90

Nile 64, 88, 92, 107
Nivelle River 163
Orthez 172
Oudenarde 40
Pamplona 162
Plattsburgh 176
Put-In-Bay 176
Pyrenees 12
Quatre Bras 186
Quiberon Bay 78
Ramillies 40, 50
Rolica 132
Saint Dominque 73, 80, 109–10
Saint Lucia 73
Saintes 44, 63
Salamanca 153, 154
San Juan 80
San Sebastian 162
Saratoga 44
Spanish Armada 5, 32
Talavera 136
Tara 91
Thames 176
Toulon 68, 71
Toulouse 172
Tourcoing 71
Trafalgar 63, 115
Trinidad 80
Ulm 114
Valenciennes 67
Valmy 52–53
Vimeiro 132
Vinegar Hill 91
Vitorio 161
Wagram 134, 135
Waterloo 2, 131, 186, 191
Yorktown 44
Znaim 135
Zurich 94
Bavaria 41, 76, 99, 114, 116, 135
Bayard, James 179
Beauharnais, Eugene 135, 164
Beauharnais, Hortense 101
Belgium 187
Bentinck, William 148, 172, 184
Beresford, William 120–21, 132, 136, 137, 139

Index

Bernadotte, Jean-Baptiste 152, 164–65, 168, 170, 171
Berthier, Louis-Alexandre 91–92
Black, William 178
Blake, Joaquin 139
Blakewell, Robert 24
Blucher, Gebhard von 168, 172, 185 186
Bolivar, Simon 145
Bompart, Jean 91
Bonaparte, Caroline 171–72
Bonaparte, Jerome 124
Bonaparte, Joseph 98–99, 106, 119, 130–31, 133, 139, 145, 161, 165
Bonaparte, Josephine 101, 186
Bonaparte, Napoleon 5, 40, 46, 59, 68, 76, 81–83, 87–88, 91, 96–97, 98–99, 100–01, 106, 109–10, 111–18, 119–28, 129–31, 133, 149–50, 151, 152, 153, 155, 163–68, 169–70, 171–73, 176, 177, 180, 182, 184, 185–87, 189
Borghese, Pauline Bonaparte 175
Bourmont, Louis, Marquis de 77
Boyle, Robert 23
Brandt, Heinrich von 140
Brazil 125, 137, 158, 192
Bridport, Alexander Hood, Lord 78
Britain: Economy 2–3, 21–30
  Agriculture 24–25, 28
  Companies and Corporations 29, 32, 34, 38–39, 43, 57, 65–66, 93, 178, 193
  Finance 2, 26, 34, 150, 178, 191
  Industrial Revolution 3, 21–30, 57
  Manufacturing 2, 21, 22, 27–28, 150
  Mining 26–27
  Societies 15–16, 20, 23, 29, 37
  Trade 3, 4, 5, 33–34, 35–38, 39, 41–42, 43, 45–46, 65, 73, 107, 126, 137, 150, 177–78, 190–91
  Transportation 27
Britain: Empire 3, 4, 31–46, 42
  America 32–33, 36, 38, 40–41, 42–44
  Australia 37
  Canada 38, 40, 41, 64, 178, 179, 181
  Cape Town and Hope 97, 120, 170, 173, 192
  Ceylon 106, 107, 192
  Gibraltar 40, 105

India 34–35, 38, 81, 87, 93, 131–32
Indians (American) 44
Ireland 12, 13, 14, 31, 90–91, 103–04, 190
Malta 4, 87, 92, 106, 110, 113
Minorca 40, 91, 102
Slavery 33–34, 160, 184
Trinidad 106, 107
West Indies 32–34, 36, 37, 38, 39, 40, 41, 44, 64, 65, 73, 80–81, 126–27, 173, 190, 192
Britain: Government 2, 3, 4, 11–20, 37
  Acts 13, 14, 25–26, 36, 32, 60, 61, 65, 74–75, 85, 90, 102, 103, 112, 127, 191
  Church of England 12–13, 14, 18, 22, 104
  Commonwealth 13
  Development 11–20
  Espionage 2, 7, 65–66, 71, 75–76, 100
  Finance 2, 16, 20, 26, 45, 55–57, 191
  Glorious Revolution 14
  Magna Carta 12
  Monarchy 11–20
  Navigation Acts 5
  Palaces 16, 17
  Parliament 12, 14, 16, 18–19, 23, 37, 38, 49, 74, 75, 78, 98, 102, 127, 136, 137–38, 183
  Political Parties 18, 74
  Power 2, 4, 40
  Whitehall 7, 16, 17–18, 37–38, 39, 49, 65–66, 75, 84
Britain: Military
  Army 7, 19, 35, 57–61, 192–93
  Navy 2–3, 4, 7, 19, 23, 55–56, 57, 61–65, 79, 83–84, 107, 112, 191
  Strategy 1–2, 3, 4–5, 5–6, 39–40, 42–43, 55–56, 64, 69, 150–51
  Subsidies to Allies 2, 66–67, 70, 71, 76, 77, 78–79, 80, 82–83, 84–85, 89–90, 93–94, 98, 113, 116, 123, 126, 130–31, 136–37, 141–42, 146–47, 148, 152, 158, 163–64, 164–65, 166, 167–68, 170, 171, 185
Britain: Society and Culture
  Academies and Societies 15–16, 20, 23, 29, 74, 75, 126
  Catholics 12, 13, 14

Dissent and Subversion 74–75
Education 19, 22, 24, 45, 55, 75
England 11, 12, 13, 14, 15, 18, 19, 28, 38, 65, 190
  Literacy 15
  Literature 15
  Nationalism 11, 15
  Population 25, 28–29
  Presbyterians 13
  Press 15, 74, 75
  Puritans 13
  Quakers 19
  Scotland 12, 13, 14, 18, 19, 24, 28, 38, 65, 190
  Wales 12, 13, 18, 19, 28, 38, 190
Brock, Isaac 176
Brown, John 15
Brunswick, Wilhelm, Duke 52–53
Brueys, Francois 87, 88
Buckingham, Richard, Duke 96–97
Brune, Guillaume 94
Bubna von Littitz, Ferdinand 163
Buckinghamshire, Robert Hobart, Earl 105
Burgoyne, John 44
Burke, Edmund 50–51, 74
Burrard, Harry 132

Cadoudal, Georges 101, 110–11
Camden, John Pratt, Marquis 112
Canning, George 97, 119, 122, 123, 124, 129, 130, 134, 138, 146
Carden, John 176
Carraffa, Juan 125
Cartwright, Edmund 27
Cartwright, John 74
Carvajal, Jose 156
Caulaincourt, Armand 171
Castlereagh, Robert Stewart 11, 16, 103, 112, 122, 138, 147, 149, 150–51, 153, 161, 163, 164, 165, 166, 167, 169, 170, 171, 172, 173, 175, 179, 181, 182, 183, 184, 185, 187
Cathcart, Charles 35, 124
Cathcart, William Earl 123, 152, 165, 166, 171
Catherine the Great 78–79
Championnet, Jean 92

Charles Archduke 114, 115, 116
Charles, Comte d'Artois 52, 83, 101–02
Charles I 13
Charles II 14, 38
Charles III 44
Charles IV 113, 129–30, 145
Charles V 32
Charles XIII 134, 152
Charles Frederick 114
Charlotte, Princess 170
Charlotte, Queen 17
Chauvelin, Bernard-Francois 53
Chile 145
China 35–36
Christian, Hugh 80
Clark, Mary Anne 137–38
Clay, Henry 179
Coalitions 2, 17, 29, 189–93
  First 2, 49–85
  Second 87–108
  Third 109–17
  Fourth 119–28
  Fifth 129–48
  Sixth 2, 149–73
  Seventh 2, 175–88
Cobenzl, Louis 89
Cochrane, Andrew 177
Cochrane, Thomas 133–34
Coleridge, Samuel 69
Colombia 145
Columbus, Christopher 32
Conde, Louis Joseph, Prince de 77–78, 83, 95
Congresses
  Aix-la-Chapelle 189
  Laibach 189
  Troppau 189
  Verona 189
  Vienna 7, 181–84, 186–87, 189
Continental System 121, 124, 125, 135, 150, 151, 177
Conway, Henry 42
Cook, James 23
Copernicus, Nicolas 22
Copley, John 16
Cornwallis, George 44, 70, 91, 106, 107
Cordova, Josef 83–84

Index

Cort, Henry 27
Cowper, William 126
Cradock, John 136
Craig, James 81, 114
Cromwell, Oliver 13, 131
Cromwell, Richard 13
Crompton, Samuel 27
Cudjoe, Captain 34
Cuesta, Gregorio 136
Cuyler, Cornelius 73

Dalrymple, Hew 132
Darwin, Erasmus 23
Decatur, Stephen 176
Defoe, Daniel 23
Denmark 4, 99, 124, 132, 152, 170
Devis, Arthur 16
Diebitsch, Hans von 163
Djezzar, Pasha 96
Downie, George 176
Drake, Captain Francis 32
Drake, Francis 76
Drummond, William 120
Duckworth, John 91, 123
Duphot, Mathurin 91
Dumouriez, Charles 53
Duncan, Adam 84
Dundas, Charles 62
Dundas, David 58
Dundas, Henry, (Viscount Melville) 1, 3, 5, 6, 54, 55, 72, 73, 89, 94, 95–96, 97, 102, 103, 112
Dundas, Robert (Viscount Melville) 62

Egypt 87–88, 93, 96, 97, 105–06, 109, 110
Elba 173, 184
Elizabeth I 13, 32, 34
Elliot, Hugh 120
Elphinstone, George 81
Enghien, Louis Antoine de Bourbon, Duc 111
Enlightenment 23
Estrade, Florez 154–55
Europe 2, 12, 19, 40, 46, 121

Ferdinand IV 92–93, 119–20, 148, 172
Ferdinand VII 129–30, 145, 169–70, 175

Fielding, Henry 15, 21, 29
Finland 134, 152
Foote, Samuel 15
Ford, John 73
Foster, Augustus 161
Fouche, Joseph 101, 186
Fox, Charles 50, 119
France 2, 4, 5, 6, 12, 20, 24, 33, 35, 39, 40–41, 44, 49, 66–85, 87–108, 109–18, 120–18, 129–49, 149–75, 181–84, 185–87, 189, 190
Francis II/I 112–13, 121, 172, 185, 187
Franklin, Benjamin 42
Frederic 114
Frederick William II 51–52, 70
Frederick William III 89–90, 115–16, 121, 123–24, 163, 165, 176, 183, 187
Frere, John 131, 142

Gage, Thomas 43
Galilei, Galileo 22
Gallatin, Albert 179
Galles, Justin 90
Gambier, James 124, 133–34, 179
Gama, Vasco da 32
Gardner, Alan 73
Genoa 82, 99, 107, 172
George I 17, 39
George II 17, 39–40
George III 11, 15, 16–17, 31, 38, 39–40, 44, 45, 52, 54, 58, 69, 74, 79, 84, 103, 104–05, 112, 119, 120, 122, 126, 136, 138, 187
George IV (Regent) 17, 138, 180
Germany 8, 82, 88, 93, 113, 116, 121, 185
Godoy, Manuel 125, 129–30
Godwin, William 74
Goethe, Johan Wolfgang von 53
Gordon, Alexander 143
Goulburn, Henry 179
Gower, Granville Leveson 123
Graham, Thomas 170
Grasse, Francois de 44, 63
Grave, Thomas 44
Gravina, Frederico 68, 115
Grenville, Thomas 89

Grenville, William 6, 18, 49, 53, 54, 55, 66, 69–70, 75, 77, 82, 84, 88, 89, 93, 94, 95, 97, 99, 101, 103, 107, 119, 122, 159, 160, 189
Grey, Charles (viscount Howick) 62, 73, 102, 117
Guichen, Luc-Urbain 63
Gustavus IV 123, 129, 134
Guttenberg, Johannes 21–22

Habsburg Empire 32
Hamilton, Alexander 181
Hamilton, Emma 92
Hamilton, William 92
Hanover 39, 54, 67, 99, 116, 168, 183, 187
Hanway, Jonas 37
Harcourt, William 67
Hardenburg, August von 115, 170, 181, 183
Hardy, Thomas 74
Hargreaves, James 27
Harriot, Thomas 23
Harrison, John 23–24
Harrison, William 176
Harrowby, Dudley Ryder, Earl 112, 116
Hastings, Warren 38
Haugwitz, Christian von 70, 79, 115–16
Hawkins, John 32
Hely-Hutchinson, John 105
Henley, Morton Eden, Baron 70
Henry VIII 12–13, 22, 31
Herman, Ivan 94
Hervilly, Louis Charles 78
Hesse-Cassel 67, 79
Hesse-Darmstadt 67
Hoche, Lazare 78, 90
Hogarth, William 16
Holy Alliance 187, 189
Holy Roman Empire 82, 121
Hood, Alexander 90
Hood, Samuel 68, 71–72
Hotham, William 72
Houchard, Jean 67
Howe, Richard 72, 84
Hugues, Victor 73
Humbert, Jean 91
Hume, David 23

Humphreys, Salusbury 160
Huygens, Christian 28

Italy 8, 81–82, 91–92, 94, 98, 99, 106–07, 111, 115, 172
Izard, George 178

Jackson, Andrew 177
Jackson, Francis 167, 171
James I 13
James II 14
Japan 8
Jay, John 159
Jefferson, Thomas 109–10, 160, 177, 181
Jenner, Edward 28
Jervis, John (Earl St. Vincent) 62, 73, 80, 83–84, 87, 88, 92, 105, 111
Joao, Prince 125–26, 137, 158
John I 12
Johnson, Samuel 15
Jourdan, Jean-Baptiste 94, 161
Junot, Jean 125, 132

Kaunitz, Wenzel von 52
Kay, John 27
Keith, George 105
Kellerman, Francois 53
Kleber, Jean-Baptiste 96, 105
Knights of St. John 4, 87
Knox, John 13
Korsakov, Alexander 94
Kutuzov, Mikhail 151

Lacy, Peter von 114
Lake, Gerald 91
Lansdowne, Henry Petty-Fitzmaurice, Marquess 119
Latin America 50, 145, 192
Lebzeltern, Ludwig 163
Leclerc, Charles 109
Lemaitre, Pierre Jacques 76
Leopold II 51–52
Lieven, Christoph 152, 163
Liniers, Santiago 121
Liverpool, Robert Jenkinson, Hawkesbury 105, 107, 112, 122, 141, 145, 150, 157, 168, 170, 171, 178–79, 180, 182, 183

Locke, John 23
Long, Robert 144
Louis XVI 44, 49–50, 52, 53–54, 100
Louis XVII 77
Louis XVIII (Comte Provence) 51, 52, 77, 83, 99, 173, 185, 186, 187
Louis Joseph, Prince Conde 52
Low Countries 82, 93, 152, 170
Ludd, Ned 150
Lujando, Jose 169
Luther, Martin 22

Macartney, George 31, 35, 42, 77
Macdonough, Thomas 176
Mack, Karl 92, 114
Madison, James 161, 177, 180, 181
Maitland, Frederick 186
Malmesbury, James Harris, Earl 70
Malthus, Thomas 25
Mansfield, William Murray, Earl 126
Maria I 125
Maria Carolina 92–93, 120, 148, 172
Maria Luisa 125, 129–30
Marie Antoinette 51, 92
Marie Louise 173, 185
Marlborough, John Churchill, Duke 40, 131
Marmont, Auguste 154
Marshall, William 27
Mary II 14
Massena, Andre 94, 115, 119, 138–39
Maximilien Joseph 99, 114, 168
McDonald, Thomas 160–61
McKenzie-Fraser, Alexander 123
McTavish, John 178
Melas, Michel von 98
Melito, Andre 139
Mendez, Luis 146
Metternich, Clemens von 163, 166–67, 168, 175, 181, 183, 187
Mexico 145, 147
Menou, Jacques 105
Mildmay, William 3
Minto, Gilbert Elliot, Earl 18, 98
Moira, Francis Rawdon-Hastings, Marquis 76–77
Mollendorf, Otto von 70
Monck, George 13–14

Monroe, James 109, 161, 180
Moore, Graham 113
Moore, John 129, 132–33, 135
Moreau, Jean 82, 98, 110
Mortier, Edouard 110
Mortimer, Thomas 3
Mulgrave, Henry Phipps, Baron 62, 95
Murat, Joachim 130, 152, 164, 171–72, 184, 186
Murphy, Arthur 15

Naples (Two Sicilies) Kingdom 66, 68, 92–93, 106, 110, 116, 119–20, 122, 148, 151, 164, 165, 166, 171–72, 184, 186, 187
Necker, Jacques 49
Neipperg, Alfred von 185
Nelson, Horatio 5, 64, 71, 72, 83–84, 88, 92, 93, 100, 115, 133, 189
Nesselrode, Charles von 171, 181, 183
Netherlands (Batavia) 2, 4, 7, 26, 28, 32, 33, 35, 39, 53–54, 55, 70, 71, 79, 81, 93–94, 99, 106, 110, 112, 113, 116, 117, 135, 151, 166, 170, 171, 183, 185, 187
Neuville, Paul Hyde de 100
Newcomen, Thomas 27
Newton, Isaac 23
Nicolson, Harold 7
Nielly, Joseph 72
Noisy, Le Clerc 76
Normandy 12
Norway 152, 166, 170

Oceans, Seas, and Islands
    Atlantic 64, 81
    East Indies 40, 65
    Indian 31, 34, 64, 81
    Mediterranean 80, 88, 91–92
    Pacific 23, 34
    West Indies 7, 32–34, 40, 41, 64, 65, 72–73, 80–81, 93, 114, 148, 187, 192
Oldenburg 151
Ottoman Empire 51, 79, 87, 88, 96, 123, 124

Paine, Thomas 50–51
Pakenham, Edward 177

Palafox, Jose 169
Paley, William 126
Paoli, Pasquale 71
Papal States 12, 13, 22–23, 82, 91, 92, 106
Parker, Hyde 72, 100
Paul I 79, 89–90, 93, 99, 100, 182
Perceval, Spencer 20, 122, 138, 150
Perry, Oliver 176
Peru 145
Philip II 32
Pichegru, Jean Charles 82–83, 110
Piedmont-Sardinia 53, 66, 68, 76, 77, 81–82, 113, 114, 116, 187
Pius VII 111
Pitt, John (Earl Chatham) 62, 135
Pitt, William (older, Earl Chatham) 45
Pitt, William (younger) 5, 20, 45–46, 49, 50, 51, 52, 54, 55, 58, 59, 69, 70, 76–77, 78–79, 84, 85, 89, 94, 96–97, 98, 101, 102, 103, 104–05, 107, 109, 112, 115–16, 117, 119, 122, 127, 189, 193
Poland (Duchy of Warsaw) 79, 124, 135, 166, 183, 187
Pomerania 170
Popham, Home 120
Portland, William Cavendish-Benedict, Duke 54, 97, 105, 122, 129, 138, 149
Portugal 2, 4, 6, 31, 32, 33, 34, 35, 122, 124, 125–26, 131, 132, 136–37, 138–39, 143, 151, 154, 158, 161, 165, 182, 190, 192
Precy, Louis, Comte de 77
Prevost, George 176
Priestly, Joseph 23, 74
Prussia 51–52, 55, 66, 70, 79, 89–90, 93, 99, 100, 113, 114, 115–16, 119, 121, 122, 123–24, 129, 151, 163–68, 169, 171–73, 181–84, 185, 186, 187, 188, 190
Puisaye, Joseph, Comte de 78

Quesada, Juan de 91

Religion
Bible 13
Catholic 12, 22–23, 32, 51, 90, 103–04, 187
Orthodox 12, 187
Protestant 90, 187
Reformation 12, 13, 22–23

Renaissance 21–22
Reynier, Jean 120
Rhine Confederation 121, 163, 166
Richmond, Charles Lennox, Duke 54
Rigaud, Andre 80
Robespierre, Maximilien 71
Rochambeau, Donatien de 73
Rodney, George 44, 63
Rome (ancient) 15
Roosevelt, Franklin 8
Ross, Robert 176
Rothschild, Nathan 181
Ruffo di Baranello, Fabrizio 92–93
Russell, Jonathan 161
Russia 2, 51, 64, 78–79, 88, 89–90, 93, 94, 95, 96, 97, 99, 101, 111, 112–13, 114–15, 119, 121, 122, 123–24, 129, 134, 135, 149, 151–53, 153, 163–68, 171–73, 176, 181–84, 185, 187, 188, 190
Russell, Jonathan 179

Saint Aignan, Auguste de 168
Saint Cyr, Laurent 115
Saint Helena 185, 186
Saint Regeant, Pierre 101
San Carlos, Jose Miquel Duque 169
Saxony 121, 183
Scandinavia 64
Schaumann, Augustus von 157–58
Scherer, Barthelemy 94
Schwarzenberg, Karl Philip, Prince 163, 168, 172
Selim III 123
Serizat, Charles 77
Shelburne, William Petty, Earl 45
Sheridan, Richard 78
Shipley, William 37
Smith, Adam 23
Smith, William Sydney 96, 105, 125
Smollett, Thomas 15
Sobremonte, Rafael 121
Soult, Nicolas 133, 135–36, 139, 153, 161–62
Sousa-Coutinho, Domingos 126, 137
Spain 2, 4, 13, 32, 33, 34, 39, 40, 41, 44, 51, 66, 68, 79, 80, 106, 113, 114, 120–21, 120, 125–26, 129–31, 134, 135–37,

138–39, 139–41, 141–45, 145–48, 149, 151, 154–58, 161–63, 169–70, 173, 182, 190, 192
Spencer, George Earl 62, 66, 84, 88, 119
Starhemberg, Georg Adam 70, 89, 134
Stewart, Charles 163, 166, 171
Steele, Richard 15
Strachan, Richard 135
Strangford, Percy Smythe 126
Stuart, Charles 137
Stuart, General Charles 80, 91, 120
Suvorov, Alexander 94, 95
Sweden 2, 4, 99, 115–16, 123, 124, 129, 134, 152, 164–65, 168, 170, 182
Swift, Jonathan 23
Switzerland (Helvetia) 76, 82, 94, 99, 107, 110, 117
Sydenham, Thomas 143

Talleyrand-Perigord, Charles Maurice 97, 106, 125, 172–73, 181, 182, 184
Thornton, Edward 152, 164–65
Thugut, Johanne 70, 89, 98
Tierney, George 103
Tone, Wolf 90–91
Tooke, John 74
Toussaint Louverture, Francois 80, 109
Townsend, Charles 24
Treaties, Conventions, and Armistices
  Alessandria 98
  Alkmaar 94
  Amiens 106–07, 109
  Campo Formio 82, 99
  Chaumont 171, 188
  Commercial 137
  El Arish 105
  Fontainebleau 125
  Fontainebleau (1814) 173
  Ghent 179–80
  Hague 79
  Jay 159
  Kalisch 163
  Leoben 82
  Luneville 98–99
  Mortefontaine 159
  Nanjing 36
  Paris (1763) 38, 41, 42

Paris (1783) 44–45
Paris (1814) 173, 185
Paris (1815) 188
Plaswitz 165
Pressburg 116–17, 119
Reichenbach 166
Reid 168
San Ildefonso 109
Schonbrunn (1805) 116
Schonbrunn (1809) 135
Sintra 132
Tauroggen 163
Tilsit 123, 129, 151, 182
Tolentino 91
Utrecht 40
Valencay 169
Westphalia 13, 23, 53, 97
Zeyes 163
Tucker, Josiah 31, 42
Tull, Jethro 24
Tuscany 99

United States 4, 7, 8, 23, 26, 32–33, 36, 38, 40–41, 42–44, 50, 72, 109–10, 145, 158–61, 176–81, 189, 190
Uruguay 145

Venezuela 145–46
Venice 77, 82, 99, 117, 187
Victor-Amadeus III 77
Victor-Perrin, Claude 136
Vikings 12
Villaba, Luis de 141
Villaret-Joyeuse, Louis 72
Villeneuve, Pierre 114, 115
Vins, Joseph de 77

Warre, William 136
Wars
  American Independence 4, 40, 41, 42–44, 55, 145, 152
  Barbary State 159–60
  Civil War (English, 1642–29) 13
  Civil War (English, 1689–91) 14
  Dutch (17th Century) 2–3
  1812 175–81
  India 35

King George's/Austrian Succession 40, 41, 42
King William's/Augsburg Succession/ Nine Years 40, 41, 42
Opium 36
Quasi 159
Queen Anne's/Spanish Succession 40, 41, 42
Seven Years/French and Indian 38, 40–41, 42
Thirty Years 13, 23
World War II 189
Washington, George 40–41, 44, 159
Watson, Brook 70
Watt, James 23, 27
Wedgwood, Josiah 23, 126
Wellesley, Henry 142, 146, 147, 154, 156–57, 169, 170, 175
Wellesley, Richard 2, 129, 131–32, 138, 142, 146, 148
Wellesley-Pole, William 138
Wellington, Arthur Wellesley, Duke 5, 61, 124, 125–26, 131–32, 133, 136–37, 138–39, 141–45, 145–48, 153–58, 161–63, 165, 167, 169, 172, 175, 179, 183–84, 185–87, 189

Western Hemisphere 32
Westphalia 124
Whitbread, Samuel 143
Whitworth, Charles 66, 78–79, 89, 93, 99, 110
Whyte, John 73
Wickham, William 1, 71, 75–76, 77, 78, 82–83, 89, 95, 99, 101, 102
Wilberforce, William 126–27
Wilkinson, John 27
William of Orange, Prince 170
William I 12
William III 14, 26
William V 93
Williamson, Adam 73
Windham, William 54, 119
Winter, Jan de 84
Wolf, Benjamin 16
Wood, John 27
Wurmser, Dagobert 77–78
Wurttemberg 99, 114, 116

Yorck, Johann 163
York, Frederick Augustus, Duke 17, 58, 59, 67, 93, 131, 137–38
Yorke, Charles 62